The

CHIEFTAIN

The

CHIEFTAIN

Victorian
TRUE CRIME
through the Eyes
of a SCOTLAND YARD
Detective

CHRIS PAYNE

To Meg, Kate and Rob

Front cover picture credit: A cartoon illustrating the weapons available to burglars and policemen. (*Punch*, 8 October 1881)

Back cover picture credit: Chief Inspector George Clarke, 1877. (Cobb, *Critical Years at the Yard* (1956))

First published 2011

The History Press
The Mill, Brimscombe Port
Stroud, Gloucestershire, GL5 2QG
www.thehistorypress.co.uk

British Library Cataloguing in Publication Data.
A catalogue record for this book is available from the British Library.

ISBN 978 0 7524 5667 6

Typesetting and origination by The History Press
Printed in the EU for The History Press.

CONTENTS

Preface   7

1   The Journey to Scotland Yard   11
2   A Murderous Year   30
3   The Fenians are Coming   66
4   Back to Basics   106
5   The Tichborne Claimant, Theft and Fraud   146
6   Suicide, Accidental Death or Murder?   167
7   The Great Turf Swindle and Police Corruption   200

Epilogue   243
Acknowledgements   247
Notes   251
Bibliography   275
Index   281

PREFACE

Many people read about detectives, and they see things upon the stage about detectives, and they think it is a very good sort of life; but when they come to try it they find it is earning your livelihood, like lifting bricks and everything else, and they get tired of it.

Superintendent James Thomson, 1877[1]

Many of us enjoy a good crime story and can readily recall the names of our favourite fictional detective, whether it be Sherlock Holmes, Sexton Blake, Philip Marlowe, Hercule Poirot, Maigret, Morse, Rebus, Wallander or many others. Fewer of us, I suspect, can recall the names or exploits of those who investigate crime in the real world. Thus when I discovered that one of my ancestors, George Clarke, had been a detective chief inspector in the London Metropolitan Police in the 1870s, it meant little to me. It was only later that I found some information that was sufficient to persuade me that his story would be an intriguing one to investigate. During my research, it soon became obvious that George Clarke had been a leading figure at Scotland Yard and was well known by the Victorian London public, especially those who crossed the boundary from legality to crime. Indeed, when it comes to Victorian detectives Clarke was the real thing, but his story has essentially remained untold until now. This book sets out to open up the world of Victorian crime and the diverse investigations of the early Scotland Yard detectives, through Clarke's eyes and experiences.

In 1840, at 21 years of age, George Clarke joined the London Metropolitan Police. After twenty-two years' service he had only achieved promotion to sergeant, but, in 1862, he was transferred to the small group of nine detectives that then constituted the plain-clothed detective department at Scotland Yard; the only detectives within the Metropolitan Police at that time. By May 1869 Clarke had risen to the rank of detective chief inspector and, by his retirement in January 1878, he had been second-in-command of the department for nine years. By that time he had become known to colleagues and to members of the criminal fraternity as 'The Chieftain' or 'The Old Man'.

During much of his time as a detective (particularly between 1864 and 1878) Clarke's career can be tracked reliably, not least because he was the only 'George Clark(e)' within the very small team in the Scotland Yard Detective Department. His involvement in major cases required the preparation of reports, several of which, bearing his clearly identifiable signature, have survived in the National Archives. In addition, the universal interest in crime as a topic for the press of the day has ensured that Clarke's activities were well reported by the national and provincial newspapers of that era. Information on Clarke's earlier life between 1818 and 1864 (the subject of Chapter One) is less readily accessible and its interpretation requires some informed speculation.

From 1864 onwards (the subject of Chapters Two to Seven), Clarke played a substantial part in many of the major criminal investigations and trials of the mid-Victorian period. These included: the hunt for the perpetrator of the first murder committed on a British train; the investigation of a headless corpse at Plaistow Marshes; the policing of Irish terrorism (including Clarke's role in the arrests of a leading mercenary and a Fenian arms organiser); investigating theft at Windsor Castle and the Earl of Cardigan's premises; breaking up gangs of foreign burglars; providing important evidence that contributed to the conviction of that greatest fraudster of his era, 'the Tichborne Claimant'; enforcing legislation for the regulation of betting and the control of turf frauds; pursuing investigations into 'baby farming'; solving a series of financially damaging arson attacks in the East End; eventually bringing to justice the murderer Henri de Tourville in a court in Austria; leading the police inquiry into the suspicious death of Charles Bravo (a case which titillated the British public in 1876 and has subsequently provided fertile ground for the imagination of several true-crime authors); and many other cases. Trusted by his superiors, Clarke was highly regarded and considered a safe pair of hands, until two ruthless and clever convicted fraudsters sought to offset their heavy prison sentences by giving evidence that corruption existed within the ranks of the Scotland Yard Detective Department.

British detectives have achieved only a passing mention in many accounts of Victorian crime despite the public prominence they achieved in the press of their day. Kate Summerscale's book *The Suspicions of Mr Whicher* is a rare exception in providing a centre-stage description of a detective's role.[2] Detective Inspector Whicher was a Scotland Yard colleague of Clarke from 1862 until

Whicher's retirement in March 1864. In the essentially chronological sequence of events that I have recounted in this book, I have likewise sought to ensure that Clarke and his police colleagues are in the spotlight again, whether their roles were heroic, merely competent, incompetent or criminal!

When trying to separate fact from fiction in the events that took place at Scotland Yard more than 130 years ago, the most important research documents have been the primary sources that have not been subjected to the 'Chinese whisper' effect of errors and misinterpretations that can be found in some secondary sources. The extraordinary range of research resources that we are privileged to have available in the United Kingdom have helped me locate many such documents, including Clarke's original reports of several cases and contemporary newspaper accounts of his investigations. I have also used additional information to place Clarke's experiences in the wider context of the events and social and political attitudes that prevailed in the mid-Victorian era. In this way, I have tried to ensure that the account that I have presented is set in context and, hopefully, objective. To help capture the atmosphere of the nineteenth century I have made frequent use of quotations from reports and newspapers, contemporary to the period, and from articles and books written by individuals who were directly involved in some of the events that are related here.

I have written this book with the general reader predominantly in mind. However, I hope that it will also prove of value to those with an academic interest in the history of policing and crime detection and, for this reason, I have included references to all documents and published texts that I have cited.

1

THE JOURNEY TO SCOTLAND YARD

1818–64

This town is paraded with policemen in blue
They carry a mighty big staff and make use of it too.
They batter your sconce in for pleasure,
In the station house poke you for fun,
They take all your money and treasure
And fine you five bob when they've done!

Tom Lawrence[1]

Early Days in Therfield

George Clarke was born in July 1818 in Therfield, Hertfordshire, a village on the ancient Icknield Way amongst the chalk hills some 3 miles south-west of Royston. He was the fifth child and fourth son of Robert Clarke and his wife Catherine (*née* Gatward). Catherine's family, which included several members who encountered the wrath of the law, had been resident in Therfield for several generations, while Robert, whose occupation was variously recorded as 'agricultural labourer' or 'gardener', had been born in the nearby village of Barley. Married in December 1807 at Therfield church, Robert and Catherine had at least ten children between 1809 and 1833 (six boys and four girls).[2]

The Clarke family must have been on the margins of poverty, though they managed to avoid the workhouse. In 1821, Robert and Catherine and five of their children were sharing a house in Therfield with Catherine's parents and six of Catherine's younger brothers and sisters; a total of fifteen people in the one house.[3] Between 1793 and 1815, the agricultural sector, and those employed in it, had profited from the need to sustain food production during the wars with France. However, after the wars had ended, peace brought only poverty to those employed on the land.[4] Under these circumstances life for the Clarkes was undoubtedly hard, and it is little wonder that several of Robert Clarke's sons explored different ways of earning a living. Amongst George Clarke's three older brothers, only Leonard, the older brother nearest in age to George, followed in his father's footsteps as an agricultural labourer, but later immigrated to Australia. The two eldest, Thomas and Robert, spent their lives in Therfield but earned their living from occupations other than agricultural labouring, albeit in allied trades. The eldest brother, Thomas, was variously a butcher, jobber and cattle dealer. Robert initially earned his living as a butcher and carrier, but by 1861 had become a shopkeeper in the village, a position that he occupied for much of the rest of his life.

George Clarke was the first member of his family to move to London to obtain work, joining an exodus of working men from the countryside to the city. He was not to be the last, as his younger brothers Henry and John Clark (sic) had followed suit by 1845 and 1856 respectively.[5] In addition, by 1861 two of his younger sisters, Susan and Jane, had married and were based in London, living in Bethnal Green and Marylebone with their respective husbands, Samuel Sitch (a carpenter) and Joseph Norton (a fruiterer).

It seems unlikely that Clarke's application to join the Metropolitan Police in 1840 was his first job in London, but the precise timing and nature of his initial move from Therfield is a matter of speculation. His police 'joining records' provide some possible clues.[6] Every applicant wishing to join the Metropolitan Police had to submit three written testimonials of character, one of them being from their last employer.[7] Clarke's testimonials came from a Thomas Garratt of Kingston House, and from two others (whose names are illegible in the records) located at Regent's Park and Portland Terrace, suggesting that Clarke was already working in London by 1840. Between 1837 and 1842, Kingston House, a mansion in Westminster, was let to Richard Wellesley, the eldest brother of Arthur Wellesley (the Duke of Wellington).[8] Between 1822 and 1832, the Duke of Wellington's youngest brother, Gerald Wellesley, had been Rector of Therfield at a time when George Clarke was growing up.[9] The Clarke children were all baptised at Therfield church and the family were probably regular churchgoers. Thus, one possibility is that George Clarke initially gained employment in London as a member of the household staff of Richard Wellesley, following earlier contact with the Wellesley family in Therfield.

London and the Metropolitan Police

The London of 1840 was crowded, noisy, smelly and dark. The population was predominantly English but had significant ethnic minorities and was becoming increasingly multicultural. Industrial premises existed cheek by jowl with crowded housing, and the principal use of coal as a fuel added to the smell and created the smoke-blackened buildings and the fog-laden atmosphere. Gas lighting had brightened up some streets and buildings. The more select areas contained the gated communities and mansions built in the Georgian and Regency periods, owned by rich merchants, politicians and landowners in London for the season. The busy streets were crowded with handcarts and horse-drawn vehicles of all shapes and sizes, but a revolution in transport had started with the opening of a primitive terminus at Euston by the Birmingham Railway Company in 1837 and the construction of the Great Western Railway from Paddington to Maidenhead in 1838. For many it was a place of brutality and hardship; child mortality was high, life expectancy low. Numerous diseases were prevalent and the arrival of cholera in 1832 simply added to the problems faced by those living in crowded and unsanitary conditions without clean water and effective sanitation or medication. In 1840, London was also in the middle of the worst economic depression that had ever afflicted Britain. In this environment, the Metropolitan Police were doing their best to maintain order and prevent crime.[10]

The London Metropolitan Police had been set up in 1829, the necessary legislation being driven through Parliament by the Home Secretary and later prime minister, Sir Robert Peel. The orthodox history of the force is that an incompetent and corrupt system of parish policing in pre-1829 London made it essential to establish a more effective and centrally organised police force for London.[11] More recent historical analyses have questioned this perception of the 'before and after', though the details need not concern us here.[12] After the enabling legislation was passed in Parliament, Peel had appointed two commissioners, responsible to the Home Office, to establish and manage the force. These were Colonel Charles Rowan and Richard Mayne. Rowan was 47, with a distinguished military record in the Napoleonic wars. Mayne was a 33-year-old Dublin-born barrister who had not held any administrative post. The appointments proved to be shrewd and effective ones and the two men worked well together right up to the time of Rowan's retirement in 1850.[13] From 1855 Mayne became the sole commissioner and operated in an increasingly autocratic manner until his death in 1868.[14] Between 1862 and 1868, after joining the detective department at Scotland Yard, George Clarke found himself working in close proximity to Commissioner Mayne and at times received his orders directly from him.

The original Metropolitan Police district was a 10-mile radius from Charing Cross, excluding the City where a previously established City Police was retained under the City of London Corporation. The Metropolitan Police headquarters was established in Whitehall Place, adjoining Old Scotland Yard. The district was managed within several divisional areas, each headed by a superintendent; seventeen divisions were operational by May 1831 and by 1834 the number of London policemen was just short of 3,400.[15] It was the two commissioners, Mayne and Rowan, who drew up and implemented the operational strategy for the force. Embodied in the early police instructions was the philosophy that the principal role of the Metropolitan Police would be to contribute towards crime *prevention*.[16] Creation of a small plain-clothes detective force (focusing on crime *detection*) was delayed until 1842, not least because of political and public concerns that this would lead to a civilian-spy system similar to those found in some European countries, and further fears that men in plain clothes were more susceptible to corruption.[17] These concerns were real in the minds of many people, and remained so for many years. James Davis, who was appointed in the 1870s as the legal adviser to the Metropolitan Police commissioner and worked on a daily basis with the detective department, expressed the following views to a Home Office Commission in 1877:

> … the principle of having police in plain clothes is, in my opinion, an evil, and I think that their being in uniform is one of the greatest guarantees for good conduct. I may say that all action in plain clothes, which is to a certain extent a disguise, and where there is no public control over the officer in question, is an evil. No doubt there are exceptional cases where the advantages outweigh the evil, but I still think that a detective force, that is to say, men going about who are police officers not in uniform, is of itself a great evil.[18]

However, Davis did not allow his personal principles to prevent him 'supping with the devil' when at work.

The accountability of the force to the Home Office, rather than to local administrative authorities in London, was justified on the grounds that the police would need to perform tasks of national importance, such as protecting the monarch, the royal palaces, Parliament and public buildings, and protecting society from terrorist threats.[19] Centralised government control ensured that functions additional to the prevention and detection of crime were added to the Metropolitan Police remit, to aid the smooth running of a variety of aspects of society. These included traffic regulation, the licensing of cabs and street-sellers, supervising the prevention of disease amongst farm animals (which were still numerous in London in the mid-nineteenth century) and implementing government legislation established to protect individuals from their own 'moral weaknesses' (including drunkenness and gambling).[20]

From the outset, efforts had been made to ensure that the all-male police was not regarded as a militaristic organisation. This started with the selection of the policeman's uniform, which initially consisted of top hats and blue swallowtail coats with the minimum of decoration, in contrast to the colourful military uniforms of the time.[21] A future police colleague of Clarke's, Timothy Cavanagh, was not impressed by the uniform, describing it retrospectively as 'a cross between that worn by the ex-Emperor Zoolooki of the Squeejee Islands, and the policeman in the pantomime'.[22] Apart from the uniform, some other operational aspects of the force were closer to a military regime, including the hierarchical structure. In addition, many of the commanding officers were former soldiers, and constables were subjected to strict discipline and had to cope with ceremonial drill and its associated cleaning and polishing.[23] One consequence of the strict discipline was a high turnover of policemen. Of the 2,800 constables serving in May 1830, only 562 remained in the force by 1834 – drunkenness being one major problem. As late as 1865 the annual staff turnover rate in the Metropolitan Police was still high at 13.5 per cent.[24]

The work was also uncomfortable and often dangerous, and recruitment mainly attracted unskilled or at best semi-skilled labourers who would be less discouraged by these features of the job and the low pay.[25] Constables were paid 21s a week, of which 2s were deducted for section house accomodation. Sergeants received 22s and 6d a week. All ranks were required to give their whole time to the service, wearing their uniforms on and off duty and, even if they matched the qualification criteria for the electoral roll, policemen were not entitled to vote.[26]

It is always difficult to make meaningful comparisons between the comparative values of salaries, not least because of the differences in living standards and taxation regimes between eras but, using one comparator, the annual salaries of a constable and sergeant in 1830 would be worth approximately £2,700 and £2,900 in 2010.[27] Little wonder that Peel's new police were regarded as underpaid by modern standards. However, for Victorian labourers (including those from the agricultural sector who would only be drawing that scale of wage in the weeks when work was available) a job in the police gave them continuity of employment, and large numbers applied to join. Of 5,056 individuals recruited into the Metropolitan Police between 1840 and 1900, 48 per cent were labourers, of which 24 per cent were from the agricultural sector. From a regional perspective only 18 per cent of all recruits were from the London area, a further 24 per cent were from the Home Counties and 42 per cent from the other English counties, with the remaining 16 per cent from Scotland, Wales, Ireland or abroad.[28]

Applications from men like Clarke were welcomed:

From the first day of the Metropolitan Police, the policy pursued, in recruiting for the force, was to endeavour to get men from the agricultural community, not only because of the superior physique of the rural worker, but because countrymen without previous experience of town life, made more trustworthy policemen than those who were London bred and might be described as knowing too much about London. The countryman's mind had the advantage, from the point of view of those who had to train him as a constable, of being fallow and not 'infertile'; the Londoner's might be more fertile, but it was usually far from fallow.[29]

The establishment of the new police in 1829 was not greeted with much enthusiasm by Londoners (and the same could be said for the press of the day). When Londoners joined they not infrequently found that their decision had distanced or even ex-communicated them from their families and friends.[30] However, by 1840 perceptions of the force had started to improve somewhat, largely through the efforts of Rowan and Mayne in establishing clear operational procedures and high standards. Indeed, as early as 1834 a Parliamentary Select Committee report described the new police as one of the most valuable modern institutions.[31] In addition, though policemen remained the butt of many a joke and still encountered some public anger, the increasing adoption by the press and public of the more affectionate nickname of 'Bobbies' for police constables (rather than the more dismissive 'Peelers') suggested that some of the initial hostility had eroded.

In 1839 a second Metropolitan Police bill extended the district of the Metropolitan Police to a radius of 15 miles from Charing Cross, and the force's manpower was increased to 4,300 to accommodate this. In 1829 the infamous Bow Street Runners had originally been retained as a distinctive body, but they had functioned more as a private detective agency than a public service and there was confusion over the powers of the Metropolitan Police commissioners vis-à-vis the chief magistrate of Bow Street. Following the 1839 legislation the Runners were disbanded and were offered the opportunity to transfer into the Metropolitan Police, though it seems that few did.[32] Other changes in the new legislation meant that the stipendiary (paid) magistrates of London lost their police role and their offices were transformed into the Metropolitan Police Courts, including Bow Street and twelve other such courts.[33] By the time that George Clarke decided to apply to join the Metropolitan Police, the essential elements that he would encounter in his career, with the exception of the creation of a detective department, had been put in place.

The Uniformed Policeman

George Clarke, warrant number 16834, formally joined the force on 6 April 1840 at Scotland Yard. Of the eight new recruits listed alongside his name that day, only George Clarke was still in the police fifteen years later, the others having variously resigned or been dismissed.[34] For Clarke to have been accepted, he had satisfied several recruitment criteria. His testimonials must have proved satisfactory, and a brief medical examination had ensured that he was physically fit and 'intelligent' and met the minimum height requirement of 5ft 7in.[35] He had also needed to demonstrate that he could read and write and was able to understand what he had read. Aged 21, he was comfortably below the maximum recruitment age of 30.[36] During the early recruitment of constables for the force, only one in three applicants met these basic criteria.[37] Successful applicants such as Clarke were then sent for basic training, during which wages were 10s a week. Each preparatory class numbered about thirty men who were required to parade at the Wellington Barracks drill ground for several hours each day, six days a week, for a fortnight. Close-order drill and sabre practice constituted the bulk of this training, which was supplemented by two afternoon lectures by a superintendent and a considerable amount of legal material to be learnt by rote. Following this, the new constable patrolled with an experienced man for about a week; he was then moved to his division and sent out on his own.[38]

Clarke was allocated to S Division (Hampstead), one of the larger divisions in terms of area and at the time relatively rural. S Division had four police stations located at Hampstead, Albany Street, Portland Town and Barnet; Clarke may have initially been located at Barnet or Hampstead, but was probably later transferred to Albany Street. Initially, as a single man, it is likely that he lived in lodgings or in a section house together with other constables.

The principal means by which the new Metropolitan Police delivered its crime-prevention strategy was to give police constables the responsibility for a 'beat', which they patrolled in a regulated fashion.[39] The day's duties started with a short parade followed by daily orders being read out by a sergeant. Constables like Clarke had to write up their reports in their own time and until 1854 they were also drilled twice a week, all year long. After that year their drill was reduced to an hour a week in good weather during the summer only.[40] Individual beats would vary in length from about 2 miles to 7.5 miles, being longer in rural areas and shorter during the night, with approximately two-thirds of the men placed on night duty at any one time. Beats had to be walked at a steady 2.5mph (to assist timed checks by supervising sergeants). During the day the constable would patrol on the kerb side of the pavement, but at night they would switch to the inner side of the pavement to enable them to check more easily the security of bolts and fastenings on properties.

Despite their training in the use of sabres these would have been issued only when dealing with serious disorder; Clarke, on his beat, would only have been armed with a truncheon and a rattle to summon help.[41]

The workload of a constable and its physical and mental demands were considerable and unremitting, and the frequent solace of drink as an alleviator of pain and boredom was to some extent understandable. They were on duty seven days a week, only had one (unpaid) week's holiday a year and no absolute entitlement to a pension.[42] The records of those retired policemen fortunate enough to be pensioned-off frequently includes the phrase 'worn out' as the sole medical reason for their retirement. However, in reality the force had little charity for malingerers and as a deterrent police absent through sickness or injury had their pay deducted by 1s a day, increasing to 2s a day after three months' absence.[43] In 1868 a Home Office departmental committee report on the Metropolitan Police acknowledged that:

> The duty of a constable is very severe; if on night duty he goes on duty at 10 p.m. and remains on his legs till 6 a.m.; he then goes back to rest, but has in the course of the day frequently to attend at the police court as a witness, and also occasionally to be at drill, walking sometimes a considerable distance to and from the drill ground. Dr Farr calculates that on average a constable on night duty walks 16 miles … A constable is 10 hours on a day beat, *viz.*, from 6 to 9 a.m. and again from 3 to 10 p.m. and during this period he walks according to Dr Farr's calculations, 20 miles.[44]

George Clarke survived the work regime of a constable in S Division for a relatively long period (thirteen years) before he was promoted to sergeant on 27 May 1853, at which time his weekly wage was increased to £1 4s. His brother Henry, who joined in March 1845, remained a constable for fourteen years in N Division (Islington) before receiving promotion. Both brothers were put in the shade, however, by youngest brother John, who joined N Division in April 1856 and became a sergeant only five years later.[45] Yet long before George Clarke became a sergeant, he had also acquired a wife.

On 18 November 1843 at the parish church, Islington, Clarke married Elizabeth McGregor, the 19-year-old eldest daughter of John and Elizabeth McGregor from Chipping Barnet. How George Clarke and Elizabeth met is unknown, but if Clarke was indeed located at Barnet Police Station they may have met on his beat (though constables were told to avoid conversation with women while on duty). There could be another explanation, as Elizabeth's eldest brother, John, was 'known to the police' having been sentenced to twelve months' imprisonment in April 1842 for housebreaking.[46]

A constable had to get permission to marry and, presumably, the authorities that vetted Clarke's future wife dismissed any concerns about her errant brother, or were perhaps kept unaware of his criminal tendencies. The marriage was unlikely to have improved their financial situation as a police officer's wife was not supposed to take paid work, further testing the ability for two to live on a constable's meagre wage, only supplemented by the regular income and a uniform. In addition, Elizabeth did not have any significant financial resources of her own. Her father was an agricultural labourer and, when he died of pneumonia in April 1855, her mother died only a few months later at the Union Workhouse at Chipping Barnet. Despite the difficulties that the young newlyweds must have had in managing on a tight budget they remained together until death intervened. Between 1845 and 1859 they had five children, three boys and two girls, during which time they rented rooms in Highgate and later St John's Wood, before moving to Great College Street, Westminster, during the 1860s.[47]

Clarke's main duties as a constable would have been in crime prevention, but there were occasions when he had to deal with individuals who had committed a criminal offence. The British legal system entitles the victims of a crime to initiate prosecutions but, increasingly during the nineteenth century, the police replaced the victim as the prosecutor in many cases.[48] Offenders were brought before one of three principal courts: petty sessions, quarter sessions or assizes. The least serious offences could be dealt with summarily by magistrates sitting alone or in pairs; in metropolitan London such offences would have been handled in the thirteen police courts established by the 1839 legislation. These courts also decided whether there was sufficient evidence in other, more serious cases to refer them to a higher court. Quarter sessions dealt with these, with verdicts being decided by juries and sentences by magistrates. The most serious cases were entrusted to judges and juries at the assizes. The London equivalent of the assizes was the Old Bailey, which had been re-housed in 1834 in the new Central Criminal Court.[49] This was a court which George Clarke would get to know well.

So, what type of criminal cases did Police Constable George Clarke get involved with? This is not as easy a question to answer as it sounds, not least because no relevant divisional records appear to have survived and, until the wider proliferation of newspapers from about 1855 onwards, press coverage was patchy. Additionally, George Clark(e) was a reasonably common name in the population so, even when case records refer to policemen with this name as investigating officers or witnesses, it cannot be certain that the reference is to 'our' man. Indeed, there were at least four other serving policemen in the Metropolitan Police with the name George Clark(e) during the 1840s and 1850s. Two of these suffered abrupt conclusions to their career. On 29 June 1846 a Police Constable George Clark was found murdered, his body shockingly mutilated and lying in a field in Dagenham. The murderer was never found.[50] In 1854 another Police Constable George Clarke (G Division,

Finsbury) also had an unfortunate encounter with the potential hazards of the job, and was retired from the force after 'an injury to the spine and testicles' following a fall on to iron railings at Dalby Terrace, City Road. By comparison, the more fortunate third George Clarke (M Division, Southwark) was pensioned off on 14 May 1853 merely for being 'worn out and unfit for further service'. The fourth only joined the force on 3 August 1858 and was located in R Division, Greenwich.[51] None of these officers served in S Division, and this improves the odds that any references involving Police Constable/Sergeant George Clark(e) within the S Division area between 1841 and 1862 are attributable to the Chieftain.

During this period Clarke's name was associated, in the press and court proceedings, with several arrests and successful prosecutions for theft.[52] Although little or nothing stands out, or helps to explain why Clarke was transferred to the Scotland Yard Detective Department, it is probable that Clarke was given the opportunity to undertake some plain-clothes work within S Division (as was occasionally available), and had impressed the divisional superintendent sufficiently to recommend him for a transfer to Scotland Yard when a vacancy arose. Another possible clue to Clarke's transfer to Scotland Yard comes from his own police contacts. In 1877, the head of the detective department, Superintendent Williamson, was to recall in evidence at the Old Bailey that he had known Clarke 'over twenty years'. Thus Williamson, who was greatly influential in the history of the detective department, might have had some specific reasons to recommend that Clarke should join the small group of detectives at the Yard. Whatever the factor that triggered his transfer, Sergeant George Clarke moved to the detective department in A Division on 19 May 1862, after a length of service at which many policemen would be seeking to leave the force. He would now receive a significantly improved salary of £2 2s a week, placing him financially just within the economic definition of the 'lower-middle classes' for that time.

The Scotland Yard Detective Department

After the disbanding of the Bow Street Runners in 1839 there was no group of detectives working in the Metropolitan Police area, though one former Runner, Nicholas Pearce, had become an inspector attached to A Division in 1840 with special responsibilities for watching the activities of London's habitual criminals and investigating certain cases of murder or other serious crimes.[53] By 1842, an appalling muddle in the police investigation of the murder of Jane Good by Daniel Good, together with some other unsatisfactory incidents, had finally encouraged the Home Office to sanction a small detective force.[54] It is not completely clear whether the earlier reluctance had been attributable to the

Home Office, to the dragging of feet by the two commissioners, or a combination of the two. However in his authoritative book on *Policing Victorian London*, Phillip Smith seems to lay the responsibility firmly at the door of the commissioners; quoting from the Victorian social reformer Sir Edwin Chadwick in the 1840s: 'I know from Sir C. Rowan and Mr Richard Mayne that they disliked detection on principle, and only yielded to its adoption on what they deemed superior authority.'[55] The new detective department was created on 15 August 1842 and it was directly responsible to the commissioners. The original staff complement was eight men (two inspectors and six sergeants), which was temporarily increased to ten in 1856 (three inspectors and seven sergeants), the same number as when Clarke joined the detectives in 1862.[56] The branch appears to have had no fixed name in those early days, being referred to variously as the detective office, department, force or branch.[57]

From today's perspective it seems incredible that in 1842 there were only eight men in plain clothes at Scotland Yard to investigate every case of crime committed in London.[58] Some plain-clothes detection work was done outside the detective department, within the divisions, from 1846 onwards, but very few specifically plain-clothes men were used in this role.[59] In addition, Commissioner Mayne's limited enthusiasm for this approach became clear in January 1854 (by which time about 100 plain-clothes men were being used across divisions), when he reminded superintendents that 'there is no regulation of the Service authorising the employment of Police in plain clothes' and asked for reports to be made when they were used.[60]

The first eight detectives employed within the new Scotland Yard Detective Department in 1842 were: Inspectors Nicholas Pearce (the former Bow Street Runner) and John Haynes; Sergeants Braddick, Stephen Thornton, William Gerrett, Frederick Shaw, Jonathan Whicher and Charles Goff.[61] Several of these men were soon to become household names (albeit in slightly modified form), as a result of Charles Dickens' interest in the detective police, which he explained in 1850 in *Household Words*:

> The Detective Force organised since the establishment of the existing Police, is so well chosen and trained, proceeds so systematically and quietly, does its business in such a workmanlike manner, and is always so calmly and steadily engaged in the service of the public, that the public really do not know enough of it, to know a tithe of its usefulness. Impressed with this conviction, and interested in the men themselves, we represented to the authorities at Scotland Yard, that we should be glad, if there were no official objection, to have some talk with the Detectives. A most obliging and ready permission being given, a certain evening was appointed with a certain Inspector for a social conference between ourselves and the Detectives, at The Household Words Office in Wellington Street, Strand, London.[62]

By the date of the detectives' visit to Wellington Street only Thornton, Shaw and Whicher of the original 1842 team were still in post (plus Inspector Haynes who was unavailable). Others attending were a new inspector, Charles Field, and two new sergeants, Smith and Kendall. In Dickens' anecdotes published after the meeting, the detectives became loosely disguised under the pseudonyms he gave them. Thus, Field became 'Wield' (and was subsequently used by Dickens as the model for Inspector Bucket in *Bleak House*), Thornton became 'Dornton', Whicher became 'Witchem', Smith became 'Mith', Kendall became 'Fendall' and Shaw became 'Straw'. Dickens also met another senior policeman, Robert Walker (to whom he gave the pseudonym 'Inspector Stalker'); Walker was not a member of the detective department but a senior member of the A Division (Whitehall) executive team.[63]

When Clarke transferred to the detective department in 1862, he would have found Thornton, Whicher and Walker still at work, and it is therefore of particular interest to see how Dickens assessed them in 1850:

> Sergeant Dornton about fifty years of age, with a ruddy face and a high sun-burnt forehead, has the air of one who has been a Sergeant in the army … He is famous for steadily pursuing the inductive process, and, from small beginnings, working on from clue to clue until he bags his man. Sergeant Witchem, shorter and thicker-set, and marked with the small-pox, has something of a reserved and thoughtful air, as if he were engaged in deep arithmetical calculations. He is renowned for his acquaintance with the swell mob [pickpockets]. Inspector Stalker is a shrewd, hard-headed Scotchman – in appearance not at all unlike a very acute, thoroughly trained schoolmaster, from the Normal Establishment at Glasgow.[64]

The Apprentice Detective

When Clarke turned up for work as a temporary detective sergeant, on the morning of Monday 19 May 1862, he would have found himself occupying a room in Old Scotland Yard which he would share with the other detective sergeants. A future colleague of Clarke's later described one aspect of the sergeant's room: 'Around the room overhead are a number of plaster casts of the heads of notorious criminals, and hanging at full length beneath some of these are the ghastly looking ropes which have been used in their execution.'[65] Aged 43, he was probably amongst the oldest of the detective sergeants when he joined the department. Indeed, on his first day at work at Old Scotland Yard he might already have deserved one of the nicknames that he was later to receive: 'The Old Man'. Unlike several of his new colleagues, he had arrived at Scotland Yard with twenty-two years' familiarity with the streets of

London, including thirteen years when he had pounded a beat and a further nine years when, as a sergeant, he would have supervised other constables engaged in that function. His capacity to cope with the physical and mental pressures associated with those tasks, and his practical experience of crime on the streets, would serve him well in his future career as a detective.

In 1862 the staffing of the detective department had gone through some further changes, but the complement of ten detectives included Inspectors Thornton and Whicher, together with Sergeants Robinson, Adolphus Williamson, Richard Tanner, William Palmer, Alexander Thomson and James Thomson.[66] Clarke filled the temporary sergeant vacancy; the temporary inspector position remained unfilled between 1859 and 1864.[67] Sergeant Palmer had earlier that year been transferred from Chatham Dockyard.[68] James Thomson had only arrived in February 1862. Regarded as a well-educated 'gentleman-copper', Thomson had originally been posted to C Division (St James) but, in less than a year, he had left the Metropolitan Police and moved first to the Devon constabulary before joining the Hampshire force. Deciding to rejoin the Metropolitan Police, he made a special application direct to Sir Richard Mayne, and was appointed as a constable in the detective department in February 1862, the next day being promoted to sergeant.[69] This was quite a different career progression to that of Clarke and illustrative of the way in which Mayne was prepared to adapt the recruitment procedures when it came to appointing detectives, creating an eclectic mix of experience and skills in the process.

Of the detectives at Scotland Yard in 1862, the most significant in Clarke's future career was Adolphus Frederick Williamson, known as 'Dolly' to friends and colleagues. Shortly after Clarke arrived, Williamson was promoted to acting inspector, at the age of only 32.[70] He was a Scot, whose father had been Superintendent of T Division (Hammersmith). Dolly Williamson's first job was as a temporary clerk in the War Department before he decided to follow his father into the Metropolitan Police in 1850. Initially working as an assistant clerk in P Division (Camberwell), he gained promotion and joined the detective department as a sergeant in 1852.[71] Williamson had worked with Inspector Whicher on cases such as the Road Hill House murder.[72] During Clarke's time at Scotland Yard Williamson was to become the head of the detective department, achieving the ranks of chief inspector, superintendent and chief constable en route. He had a great capacity for hard work, combining it with a dry sense of humour. As time permitted he is said to have been a powerful sculler and a devotee of the annual Oxford-Cambridge boat race but, like Wilkie Collins' 'Sergeant Cuff', Williamson's principal relaxation was gardening.[73] Though Clarke was about twelve years older than Williamson, and always at a lower rank, the two men were to develop a close relationship as colleagues and friends. Indeed they eventually lived very near to one another,

with Clarke's house at 20 Great College Street, Westminster (which he rented
from the late 1860s), being just round the corner from Williamson's in Smith
Square. Their relationship was to stand Clarke in good stead throughout his
next thirteen years at the Yard, and particularly when times got hard, as they
certainly did in August 1877. Richard Tanner also worked closely with Clarke
in the early stages of Clarke's detective career. Thirteen years younger than
Clarke, he was described by a friend and colleague as keen and lively, and a
favourite of the commissioner.[74]

In 1862 Commissioner Mayne was the dominant figure who loomed over
the small detective team. He directed the strategic priorities of the detectives,
as well as the uniformed force, and was known for his long working hours and
attention to detail. Under Mayne's overall direction all serious investigation of
crime in the metropolitan area involved the men of the detective department.
If anything serious happened in a division it was notified to the Scotland Yard
Detective Department and a detective officer was ordered to make enquiries
and to report.[75] On occasion, a detective would also be deployed to help with
serious crimes committed outside of London.[76]

As a new detective sergeant, Clarke probably shadowed the two inspectors
for his first few weeks in the job. The daily operational procedures of the
detective department in 1862 are not well documented but, by 1877 at least,
men were expected to report daily to their superior officer and to enter into
an entry book in their own handwriting the work that they were engaged on
each day.[77] In addition, office records were kept in a case book and office diary,
and regular case reports were written by individual officers for the senior
officer in the department, and for the commissioner.[78] Attributes that Clarke
would have needed to develop would have included surveillance skills and
useful contacts, including informers. Out of the office, the surveillance of suspected criminals was a regular chore on many cases. As Andrew Lansdowne
(another future colleague of Clarke's) commented: 'watching is always a tedi-
ous business; when, day after day, no result appears, it is enough to discourage
the most sanguine; but one must accustom oneself to monotony to get on as
a detective.'[79] During such activities, the use of disguises was not encouraged
by Mayne or Williamson.[80] Informers were regarded as an essential part of the
detectives' toolbox, though to be used with caution. Writing in 1904, George
Greenham, a colleague of Clarke's from 1873 onwards, explained his viewpoint on informers and their associated problems:

> One of the pests of society an officer has to meet with is the voluntary
> 'informer', who for monetary consideration offers to discover the criminal
> wanted. To place too much confidence in such a person is, to say the least, risky,
> for he will often draw small sums on account for current expenses, and finally
> deceive you. And yet one cannot altogether ignore him or do without him.[81]

The costs of informers and the recovery of these costs and other work-related expenses often left the detectives out of pocket, as the reimbursement of expenses by the Yard's administrators appears to have been a challenging process. Williamson commented in 1877: 'I am perfectly certain that men often will not put down items of expenses, because they know that they will be disputed, and they would rather lose money than enter into a dispute upon them ... I consider it most unfair.'[82] It seems likely that the grudging attitude towards expenses stemmed from Mayne's attitude to these matters ('it is a mistake to give men too much money'), implemented by an eagle-eyed chief clerk.[83] The consequences of this approach were considerable. At one extreme, Edwin Coathupe, who became a sergeant in the department in 1863, stated that 'I had £2 a week and used to spend £3 of my own money to be able to keep myself respectable'.[84] As a man of independent means, Coathupe had that luxury. Others (including Clarke) did not have that elasticity in their own finances and either had to fight their corner on the expenses issue or had to rely on additional sources of income to offset their expenditure. One such source was gratuities from those members of the public who wished to acknowledge good service. Subject to the approval of the commissioner, these gratuities could be retained by the individual detectives, and many saw them as an essential subsidy to compensate for the difficulty of recovering their full expenses. The consequences were almost inevitable:

> [Gratuities] used to be the great evil of Scotland Yard; not one of the officers of Scotland Yard would ever look at a case of picking up a thief in the streets; it was beneath them. 'It does not pay' used to be the answer. 'I can wait and get a case from Mr So-and-so, or Mr So-and-so's solicitor which will bring me in £5 or £7'. Those people would hang about the office for five or six days with the hope of getting a case of that kind.[85]

Such was the world in which Clarke now worked, and in which he had to learn on the job because, like others who found themselves in the detective department in the 1860s, he would not have received any formal training in detective work. Fortunately, he must have done enough in the first few months to satisfy his superiors, as his post was made permanent on 29 November 1862.[86]

The first press reports of cases involving Clarke after he joined Scotland Yard appeared early in 1863 and involved crimes in cities in the north of England. The first of these was a bank robbery in Manchester carried out by two men, Potter and Welby, who had drilled through to the bank vaults from an adjoining cellar. Having removed some £1,000 in gold and silver (worth £43,000 today), the men were seen to catch a train to London. Likely train destinations and police forces were alerted by telegraph. Welby got off the train at Crewe and was immediately arrested; Potter was arrested by Clarke at

Camden Town station (where the trains always stopped for ticket inspection). Clarke found that Potter was carrying a portmanteau containing £346 4s 7d from the robbery. He gave evidence to this effect at the magistrate's hearing in Manchester and at the Crown Court trial, when both men were found guilty and each was sentenced to twenty years' penal servitude.[87]

The second case involved David Charles Lloyd, who had worked as a clerk for a share broker in Newcastle and had dealt with the purchase of £600 of stock in the North Eastern and Berwick Railway Company for a client, James Oliver. After leaving his employment Lloyd had approached the registrars of the stock, claiming to be James Oliver, and asked for a new stock certificate, 'as he had lost his during a recent move to a new address'. On receipt of the certificate, Lloyd had then attempted to sell the stock, forging James Oliver's signature in the process, in an attempt to realise the £600 plus any profit. However, an alert clerk suspected fraud and the sale was stopped at the company's office. Superintendent Hawker of the North Eastern Railway police was then asked to track down the fraudster in collaboration with Clarke. The two men tracked Lloyd to the Gloucester Hotel, Brighton, where Clarke arrested him on 2 June 1863. Clarke gave evidence at the Bow Street Police Court hearing on 9 June and at the Old Bailey trial on 13 July; Lloyd was found guilty and received a sentence of five years' penal servitude.[88] Forgery was also the basis of a third case, where Clarke travelled to Hull on 10 January 1864 to arrest Charles Alberti for 'forging two checks [sic]' for £94 and £214. Alberti pleaded guilty at his trial at the Old Bailey and he was also sentenced to five years' penal servitude.[89]

It seems more than a coincidence that Clarke's first three documented cases after joining the detective department involved a link with the north of England, and it may be that each detective sergeant had some liaison responsibility for different sectors of the country. Likewise, all three cases had a link to financial institutions, and it is probable that some 'division of labour' was established within the detective department on the nature of the cases that individual detectives would take responsibility for. However, as Clarke's career developed, he would become involved in investigations of a very diverse range of crimes.

During 1863 and 1864 some further staffing changes were made at the detective department. Inspector Whicher retired on 19 March 1864.[90] Whicher later became a private detective and Clarke would meet up with him again, in a major investigation in 1873. Whicher's position was filled by the promotion of Sergeant James Thomson who, like Williamson earlier, had clearly been marked out for fast-tracking.[91] Williamson's own promotion to inspector was confirmed on 6 August 1863 and Richard Tanner was also promoted to acting inspector on 25 March 1863, an appointment that was confirmed later, in March 1864. These changes restored the full complement of three inspectors.

With some sergeant vacancies also arising during 1863 and 1864, Mayne took the unusual step of appointing Sergeant Coathupe as a direct entrant to the detective department in April 1863. Coathupe had no previous experience as a policeman but had applied indirectly to Mayne through a family friend; he had previously qualified as a surgeon and had been practising as such in Chippenham. Though perhaps the first direct entrant to the department, Coathupe would not be the last.[92] Such appointments undoubtedly created tensions; one later appointed direct entrant, George Greenham, confirmed that there was internal jealousy of those men brought in from outside, and James Thomson, one of the 'insiders' (though with much less police experience than Clarke), expressed the view that 'taking people into the service who have no police experience is a great mistake'.[93] Coathupe only stayed in the department for three years before becoming head of the detective force at Manchester and, later, head constable in Bristol. Despite this rapid career progression, James Thomson (who seems never to have been at a loss for a robust and dismissive comment on anything and anybody) commented that Coathupe 'was an amateur policeman and he will be an amateur policeman to the end of his days'.[94]

Sergeant Coathupe's arrival was followed by the appointment in October 1863 of 22-year-old Nathaniel Druscovich to fill the sergeant vacancy created by Tanner's promotion.[95] Druscovich, formerly and briefly a constable in C Division, was born in England but had a Moldavian father and an English mother. He also spent some of his youth in Wallachia.[96] He was fluent in several languages, albeit not in English, and his appointment caused a further flutter in the Scotland Yard dovecote. Speaking in 1877 with the benefit of some recent hindsight, James Thomson said:

> My individual opinion is that it is unwise to let foreigners have anything to do with our police. They think a great deal of themselves, they take too much upon themselves and they get into difficulties. I was strongly opposed to Druscovich coming to Scotland Yard and I advised them at the time not to have him … I thought there was a good deal of the foreigner in him, because when he first came to Scotland Yard … his English was almost broken English.[97]

To complete the staff changes, Sergeant John Mulvany was transferred to the department in April 1864 from S Division. Born in Chelsea, Mulvany had joined the police in 1848 and was now 37 years old and therefore, like Clarke, one of the 'old guard'.[98] Precisely what Clarke thought of his new workmates is not recorded but, with almost twenty-four years' police experience under his belt, he had more in common with Mulvany than with Coathupe or Druscovich. By 1864 the department contained a very diverse range of natural ability, experience and skills. Williamson, Clarke, Druscovich and Palmer would remain together for the next thirteen years.

While the detection of crime was the principal objective of the department, not all of its responsibilities were restricted to dealing with criminal cases. There were also activities of national and imperial importance to deal with, including State visits by royalty and international political figures. The detectives were also frequently deployed to work with the uniformed police in the management of public order both in London and at the major horse-racing meetings. In addition, private citizens were entitled to purchase the services of the police for investigations or for the policing of events, subject to the agreement of the commissioner.

During Clarke's first two years at Scotland Yard, the most important political visit was by Giuseppe Garibaldi in April 1864. Garibaldi, the Italian freedom fighter, was a popular hero amongst the anti-Catholic majority of Victorian Britain.[99] However, the Irish-Catholic community did not share this enthusiasm and, in September and October 1863, the Metropolitan Police had found it difficult to deal with violence in Hyde Park when pro-Garibaldi demonstrators were attacked by Irish-Catholics.[100] It was therefore likely that the detective department were working behind the scenes to help prevent further violent outbreaks during his visit in 1864. Despite Garibaldi attracting large crowds, events seemed to have passed off reasonably peacefully, partly due to the fact that Garibaldi cut short his visit on health grounds.

There is no doubt that Clarke was actively involved during his detective career in the management of betting crime and other villainy at horse-racing meetings. Williamson is recorded as saying that 'you want a man who is a little rough to go to races, and who will hold his own', and it seems that Clarke and Tanner both fitted this description.[101] Tanner was the detective who was most frequently deployed to take the lead at the major race meetings, until he retired in July 1869, and Tanner and Clarke were often on duty together at racecourses.[102] The Epsom meeting, in particular, was a huge public event; Derby Day was the highlight, invariably patronised by the Prince of Wales and by the swell-mob and other assorted criminals and 'roughs'. For the police present, such events could present a challenging and hostile environment. Tanner recorded in his personal notebook such an occasion at Epsom in 1857:

Robert Travers a pugilist apprehended by myself on the 29th May 1857 for violently assaulting me on Epsom Race Course (Oaks Day); taken before B. Coombe Esq. at Southwark Police Court and fined 40/- [shillings] or one months imprisonment. Remarks. The Races were over and a fight was got up between two roughs. Travers was seconding one, and Inspector Henry Smith and myself went into the crowd, when Plumb the jockey and Smith fell out. Plumb told Travers his grievance and he came and struck me to the ground insensible.[103]

Precisely how Tanner, from his unconscious state, then apprehended Travers is not explained. However, such events were not uncommon, as another detective, John Meiklejohn, also described. After arresting a man at Epsom on Derby Day who had already thrown him to the ground once, Meiklejohn recalled:

> Perhaps I had somewhat relaxed my vigilance on the prisoner's assurance that he would accompany me quietly. At any rate, we had not gone many yards when, by a sudden wrestling trick with which I was unfamiliar he again brought me to the ground with a crash. I was dazed but still retained my grip. There was no hope of assistance in such a crowd. It was rather hostile than otherwise. But regaining my feet I concluded to bring matters to a decided issue, and set about him until he was as tame as a rabbit. When after some further difficulty I got him to the station at the back of the Grandstand, my clothes were hanging in ribbons and his eyes were completely bunged up. Even then he was not entirely subdued, for when the Serjeant [sic] attempted to search him he sent that valued officer rolling down the steps of the Station like a football.[104]

Like Tanner and Meiklejohn, Clarke must have learnt how to handle the more physical elements of his job. However, physical hazards were not the only concern, and Coathupe was later to comment that the employment of detectives at racecourses exposed them 'to such temptations that they were liable to become mixed up with transactions which were not creditable'.[105]

As a further illustration of the nature of Scotland Yard detectives' work, their services could be purchased by private individuals with the commissioner's permission. One such occasion arose in June 1864 when Tanner and Clarke were sent in plain clothes to attend and provide security at the fête and fancy bazaar at Orléans House, Twickenham, arranged by the Duc d'Aumale. The Duc's father was the last King of France, whose abdication in 1848 had led to the French Second Republic when Prince Louis Napoleon Bonaparte was elected president and later became Emperor Napoleon III.[106] The Duc and his family had sought sanctuary in England, and required a detective presence to help dissuade and to deal with any discontent French republicans who might appear at the fête. Fortunately, it seems that the fête passed off peacefully.

By June 1864, Clarke's 'apprenticeship' as a detective had come to an end, and he was shortly to be moved on to bigger and better things.

2

A MURDEROUS YEAR

1864

Another base and dreadful murder
Now again, alas has been,
One of the most atrocious murders
It is, as ever yet was seen;
Poor Thomas Briggs, how sad to mention
Was in a first-class carriage slain,
Between Old Ford and Hackney Wick,
Which caused excitement, care and pain

Anonymous[1]

The North London Railway Murder

On the evening of Saturday 9 July 1864 in the gathering dark at Hackney Wick station, two bank clerks, Henry Vernez and Sydney Jones, entered an unoccupied first-class compartment of the slightly delayed 9.45 p.m. train from Fenchurch Street to Chalk Farm. Noticing a bag on the seat near the door, Jones moved it before sitting down, only to discover that there was fresh blood on his hand. Alerted to this, his colleague immediately called the train guard Benjamin Ames who, with the aid of his hand lamp, found in the compartment a hat and walking stick in addition to the bag. There was blood on all these items, on the seats and trickling down the glass of the window.[2] In the words of a subsequent newspaper report, the compartment 'was saturated with blood'.[3] Not unreasonably suspecting foul play, Ames locked the compartment doors, telegraphed Chalk Farm station and stayed with the train to its final destination before providing a full report to the stationmaster.

That same night, on the London-bound track, a train of empty carriages left Hackney Wick station at 10.20 p.m. Before reaching Bow station the engine driver, Alfred Ekin, noticed a large dark object lying between the tracks. Alerting his guard, William Timms, who was in the brake van, the train was stopped and reversed. Between the tracks the two men found the unconscious body of a man lying on his back, with his head towards Hackney. With the help of others who had arrived at the scene, including P.C. Edward Dougan, the body was carried to the Mitford Castle public house nearby. P.C. Dougan searched the man's pockets:

> and found four sovereigns and some keys in the left-hand side trousers pocket, and in the vest pocket a florin and half of a first-class ticket of the North London Railway. In the right-hand side trousers pocket there were 10s. 6d. in silver and copper, some more keys, a silver snuffbox, and a number of letters and papers, and a silk handkerchief, and a diamond ring on the little finger which I took away. There was a gold fastening attached to his waistcoat, but I could not undo it.[4]

By 11 p.m. a local surgeon, Alfred Brereton, had arrived. He found that the man had many serious head wounds but was still alive. The surgeon's attempts to revive the patient failed and he remained unconscious. The head wounds had arisen as a result of two main traumas; those on the top of the head had been caused by a blunt instrument while those on the left side of the head were consistent with a fall from a moving railway carriage. Clearly the man had been the victim of a violent assault, and it took little time for the connection to be made between the blood-soaked train compartment and the body on the railway track.

During the early morning of Sunday 10 July the man was identified as Thomas Briggs, 69 years old, a highly respected chief clerk in the bank of Messrs Robarts, Curtis & Co. of Lombard Street, coincidentally the same bank as that which employed the two clerks who had first entered the blood-splattered train compartment at Hackney. Briggs was well known as a frequent traveller on the North London Railway between Fenchurch Street and Hackney Wick. His son, Thomas James Briggs, was quickly contacted and arrived at the Mitford Castle at 2 a.m. Arrangements were made to transfer Briggs to his home at Clapton Square, Victoria Park, where he died at a quarter to midnight on the Sunday night. The police now had a murderer to find, and also had to cope with the considerable public reaction to the fact that this was the first murder that had taken place on a British train.

George Clarke would soon have heard the news of the murder at the office in Scotland Yard. However, he would not have immediately appreciated the ultimate extent of his involvement in the case. Indeed, Clarke was not involved in the initial inquiries. As the murder had occurred in East London, the first responsibility for the case fell on K Division (based at West Ham), under Superintendent Howie. Howie had been a policeman for twenty-eight years, and superintendent for twelve of them, and was only nine months away from his retirement, but his last few months were to prove eventful.[5]

Inspector Walter Kerressey, of Bow Police Station, was the first senior officer on the scene having been called at an early stage to the Mitford Castle by P.C. Dougan on the night of 9 July. Kerressey, a 43-year-old Irishman from Cappoquin, had joined the Metropolitan Police ten years after Clarke but had already been an inspector for five years.[6] On the morning of Sunday 10 July, Kerressey examined the train compartment at Bow station before visiting Briggs at his home, where 'he was then alive but insensible'.[7] The items recovered from the train compartment were shown to 'young Mr Briggs' who identified the stick and bag but, to everyone's surprise, told the police that the hat, a black beaver, was not his father's.[8] It also became clear that a valuable gold watch and chain that had been regularly worn by the elder Thomas Briggs had not been found on the body. This suggested that theft was one possible motive for the murderous assault, albeit that more than £4 in cash had been found apparently untouched in Briggs' pockets. From these early observations the search was set in motion to locate Briggs' missing watch and chain, to identify the person who had left an unknown hat at the scene of the crime and to locate a bell-crowned hat, made by the hatter Daniel Digance of 18 Royal Exchange, which Thomas Briggs was known to have been wearing on the day he was assaulted. As later events proved, it was the hats and the watch that provided the key evidence, ultimately linking the murderer and the railway compartment. While K Division led the initial enquiries, they did not hold this responsibility for long. On Monday 11 July Commissioner Mayne appointed Inspector Tanner to take over the investigation.[9] He was to be assisted in this task by Clarke and the K Division team.

The extent of public concern about the Briggs murder was soon evident from the reaction of the press, highlighting the public fear of being attacked in railway compartments which, in those days, were cut off from one another and had no emergency communication system. *The Times* was amongst the first to comment on this aspect:

> ... all of us are liable to find ourselves in positions where we might easily be murdered for the sake of a purse or a gold watch. A railway carriage is a place where we are cut off for a time from all chance of assistance, and this feeling of helplessness in case of emergency has been a bugbear to many nervous travellers, male as well as female. Without the means of communicating with the guard we are almost at the mercy of fire, collisions, and fellow-passengers. This

last danger is to most minds by far the most intolerable of the three. The idea of … being shut up with a murderer is still more intolerable. Highwaymen were bad enough, but they rushed out at you from behind a hedge, instead of quietly taking their tickets and seating themselves beside you in the same carriage … For some months to come travellers by night trains will probably scan their companions narrowly before entering a railway carriage. The best antidote to any such panic would be the speedy apprehension of the criminals, and this we trust we may very shortly have to report.[10]

Fortunately, an important witness came forward on 12 July after a combination of intense newspaper coverage and the posting of bills describing the missing watch and chain and offering a reward totalling £300. A silversmith and jeweller of 55 Cheapside, with the somewhat unfortunate name of John Death (which he apparently preferred to pronounce as 'Deeth'[11]), contacted the police to report that on 11 July a man had been served by his brother Robert who had exchanged a 15-carat-gold watch chain resembling the one stolen from Thomas Briggs. Robert Death's description of the man was 'about 30 years old, 5 feet 6 or 7 inches high, with a sallow complexion and thin features. He is a foreigner, and is supposed to be a German, but speaks good English. He wore a black frock coat and waistcoat, dark trousers, and a black hat.'[12] In exchange for the £3 10s value of the watch chain, the man had purchased another chain and a ring which had been taken away by the foreigner in a small box.

There then followed some frustrating days for the police investigation with plenty of false leads being received from the press and public, or as the papers of the day expressed it: 'the police have of course received the usual number of communications from madmen and practical jokers.'[13] It does not take much imagination to paint a mental picture of the workload of Clarke and other members of the small police team, spending long hours ploughing through piles of correspondence, looking for new leads, locating and interviewing potential new witnesses and following up information on suspects from as far afield as Scotland. At least one individual was arrested and Robert Death was called in to identify him, but it proved not to be the prime suspect that they were seeking. However, things took a turn for the better on 18 July when a London cabman, Jonathan Matthews, emerged with evidence that was to transform the course and location of the investigation.

Matthews' evidence identified a young German, Franz Müller, as the prime suspect. Müller was a tailor and a regular visitor to Matthews' home. Indeed, only the previous Tuesday (12 July), Müller had visited and had given Matthews' youngest daughter a small cardboard box, 'such as jewellers put their various wares in', bearing the name and address of John Death.[14] Matthews was also able to provide a photograph of Müller, and informed the police that he had bought Müller a hat a few months ago, similar to one of his own, which Müller had paid for in kind by making Matthews a waistcoat. Without delay the police took the cardboard box and photograph to John Death's silversmith premises in Cheapside. Robert Death identified the box as being of the type that he would have used to pack a watch chain and ring, and, on seeing the photograph of Müller, recognised him as the foreigner who had exchanged the gold watch chain for those items. Meanwhile, Matthews was taken to Scotland Yard and shown the hat found in the railway compartment, which he duly identified as the hat that he had bought for Müller.

Why it took Matthews so long to come forward with his information remains a question even today. His explanation was that he simply hadn't heard about the Briggs murder despite the extensive newspaper coverage, street gossip and widespread bill-posting.[15] This issue and other aspects of Matthews' evidence were later to be challenged by defence lawyers at the Old Bailey. However, for Inspector Tanner and his team it provided the best information received so far on the identity of the possible murderer. Tanner promptly proceeded to Bow Street Police Court to obtain a warrant for the arrest of Müller. Matthews had also provided the police with details of the address where Müller lodged, at 16 Park Terrace, Victoria Park. Here, the landlady Mrs Ellen Blyth confirmed that Müller had stayed there for some seven weeks, but had informed her about fourteen days previously of his intention to leave England for America. Having somehow raised sufficient money for a steerage passage, he had boarded the sailing ship *Victoria* on Thursday 14 July, which had left London the next day, headed for New York. Mrs Blyth had already received a letter from Müller dated 16 July and postmarked 'Worthing':

> On the sea, July 16 in the morning. Dear Friends, – I am glad to confess that I cannot have a better time, as I have; if the sun shines nice and the wind blows fair, as it is at the present moment, everything will go well. I cannot write any more, only I have no postage; you will be so kind to take that letter in.[16]

So, the suspected murderer had escaped – or had he? For sailing packets, such as the *Victoria*, the average Atlantic crossing time from England to the east coast of America was about thirty-six days. Isambard Brunel had shown as early as 1838, with the *Great Western*, that the journey time could be reduced to as little as fifteen days if the traveller went by steamship.[17] Having hurriedly packed and bidden farewell to their families, Tanner and Clarke headed out of Euston station on Tuesday 19 July on the 9 p.m. train for Liverpool. They were accompanied by the two main witnesses, Robert Death and Jonathan Matthews. On 20 July, the four men boarded the Inman Line steamship *City of Manchester*, which departed from Liverpool Docks for New York at 11 a.m.[18] Inspector Kerressey stayed behind to obtain a further warrant and followed Tanner and Clarke on 22 July, sailing from Liverpool on another of the Inman Line's fleet of steamships, the *City of Cork*.[19] The chase was on to get to America before Müller.

The sixteen days it took Tanner and Clarke to reach New York provided them with time to take stock of the case, and to plan their strategy once they arrived. They had to be self sufficient, as there was no opportunity for communicating with their colleagues in London while on the ship. In 1864 the use of wireless telegraphy was many years away, and wireless communication did not impact on the international tracking-down of criminals at sea until its use in the arrest of Dr Crippen on 31 July 1910. In addition, it was only in 1866 that lasting cable telegraphic links were established between Britain and America, so, even when they reached New York on 5 August, Clarke and Tanner were only able to contact Scotland Yard through messages sent by steamship.[20] Despite the relative isolation in which the two detectives had to make their decisions, the absence of an effective means of communicating between ship and shore was also beneficial for them as Müller would not be able to hear the news that he was being pursued unless the *Victoria* called in at another port en route. Events back home suggested that this would be unlikely. Before they had left England, the Victorian equivalent of an 'all ports alert' for the *Victoria* had been put out by Scotland Yard, informing police in British (including Irish) ports where the *Victoria* might call in, 'to search for and arrest Franz Müller'.[21]

On board the *City of Manchester*, Tanner and Clarke must have wondered what reception they would receive when they reached New York. America was in the throes of a prolonged and bloody civil war. While Britain had maintained a formal position of neutrality, the political and economic tensions were considerable. The war had produced adverse effects on some sectors of the British economy, particularly the textile industry of north-west England, since 1861, when there had been an interruption in the imports of baled cotton from America's southern states. One consequence was that large parts of Lancashire's workforce went from being the most prosperous workers in Britain to the most impoverished.[22] This had led to some overt support in Britain for the Confederacy, which had been exacerbated in the eyes of Union politicians by the manufacture in Britain of some warships, including the *Alabama*. The ship had been built in secret at Birkenhead in 1862, through the collaboration of a Confederate agent and a cotton broker in Liverpool. Launched in July 1862 as the *Enrica*, it had sailed with a civilian crew to the Azores, where it was commissioned as the *Alabama*. Operating with a crew that still included some British nationals, the *Alabama* had served for two years as a commerce raider, attacking Union merchant and naval ships in a total of seven expeditionary raids. In this time, she boarded nearly 450 vessels and captured or burned sixty-five Union ships, but had finally met her end off Cherbourg on 19 June 1864 under the guns of the United States' Ship *Kearsage*.[23] Tanner and Clarke would have known of the recent demise of the *Alabama* before they left for America, and must have wondered whether the wounds inflicted on the Union cause by a British-manufactured, and partly British-manned ship, would affect their reception in New York.

Their voyage was also not without incident. On 23 July Tanner fell down a stairway and injured his back. Whether he had not yet gained his sea legs or had over indulged on the ship's rum we will probably never know, but the accident confined him to his bunk for four days and, despite on-board treatment, he required further treatment for his injury after arriving in New York.[24] On 5 August, the *City of Manchester* finally berthed at Manhattan.

Tanner's first substantive report to Mayne was sent on 9 August, relaying the information that the *Victoria* was not expected to arrive until 20 August at the earliest.[25] Tanner also reported a visit to the British Consul, who had advised him to communicate with the chief of police in New York, Superintendent Kennedy, and with the legal counsel for the consulate, Mr Marbury. Tanner met with Kennedy and Inspector Carpenter of the New York Metropolitan Police and had been assured that he would receive all the aid he required.[26] Marbury had informed the detectives that the arrest of Müller in American territory must be made by an officer deputed by the New York police. With Kennedy's agreement, Sergeant John Tiernan had been selected for this responsibility as he was stationed 8 miles up the bay, at Sandy Hook, alongside the medical officer whose duty it was to board each ship before the captain was able to enter the harbour and disembark the passengers. If arrested, the prisoner would need to be taken before a commissioner for the extradition hearing. Tanner also informed Mayne that he was taking every possible step to prevent Müller escaping. To reduce the chance of escape happening a reward of £5 had been offered to any ship's pilot who boarded the *Victoria*, to ensure that they communicated only to the ship's captain the police plans to board the ship and arrest Müller. Tanner had sent Clarke and Kerressey about 7 miles up the bay, to Staten Island, to locate all potential ships' pilots. From here they could also give early warning of the *Victoria's* impending arrival and do everything possible to prevent Müller's escape, rescue or kidnapping by bounty hunters; all of which were seen as real dangers.[27]

By the time of Tanner's report of 16 August, the impact of the Civil War was starting to introduce worrying complications, and the New York summer weather was adding to the problems:

> ... the Victoria has not yet arrived, or since the 25th July been heard of. My arrangements are very much (just at the present time) complicated, for a Confederate vessel named Tallahassee paid a visit outside New York harbour and destroyed several ships, one of which the Adriatic belonging to same owners as

the Victoria, and I fear, the Victoria will share the same fate … We are all well, but suffer somewhat from the very great heat.[28]

Tanner was right to be concerned about the Confederate ship. The *Tallahassee* was yet another British-built ship. It had only been commissioned in the Confederate navy as recently as 20 July 1864, the same day as Tanner and Clarke had sailed from Liverpool. Under its new flag it ran the Union blockade of its home port, Wilmington, North Carolina, on 6 August and then undertook a spectacular nineteen-day raid off the Atlantic coast as far north as Halifax, Nova Scotia, destroying twenty-six ships and capturing seven others. Amongst them the *Victoria*'s sister ship, the *Adriatic*, had been seized and burned, though the *Tallahassee* lost her main mast in the process.[29] There had been no casualties amongst the passengers and crew of the *Adriatic*, but they had suffered a considerable ordeal. They had been transferred to a small barque which took two days to reach land, had inadequate food and water, and provided standing room only for the passengers. In addition, most of the passengers had lost their possessions, which had been burned with the *Adriatic*.[30] If such a fate befell the *Victoria*, what chance would Tanner and his colleagues have to arrest Müller and to locate any incriminating evidence that he might have been carrying in his luggage? Fortunately, as events turned out, the Confederate vessel headed north and did not interfere with the *Victoria*'s passage.

On 23 August, Tanner was still waiting. 'Up to this date we have no tidings of the ship *Victoria* she is now 40 days out and may be hourly expected.'[31] Shortly after he had sent this message he received a telegram from Sandy Hook, that the *Victoria* had at last been sighted off the coast. Once the ship was in American waters (and only then), Tanner was able to obtain a warrant for the arrest of Müller from Commissioner Charles Newton. Despite various efforts on the part of the British detectives to prevent the news of the arrival of the *Victoria* becoming widespread knowledge, there were soon reports of groups of people in boats and on the shoreline, hailing the ship with shouts of 'How are you, Müller the murderer', 'Throw the murderer overboard' and similar expressions.[32] Fortunately, these were not heard or understood by the man himself. At last, on the evening of Wednesday 24 August, Sergeants Clarke and Tiernan climbed on board the *Victoria* from the medical officer's boat in Staten Island Bay. They found that Müller was unaware of what was about to happen. Clarke later described Müller's arrest:

On 24th last August I went on board the ship *Victoria* at New York. Mr Tiernan, an officer of the New York police, was in company with me. The prisoner was on board. He was called to the after part of the ship by the captain. I seized hold of him by his arms. He said 'What is the matter'. Tiernan said,

'You are charged with the murder of Mr Briggs'. I found that Tiernan did not remember the particulars, and I followed by saying 'Yes, on the North London Railway between Hackney Wick and Bow, on 9th July'. The prisoner said, 'I was never on the line'. I do not know whether he said, 'that night', or whether he said 'I never was on the line'. I told him my name, and that I was a policeman from London, and pointing to Mr Tiernan, that he was a policeman of New York. I then took him down stairs into the saloon. Tiernan searched him in my presence. A key was taken from his waistcoat pocket. I have it here. I took possession of it and said, 'What is this the key of?' He said 'The key of my box'. I said 'Where is your box'. He said 'In my berth'. In consequence of what the captain told me, I went to No. 9 berth and found a large black box which I brought into the saloon where the prisoner was standing. He said 'That is my box'. I unlocked it with this key that I had taken from his waistcoat pocket, and in a corner of the box I found this watch (produced). It was then sewn up in a piece of leather. I have the piece in which it was sewn up. I said to the prisoner, 'What is this?' believing it to be a watch as I felt it in my hand. He said 'It is my watch'. I then took up the hat that was standing in the box, and said 'Is this your hat?' He said 'Yes, it is the hat' (produced). I said 'How long have you possessed them?' He said 'I have had the watch about two years, and the hat about twelve months'. I told him he would have to remain in custody and be taken to New York. I kept him on board all night. Inspector Tanner came in the morning and I then gave him over to him.[33]

Clarke then questioned members of the crew and some of the other passengers to establish how Müller had behaved during the journey. The reports that emerged suggested that Müller had been better behaved and more popular than some passengers. There had, however, been some trouble which was attributed to his 'overbearing manner' and, on one occasion, he received a black eye for calling a fellow passenger 'a liar and a robber'.[34]

Tanner, when he arrived on board, had brought Death with him and conducted an 'identification parade' in which Müller was placed amongst a group of eight other steerage passengers in a cabin. Death duly picked out Müller as the man who had exchanged Briggs' watch chain on 11 July.[35] Tanner briefly reported progress to Mayne: 'The *Victoria* has arrived at New York and Müller has been arrested. The hat and watch of Mr Briggs were found in his possession. Müller protested his innocence and the legal proceedings in reference to his extradition are progressing.'[36] The news of the arrest did not arrive in Britain until 7 September. When it was received, newspapers across the country devoted numerous column inches to the story. Few of the press reports sought to present a balanced picture of the case, with Müller's presumed guilt being implicit in every story. Several articles contained the first descriptions of Müller:

He is apparently about five feet six or seven inches in height, compactly built and about twenty-four or twenty-five years of age. His forehead is well developed, hair light, no whiskers or moustache, and eyes blue, but very small and very deeply set in his head; while his mouth is decidedly repulsive from its extreme width and protuberance, impressing one with the idea of dogged obstinacy and vindictive relentlessness.[37]

The extradition hearing was the next hurdle for Tanner and Clarke to overcome. Mr Marbury presented the case for the British Consulate and Müller was represented by Messrs Shaffer and Blankman, thanks to the German Legal Protection Society of London who paid for his defence. The first day was filled by prosecution evidence and the cross-examination of Tanner, Clarke, Kerressey, Tiernan, Death and Matthews. The second day was to prove to be a memorable day of courtroom theatre. It started quietly enough with Müller's counsel seeking an adjournment to give them further time to prepare the defence. When this was refused, Chauncey Shaffer played the *Alabama* 'card':

He was not present to-day to quarrel with the policy of England, but here he would fearlessly state at the outset that he did not regard the treaty under which it was sought to extradite this man as anything else than a violation of the Constitution of the United States and utterly inoperative … He would show conclusively that it [the Treaty] was at present suspended by the act of the British Government … There is that hostility on the part of English subjects towards this country which writers on international law denominate 'mixed and unsolemn war' … England cannot say she is neutral in this matter when she furnishes our rebellious subjects with vessels of war, mans them, opens her ports to them, furnishes them with arms and ammunition and sends them forth on their errands of destruction, burning merchant ships and destroying the commerce on the seas of a friendly Power. The *Alabama*, built and armed in England, and manned by Englishmen, sunk and burned 120 of our ships … But as in the case before the Court, when a man is found murdered near London, they pursue the supposed murderer to our shores and cry 'Treaty, treaty, treaty'. They tore that treaty to pieces three years ago (Applause). Nay, more than that, great argosies, laden with the choicest treasures of the nation, have been sunk in countless numbers with connivance and consent of the neutral, friendly Power … England, to claim this man [Müller], must come into court with clean hands. She must not come here and ask to honour her justice when she dishonours her own justice, breaks her treaties and cries peace and neutrality, while at the same time she lets slip the dogs of war.[38]

Shaffer's tour de force must have been a painful experience for the Englishmen in court that day. Fortunately, Marbury resisted the temptation to argue on the same political ground as Shaffer and concentrated on the evidence, present-ing a telling claim that there was a complete chain of evidence that justified Müller's committal and extradition. He was rewarded for his restraint by the verdict delivered by Commissioner Newton. While complimenting Müller's defence team for their performance, Newton concluded that there was suf-ficient evidence to commit Müller.[39]

Tanner waited for the newspapers to emerge on 28 August before reporting back to Mayne:

> I beg further to report that yesterday the final examination of Müller took place when the Commissioner decided that it was a case in which he should certify for a warrant of extradition. It will be seen by the newspapers which I send also by this mail that strong language was used by the prisoner's counsel in reference to England and the applause it gained. When the papers are ready I go on to Washington to obtain the warrant from the President [Abraham Lincoln] to take the prisoners home. I do not know how long it will take but I shall endeavour to leave here by the steamship, *Etna*, on the 3 September for Liverpool. I beg also to state that extraordinary as it may seem, strong sympathy is felt here for the prisoner and it is rumoured that an attempt to rescue him from my custody will be made.[40]

While Tanner, and possibly Clarke, travelled to Washington to collect the extradition warrant from the president's office, Müller was held in the aptly named Tombs Prison in New York. Tanner left Washington with the warrant on 31 August and Müller was surrendered into his custody in time to board the *Etna*. To reduce the risk of Müller being rescued, an announcement was placed in the local papers that he would be leaving on another ship that was due to sail on 7 September. The plan was successful, although several thousand people still crowded the quayside; most of them arriving after Müller had been placed on board, in the ship's hospital, where he was guarded by Clarke and Kerressey.[41]

The newspaper reports that emerged of the voyage back to England sug-gest that Müller was a model prisoner, and that Tanner, Clarke and Kerressey behaved humanely as his gaolers, even providing two Charles Dickens' novels for Müller to read. Delayed by bad weather, the steamship finally entered Liverpool harbour on 16 September. Anticipating the crowds that would gather, plans had been put in place to take Müller and the accompanying police off the *Etna* before the ship docked.[42] That night, Müller was detained at Liverpool Police Station while Tanner, Clarke and Kerressey spent their first night back in England at the Crooked Billet public house. Early the next day, Müller was taken to Edgehill railway station, rather than the main rail terminus at Lime Street, where large crowds were again expected. The party was allocated an entire carriage on the London and North Western Railway train for their journey back to London. Nearing Euston, the train stopped briefly at the Camden ticket platform where 'there was a tremendous rush of people from all directions', and the party was joined by two other members of the Scotland Yard Detective Department, Inspector Williamson and Sergeant Thomas. With the detectives guarding the doors, 'the prisoner Müller as he occupied his seat looked exceedingly pale and agitated'.[43] The train finally arrived at Euston Square station at 2.44 p.m., where 'the excitement of the crowd was immense'.[44] After a struggle by the police to clear a route through, Müller was loaded into the waiting police van and driven off to Bow Street:

A desperate rush was made at the van as it drove down Bow-street up to the door of the police station. And at one time there appeared some risk of its being turned over; but a dozen or two of the constables pushed against the nearside of the van, and its equilibrium was fortunately not disturbed. It was some little time before a passage could be cleared for the transit of the prisoner and his attendants, but at length the door was opened, and the first person to alight from the van, with a light, jaunty step was Franz Müller himself. Then arose a storm of hissing and groaning of a most unmistakable character, but it did not in the slightest degree disconcert the prisoner. The people seemed surprised at the slight, mean, and shabby appearance of the man who had been so long the theme of universal discussion. Far below the middle height, excessively plain-looking and ill-featured, and with light-coloured hair projecting from under his hat, garments thin and seedy, and wearing a white broad-brimmed and somewhat weather-beaten straw hat, he really was not 'equal to the occasion' in the estimate of the crowd, who freely commented on the disappointment which they had experienced. 'What!' said one stalwart ragged denizen of Seven Dials, '*he* murder Mr Briggs, *he* chuck a big man out of the carriage! Why he couldn't do it'.[45]

Though proving a disappointment to the Bow Street mob, Müller was charged and held in the cells of the heavily guarded police station.

During the absence of Tanner and Clarke in America, responsibility for the continuing investigations in London had been taken on by Inspector Williamson. Anticipating the return of his two colleagues from America, Williamson had prepared an updated summary of events on the Briggs murder case.[46] There was little new information. However, Müller was now known to have made occasional use of the North London Railway between Bow and Fenchurch Street, despite his assertion to Clarke, when arrested, that he had not been on that line. It had also become clearer how Müller had raised the money to buy his steerage passage on the *Victoria*. In the original transaction which Müller had with the Deaths, Brigg's watch chain had not been exchanged for cash, but for another watch chain and a ring. Further investigation had revealed that there had been other dealings with pawnbrokers and with work colleagues and friends, which had allowed Müller to raise about £4 5s in cash with which he had been able to buy his £4 passage. In addition, further information had been obtained about Müller's background: 'Müller was a native of Saxe-Weimar, twenty-five years of age. Apprenticed as a gunsmith in his native country, he had come over to England about two years before the murder of Mr. Briggs. Failing to get work as a gunsmith, he had turned tailor.'[47]

The remaining issues for the detectives were to establish the origin of the hat that Clarke had found in Müller's trunk, and to locate any evidence that would specifically place Müller on the train at the time that the murder occurred. Tanner had confidently reported back from America that the hat in the trunk was the one which Briggs had been wearing on the night that he was murdered. However, despite containing the correct maker's name (Digance), closer inspection had revealed that the hat was noticeably shorter than the original description of Briggs' hat had suggested. A visit to the hatter was required and Digance duly solved the riddle. In evidence that he later gave at the Old Bailey, he explained that:

> Mr Briggs has been a customer of mine for the last five-and-twenty or thirty years … I made a hat to order for Mr Briggs in September, 1863. According to the description in the book the hat produced does not correspond … I should say the hat has been cut down from 1 inch to 1½ inches. The bottom part of the leather has been cut off, and it has been sewn together again, and the silk has been pasted on again. It has not been cut down as a hatter would do it … The hat has been neatly sewn, and I should say it was done by a person who understands sewing. With the exception of the cutting down, the hat corresponds with the hat of Mr Briggs.[48]

So the supposition became that Müller, using his tailoring skills, had modified Briggs' hat to disguise it.

The task of finding evidence that placed Müller on the 9.45 p.m. train from Fenchurch Street on 9 July 1864 proved much more elusive, and no satisfactory conclusion was reached. One witness, Thomas Lee, emerged late and clouded the issue as far as the police were concerned by claiming that he had seen two men sitting in the compartment with Mr Briggs. Lee could not confirm (or deny) that Müller was one of them, and his evidence was not used by the prosecution. Müller had been out in London that night as he had travelled south of the Thames to call on a young lady, Mary Ann

Eldred, in Camberwell. However, no one came forward with evidence that they had seen Müller and Briggs together, or even that Müller had been on the same train. Clearly, the assiduous protection of the train compartment as a scene of crime by Ames, the train guard, would have yielded more clues for the police to work with if some of the modern technologies now used by forensic scientists had been available in Victorian times. As it was, fingerprinting and blood analysis were still decades away from being understood and implemented, and DNA fingerprinting techniques were only to emerge more than a century later. Thus, without a confession (which was not forthcoming), the evidence that the police had been able to obtain against Müller was entirely circumstantial.

The next step was to persuade the Bow Street magistrate that there was a sufficient case for him to commit Müller for trial. The magistrate's hearing was convened by the presiding magistrate, Mr Flowers, at Bow Street Police Court on Monday 19 September, less than two days after Müller had arrived back in London. The magistrate, 'Jimmy' Flowers, was described by a contemporary lawyer as 'one of the most kind-hearted creatures that ever lived', but it probably didn't feel that way to Müller.[49] With the continuing high level of public interest, there was a strong body of police stationed at each end of the street and, in the court, the limited space devoted to the public was occupied almost exclusively by the representatives of the English and foreign press, the artists of the illustrated papers and a few notable gentlemen in the literary world.[50] Clarke was the last witness to give evidence on that day, and the case was remanded for a week when its continuation was to clash chaotically with the resumed inquest on the murder of Mr Briggs.

The inquest (a 'ticket-only' affair for members of the public), which had been initiated before Clarke and Tanner had gone to America, was resumed at 8 a.m. on Monday 26 September in the Town Hall at Hackney. Müller was brought in, though he had nothing to say. After Müller had been duly identified the coroner addressed the jury, summing up the information that had been presented on previous days, and asked the jury to retire to consider their verdict. After only twenty minutes the jury concluded 'that the deceased died from the effects of foul violence administered in a railway carriage on Saturday, the 9th of July, and we find that Franz Müller is the man by whom that violence was committed'. They then expressed their dissatisfaction with 'the present state of railway accommodation at affording facilities for the perpetration of various crimes and offences; and earnestly desire to call the attention of the home government to the subject, and to the necessity of enforcing the adoption by railway companies of some more efficient system of protection to life, character and property'.[51]

There was then a mad dash for the prisoner and witnesses to get from Hackney to Bow Street for the resumed magistrate's hearing due to start at

11 a.m. *The Times* noted that 'the coroner had deprived the witnesses of all chance of rest or refreshment before being exposed to another long examination and the occurrence was the subject of bitter complaint'.[52] At the end of a disgruntled day's proceedings, Mr Flowers formally concluded that there was sufficient evidence to warrant a trial by jury and committed Müller for trial at the next sessions of the Central Criminal Court, on the charge of wilfully murdering Mr Briggs. Müller was then transported to Newgate Prison, where the mob was waiting for him outside.

Müller's trial started at a crowded Old Bailey on Thursday 27 October. The prosecution team for the Crown consisted of the solicitor general, Sir Robert Collier (Liberal MP for Plymouth and later to become attorney general).[53] He was assisted, amongst others, by Serjeant-at-Law William Ballantine and Hardinge Giffard, later Earl of Halsbury and a lord chancellor.[54] Müller's defence team was led by Serjeant-at-Law John Humffreys Parry, a senior barrister and popular and successful advocate.[55] As was the practice at that time, there were two judges, the more senior of whom was the Lord Chief Baron of the Exchequer Sir Frederick Pollock, a previous attorney general in the Tory administrations of Sir Robert Peel.[56] The junior judge was Baron Martin. 'The judges having taken their seats the prisoner Müller was placed at the bar … He was neatly dressed in a plain brown-coloured morning coat, which he wore buttoned on the chest. His manner was quiet, self-possessed, and respectful. For some time at first his countenance was pale, but at length assumed what appeared to be its natural hue.'[57]

Müller pleaded 'not guilty' to the charge of murder and, somewhat surprisingly, elected to be tried by twelve Englishmen rather than a jury partly composed of foreigners which, in view of his nationality, he was entitled to elect for (an entitlement that ended in 1870). The case for the Crown was opened by Collier who began by entreating the jury to remove from their minds any of the hostile press coverage that had been so prevalent.[58] Collier then proceeded to summarise the key issues of the Crown case: that Thomas Briggs had been murdered by Müller, and that the motive was the theft of his watch and chain. Müller had been keen to travel to America but needed money to do it. Through a sequence of financial transactions involving several pawnbrokers, he had raised the money he needed for his passage. Mistakenly removing Briggs' hat from the railway carriage and leaving his own, he had modified Briggs' hat in an attempt to disguise it. When arrested on board the *Victoria*, his trunk was found to contain both Brigg's watch and his hat. Though Müller had not been observed in the train compartment where Briggs was murdered, he had been in London on the night of 9 July and had the opportunity to commit the murder.

The individuals that were called to provide evidence on behalf of the Crown on the first day of the trial included relatives of Briggs (with whom he had been dining on 9 July before travelling homeward), the two clerks who had first entered the blood-soaked compartment at Hackney Wick, the railway staff, the medical men and the police from K Division. These were followed by John and Robert Death and by Müller's landlady and landlord, Mrs Blyth and her husband. The Blyths bore sympathetic testimony to the quiet and inoffensive disposition of the prisoner. They also mentioned that, on 9 July, Müller had discarded one of his boots and replaced it with a slipper because he had injured his right foot; a feature that one assumes should have made him more noticeable as he travelled round London on that day. Important evidence was presented by the next witnesses, Mrs Repsch and her husband, a fellow German and work colleague of Müller. The couple were regularly visited by Müller, with whom they were on friendly terms. When Müller had visited them on 11 July, he had shown Mrs Repsch a new watch chain which he claimed to have bought at the docks. When the chain that had been purchased by Müller at Death's silversmiths was shown to her in court, Mrs Repsch identified it as the one shown to her by Müller. In addition, she stated that Müller had been wearing a new hat on that Monday, and she had chided him for his extravagance. She also described Müller's previous hat, her description being consistent with that found in the railway carriage. By 5 p.m., with seven or eight Crown witnesses still to be examined, the court was adjourned and the jury 'in accordance with custom, were escorted to the London Coffee-House in Ludgate-hill to stay over night'.[59]

On the following day the trial resumed with the examination of further prosecution witnesses, including several pawnbrokers who gave evidence of the financial transactions that had taken place between them and Müller. But the court (which was again crowded, with hundreds of people congregated outside) was most keenly anticipating the appearance of the key witness, Jonathan Matthews. Would the defence team suggest that Matthews rather than Müller was the guilty man? Was the hat found in the railway compartment really Matthews' hat rather than Müller's? Was Matthews making things up, simply to claim the £300 reward? As events turned out, Matthews stood his ground and persisted with his claim that he had not heard about the murder until the day (18 July) on which he had first contacted the police. Parry provided evidence that Matthews had been previously convicted of theft in 1850 (serving a prison sentence of twenty-one days for the offence), but the consensus view seemed to be that 'severe as was the cross-examination of Matthews, in the judgement of those who heard it, it had not shaken the weight of his evidence in any material degree'.[60]

Later in the day the evidence of Müller's arrest given by Clarke and Tanner came as something of an anti-climax, with all the essential details being well known. However, Parry did probe Clarke on whether Müller had said 'I never was on the line' or 'I never was on the line that night'. Clarke couldn't remember, but, when pressed, told the court that 'I am quite certain that if the passage quoted is in the deposition, the prisoner used it'.[61] Clarke was also recalled during Tanner's evidence and asked whether Müller had sold any clothes during the voyage (yes, a waistcoat that Müller had subsequently bought back), and whether his clothes had been forensically analysed (no). The prosecution evidence was then concluded by the witnesses Thomas Briggs (the younger) and the hatter, Daniel Digance.

It was now the turn of Müller's defence team to present their case. The legal procedures of the time dictated that the speech for the defence was made before calling any witnesses. The prosecution then had the right to reply to the case presented by the defence team, and often exercised that option. Defendants were also not allowed to give evidence in their own defence at Crown courts, so Müller could not be called into the witness box even if his counsel had thought that would help his cause. Müller's counsel delivered a speech which ended with applause from sections of the courtroom.[62] As expected, he first reminded the jury that they should disregard the comprehensive newspaper coverage of events before the trial and chastised the press:

> I must say that it is for the most part unusual when a person has been arrested on a charge on which, if found guilty, his life must be sacrificed [the death penalty was the mandatory sentence for murder], to find writers, not in insignificant journals but in the most respectable and the most eminent parts of the press, commenting on the likelihood of the guilt or the innocence of such a person.[63]

He then concentrated on undermining the credibility of two of the key prosecution witnesses, Mrs Repsch and Jonathan Matthews. With Mrs Repsch, who had damagingly identified the hat found in the train compartment as being one that she had seen Müller wearing, he implied that the prosecution may effectively have 'trained' her into its recognition, though 'he cannot conscientiously charge her with perjury'.[64] Sailing close to the wind, he moved on to Matthews:

> If I were to point to Matthews as having been guilty of the murder, or a party to it, I should be a disgrace to the profession to which I am proud to belong. There was no such stuff in my thoughts; but this I will say of Matthews, that he is a man whose evidence is entirely untrustworthy, who gave his evidence in a most unsatisfactory manner, and to whose testimony I am sure no educated man, having the responsibility of the life of a fellow-creature on his shoulders would pay any attention for a moment. He is obviously actuated by a desire to obtain the reward offered for the murder of Mr Briggs.[65]

Parry then stated that the prosecution evidence had not been sufficient to confirm beyond reasonable doubt that the hat found in the train compartment was Müller's, or that the hat found in Müller's trunk was originally Mr Briggs' hat. He stressed that Müller 'was always chopping and changing, buying and selling'.[66] Clearly, Parry hoped to leave the thought in the jury's mind that Müller could have purchased the incriminating items from another person, rather than committing the murder himself. He then turned to the issue of Müller's slight physique and whether he would have had the strength to beat and rob Briggs, and throw him out of the compartment:

> there is, I say, one part of this inquiry which I almost defy you to reconcile with the guilt of the prisoner. Mr Briggs seems to have been a man of about 12 stone weight and 5 feet 9 inches in height … in robust and vigorous health. Compared with Mr Briggs the young man at the bar is a mere stripling … Could, I ask you, the struggle which ended in the death of a powerful sober man of considerable weight and with all his faculties about him, have been perpetrated by a young man such as he whom you now have before you?[67]

Suggesting that the murder must have been committed by more than one person, Parry indicated that he would be calling a witness who would confirm that he had seen two men in the railway compartment with Thomas Briggs on the evening of 9 July. Finally, he stated that he would be calling alibi witnesses who would confirm that Müller could not have been on the 9.45 p.m. train from Fenchurch Street as he had been elsewhere at that time.

On Saturday 29 October the first defence witness called was Thomas Lee, who had been previously discarded as a witness for the prosecution. Lee said he had seen two other men in the compartment with Mr Briggs at Bow station, but his evidence lacked credibility on cross-examination.[68] The alibi witnesses also failed the credibility test. It emerged that Müller had been a regular caller at a house in Camberwell where a young lady called Mary Ann Eldred was lodging, and it was claimed that he had called to see her in her lodgings on the evening of 9 July, only to find that she had gone out. The landlady, Elizabeth Jones, gave evidence to this effect and stated that Müller had not left until at least 9.30 p.m. according to her clock (which, if correct, would have meant that he would have been unable to catch the train on which Briggs had travelled). Once it became clear that Elizabeth Jones' house was a brothel, and that Mary Ann Eldred was a prostitute (although, by all accounts, fond of 'her little Frenchman', as she called Müller), these witnesses did not help Müller's case; neither did a bus conductor, Charles Forman, who remembered seeing a man on his bus who was wearing a slipper, but could not remember whether he had seen him in July or August.

In his reply to the defence case, the solicitor general responded to the attempt to compromise Mrs Repsch's testimony by commenting that 'a fairer or more straightforward witness never appeared before a jury'. With serious intent, but with legal tongue-in-cheek, he expressed his pleasure that 'my learned friend most honestly, candidly, and eloquently disavowed any intention – the remotest idea – of imputing to Matthews that he was concerned in the murder'. On the subject of Müller's alibi, he questioned the time-keeping and accuracy of the brothel clock by asking the jury if they thought that Elizabeth Jones' 'respectable and well conducted establishment were so ordered that the goings out and the incomings of its inmates were regulated by clockwork?'[69]

At 1.30 p.m. the senior judge Lord Chief Baron Pollock commenced his summing-up to the jury; 'Though scrupulously fair and dignified in tone, it was decidedly unfavourable to the prisoner'.[70] The jury members retired to consider their verdict at 2.45 p.m. and, after only fifteen minutes' deliberation, they returned a verdict of 'guilty'. It was a considerable surprise when, 'directly the fatal word was pronounced, the lord chief baron burst into a flood of tears. He placed his hands over his face, and raised his elbows on his desk, and a profound silence reigned throughout the court.'[71] The black cap was placed on the head of Baron Martin who sentenced Müller to death by hanging. Müller, who had continued to display surprising firmness and self-possession, said:

'I should like to say something. I am, at all events, satisfied with the sentence which your Lordship has passed. I know very well it is that which the law of the country prescribes. What I have to say is that I have not been convicted on a true statement of the facts, but on a false statement.' The prisoner had not completed the last sentence when his iron resolution and the stern self-command which ... he had maintained throughout the trial with an imperturbability which showed him capable of the most desperate deeds, entirely gave way, and the miserable man left the dock dissolved in tears.[72]

There is no surviving record of how George Clarke, the police of K Division and the other detectives at Scotland Yard reacted to the verdict and sentence. Whether they got together at a nearby hostelry for a glass of porter, or some other appropriate libation, to celebrate a successful conclusion to their work is therefore left to the reader's imagination. Whether Clarke, Tanner or Kerressey felt any pity for Franz Müller, with whom they had spent much time during the voyage back from America, is also unknown.

For Müller or any other convicted prisoner at that time, there was no formal process of appeal. However, it was possible to submit representations for mercy to the Home Secretary, and these were duly received from the German

Legal Protection Society. In addition, there were reports of submissions from Germany to Queen Victoria (who of course had German ancestors), which were treated with indignation in sections of the British Press.

Müller's landlady, Ellen Blyth, submitted a letter claiming that on 10 July (the morning after the murder), Müller had breakfasted with her and her husband and wore the same clothes that he had worn on 9 July and 'such clothes were clean and spotless from mud, dirt, stain or anything calculated to excite attention'.[73] A new witness, Baron de Camin, swore under oath at Worship Street Police Court that, on the night of 9 July, he had seen a 'man blooded from head to foot' on the railway embankment between Bow and Hackney Wick stations, and stated that he had told these facts to Sergeant Clarke.[74] This prompted a swift rebuttal from Scotland Yard; in an internal memorandum to Mayne, Inspector Williamson reported that 'I have seen Sergeant Clarke respecting the remark in Baron de Camin's affidavit but the Sergeant states that he has no recollection of any person making such a statement to him at anytime'.[75]

In the event, none of these representations swayed the Home Secretary towards granting a respite or commuting the sentence. *The Times* reported that the death sentence would stand, adding that 'the excitement caused by the near approach of the execution is almost unprecedented'.[76] On the same page of the newspaper there was a report of investigations into another gruesome murder case under the headline 'The Murder in Plaistow Marshes'.[77] This report made reference to 'Sergeant Clarke, of the detective force'. George Clarke was indeed already working on his next murder case and it seems likely that he was not in attendance at Müller's execution, being otherwise engaged in the new inquiry. If so he was probably relieved not to be at Newgate, judging by the reports of the events that took place on 14 November.

Müller's public execution was an unedifying affair, particularly so to modern sensibilities. As early as Friday 11 November, when crowd-control barriers were already being placed in the streets around Newgate, 'a dismal crowd of dirty vagrants kept hovering around'.[78] At dawn on the morning of 14 November, an estimated 50,000-strong crowd had gathered:

> Among the throng were very few women; and even these were generally of the lowest and the poorest class, and almost as abandoned in behaviour as their few better dressed exceptions. The rest of the crowd was, as a rule, made up of young men … of what may be almost called as low a grade as any of the worst there met, the rakings of cheap singing-halls and billiard-rooms, the fast young 'gents' of London … Only as the sun rose clearer did the mysterious dull sound so often explain itself … It was literally and absolutely nothing more than the sound caused by knocking the hats over the eyes of those well-dressed persons who had ventured amongst the crowd and, while so 'bonneted', stripping them and robbing them of everything.[79]

The public hangman at the time, and since 1829, was William Calcraft who, while working as a pie vendor at an earlier public execution in 1828, had expressed his willingness to take to the hangman's line of business.[80] Perhaps not surprisingly, he was not well regarded:

> Calcraft inspired neither respect nor confidence. A small man of sallow complexion, dead-fish eyes and shuffling gait, he had the decrepitude of age, but none of its sweet benevolent characteristics. His faith in a short rope saw many of his victims survive the drop, obliging him to complete their strangulation by hanging on their backs or yanking on their legs. It was also his unseemly and mercenary custom to sell small pieces of the ropes used to hang notorious criminals.[81]

Müller is reported to have accepted his fate at Calcraft's hand with considerable bravery. As he approached the gallows, accompanied only by a German Lutheran minister, the Reverend Dr Cappel, 'his face was very pale indeed, but still it wore an easy and, if it could be said at such a time, even a cheerful expression, as much removed from mere bravado as it seemed to be from fear'.[82] Although Müller had previously and repeatedly expressed his innocence of Briggs' murder, Dr Cappel claimed that Müller's final words on the gallows were '*Ich habe es gethan*', which translates as 'Yes, I did it'.[83] For once, Calcraft's arrangements did not prolong the agony of the victim, although he managed to bungle the cutting down of Müller's body to the hisses of the crowd.[84] After the body had been removed, as was the practice at the time, a cast of Müller's head was made, which to this day remains on a shelf of the crime museum at New Scotland Yard.

The Briggs murder and Müller's execution had several important social consequences in Victorian Britain. Ticket sales for the steamship journey to New York increased as the transatlantic steamship companies basked in the free advertising from Tanner and Clarke's speedy journey across the North Atlantic. The substantial criminal activities of sections of the crowd that assembled on Müller's execution day strengthened the political will that placed capital punishment behind closed doors from mid-1868 and eliminated executions as spectator sport; a small step towards the much later abolition of capital punishment in 1969.[85] The request of the Briggs inquest jury to improve passenger safety on the railways did eventually lead to improvements. The South Western Railway was the first to act, by installing small portholes in the wooden walls that divided railway compartments from each other. Christened 'Muller lights', they were not as well received as the railway company expected, as they provided opportunities for Peeping Toms. From 1868 or so, versions of 'communication cords' were beginning to be introduced in railway carriages.[86] Enterprising hatters decided to start producing the cut-down versions of the bell-topped hat discovered by Clarke in Müller's trunk, and found that they had a ready market for their 'Muller hats', a style that was later to lead on to bowler hats. Müller's name has also lived on in the East End vernacular, with 'muller' being used as a slang term for 'murder', and has now evolved further in the slang of younger generations to represent drunkenness – as in 'he was mullered'.[87]

The Metropolitan Police and the investigating police team, particularly Inspector Tanner, emerged with considerable credit and public recognition for their work. On 8 February 1865 the team was recognised by the payment of rewards for their 'zeal, expertise, extraordinary diligence and exertion' in the detection of Franz Müller.[88] A total of nine awards were made, with Tanner receiving £20 and Clarke £10. By the time Clarke had received his useful bonus he had also been rewarded for the work that he had undertaken on his next case, the Plaistow Marshes murder.[89]

The Plaistow Marshes Murder

On 8 November 1864 while London was still awaiting Franz Müller's execution, Richard Harvey, a young shipwright's apprentice from Poplar, was out on Plaistow Marshes with a work colleague, Josiah Gaster, a ship joiner, and several other men. They were there to shoot birds for the pot. The day had started foggy but, with the help of a westerly wind that had picked up during the morning, visibility had improved. Harvey was not carrying a gun but was helping the group by keeping his eye out for wildfowl, with the intention of driving any he spotted on to the guns. At about 1.20 p.m. he was about 50yds from the bank of the Thames where the reeds were at a height of between 7 and 10ft. Walking down a narrow path through the reed bed, he spotted a large object among the reeds a few yards from the path. When he got closer he realised that it was a man's body: 'it was lying on its back, with the left hand on the breast – there was only a pair of trousers and a pair of Wellington boots on it, and his shirt was half off his body; it was only part of a shirt.'[90] The body also had no head. Harvey called out in horror to his colleagues; Gaster then fetched the police.

Sergeant William Bridgeland, K Division, was the first policeman to reach the location. He later described the scene:

[the body] was dressed in a pair of black trouser, Wellington boots, and a small piece of shirt with the letters 'O.B.C.' in ink … I searched the pockets and found a farthing and a small piece of paper. The body was lying on its back, with the legs quite straight. The right arm was lying over the chest, and the left was lying down by the side, with the hand extended. I observed the condition of the neck where the head had been severed from the body. There was a dent in the earth, apparently where the back of the head had been. Small pieces of bone were lying by the neck, and a small portion of brain. The flesh had been eaten all round the bone, apparently by rats. The body appeared quite fresh, but there was no blood, or scarcely any. I had the body removed to the Graving Dock Tavern.[91]

Police regulations at the time stated that dead bodies should be transported to the nearest 'Dead House' or to the nearest public house, which was in this case in Silvertown. A stretcher had been obtained from the Victoria Docks nearby to transport the corpse to the tavern, where it was placed in the stables.[92]

The body had been found within the area of London for which K Division was responsible. The divisional superintendent, Daniel Howie, must have wondered what he had done to deserve another gruesome murder on his patch, particularly when he quickly realised that the case involved more German immigrants. Having promptly instituted inquiries, Howie already had two suspects locked in the cells by night-time. He reported progress to Sir Richard Mayne early on Wednesday 9 November:

> From enquiry instituted in the neighbourhood where the body was found, I ascertained that a young German named John Führhop had been missing since Thursday last from the house of another German named Karl Köhl, at Roscoe Town, and further inquiries satisfied me that the headless body was that of Führhop who had been murdered and that there were circumstances of a suspicious nature which would justify me in arresting Köhl on the charge of having committed the murder. I accordingly took him into custody, as also his wife, who is charged on suspicion of being concerned with him in the murder. The prisoners will be brought before the Essex Magistrates this morning at Stratford. I have placed their house in charge of the police and have applied for and obtained the assistance of Police Sergeant Clarke of the Detective Department to aid me in the enquiry.[93]

With suspects already in the cells, Howie probably felt that he didn't need a detective inspector on the case, such as Tanner, but he did need an experienced and reliable detective sergeant who would do the leg work and collect evidence. Clarke arrived at Plaistow Police Station at 11.45 p.m. on the same day that the body had been found. The first thing that Clarke did was to arrange for Köhl's clothes to be removed and searched. He found a peculiar key in Köhl's trouser pockets, a small amount of cash, a sixpence, a penny and a farthing, and a purse containing four duplicates (receipts) from William Darlow's pawnbrokers of Victoria Dock Road, for items pledged between 11 and 19 October. Moving on to Köhl's house, at 4 Hoy Street Plaistow, Clarke found five more pawnshop receipts for items pledged between 12 and

28 October. Amongst other items in the house that were to prove significant in the inquiry were two wooden boxes, a portmanteau and two hat boxes, which were the possessions of 'John Führhop', the suspected victim who, it emerged, had been lodging in Köhl's house.[94]

It was clear from the receipts that Köhl had been busy pawning items during the last month. Though this was not unusual in the Victorian era, where pawnbrokers were often the bank of first resort for the working class, it was a starting point for further investigation to see if there were any transactions that were associated with the victim. It was beginning to look as if this was to be another case, like the Briggs murder, where Clarke and other police would have to trudge round a number of East End pawnbrokers. At least this time they knew from the receipts which pawnbrokers to visit. However, the highest priority was to find the victim's head, to help confirm his identity.

The head was discovered at about 7.30 a.m. on 9 November. Inspector George Goode of the Thames Police, whose knowledge of the river stretched back more than thirty-five years, had been sent to search the reed bed and was alerted by a lighterman who had been working in the area to a hole in the mud where blood could be seen. Careful digging and removal of the mud revealed a man's head.[95] As with the body, rats had found parts of the head to their taste. It was taken to be reunited with the body and both were examined by a local surgeon, Edward Morris, who drew several conclusions from what he saw. Firstly, two instruments had apparently been used to remove the head: a sharp blade such as a knife and a hatchet or chopper. Secondly, from the non-contracted state of the neck muscles, the head had only been removed some time after the man had died. Thirdly, the man had several extensive wounds on the head, which were probably the initial cause of death. Fourthly, the body had probably been dead for four or five days before its discovery.[96] The body without the head had been provisionally identified the previous evening from its boots by a local shoemaker, Heinrich Zülch. With the head now available others, including a former landlord of 'John Führhop', James Warren, added their confirmation to the identification.[97] They weren't the only people to view the body:

> The murder has caused extraordinary excitement in the neighbourhood of Silvertown. Four thousand persons yesterday went to view the body. They were in most instances permitted to see the remains of the deceased, not only to endeavour to corroborate the identification by means of the clothes, but also to give an opportunity of ascertaining whether any person had seen the deceased walking towards the river bank through the marsh on the day of the murder.[98]

As in the Briggs case, information of interest had passed with almost lightning speed in the Victorian working-class community.

On the same day as the head had been found, the two prisoners were due
to appear before magistrates at Stratford Police Court. Köhl, referred to as a
'sugar-baker' and now known to be Ferdinand Edward Karl Köhl ('Charley'
to his English acquaintances), and his wife Hannah duly appeared in a densely
crowded court:

> Köhl is a dull, heavy-looking man, about 27 years of age. He did not seem in the
> dock to pay much attention to the proceedings. His wife, on the other hand, a
> girl of 18, showed that she acutely felt the position in which she was placed. She
> is the daughter of poor, but respectable parents at Plaistow.[99]

A 'sugar-baker' was someone employed in the refining of sugar from sugar
cane which, in London, was imported from the Caribbean into the West India
Docks. In view of its location, London's East End was the centre of sugar
refining in Victorian London, and the industry provided employment for several thousand men. However, the industry 'was looked on with such dislike
that even that pattern of patient drudgery, the Irish labourer, could by no sort
of persuasion be brought to undertake it. I was credibly informed that the
bribe offered had even taken the seductive form of beer unlimited; but that
still, marvellous to relate, the Emerald Islander remained obdurate, and the
sugar-bakers were compelled, as has ever been the case, to resort for "hands" to
the German labour market.'[100] In a sugar-refining factory 'The heat was sick-
ening and oppressive, and an unctuous steam, thick and foggy, filled the cellar
from end to end … Regarding the close, reeking, stifling place, the disgusting
atmosphere, the incessant toil and the disgusting conditions of it, the valid-
ity of the Irish labourer's objection became manifest.'[101] This had been Köhl's
employment before he had chosen to leave a few weeks previously. It was a job
that few would do from choice and some who were employed in the industry
might certainly try to find alternative ways of making some money.

At the magistrate's hearing the police had assembled their witnesses,
including those who had discovered and examined the body. The first witness
was Elizabeth Warren of 3 Nelson Place, Plaistow, who had known Köhl as a
former lodger at her house. She informed the court that Köhl had brought
the murder victim, whom she knew as 'John', to her lodgings where he had
stayed for some days. She described him as 'a very handsome young man'
of about 21–22 years of age who (in an uncanny echo of Franz Müller) was
planning to travel to New York.[102] John was also German and did not speak
good English. She described Köhl's introduction of John to her:

> He asked me if I could oblige this young man by taking him into my place, and
> he told me that he was a gentleman. I said, 'Well Charley, if he is a gentleman,
> our place is only for poor men lodgers' … I told the prisoner that my lodging

was not fit for a person in that station. I ultimately agreed to take him in, and he came. After he had been with me for some time, he asked me to take care of some things for him.[103]

John was obviously a trusting soul, as he left Mrs Warren to look after several sovereigns and a gold watch and chain amongst other items; she seems not to have betrayed his trust. After some days with the Warrens, John had moved out to lodge with the Köhls. Although there had been some disagreement on the amount of rent due, it did not appear to have changed Mrs Warren's belief that John was a very nice young man.

The next witness was Superintendent Howie, who described his 7 p.m. visit the previous evening to Köhl's house. The contemporary press report of the magistrate's hearing did not make it clear what had prompted this visit. However, it subsequently came to light that Köhl had joined the crowds assembling at the Graving Dock Tavern when the body was found. The landlord, William Richardson, had then alerted the police to Köhl's unusual reaction when shown the body:

I pointed out to him where the first blow had been struck in the neck; it was within about a sixteenth of an inch of being through. Directly he saw that, he made a turn and took himself to the wall, to take himself away from the body altogether. I said 'From your appearance I think you know something of this affair'. He had become deadly pale. I had shown the body to other parties previously, but saw no one to resemble the same countenance as the prisoner. I put my right hand on his shoulder, and told him I should apprehend him on suspicion of being concerned in the murder. He dropped his hands and fell against the wall. He never made any reply at all. I then brought him through the house and called Police Constable Wills, and directed him not to lose sight of him.[104]

During questioning by Howie, Köhl said that he hadn't seen 'John Führhop' since Thursday 3 November. On that day, Köhl said that the two of them had gone towards London, down to Commercial Road, and Köhl had gone into a sugar-bakers' factory to enquire about the possibility of work. According to Köhl's account of events, when he came out John had disappeared; he made a search for him but had not seen him since.

As this information emerged in court, it was becoming clear that 3 November would be a critical date in the police inquiries. The penultimate witness at the hearing was to throw some further light on that particular day. That witness was a young labourer, Henry Lees, some 13 years of age:

Last Thursday morning, the 3rd inst, about 10 o'clock, I was at work at Plaistow, and I saw the male prisoner and the young man 'John', whom I believe to be the deceased, walking along the river-wall, near the sugar-house, towards Silvertown … I have not seen the young man since … It would be about four minutes' walk from the spot where I saw the deceased and the male prisoner to the reed beds where the body was found. I saw the prisoner at half-past 4 in the afternoon of the same day, and he said to me that the young man was missing. I replied to him that 'I saw you and the young man this morning about 10 o'clock walking by the river bank'. The prisoner said nothing at all in reply.[105]

No evidence was presented against Hannah Köhl and at Howie's suggestion she was discharged by the magistrates, leaving the courtroom in a swoon in her brother's arms. In contrast, 'Charley' Köhl was remanded for further inquiry, handcuffed and transported to Ilford Gaol. A large crowd was in the vicinity of the court and it was with some difficulty that the prisoner was conducted to the cab. As Köhl headed off to gaol the rumour mongers in the area were busy; the motive for murder was being suggested as jealousy over Hannah Köhl, rather than theft.

The following day the inquest into the death of 'John Führhop' was held at the Bell and Anchor Tavern, near the Victoria Docks, starting at 6.30 p.m., with many of the same witnesses appearing:

> Very little additional evidence to that produced before the magistrates … has as yet been obtained, but it is understood that Sergeant Clarke of the detective department of the metropolitan force has elicited several important facts which will throw light upon the motives which have led to the commission of this horrible murder, but which at present it is not advisable in the interests of justice to disclose.[106]

After the coroner and jury had heard from all the witnesses, and had had the opportunity to question them, the coroner adjourned the inquest for a week.

Behind the scenes the police were already making further progress in establishing the true identity of the victim. Howie reported to Sir Richard Mayne that 'from papers found in the trunk of the deceased I believe his name to have been Theodor C. Führhop, late a corresponding Clerk in the house of Neumann and Böcher of Hamburg'.[107] He suggested that the police authorities in Hamburg should be contacted to help confirm this. In addition, Howie had set in motion a further search of the reed bed in the hope of discovering the murdered man's missing garments and 'the "knife or weapon" used by the assassin'.[108] The initial proceedings of both the magistrate's hearing and the inquest had demonstrated that the police had reasonable grounds for arresting Köhl, but there was clearly further work to be done to investigate the case against him. Firstly, what weapon(s) had been used to commit the murder? Secondly, could any direct forensic evidence be found to link Köhl to the murder? Thirdly, what was the likely motive for the murder? Fourthly, would Köhl's alibi – that he had been in the Commercial Road with Führhop on 3 November – stand up to further investigation? These were the main topics on which Superintendent Howie and George Clarke would focus their attention.

The search of the reed bed on 10 November unearthed a 'wooden handle of what appeared to be a hammer', but no hammer head or blade. On the same day another witness, Thomas Hudson, came forward to report that he had seen Köhl and Führhop together in the marshes on 3 November, even closer to the reed bed location where the body was found, than the witness Lees had reported.[109] On 12 November two further key witnesses were interviewed by the police, probably by Clarke. These were Mary Wade and Eliza Whitmore, both of whom, with their respective husbands, were lodgers at Köhl's house at 4 Hoy Street. Both reported that they had seen Köhl in a muddy state in the early afternoon of 3 November. In a newspaper report of the resumed magistrate's hearing on Saturday 12 November, Mary Wade's evidence was summarised as follows:

> She recollected Thursday the 3rd inst., when the prisoner left home about half-past nine o'clock. The young German, 'John' accompanied him, but they did not return together. The prisoner Köhl came back alone and witness let him in. When he entered she said 'Good gracious Charley, where have you been to in the mud'. The back of his coat, the elbows, and trousers were dirty. He then asked witness where his wife was, and witness replied 'She has gone to mangle'. He then went off to the back yard, and brushed off the mud from his clothes.[110]

Whitmore's evidence was consistent with this, confirming that she had also seen Köhl brushing his clothes in the back yard.

The next piece of new evidence concerned the possible murder weapon. When questioned by the magistrates at the hearing on 12 November, Mary Wade added considerably to the evidence accumulating against Köhl:

> 'I have lent the prisoner my chopper, which he borrowed every day. He used to keep the chopper two or three days sometimes. He used to keep the chopper in his kitchen … The chopper when I found it was painted over with red paint. It was not so when I lent it to him.' Sergeant Clarke, the detective officer, here produced the chopper, when the Chairman [of the magistrates] said 'Why, that is a butcher's pole-axe!' Sergeant Clarke answered in the affirmative, and when examined it was found that the chopper had a round head similar to a hammer on the back part of the blade.[111]

The chopper was promptly sent for forensic analysis to Dr Henry Letheby, Professor of Chemistry at the London Hospital, who later appeared as a prosecution witness. Meanwhile, Köhl, who had no legal representation and who clearly had failed to understand all of the day's proceedings, was again further remanded in custody until 19 November. The prisoner was then heard to say: 'What for then I come to-day? Why you not settle and I go away?'[112] There then followed a conversation between the prisoner, the magistrate and Superintendent Howie in which the magistrate commented that 'it is a great pity he has not got any legal assistance'.[113]

For a day or so prior to the hearing on 12 November, Clarke had probably been distracted by having to deal with Baron de Camin's intervention into the Briggs murder case, but on 14 November (the date of Müller's execution) he was again actively involved on the Plaistow Marshes case.[114] There was still work to be done on the motive for the murder, and on Köhl's alibi, as well as further confirmation of the identity of the victim. On this last point, Captain Harris, an assistant commissioner of the Metropolitan Police, had been in contact with the police authorities in Hamburg and had just received information that 'George Führhop … brother of Theodore C. Führhop … declared that by the description received … he undoubtedly recognises his brother'.[115]

Between 14 and 16 November, Clarke investigated the large number of pawnbroker receipts that he had found in Köhl's clothes and at Köhl's house on the night after the body had been discovered. The detail that materialised from Clarke's visits to the pawnbrokers was presented in evidence later at the magistrate's hearing on 25 November and at the Old Bailey trial. In short, the majority of items pledged had been taken into the pawnbrokers by Köhl and his wife using lightly disguised versions of their names. But to whom had these items originally belonged? This aspect would take further work to disentangle. Clarke had one apparently reliable witness, Elizabeth Warren, at whose house Führhop had first stayed when he arrived in London. She had a reasonable knowledge of Führhop's effects as he had asked her to look after some of his things, and indeed she was able to identify some, but not all, of the pawned items as having belonged to Führhop. Führhop's relatives would presumably have more knowledge of his possessions, but they were all living in Germany. Finally, and as pointed out in one of Howie's reports to Mayne, with one exception, all the receipts were for items pawned before Führhop had been murdered. Had Führhop therefore intended them to be pawned or was he unaware that they had been?

Literally and metaphorically, Clarke already had the key to help answer some of these questions – it was the unusual key that he had found in Köhl's pockets in Stratford Police Station on the night of 8 November, which proved to be the key to Führhop's boxes.[116] Clarke and Howie had also realised that they had some important potential witnesses amongst the family of Köhl's wife, Hannah. As early as 16 November, Howie commented to Mayne that 'from what I have seen of the wife of Köhl and her relations I am inclined to think that they are more likely to assist the prosecution than to aid the prisoner in a defence'.[117] That was to prove to be the case. Clarke had already heard from the women, Mary Wade and Eliza Whitmore, that, on the night of 3 November after Führhop had gone missing earlier that day, Köhl went up and broke into Führhop's boxes using a poker after expressly asking his wife's cousin, Joseph Skeldon, to go with him. Skeldon later confirmed, as a prosecution witness, that he had seen that the two boxes broken into contained very few items, only a few collars and some old clothes, which would be consistent with the increasing evidence that Köhl had pawned several of Führhop's belongings well before 3 November.[118] Köhl accounted for the almost-empty boxes as evidence that Führhop had left, taking most of his things with him. The reason why Skeldon had specifically been asked to accompany Köhl to break into the boxes was now seen by the police as a ploy to disguise the earlier removal of Führhop's clothing if, as they had concluded, Köhl had acquired the key to Führhop's boxes early in October.

Other members of Hannah Köhl's family, her mother Esther Williams and her brother Thomas Williams, eventually gave evidence for the prosecution, stating that Köhl was always short of money and that he had either borrowed money from them or had obtained money from them through Hannah. Esther Williams confirmed that 'he never did any work after his marriage with my daughter. He never repaid me any of the money that had been borrowed.'[119] So Köhl had been unemployed since returning from Germany, was financially hard-pressed and had directly and indirectly tapped his in-laws (and others) for cash on several occasions. By asking around the shopkeepers in the immediate area in Plaistow, the police team also unearthed at least one shopkeeper who had seen Köhl with more money than usual on 5 November.[120] It was looking increasingly likely that theft was the principal motive behind Führhop's murder and, as with the other evidence, the finger pointed directly at Köhl.

Between 17 and 26 November both the inquest and the magistrate's hearing were resumed. At the inquest on 17 November the evidence that had emerged from the witnesses Mary Wade, Eliza Whitmore and Joseph Skeldon was presented; about the muddy state of Köhl on 3 November and his opening of Führhop's boxes on the same day. The other significant new information for the jury came from Clarke – whose evidence on the pawned items had previously been deferred – and from a new witness, John Atkinson, who reported finding a clasp knife about 20ft from the location of Führhop's body on 9 November. The knife had subsequently been identified as belonging to Köhl, by Mary Wade, who also stated that she had seen Köhl using it at his home as late as Sunday 6 November. When the inquest was again resumed for the final time on 23 November, Köhl appeared before the inquest jury for the first time, and Dr Letheby of the London Hospital presented the findings of his forensic analysis of the chopper and of Köhl's clothes. On the chopper he had found wool fibres from clothing, blood (though he was unable to confirm that it was human blood) and human skin; on the clothes he had also found some drops of blood. After the coroner's summing-up, the inquest jury concluded their deliberations with a verdict of wilful murder, against Köhl.[121]

The magistrate's hearing was concluded two days later at Ilford Gaol, with a similar outcome. For the first time Köhl was represented by legal counsel and the prosecution was led on behalf of the Crown by Hardinge Giffard. The most interesting new witness was Mary Cooper, who had come forward to say that she had seen Köhl near the reed bed on Monday 7 November, the day before the body was discovered. The potential implication of this evidence was that this could have been the day on which the head was removed from the body. Satisfied with the prosecution case, the chairman of the magistrates committed Köhl for trial at the next sessions of the Central Criminal Court, 'for the wilful murder of Theodor Christian Führhop'.[122]

Following this satisfactory outcome as far as the police were concerned, Superintendent Howie produced a summary report of the case for Mayne and for the Treasury Solicitor's Office. There had been some investigation of Köhl's German background, which confirmed that he was a native of Splietau near Dannenberg, and had returned from Germany to Britain on board the ship *Berlin* in company with Führhop.[123] During the next few weeks Clarke and Howie spent time with the Treasury Solicitor's team, helping to build the case for the prosecution. This included some work on Clarke's part to investigate the alibi that Köhl's defence team would present on his behalf – more of that later. The Treasury also reconsidered the need to obtain further background information on Köhl and the identification of Führhop's effects.

> In the Plaistow Murder Case some further evidence has been thought necessary for the identification of the clothes and effects of the deceased – and as to the previous acquaintance of the prisoner and the deceased, and the relations exist-ing between their families. For this purpose it is proposed to send an intelligent and trustworthy person to Hamburg – Probably no better person could be sug-gested than Mr. Clarke (in the Detective Force) who has been engaged in the case throughout. But if you could suggest a better man and would kindly allow us his services we should be extremely obliged.[124]

On 21 December, following confirmation from Inspector Williamson that no better man could be found, Clarke headed off on his international travels again, this time to Germany. Clarke subsequently reported his visit:

I arrived at Hamburg on the 23rd and delivered the letter of introduction to Mr. Ward, Her Majesty's Consul in that town, who granted me every assistance. I shewed [sic] the property to the family of the deceased and it was all identified by Carl Henry Theodor Fuhrhop, the youngest brother, who I brought with me to London. On the 25th I left Hamburg for Splietau in Hanover, accompanied by an interpreter for the purpose of ascertaining the antecedents of the prisoner 'Köhl' which I found to be generally bad. He enlisted in the Kings Regiment of Hussars in 1860 for ten years but after serving 2½ years he was convicted and sentenced to three months in a Military Prison for stealing from his comrades, and was then dismissed the service. In the early part of 1864 he was charged with stealing a quantity of harness at Ledorf near Splietau, but he then absconded to avoid punishment and came to England.[125]

These days, a journey of that nature might be straightforward. In the middle of winter in 1864 it was undoubtedly less so, and Germany was not at that stage an integrated country. The village of Splietau, to which Clarke travelled to seek further information on Köhl, was in the county of Dannenberg (Lower Saxony) and was part of the Kingdom of Hanover until it was later annexed by Prussia in 1866. Hamburg, where Führhop's family were based, was one of thirty-nine sovereign states of the German confederation.[126]

Clarke's expenses claim for the visit totalled £39 19s 10d (about £1,750 today). It included 17s for the purchase of a lockable packing case for Führhop's property; £1 4s 6d for the cost of transporting the extra luggage around northern Europe; £3 6s for extra pay while outside the London area (6s a day for eleven days); and £1 10s 'paid to four persons for loss of time and refreshments whilst assisting me in gaining information of Köhl's antecedents'. It took some persuasion for the authorities to fully reimburse him, and he was asked to supply further information on expenses claimed 'which are not strictly in accordance with the Regulations'. Inquisitions in relation to expenses claims were indeed a thorn in the flesh for the poorly paid detectives, but Clarke on this occasion was reimbursed in full.[127]

Köhl's trial at the Old Bailey started on Wednesday 11 January 1865. Lord Chief Baron Pollock was the senior judge, as he had been at the Müller trial, but on this occasion was assisted by Mr Justice Blackburn. The prosecution team for the Crown contained some other familiar faces from the Müller trial, including the solicitor general Sir Robert Collier, Serjeant-at-Law Ballantine and Hardinge Giffard. Köhl was represented by Mr Best of the Oxford Circuit and Mr Palmer. The start of the trial was described by *The Times*:

The prisoner is 26 years of age, and was described as a sugar baker. He is a short thick-set man with dark-brown hair and somewhat florid complexion.

When asked to plead, he replied 'Not Guilty' in an emphatic tone of voice, and speaking in English. He elected to be tried by a mixed jury, and one, composed half of Englishmen and half foreigners, was impanelled, the foreman being Mr Julius Schullze. He folded his arms on the front of the dock and listened with intense interest to the opening statement of the Solicitor General, at parts of which he smiled. At times during the day his manner was unbecoming, and he appeared to have no adequate sense of the peril in which he stood.[128]

In his introductory statement, the solicitor general emphasised Köhl's poverty, clearly perceiving that as a contributory factor in the murder. Although Köhl had claimed that he had known Führhop for a long time, the prosecution case was that the two men had met for the first time on the steamer *Berlin*, when Köhl was returning from Germany. With regard to the mud that had been seen on Köhl's clothes on 3 November, the solicitor general emphasised that it was a lightish colour (consistent with Plaistow Marshes) and not like the mud 'found on the streets of London'.[129] This comment was clearly included in the prosecution's introductory statement to deal with Köhl's alibi that, on the morning of 3 November, he and Führhop had gone to Commercial Road where Köhl claimed to have visited a sugar-bakers' to look for work. After the prosecution statement had been concluded, the battery of witnesses that had been assembled for the earlier magistrate's hearings were paraded before the court, including Clarke. Köhl's defence counsel failed to dent the credibility of any of the prosecution witnesses. The few witnesses that had not appeared at any of the preliminary hearings now included Führhop's brother, who Clarke had brought to England. Carl Führhop confirmed that his brother had left for England in September with plenty of money and clothes for his short-term needs. He recognised the pawned items as having belonged to his brother, and he stated that he did not recognise Köhl as someone who had met his brother when he was living in Germany. Three new witnesses were called to deal with aspects of Köhl's alibi for the morning of 3 November. James Longman, a gatekeeper at a sugar bakery at Church Lane, Whitechapel, gave evidence that he had never seen Köhl at any time, as did James Thomas, the general manager of a sugar bakery on Commercial Road. Finally, Frederick Kaiger, a surveyor, indicated that the distance from the Plaistow Marshes location, where Köhl and Führhop had been seen together by Lees at around 10 a.m. on the morning of 3 November, was 40yds short of 5 miles from the sugar bakery off Commercial Road, where Köhl claimed to have been that morning. The implication being that Köhl would have had to make a return journey of almost 10 miles, plus visit a sugar bakery, all in two hours or so. The court then adjourned until the following morning.[130]

In Köhl's defence his counsel Mr Best made a statement, but called no witnesses. Best emphasised that Köhl's reaction when seeing Führhop's body was simply the reaction of a close friend. Likewise, when Köhl had pawned some of Führhop's possessions, it had been a helpful gesture by a friend for someone who spoke little or no English. He pointed out that the knife found in the reed bed was of a commonplace style and could have belonged to anyone. He stressed that none of the witnesses had noticed any substantial amounts of blood on Köhl's clothes, and that Führhop's missing clothes when murdered had not been traced to Köhl. He also suggested that the journey that Köhl had claimed to have made on 3 November was feasible if he had travelled in a butcher's cart, which Köhl said he had done. The jury's deliberations lasted half an hour, including seeking some further information on the distances between places, from the surveyor Kaiger. They returned to the court with a 'guilty' verdict. This time restraining any tearfulness on his part, Lord Chief Baron Pollock sentenced Köhl to death and committed him to the custody of the High Sheriff of Essex.[131]

Unlike the Müller case, there is no evidence in the contemporary newspaper coverage (which was much more low-key than for Müller) that any pleas for a respite or for mercy were made on Köhl's behalf. The Reverend Dr Cappel, who had been at Müller's side in his last moments, also visited Köhl, and was with him on execution day. During his final days at Springfield Gaol, Chelmsford, Köhl continued to protest his innocence. He asked if his sentence might be commuted to transportation, and later acted with anger and aggression, including a suicide attempt in which he kept hitting his head against a wall before he was restrained. On his way to the gallows on Thursday 26 January 1865, Köhl is reported to have said that 'I had no hand in it; I die an innocent death'.[132] Cappel did not at the end receive any confession from Köhl, who became the last person to be executed in public at Springfield Gaol. George Clarke was probably not in attendance at the execution; he was already working on his next case, a theft at Windsor Castle.[133]

The Briggs and Führhop murder cases demonstrate several aspects of the effectiveness of the Metropolitan Police in the mid-Victorian era. Not least, they illustrate the speed in which decisions could be made and actions put in place. Particularly in the Briggs inquiry, when in less than forty-eight hours from receiving important new evidence, two detectives and two witnesses equipped with arrest warrant and new passports were on a 'fast' boat to America; all achieved without our modern benefits of telephone, fax and e-mail. The intense public and media interest surrounding the murder of Thomas Briggs also illustrated the challenges that the police faced from the efficiency of the 'bush telegraph' in spreading information amongst the population and 'mobs' within city communities, whether it be London, Liverpool or New York. However, in all but the incidents associated with Müller's execution, the policing strategy fulfilled its objectives. Both cases also demonstrate that, by 1864 at least, the police were prepared to operate on an international scale when the need arose, using the network of British consulates to assist their inquiries and, as in the Briggs case, achieving the successful extradition of a suspect despite the political difficulties prevailing at the time.

The legal system in place in 1864, and the manner in which trials were conducted, clearly differed in a number of aspects from the manner in which such trials would be conducted today. For example, there was no Director of Public Prosecutions in place, and many criminal cases less serious than the two murders described above would have been brought to court by the police themselves or by private individuals. In situations where it was felt to be in the public interest for the Crown to be the prosecuting body, then this was dealt with by the solicitor general's office in the Treasury, as with both the Briggs and Führhop murders. There was no formal legal aid system and, by comparison with the arrangements in place in the twenty-first century, it could be considered that Victorian defendants were at a disadvantage as a consequence. In addition, defendants were not allowed to enter the witness box to give evidence on their own behalf, although this was sometimes a mixed blessing for the defendant's case during their cross-examination by the prosecution; this situation did not change until the passing of the Criminal Evidence Act in 1898. Finally, in 1864, defending counsels had to make their statements before calling any witnesses for the defence; however, this was to change from 1865 onwards, when witnesses were called before the defending counsel's statement.

The two murder investigations undoubtedly brought George Clarke's name into the public arena and consolidated his position within the detective department at Scotland Yard. Although no 'high flyer', the skills that he had developed during his twenty-four-year-long service in S Division, and since 1862 in A Division, had contributed significantly to the successful completion of both investigations. It is often difficult from the available contemporary records to tease out the individual contributions of the members of the police teams on a major case. However, it is clear that in the Briggs murder case Clarke carried out much of the work involved in contacting the pilots on Staten Island, and of course directly participated in the moment of Müller's arrest. While Tanner has historically taken (and probably deserves) much of the credit associated with the arrest and conviction of Müller, some authors have suggested that Clarke's contribution deserves greater recognition than it has historically been given.[134] On the Führhop murder inquiry, Clarke undertook on his own the information-gathering visit to Germany over Christmas 1864 and undoubtedly led the specific inquiries into the fate of Führhop's possessions. Though pawnbrokers don't always get a good press, their contribution to both the Briggs and Führhop inquiries was such that Clarke could well have echoed the words of a contemporary of his, Superintendent James Bent of the Manchester Police, on this subject: 'Few men have had more extended or extensive dealings with the pawnbroking class than myself, and I am ready and glad to bear witness to the fact that the police are often indebted to them far more than the public would imagine for the speedy detection of crime.'[135] If determination and devotion to duty were amongst the principal attributes of Victorian detectives, then George Clarke did not fall short on either front. His superiors and the Treasury Solicitor undoubtedly appreciated his value. Clearly, by the beginning of 1865, Clarke's star was in the ascendant.

3

THE FENIANS ARE COMING

1865-68

Wherever we go, wherever we be,
Some wonders of wonder we daily do see;
All classes through Britain are trembling with fear.
The Fenians are coming – oh, don't things look queer?
The land of old Erin looks bashful and blue,
Colonel Catchem and General Doodlem doo,
Has crossed the Atlantic, poor Erin to sack,
And carry Hibernia away on their back.
Chorus
There's a rumpus in Ireland by night and by day,
Old women and girls are afraid out to stray;
Cheer up and be happy on St Patrick's day,
The Fenians are coming, – get out of the way!

Anonymous[1]

On 21 January 1865, Commissioner Mayne received a letter from the Treasury stating that Detective Sergeant Clarke 'had proved himself very useful' in the Führhop murder inquiry, and that they proposed to provide Clarke with a £3 gratuity, subject to Mayne's approval.[2] On the same day, Clarke was attending a magistrate's court hearing at Windsor Town Hall. The hearing was linked to an event that had occurred some two days previously, when Scotland Yard had been contacted by Oxenhams auction house, Oxford Street, about a suspicious parcel that they had received from Windsor Castle containing some particularly fine silk bed furniture, together with a request that the items should be sold at auction. Clarke had been asked to make enquiries and had visited Oxenhams to collect the parcel, finding it to contain several pieces made from Indian silk, plus two embroidered silk curtains and matching valances. Travelling to Windsor Castle to pursue enquiries, Clarke interviewed two men and arrested both of them.

One was William Wilson, foreman of the castle's upholsterers, who had been in post for nine months and had been recently told to overhaul the stores. The second was George Hammond, a long-serving head porter in the lord chamberlain's stores, who had taken the parcel to Windsor station at Wilson's request. At the magistrate's hearing on 21 January the case 'excited great interest and the court was crowded during the examination of the prisoners. The articles stolen were of the richest possible character, and the bed furniture is said to have belonged to the marriage bed of King George IV'.[3] At their trial at Reading Crown Court on 27 February, Wilson pleaded guilty and was sentenced to twelve months' imprisonment. The jury acquitted Hammond, who had been of good character, had worked at the castle for nine years and claimed to have been unaware of the contents of the parcel he had been asked to send.[4]

From a case in which the criminal had been readily located, Clarke and his Scotland Yard colleagues were about to find themselves tackling a completely new challenge that was to dominate their lives for the next three years. The cause was a resurgence of Irish Nationalism, historically recorded as the 'Fenian Conspiracy'. This was to involve political-policing activities that, in the present day, would probably be within the purview of Special Branch, a section of the police that did not exist in the 1860s and 1870s. The public record of the activities of Clarke and his colleagues between 1865 and 1868 is scanty and incomplete. However, a police document published on 7 November 1868 provides evidence of the extent of the department's involvement: 'Gratuities to Detective Police. – Fenian Conspiracy. – The Secretary of State, on the recommendation of the Commissioner, has been pleased to allow the following gratuities to the several Officers of the Detective Force, on account of duties performed beyond the Metropolitan Police District in connection with the Fenian Conspiracy.'[5] There followed a list of awards, totalling £160, to thirteen men of the detective department: the largest amount, £58 19s 10d, to Inspector Williamson; and the second-largest sum, £38 13s, to Sergeant George Clarke. The money Clarke received represented about 35 per cent of his annual salary as a sergeant; it was therefore clear that the Fenian conspiracy involved Clarke (and others) in a considerable amount of work, much of it scarcely reported in the press and little retained within the surviving archival records.

Before concentrating on the events of 1865–68, it is necessary to provide some background on the Fenians by way of a concise introduction (which for the reader interested in pursuing the subject in more detail can be developed further by exploring several excellent books on the subject).[6]

The Fenians

During Clarke's lifetime Ireland was part of the United Kingdom, electing parliamentary representatives to the House of Commons in London. The Act of Union of 1800 had abolished the Irish Parliament and had united (in practice if not always spirit) Britain and Ireland.[7] Popular agitation for the repeal of the Union flourished in Ireland in the early 1840s, but concerted efforts were temporarily halted by a greater emergency. In the summer of 1845 the staple carbohydrate source of the Irish population, the potato, was devastatingly attacked by the fungal disease potato blight, with an estimate of 33 per cent crop losses that year and 75 per cent in 1846. Though the worst was over by 1850, there had been approximately 1.1 million deaths from starvation in Ireland, with the government's free-market approach exacerbating the problem.[8] One possible escape from the grinding poverty and hunger was emigration to other destinations in the UK, to continental Europe, North America and Australasia; many Irish-born men, women and children with the necessary courage and physical resources took that option (about 1.5 million).[9]

In the summer of 1848, a year in which much of Western Europe was gripped by serious social and economic crisis, a militant group known as 'Young Ireland' confronted Irish police at Ballingarry, County Tipperary. The so-called 'Rising of 1848' was soon put down, but one of the young men involved, James Stephens, escaped to Paris to fight another day and was joined by, amongst others, John O'Mahony, who had encouraged an attack on Glenbower Constabulary barracks later in the same year.[10] In Paris the men found an environment of revolutionary republicanism, involving oath-taking and secret fraternities, that would become part of their lives.[11] According to a later colleague (John Devoy), Stephens participated in fighting at the barricades during his time in Paris. 'Stephens was very proud of his participation in the Paris affair, and thought it qualified him to pronounce judgement on military questions. This was unfortunate for Ireland.'[12] Both Stephens and O'Mahony were intellectuals in their republican sentiments, but there the likeness ended. Robert Anderson, a future assistant commissioner of the Metropolitan Police who was employed by the Home Office at a critical point in the Fenian conspiracy, commented: 'O'Mahony, I believe was honest; just the sort of man who might have been won by conciliatory and just measures. But Stephens was a vain, self-seeking impostor, whom any competent government would have either bought or suppressed.'[13]

O'Mahony left Paris for North America in 1853 and Stephens returned to Ireland by 1856. On St Patrick's Day 1858, in a Dublin timber yard, Stephens founded a secret society dedicated to the establishment in Ireland of an independent democratic republic. Stephens did not initially give the society a name but it eventually became known as the Irish Republican Brotherhood (IRB).[14] O'Mahony had been a driving force behind the 1856 foundation in New York of the Emmet Monument Association, the precursor of the Fenian Brotherhood (FB) that in 1859 became the American counterpart of the IRB under his leadership.[15] The term 'Fenians' soon emerged as the universal designation for Irish republican revolutionaries on both sides of the Atlantic.

Stephens established the IRB along the lines of various continental secret societies:

> He adopted the cellular principle that had been a feature of the *Societé des familles*, which flourished in France in the 1830s. Thus the new organisation was to consist of circles each headed by a centre or A, known only to the officers immediately below him, nine Bs; each B would command nine Cs and would be known to them alone; each C would be responsible for, and known only to nine Ds, the rank and file ... Like members of every secret society, Stephens's followers were to be oath-bound ...[16]

Stephens himself became known as the head centre and chief organiser of the Irish Republic. The oath that IRB members had to swear took a general form (with local variations): 'I promise by the Divine Law of God to do all in my power to obey the laws of the Society and to free and regenerate Ireland from the yoke of England. So help me God.'[17] Somewhat in contrast, the FB in America was an open and legal organisation, keeping only its inner policies and contacts with Ireland as secret as possible, and was seen by Stephens as the principal source of fundraising to support an insurrection in Ireland.

Leaving others to encourage the swearing-in of members in Ireland, Stephens travelled to America in late 1858, spending six months there to raise money, before travelling to Paris as he feared arrest if he returned to Ireland. Meanwhile in Ireland, newspaper reports of a new secret society in the southwest began to emerge in November 1858, and a £100 reward was issued by the government for information about oath taking, which led to several arrests including one of Stephens' leading associates, Jeremiah O'Donovan Rossa.[18] By 1860, with Stephens still in France, the IRB had become virtually moribund, but its regeneration started with a visit to Paris and Ireland by O'Mahony and, after his prompting, Stephens agreed to return to Ireland. During O'Mahony's visit, the two leaders reached agreement on the numbers of men, officers and weapons that would be required as a pre-requisite of any rising by the Irish people.[19] The return of Stephens to Ireland helped to enhance recruitment to the IRB there. In America the Civil War (1861–65) undoubtedly caused a setback as priorities shifted towards the men and arms needed for that conflict. However, membership of the FB still made progress, fuelled by the considerable anti-British feeling that Clarke and his colleagues had themselves encountered in August 1864 in New York.

Back in Ireland, two new Fenian initiatives were developed. The first of these was to try to subvert the very large Irish-Catholic element of the British military garrison in Ireland.[20] By the mid-1860s there were an estimated 15,000 Fenian members in the British army recruited by agents such as Patrick 'Pagan' O'Leary and John Devoy.[21] In the second initiative, a Fenian newspaper was launched; the first issue of the *Irish People* appeared on 28 November 1863. The principal staff of the paper were Thomas Clarke Luby (nominal proprietor), John O'Leary (editor), Jeremiah O'Donovan Rossa (publisher) and Charles Kickham; all members of the Fenian leadership. It was widely read in Ireland and particularly in regions in Britain where Irish emigrants had concentrated.[22]

Stephens had encouraged the view within the IRB and FB that 1865 should be the year in which an Irish rising occurred. Funding from the FB in America had improved and, by early in the year, Stephens estimated that he had some 85,000 men organised in Ireland, including a significant number of 'seduced' soldiers, but was still insufficiently armed.[23] The American Civil War was moving towards its conclusion and there would soon be a considerable quantity of arms available at competitive prices, together with a substantial number of trained and battle-hardened men being discharged from the Union and Confederate armies (including an estimated 190,000 men of Irish parentage).[24] In addition, 'relations between Washington and Westminster were so poor for a few years that Anglo-American war was a credible prospect in many eyes', a situation that was of considerable potential advantage to the Fenians.[25] So, by early 1865, the Fenian threat appeared to be a substantial one and at this point in history we rejoin Clarke and the other detectives at Scotland Yard.

Scotland Yard and the Fenians

February 1865 – July 1866

Before 1865 investigations of the Fenians appear to have been the responsibility of the Irish police, under the direction of politicians and civil servants at Dublin Castle. The Constabulary Act had divided Ireland into four distinct police areas. The cities of Belfast and Derry each had their own police force. Dublin (the capital) had the Dublin Metropolitan Police (DMP), while the rest of the country had the Irish Constabulary (into which the Belfast and Derry forces had merged by 1870). In 1843, the DMP had set up G Division, a plain-clothes detective unit, and had the foresight to divide the unit's activities into two parts; one dealing with ordinary crimes and the other with political crimes. G Division was later to prove its worth in the field of political espionage and it was said that their detectives knew every dangerous political activist of the day by sight.[26]

Scotland Yard's interest in the Fenians seems to have coincided with the ending of the American Civil War, and may have involved Clarke from the outset. On 20 February 1865, Sir Richard Mayne wrote to Major John Greig, the chief constable of Liverpool: 'I beg you will cause assistance to Serjeant Clarke of the Detective Force to enable him to make effectual enquiry confidentially on the matters he will mention to you.'[27] From the point of view of informative detail the letter is somewhat lacking, but it does provide considerable scope for speculation. Firstly, the lack of any detail in the letter suggests that the enquiries related to highly confidential matters; investigations into Fenians would have been categorised in that way. Secondly, at that time Liverpool was the principal English port for arrivals from America, and also an important port of entry for travellers from Ireland. Clarke may have been involved in helping to put into place or carry out some surveillance activity for known Fenians. Whether this speculation has any substance in fact is not certain, but what is known is that O'Mahony did send several FB military envoys from America in 1865 including, in March, Thomas Kelly (who was to have a major role in subsequent events), Francis Millen (in April) and William Halpin (in October), who were to report back to O'Mahony about Stephens' plans and the resources available for a rising.[28]

Scotland Yard's involvement in Fenian investigations became more clear-cut in April 1865, when Mayne received a report from Dublin, suggesting that James Stephens might be in London and requesting help in watching him. A detailed description was provided by the Irish police:

Stephens appears 40 or 45 years of age, about 5 feet 7 or 8 inches high, pretty stout build, rather active appearance, wears all his beard which is pretty long and inclining to grey, eyes red and sore-looking are remarkably so, but this defect in the eyes is not constitutional. Accent and demeanour of a Frenchman, and speaks French tolerably well, as he has resided for a long time in France. He is an Irishman by birth and his French accent may be affected so as to suit his purpose; he dresses very respectably, chiefly in dark clothes and wears a silk hat and cloth cap and when travelling he generally has a brown cape; in damp or wet weather he wears gaiters, and carries a small black leather bag in his hand. He is generally accompanied by his wife who is a pretty neat looking person apparently much younger than he is, and less size; when habitting she wears a dark felt hat with white feather and a shepherds plaid shawl and all times dressed very respectably, chiefly in silk of a color suited to the season; when last seen she wore a black silk dress. Stephens assumes different names in different places and in Dublin he is known as Mr Power – in Cork, Mr Pillar.[29]

The Scotland Yard detective team were placed on a high level of watchfulness. Though Mayne reported back on 10 May that 'careful enquiry has been made', there had been no sightings of James Stephens in London.[30]

In June 1865, American officers from both the Union and Confederate armies, recognisable by their felt hats and square-toed boots, were beginning to make their way across the Atlantic to Ireland.[31] Meanwhile, Clarke was fulfilling his usual role at the Epsom Races, and played a bit-part in an inquiry led by Inspector Thomson into the forgery of Russian rouble notes, which concluded in December that year with convictions and sentences of five to twelve years' penal servitude for five men.[32] On the face of it, the Metropolitan Police was continuing with business as usual.

By September 1865 Ireland was tense. There was continued talk of the Fenians everywhere in the Irish and English press and instances of Fenian marching and drilling became more and more blatant.[33] Fenian plans for a rising in Dublin were mislaid and ended up in the hands of Superintendent Daniel Ryan of the DMP and, on 15 September 1865, a government decision to suppress the Fenian newspaper, the *Irish People*, was implemented by a DMP raid on their offices and the arrest, amongst others, of Thomas Luby, Jeremiah O'Donovan Rossa and John O'Leary; with further arrests in Dublin and Cork and the discovery of further treasonable correspondence.[34] The three men were tried on charges of 'treason felony' and, in December, were sentenced to long terms of penal servitude. Although the London Metropolitan Police had played little or no part in this, Mayne, in a rare moment of emotion, included in a letter to Sir Thomas Larcom (the undersecretary to the Lord Lieutenant of Ireland) the words 'I rejoice to hear of the conviction of Luby'. In the same letter Mayne also asked Larcom for a description of the Fenian leader in America, and reported that 'The Police still keep under observation the person here ...'.[35] Who that 'person' was is uncertain; it may have been a reference to a senior Fenian but there were also concerns about possible links between the Fenians and continental republican revolutionaries based in London, as well as with radicals within the Reform League (which had been established in February 1865 to promote the cause of parliamentary reform, including extended suffrage and a secret ballot).[36] One of the leading London-based continental revolutionaries was Guiseppe Mazzini, who Scotland Yard had under surveillance at about that time.[37]

In October 1865 Scotland Yard concerns had focused on the signs of an increasing arms trade. 'There are five Irishmen in this town buying up all the cheap rifles and revolving pistols they can obtain', the Mayor of Birmingham wrote in his letter to the Home Office of 20 October. Further correspondence, including letters to Inspector Williamson, highlighted an arms trade that was truly international and not infrequently involved Jewish middlemen.[38] The principal Fenian link in this trade was Ricard O'Sullivan Burke who had settled in Birmingham as 'arms agent' to the conspiracy in 1865.[39] Burke, originally born in County Cork, had immigrated to America and had served in the Union army in the 15th New York Engineers. Under different aliases, he negotiated commercial-scale purchases of arms and ammunition on behalf of the IRB and was to be an important player in future events.[40]

Meanwhile, Scotland Yard's surveillance activities of Fenians in London continued and, on 29 October 1865, Williamson submitted a report to Ireland of Clarke's investigations on alleged Fenian gatherings in London:

> … he and PC Campbell of G Division have watched Farrell, Hennessey, Butler and others; they haven't left London, and still hold meetings at a beer shop on Cleveland Street every Saturday and Sunday evenings – usually about 50 men attend, mostly of labouring classes. Men are told to hold selves in readiness as things are progressing well and action is not far off. The information respecting the language used at the meetings is received from George Tully, a police constable on the great Eastern Railway, who is admitted to the meetings. Clarke thinks that beside these meetings there are no other Fenian meetings in London.[41]

Whether or not Clarke was right in his presumption that so few Fenian meetings were taking place in London or was unduly complacent, there is no doubt that Fenian activity in London increased in later years.

By early November 1865 the Home Office was presenting a stark picture of the level of support for the Fenians, with estimates (probably overstated) that there were the following numbers of sworn Fenians in the individual countries of the United Kingdom: England 7,000; Scotland 8,000; Wales 3,000; Ireland 400,000; and a further 681,000 in the United States of America. It was also estimated that 10 per cent of the Fenians in Britain were sworn for 'special service', i.e. 'the destruction by fire of the cities, manufacturing towns, barracks, arsenals, shipyards and docks throughout England and Scotland'.[42] The Home Office mood must presumably have been lifted by events on 11 November when the DMP located and arrested James Stephens and transferred him to prison at Dublin's Richmond Bridewell. The Irish-American-dominated military council of the Fenians, including Thomas Kelly, Frederick Millen and William Halpin, met on 15 November and appointed Millen as provisional head organiser of the Irish Republic.[43] However, he was not to stay long in that post as, in an operation engineered by John Devoy and Fenians in the prison service, Stephens escaped from prison on 24 November

and went into hiding in Dublin.[44] Thus, any euphoria in government depart-
ments and police forces was short lived.

While Stephens' escape boosted Fenian morale, the events between
September and November had persuaded him that the proposed Irish rising
should be postponed and, despite opposition to any delay amongst some on
the military council, Stephens won the day.[45] One of the consequences of
the postponement of the rising was that O'Mahony was deposed as president of the Fenian Brotherhood in America, his position being taken over by
William Roberts who favoured the strategy of undertaking raids on Canada
as a way of potentially stirring up further antipathy between the United States
and Britain; thereby encouraging a political environment that could enhance,
indirectly, the Fenian desire for delivering an independent Ireland. This shift in
strategy quickly led to two factions developing amongst the American-based
Fenians: one that supported the O'Mahony stance of directly supporting an
insurrection in Ireland; the other the Roberts approach. This had the potential to dilute the American-based financial support available for Stephens and
his colleagues.[46]

The year 1866 started quietly. There is evidence that the Scotland Yard
detectives were still maintaining surveillance of Fenian movements between
London and Ireland, and reporting on attempts that had been made to induce
some marines to join the Fenians.[47] However, the commissioner at least had
sufficient time to focus on other 'vital' tasks, including a request to superintendents 'to report on what arrangements they propose to make to preserve
order and prevent snow balls etc., being thrown in parks and streets on
Sunday next'.[48] In Ireland, however, radical approaches were being planned
and implemented to stem the Fenian threat; these have been succinctly summarised by Vincent Comerford:

> Finding that the arrest and trial of the leaders and the uneventful passing of
> 1865 – the promised year of action – had not noticeably shaken the strength
> of the conspiracy, Dublin Castle resolved to abandon the attempt to combat
> subversion by ordinary legal processes. The securing of a handful of convictions
> that were supported by masses of incriminating documentation had been tedi-
> ous work. It would be impossible, simply relying on the courts, to pin anything
> on the hundreds of brazen Fenian activists throughout the country known to
> the police, or on the scores of returned Irish-Americans standing around the
> street corners of Dublin in their square-toed shoes awaiting the call to action.
> The only answer was the suspension of *habeas corpus*: a bill was rushed through
> parliament on 17 February 1866 permitting the indefinite detention of any
> person in Ireland on warrant of the Lord Lieutenant. The haste was intended
> to give the Irish police the advantage of surprise. Hours before they could have
> received confirmation of a formal enactment they had moved against scores of

suspects; within a week hundreds were in detention. For every one Fenian held an incalculable number fled to America (or Britain, where the immunities of the subjects were untouched), went to ground, or simply abandoned the conspiracy. The suspension of *habeas corpus* wreaked havoc on Fenianism in Ireland, shifting the odds in favour of the authorities.[49]

By July 1866 the total number of arrests under the *habeas corpus* suspension was 756 and, during the summer of 1866, Ireland was more peaceful than it had been for years.[50] John Devoy was one of the many Fenians arrested, and was later tried and sentenced to fifteen years' penal servitude. James Stephens and Thomas Kelly (by now the IRB's 'Chief of Staff') successfully remained in hiding in Dublin and were eventually smuggled out of Dublin in March, and arrived in New York in mid-May 1866. Shortly after they arrived, 800 members of the Fenian Brotherhood, commanded by Colonel John O'Neill, 'invaded' Canada, crossing the Niagara River and occupying the village of Fort Erie. In a short battle there were fifty-two Canadian casualties (including twelve dead) and twenty-eight Fenian casualties (including eight dead), with approximately sixty Fenians captured and many desertions. O'Neill withdrew his forces and the United States authorities, implementing neutrality laws, seized the Fenians' weapons and sent them home with paid passages. This ineffective display by the Roberts-led faction of the Fenian Brotherhood lent force to Stephens' arguments that the 'rising' should be in Ireland.[51] Though there would be two further (and equally ineffective) Fenian raids on Canada in subsequent years, they did not achieve the aim of raising USA-UK relations to a state of war.

Back in London, the suspension of *habeas corpus* in February 1866 probably provided a short respite for those detectives at Scotland Yard who had been working on Fenian-related matters. Clarke at least was diverted on to another investigation; as it turned out he might have preferred to have remained on Fenian surveillance, as the case proved not to be his finest hour.

A Diversionary Task for Clarke – The Case of the Missing Cheques

On 1 March 1866, following an approach to Commissioner Mayne, George Clarke was hired by Lord Cardigan to investigate the disappearance of two letters containing cheques sent by the Countess of Cardigan. The 7th Earl of Cardigan, James Thomas Brudenell, was a man who had been both hated and fêted during his lifetime. Born in 1797, Brudenell had been educated at Harrow and Oxford University. Having purchased a commission in the army, he had a chequered career. He was charged in June 1824 by a Captain Johnstone of having debauched Johnstone's wife Elizabeth, whom Brudenell later married in 1826 after divorce proceedings had been completed. In 1837, after his father's death, he inherited the earldom and the Deene estate in Northamptonshire, a mansion in Portman Square and an annual income of £40,000. In 1840 he fought a duel on Wimbledon Common with Henry Tuckett (a former army officer); Tuckett was seriously wounded and Cardigan was charged with 'intent to murder'. As a member of the House of Lords, Cardigan was eligible to be tried by peers and elected to do so, receiving a 'not guilty' verdict, essentially on a legal technicality. By 1840 his public image was so bad that his appearance in the audience at Brighton's Theatre Royal provoked a storm of hisses which lasted at least half an hour and, to enable the performance to begin, he was forced to leave.[52]

When the Crimean War started in March 1853, Cardigan was given command of the Light Cavalry Brigade under his brother-in-law Lord Lucan; the two men were not bosom friends. On 25 October 1854 Cardigan led the famous 'Charge of the Light Brigade' at Balaclava. Ambiguity in the orders that he received meant that the brigade rode at the wrong target, directly at a battery of Russian guns rather than at British guns which were in the process of being captured by the Russians. Out of some 676 mounted men, the total casualties were 21 officers and 257 other ranks (including 158 killed or captured), and about 335 horses were killed or had to be destroyed. Nonetheless, the reports that reached home indicated that Cardigan had led the charge with great bravery and on his return to Britain he was greeted by cheering crowds. Later, rumours began to circulate that his conduct may have been less than heroic, particularly in the context of a premature retreat up the valley after he had reached the rear of the Russian guns.

Cardigan had separated from his first wife in 1846 after an unsatisfactory relationship in which neither partner remained faithful; Elizabeth died in July 1858 and later that year Cardigan (by then 60) married the 33-year-old Adeline de Horsey who had openly become his mistress in 1857. This was a situation much frowned upon by Queen Victoria and contemporary society, which left Adeline a social outcast. Such was the colourful background of the couple that Clarke now found himself working for.

In February 1866 the Countess of Cardigan had written two letters enclosing uncrossed cheques for £18 16s and £1 10s, for goods supplied. She had then handed the letters to Robert Lilley, the groom of the chambers (a position in the household staff only second to that of the steward), requesting that they be registered and posted. Lilley was a long-serving member of the household staff who had been employed by Cardigan prior to his marriage to Adeline. A week later, surprised that she had received no receipts for the cheques, the countess contacted the addressees and discovered that they had not received the letters or the cheques. She was then told by her bank that the larger of the two cheques had been cashed on 14 February in London by someone who had been handed a £5 note, and the balance of £13 6s in gold and silver. Fortunately, as was the habit in those days, the bank had kept a record of the number of the £5 Bank of England note. The bank advised the Cardigans to contact the police, and Clarke was sent across to Portman Square on 1 March to investigate the situation. Realising that the £5 note needed to be traced, Clarke visited the Bank of England on 2 March and provided the number of the note and asked to be notified if it was traced. Clarke then interviewed the Cardigans and the substantial number of 'below-stairs staff' at Portman House. During his interview with Lilley, the somewhat truculent groom of the chambers claimed that he could not remember being handed the two letters by the countess in the first place.[53]

On 9 or 10 March, the all-important £5 note was traced to Thomas Hobson, the proprietor of Cole's truss shop at Charing Cross, who had received the £5 note from a man calling himself William Gaskell. Gaskell had told Hobson that he was a hall porter in a nobleman's family. Further inquiries revealed that the true identity of William Gaskell was in fact John Hayes, the hall porter at Cardigan's house in Portman Square, who had been employed by the Cardigans for only a few months. However, on 12 March, when Clarke took Hobson to Portman Square, Hobson did not immediately recognise Hayes as the man to whom he had sold the truss, possibly because Hayes was by then dressed in full livery with his hair powdered. Nevertheless, Hobson later mentioned in court that 'Hayes [later] came to me and said he was the man who changed the note, and hoped I would say nothing about it, as he would have to criminate one of his fellow-servants'.[54] Indeed that was precisely what Hayes did, by informing Clarke that Lilley had asked him to change a £5 note, and he had handed over 5 sovereigns in exchange for it.

By 13 March, Clarke had clearly decided to focus his attention on Hayes and Lilley, and, together with Lord Cardigan, re-interviewed the two men individually. Hayes repeated his assertion that he had received the £5 Bank of England note from Lilley, and Lilley denied it. Clarke later recalled in court that 'Lord Cardigan appealed to me in the room to know what was to be done. I think I said "My Lord, if all this is true, Lilley must have stolen the letter".'[55] Though this does not sound like a deep conviction of Lilley's likely guilt, Clarke nonetheless arrested Lilley that evening and, together with Lord Cardigan, took him to Marylebone Police Station where Lilley was charged with stealing the letters, later appearing at two hearings at the Marylebone Police Court when he was committed to trial at the Middlesex Sessions in June, and bailed.

The case was heard at the Guildhall, Westminster, on 2 June in front of a jury, Mr Bodkin (assistant judge) and several magistrates. Harry Poland appeared as counsel for the prosecution, for whom the main witnesses were the Countess of Cardigan, Hayes and Clarke.[56] The countess, who seems throughout to have been convinced that Lilley was the guilty party, insisted that her memory was particularly accurate and that she clearly recalled handing the two letters to Lilley. However, in cross-examination by Lilley's counsel, her memory came into question when she admitted that there had been a previous incident in which her rings had gone missing; she had insisted that they had been stolen and a policeman had been called, but the rings had been found in a pocket in her dress. The credibility of the hall porter, John Hayes, was completely compromised in cross-examination, not least by his attitude in the witness box and the disquieting information that Hayes had left his former employer (the Reform Club) under a cloud, as he was suspected of financial irregularity. In addition, he had left his previous rented accommodation owing his landlord £20. By the time that he had completed his evidence Lilley's defence team seemed to have right on their side when concluding that: 'Hayes had the strongest motives for sheltering himself by accusing someone else …'[57]

Before the summing-up, several 'below-stairs' members of the Cardigans' household were called to give evidence in Lilley's defence, but after Hayes' evidence their journey to the court hardly seemed necessary. The jury returned a 'not guilty' verdict, and Lilley was released. No prosecution appears to have been taken against Hayes. However, the issue returned to haunt Clarke the following year.

In June 1867, Lilley brought a case against Lord Cardigan for false imprisonment and malicious prosecution that was heard over two days at the Court of Queens Bench. Much of the same ground was covered again, with the countess continuing to stress the excellence of her memory. No further evidence from Hayes was forthcoming as he had died the previous January, but Clarke was called and responded to questions about his investigation. Lord Cardigan confirmed Clarke's version of events and appears not to have displayed any criticism of the handling of the case by Clarke.[58] The jury, finding for Lilley, awarded him £400 damages in addition to the £45 that Cardigan had already paid into court.

With the benefit of hindsight, it is difficult to understand why Clarke recommended Lilley's arrest, rather than that of Hayes. Of course, whether Hayes was guilty of the offence or not was never tested in court, but Clarke was probably the butt of a few jokes back in the sergeants' office at Old Scotland Yard. For Lord Cardigan, the £445 plus legal expenses and the costs of reimbursing the Metropolitan Police for Clarke's services would have represented only a small proportional increase in the costs of his lavish lifestyle. However, after his death in March 1868 the countess had to pay off debts of about £365,000 by realising capital assets. The countess remarried and lived into the twentieth century but, in her memoirs published in 1909, did not mention the case of the missing cheques; perhaps she had forgotten.[59]

Scotland Yard and the Fenians

August 1866 – January 1867

At the end of June 1866, the defeat of a reform bill drafted by Lord Russell's administration catalysed the resignation of the government; the subsequent General Election brought in a Conservative administration led by Lord Derby, with Spencer Walpole as Home Secretary and a new chief secretary in Dublin Castle, Lord Naas (soon to inherit the title of the Earl of Mayo). This last appointment introduced a fresh attitude to the policing of Fenianism, including a greater use of undercover detectives and political surveillance in Britain and other locations (e.g. Paris) where the Fenians were known to be active. Soon after his appointment, Lord Naas also asked a young barrister, Robert Anderson (who had been working closely with his brother, Samuel Anderson, the Crown solicitor in Ireland), to prepare a précis of secret and other documentary evidence on the Fenians.[60]

In July, the new government and the Metropolitan Police were rudely awakened by the activities of the Reform League who, after a peaceful meeting in Trafalgar Square on 2 July, went ahead with a further meeting in Hyde Park on 23 July 1866 despite a ban on the meeting being imposed by the Home Secretary. On the day, thousands of people turned up. Finding the park gates closed, the mob pulled down the railings; the police were overwhelmed and soldiers were sent in. Mayne himself was wounded and many policemen seriously injured, but Mayne's subsequent offer of resignation was refused. Some described the events that day as almost the last great expression of the traditional London crowd, and others viewed it as a revolution narrowly averted.[61] The extent of involvement of Clarke and his colleagues in these events is unclear, but these were difficult times for the police.

Lord Naas started to apply pressure in August for changes in the strategy of policing Fenianism, by suggesting to the Home Secretary that 'from four to six detectives from the Police Forces in England be assigned to Glasgow, Liverpool and Manchester to ascertain whether Fenian agents are being actively engaged in carrying on the conspiracy'.[62] Perhaps lulled by a false sense of security created by the withdrawal of *habeas corpus* in Ireland, Walpole refused but, shortly after, directed Mayne to explore the Fenian issue in Liverpool. Mayne then wrote to the Liverpool chief constable, Major Greig, early in September and sent on this occasion Inspector Williamson and Sergeant Mulvany 'to co-operate with your officers and those sent from Ireland in discovering the Fenian Conspirators'.[63] On 15 September, Williamson reported back that house searches had only revealed 'a few treasonable songs and some drill books'. He added: 'Although the Fenian spirit exists in Liverpool, there is no extensive organization, and no drilling or meetings of Fenians in numbers takes place … For some months past the Fenian cause has been in a depressed state in this town.'[64] Further activity in October suggested that this was an unduly complacent assessment, as Mulvany had to return to Liverpool to deal with the case of four men who were arrested in Liverpool when unable to account for the possession of a number of rifles, bayonets and phosphorus (used in incendiary devices), apparently obtained from military sources.[65] The items had probably been stolen from military bases in England, or 'liberated' from them by soldiers who had been seduced into the Fenian camp. Indeed, the modern perspective is that Liverpool was the centre of the Fenian conspiracy in England at that time and, when an informant finally provided details of an extensive Fenian organisation in Liverpool, even Mayne was convinced of the seriousness of the problem.[66]

In September, Lord Naas suggested deploying experienced army personnel on mainland Britain, including Captain William Whelan, who had been working to help root out Fenianism in the army. Apparently this idea was also rejected though it seems that Whelan did unofficially deploy informers on the mainland and Mayne certainly wrote two letters to Whelan in mid-September 1866 asking him to communicate to him the enquiries he had been making about the Fenian conspiracy.[67] Unfortunately, details of Clarke's role in the policing of the Fenian conspiracy during 1866 are unknown, as no specific mention of him was found in any of the surviving archived reports or newspaper accounts on the Fenians that have been located relating to this period. He only emerges publicly again, in the Fenian context, in January 1867. However, as Clarke's name also only appeared in the national newspapers in relation to two criminal cases during 1866, it seems likely that he was engaged for much of the rest of his time on some form of unpublicised anti-Fenian activity. Meanwhile, as 1866 moved to its conclusion, events in America were developing in ways that would bring Clarke more into the Fenian limelight in 1867.

In New York, Stephens and the Fenian military council had started to strengthen their military leadership by attracting some senior officers with Civil War experience who were dedicated to revolutionary republicanism. Of these, Gustave Paul Cluseret was appointed 'Commander-in-Chief' of the Fenian insurrectionary force. Cluseret was a Frenchman who had been an officer in the *garde mobile* during the revolution of 1848 and later served in Algeria, before joining Garibaldi's volunteers in Italy in 1860. This was followed by service in the Union Army in the American Civil War, where he achieved the rank of brigadier general.[68] On appointment by Stephens, Cluseret selected two other foreign veterans of the Civil War as his military adjutants, Octave Fariola and Victor Vifquain.[69] Fariola and Clarke were later to become briefly acquainted and, because Fariola has left probably the most extensive archival and newspaper record of the Fenian conspiracy between

August 1866 and November 1867, the following account will draw heavily on his experiences. The two main sources of Fariola's recollections were intended for quite different audiences: firstly, a statement or 'confession' given to the British authorities in late 1867 or early 1868 (now held in the National Archives); and secondly, a series of newspaper articles written by Fariola and published in late 1868 in the Fenian-supportive newspaper *The Irishman*.[70] The following account tries to tread the common path that emerges from these different sources.

Octave Fariola (full name Octave Louis François Etienne Fariola de Razzoli) was born in 1839. He was a Swiss citizen but was brought up in Belgium where he attended the military academy in Brussels, being commissioned as a lieutenant in about 1856, before assisting in Garibaldi's campaign in Italy in 1859–60, where he acquired his revolutionary republican credentials and contacts. Married in Brussels in 1863, Fariola and his wife immigrated to Louisiana where he joined the Union army at New Orleans on 10 July 1863 as a staff officer for General Nathaniel Banks, before serving in the 2nd Engineer Corps d'Afrique. He was honourably discharged as a lieutenant-colonel on 29 January 1866, and was living as a planter in Louisiana with his wife and young son when he received a series of letters from Cluseret, between August and October that year, inviting him to become Cluseret's chief of staff in a new enterprise. When Fariola's crop (probably cotton) in Louisiana was destroyed by caterpillars (a common fate) he finally decided that he needed to find other sources of income and travelled to New York in early November to meet Cluseret, only on arrival discovering that the object was the liberation of Ireland by the Fenians, and that his role would be the organisation of the Fenian insurrectionary force.[71] Before agreeing to accept the post, he had a long interview in New York with James Stephens. In his later confession Fariola reported that: 'The whole of his statement was so extra-ordinary that I came to the conclusion that if he was not telling the truth he must be a fool or a scoundrel of the worst character.'[72]

In his newspaper articles Fariola also echoed the concerns that John Devoy had expressed on Stephens' military proficiency: 'I do not profess to be a competent judge of a man's abilities; still if I might venture to give an opinion on Mr Stephens's it is that they are of a very high order in most things. *I except military matters* [Fariola's italics] in which he is worse than incompetent.'[73] Stephens, possibly believing his own propaganda, informed Fariola that the Fenians had 50,000 organised men on Irish soil, three steamers, funds for 20,000 rifles, as well as torpedoes and Greek Fire (an incendiary compound based on white phosphorus). Fariola would be paid £60 a month, six months in advance. He was only later to discover, when he reached Europe, that little or no money was forthcoming and that the Fenians only had one very old steamer which was sold for $14,000 – the only money that was left in the

Fenian exchequer by the end of 1866.[74] Before he agreed to accept the job of chief of staff, he sought certain conditions:

> I should not be called upon to take any share in the insurrection until it would have been clearly demonstrated that the majority of the Irish people were intent upon the overthrow of both aristocracy and monarchy … [and] … the establishment of a *de facto* Government having some degree of organization, and a certain extent of territory of its own. I objected in doing anything for the conspiracy within the British jurisdiction [on the British mainland], and this was a *sine-qua-non* condition.[75]

Receiving Stephens' agreement to these terms, Fariola left New York on 14 November 1866 on the SS *England*, arriving in Liverpool where he narrowly avoided being arrested, before travelling via London, where he purchased a revolver, to Paris. Arriving on 3 December 1866 and finding no money waiting for him, he raised funds from his wife's family and by pawning his watch.[76]

Despite the clear evidence that the availability of funding and the organisation of Fenian activities did not match Stephens' hyperbole, Fariola persisted in his task. Before he left America, Fariola had learnt that the plans for the rising involved Stephens leaving for Ireland at the end of December or beginning of January:

> … with a number of officers, arms, and ammunitions in quantity. [Stephens] pledged himself that within three days of his making his call upon the Irish Republican Brotherhood he would have 30,000 men assembled in three bodies, in three given points, and provided with arms and ammunition; which being done it remained for the Military Commander, at the head of such an army – for they were drilled men, officered by American officers – to wrest Ireland from English clutches … The plan of the C.O.I.R. [Chief Organiser of the Irish Republic] was, in my view, utterly absurd, and I ventured to point that out.[77]

The absurdity, as far as Fariola was concerned, was that 30,000 assembled men would only become an effective army through a process of training and organisation that would take time. In his confession, Fariola clearly indicates that his own proposals (influenced by his experiences with Garibaldi), if implemented, would have established an insurgency in south-west Ireland using guerrilla tactics involving small groups of no more than thirty men; cutting railway lines and telegraphic communications; establishing barricades and attacking the constabulary when found in inferior force. However, despite the suitability of Fariola's tactics to the Irish countryside, and the number of volunteers available, his instructions were abandoned during the last stage of preparations.[78]

As 1866 was coming to an end, intelligence from British consulates in America and other informers indicated that a Fenian rising was soon to break out, and that US-based Fenians were in a state of readiness to proceed to Ireland. Mayne was busy circulating a photograph and description of Stephens and requesting information from Dublin to assist in identifying known Fenians likely to travel from America. In addition, in late December 1866 and early January 1867, police from the London Metropolitan force were keeping a watch for Stephens at several ports; it is highly likely that Clarke was engaged in these duties.[79]

At a meeting of senior Fenians in New York in mid-December Stephens decided, belatedly, that the financial support and preparations needed for a successful rising were not in place and that it should again be postponed. By 29 December the 'hard men' of the military council had had time to digest the news and, accusing Stephens of incompetence, insincerity and dishonesty, they deposed him, installing Thomas Kelly as the effective leader. Kelly was later assessed as being as reckless as Stephens was timid.[80] It was probably mid–late January before the British authorities fully appreciated the changes that had occurred. Meanwhile, Kelly, who was determined to deliver action, left America in mid-January, arriving in Paris on 25 January and managing to slip through any surveillance that the police had in place. Cluseret and Vifquain travelled with Kelly, while Godfrey Massey had sailed to Liverpool a day earlier. Massey, who had been brought up under the name of Patrick Condon, was a late arrival on the Fenian scene, having joined only in 1865. Born in Ireland, he had served as a private and as a non-commissioned officer in the British army in the Crimea, before immigrating to America and fighting in the Confederate army where he rose to the rank of colonel.[81]

In Paris, Kelly and Cluseret met up with Fariola and soon travelled to London to set up their operational headquarters. 'Sprawling London, with its Irish areas no doubt seemed a safer refuge than informer-riddled Dublin, or even Birmingham, Manchester or Liverpool.'[82] In addition, *habeas corpus* was not suspended in mainland Britain; therefore, unless the men committed a criminal offence in England, had a warrant in place for their arrest from another country within the United Kingdom (including Ireland) or from their own country of origin, then the police had no grounds on which to arrest them. Kelly and Halpin (who had also reached London) took rooms off Tottenham Court Road and used aliases. Likewise Ricard Burke (the arms organiser) and Godfrey Massey were at 7 Tavistock Street, and Cluseret and Fariola at 135 Great Portland Street, staying there until 28 February 1867. During this time the Fenians held several meetings to discuss the insurrection, including one that led to the establishment of a Provisional Government for Ireland. A provisional date for the rising, of 11 February, was cancelled and a new date of 5 March was set. Fariola and Massey also made contact with one group of Irish-American Fenians (generally referred to as 'The Directory') who had been based in London for several months at Stephens' request, but who had received inadequate information and funds during that time. Nonetheless, under the leadership of Captain John McCafferty, The Directory had developed their own plans for action in February: a proposed raid on Chester Castle to seize arms and transport them to Ireland.

In the busy two months of January and February 1867, secret discussions were also held (involving Fariola) with other republican groups based in London to try to establish common cause with them. These included meetings with the senior members of the Reform League, Charles Bradlaugh and George Odger, who 'were prepared to offer their support only if Fenian principles were merely democratic and not anti-English'.[83] Fariola also met Guiseppe Mazzini who told him 'that he disapproved of Fenianism [because of] his mistrust of the principles of its leader [and] because he deemed it doomed to be a failure'.[84] Ultimately these discussions yielded nothing of benefit to the Fenians. However, in a scarcely credible breach of security, Fariola and Cluseret were able to build up their understanding of the British military machine by undertaking official visits to Woolwich Arsenal, Aldershot and the War Office. They were able to do this under the guise of a commission of the governor of New York State, obtained by Cluseret, to enquire into the organisation of militias in Europe.

All this was happening under the nose of the London Metropolitan Police, who were either unable to act until there was evidence that a criminal offence had been committed, were unaware of what was going on or were simply slow in obtaining and acting on the necessary intelligence in time. However, by no later than late February the detective department was certainly on the trail of at least Massey and Burke. This is known from evidence later given by their landlady, Eliza Lambert, who stated that 'Mr Clarke, a detective officer, came to me after they both had left'.[85] So Clarke was clearly following the trail of senior Fenians at that point. He may have been one to two weeks behind them, or had deliberately delayed his overt enquiries until the men had left as there was no specific charge to bring against them at that stage. On the other hand, Clarke had also been put on another investigation: a strange case in Ely, Cambridgeshire, where two horses had been found dead on 21 January, apparently as a result of having been fed bran containing strychnine.

This further diversion must have decreased Clarke's availability for Fenian investigations. In addition, the numbers of Scotland Yard detectives available in England had been depleted further by an edict from Home Secretary Walpole to assign detectives to Paris to watch out for James Stephens, who was now believed to have travelled (and indeed had travelled) to Paris. Despite having been deposed as chief organiser, Stephens was still considered a sufficient threat to security that his movements should be watched; the police were probably also aware that other Fenians used Paris as a bolt-hole. There had been times during 1866 when Mayne had strongly resisted the deployment of British policemen to undercover operations in France but, early in 1867, two Scotland Yard detectives were finally sent.[86] Fariola refers to their presence in Paris at the end of January 1867: 'the English detectives were already on the scent.'[87] Most of this surveillance work in Paris was undertaken by Sergeants Druscovich, Mulvany and Manners; Inspector Williamson is also known to have spent some time there and Inspector Thomson may have been involved, but there is no mention that Clarke was ever sent to France at this time.[88]

With the benefit of hindsight, it does seem strange that, at a critical time for Fenian activity in London, Clarke was allocated to a relatively low-priority case outside the Metropolitan area. As a result of Clarke's investigations in Ely, Dr Henry Hume Pearson, a physician of some twenty years' standing, was charged with the apparently motiveless poisoning of two horses, the property of George Hall, a solicitor. The case came to trial at Cambridge Crown Court on 19 March. There were four key pieces of evidence that Clarke had accumulated. The first, a witness who had seen Pearson entering the stables on the day that the horses were later found dead. Secondly, the discovery by Clarke of strychnine hidden behind a mirror at Pearson's house – in a form identical to that which had caused the death of the horses, and which was only available to members of the medical profession. Third, witnesses who had heard Pearson ask how much strychnine would be needed to kill a horse and, fourthly, evidence that he had practised by killing a pig with strychnine on his own property first. After a 'guilty' verdict was delivered, Pearson was sentenced to five years' penal servitude.[89]

The Raid on Chester Castle and the Fenian Rising

February 1867 – June 1867

On the morning of 11 February 1867, the Home Office received a telegram from the Mayor of Chester:

> There are about 500 Fenians arrived in Chester by various trains. It is reported from Liverpool Police that 700 more will be there before tonight. There are about 100 men of the 54th regiment at the Castle and about 200 militia staff and 130 police. Further military assistance urgently needed to protect the arms and ammunition at the castle and also to protect the city.[90]

The venture led by Captain John McCafferty had begun. The bold plan was to attack the castle, remove arms and ammunition and transfer them by train to Holyhead and by boat to Ireland. However, like so many of the Fenian plans, it was to be compromised by informers. The night before the proposed attack one of Stephens' most trusted agents, John Joseph Corydon, provided details of the Chester Castle raid, giving the military just sufficient time to reinforce the garrison. By 1 p.m. Fenian leaders realised that the authorities had been alerted to their plans and the operation was called off. The Fenians that had gathered in the town 'melted away', often leaving weapons and ammunition that they had brought with them (including agricultural implements, pikes and muskets) in the surrounding countryside. Amongst them was a young one-armed Fenian, Michael Davitt, who we will hear more of in a later chapter. Unable to use a weapon because of his disability, he had carried a bag of bullets to the scene.[91]

Intriguingly, it seems that Williamson and Clarke were called in and even given some credit for the way that things turned out. A cryptic newspaper article published later that year can only be a reference to events at Chester (without specifically mentioning the city by name):

> Certain trustworthy information had been given to the heads of the police that bands of men, under pretence of making agricultural work, were gathering round a city in which Government arms are stored. The Chief of the London detective branch of police, at Scotland-yard, Inspector Williamson, is in Manchester with another experienced officer from head-quarters, Sergeant Clark [sic], and the two were advised by telegraph of all the circumstances in good time, as now appear from facts that have been discovered. The place round which great numbers of Irishmen, hugely in excess of any present demand for field labour, and suspiciously well-provided with reaping implements, had congregated, is in an adjoining county, and is distant from Manchester about forty miles. The two London officers who are looking after Fenian affairs principally in this city [Manchester], took rail for the place which I have not precisely indicated, though there would be no fear of harm in naming it, and were back again before their absence had been noticed here. The visit, brief as it was, sufficed to counterplot a desperate enterprise, and to avert bloodshed in the midst of a very peaceable and rather dull community.[92]

The raid organiser, John McCafferty, was arrested in Dublin harbour on 23 February having escaped from England via Whitehaven. At his subsequent trial for treason he was sentenced to death, later commuted to life imprisonment not least because of public and government misgivings about enforcing the death penalty for a 'political' offence.[93] Meanwhile in London, plans for the Irish rising were continuing. Massey (who had been given military command of the rising itself) had visited Ireland and expressed the view that there were inadequate arms for the rising to be successful. However, he was overruled by others and planning proceeded for 5 March. General William Halpin was given responsibility for the Dublin area and, amongst others, Vifquain for the west of Ireland and Ricard Burke the Waterford district, all subordinate to Massey. Fariola travelled to Cork, arriving on 1 March, to put the finishing touches to the arrangements with local commanders.[94] When hearing Massey's final plans, Fariola felt them: 'so utterly absurd and in disregard of my instructions that I requested him in the name of the Provisional Government to stop all future proceedings, and told him that he had ruined the cause … Massey would not; he did no longer recognise the Provisional Government except Kelly and declined to comply with my advice.'[95] The last straw for Fariola was on 4 March when he was given a message from Massey, via a Miss O'Leary, telling him to go to Connaught to take command there – Fariola refused to take what he regarded as a subordinate command, an attitude which: 'vexed Miss O'Leary, who has kept a grudge against me, and taxed me afterwards of cowardice, and vexed also Massey who did not wish to admit of his being not the Chief Commander.'[96] 'Miss O'Leary' was Ellen O'Leary, sister of the imprisoned Fenian John O'Leary. She was an Irish poet and later a mentor of W.B. Yeats; in 1867 she was a leading member of the formidable Ladies Committee for the Relief of State Prisoners and was described by Clarke in one of his later reports as 'one of the most active of the female agents'.[97]

Meanwhile, events were about to make the disagreements between Fariola and Massey irrelevant. Apparently unaware that the plans for the rising had already been passed on to the Irish authorities on 27 February by the prolific informer Corydon, Massey was arrested on board a train at Limerick Junction at 10 p.m. on 4 March, followed later by the arrests of other Fenians involved in the rising.[98] Prior to the trials of those arrested, Robert Anderson recorded that he was asked to secure one or more important prisoners to turn 'Queens Evidence'. 'It did not take long to discover that Godfrey Massey was incomparably the ablest and best informed of the prisoners', and Anderson claims to have persuaded him to turn informer.[99] Fariola had a different perspective, albeit one that displayed a strong personal dislike of Massey:

> When did this being commence his career of traitorism? Before or after his arrest? I now think it was before his arrest, for in his preliminary tour over the island he had taken care to disorganise and derange all our plans, he had given orders directly opposite to his line of instructions, and it must have been for the sole purpose of making the assurance of our discomfiture, and of his own security in his treachery, doubly sure.[100]

Hearing about the betrayal of the plans, Fariola hastily left his Cork hotel, leaving behind his revolver and an unpaid bill, and undertook an eventful journey via Limerick to Dublin, London and Paris.[101] Others were unaware of the disaster that had overtaken the Fenian high command, and the Irish Republican Army was on the march in Dublin, Drogheda, Cork, Tipperary, Clare and Limerick. Discipline and morale do not appear to have been high in some areas; lack of orders and senior commanders also led to men dispersing. Although there were clashes and some modest successes for the Fenians, the last significant action took place on 31 March by which time mopping-up operations by the army and police were essentially completed. Apart from an abortive attempt to ship in additional arms and men from America, these events ended the long-awaited Fenian rising in Ireland, undermined by informers, internal conflicts and inadequate preparation.[102]

Arrests, Escapes, Trials and Promotion

July 1867 – November 1867

While the Irish police forces had arrested large numbers of the rank-and-file Fenians during March, many of the leaders had escaped. Apart from Fariola, these included Gustave Cluseret, Ricard Burke, Thomas Kelly and William Halpin – amongst others. Warrants were soon issued by Dublin Castle for their arrest, and these individuals must have been high up the list of the 'wanted men' at Scotland Yard. However, in June and July 1867 Clarke had to fit in his court appearance in the Lilley *v.* Earl of Cardigan action, and also an investigation into a series of robberies of banknotes, gold watches and rings in the officers' quarters at the Tower of London. These enquiries during June led to his arrest of Charles Stuart, a corporal in the 1st Battalion of the Grenadier Guards, who was tried and found guilty at the Old Bailey on 8 July.[103]

Soon thereafter, Clarke was back on Fenian duties and, together with 'Dolly' Williamson, made a breakthrough by arresting Fariola. The young chief of staff had returned from Paris in May and was now living in London under the name of Eugene Liebehrt. Fariola subsequently published his own account of the arrest on Saturday 13 July 1867 in Regent Street, facilitated by yet another informer:

> We walked along in the twilight, chatting on the approaching meeting, when suddenly I felt conscious of a tap on my shoulder.
> 'I arrest you in the Queen's name!'
> 'What d'ye mean? Show me your warrant.'
> 'Come, come, none of that. How do you call yourself?'
> 'Eugene Liebehrt.'
> And then the Inspector turned to Mr. Frawley.

'Who are you?'

'No necessity to tell you. Look at my number, I'm a commissionaire.'

'And who's that with you?'

'Why – why that's General Fariola!'

Now, it's just within the range of possibility that the Inspector came upon me by hap-hazard; but it does strike me as suspicious that Mr. Frawley was so pat with my name, and that his explanation had been so readily accepted, and also that a thick posse [sic] of well-armed constables was at hand to the Inspector's call, as if in preparation for possible resistance to capture.[104]

The arrest was at a rather inconvenient time as Clarke and the three inspectors, Tanner, Thomson and Williamson (who had recently been promoted to chief inspector), were busy with police arrangements for the State visit of His Imperial Majesty the Sultan of the Ottoman Empire Abdülaziz I, who had arrived in London only the day before.[105] Although the Ottoman Empire was in decline, this first visit of a sultan to Britain was of considerable importance politically and as a public event.[106] Despite the State visit, someone at Scotland Yard had the job to transfer Fariola to Kilmainham Prison, Dublin, and that task fell to Inspector Thomson who, according to Fariola, 'was as kind to me as his duties permitted'.[107] In gaol, Fariola joined William Halpin who had been arrested by the Irish police earlier in July on board the *City of Paris* in Queenstown harbour where he was en route to New York from Liverpool. Tipped off by a Liverpool source, the police had been accompanied by the informer, Corydon, who had pointed out Halpin to the arresting officer. To add further substance to Halpin's identity, Clarke later visited Dublin, together with at least one witness, Emma Muntz, who had lived in the lodgings occupied by Halpin and Kelly in February; Muntz identified Halpin in prison as the man she had known as 'Mr Fletcher'.[108]

Fariola appeared in front of magistrates at Castle Yard, Dublin, on several occasions in July. Clarke gave evidence that he had 'arrested the prisoner in Regent-street, when he denied he had ever been in the American army, and said he had only just arrived from Paris'.[109] The fact that Clarke gave evidence of the arrest rather than Williamson suggests that he, rather than Williamson, was the 'inspector' referred to in Fariola's description of the arrest. Mayne, sensitive to concerns that Fariola's trial might make public the fact that the Metropolitan Police had detectives on covert surveillance duties in Paris, wrote to Lord Naas that he didn't want Sergeant Manners (one of the detectives based in Paris) used as an identification witness in Fariola's case, and that he had therefore asked the lodging-house keeper at Great Portland Street to be sent to Dublin for this purpose.[110] When Fariola was finally arraigned before the Special Commission Court in Dublin in November he had decided to plead guilty. Not surprisingly, in his own account in *The Irishman*, Fariola

strongly rebuts the idea that he acted as an informer or gave useful information to his captors, and it does seem that most of the information presented in
his confession is likely to have been known to the Irish and English authorities. Even so, the confession was regarded as 'extremely interesting' by Samuel
Anderson, Ireland's Crown solicitor, and in Benjamin Disraeli's words was 'the
only complete account of the plans and resources of the Fenian Conspiracy'.[111]
Indeed, Fariola's confession and his articles in *The Irishman* remain fascinating
and unputdownable first-hand accounts of the Fenian rising, as fresh today as
when they were written.

In early 1868, Fariola's confession delivered what he desired, an early
release and a passage for Fariola, his wife and child to Australia. In contrast,
his former colleague William Halpin, who was put on trial immediately
after Fariola, pleaded 'not guilty' and was rewarded with a sentence of fifteen
years' penal servitude for his part in the conspiracy.[112] After Fariola's release,
his engagement with revolutionary republicanism appears to have ceased.
His experiences with the Fenians probably provided enough politics, economic hardship and in-fighting for a lifetime. He stayed in Australia for about
twenty-six years, working as a planter and later as an engineer. By 1894 he
was living in Siam and, just before his death, in Sicily. As a former officer and
wounded American Civil War veteran (he had received a bayonet wound in
his foot) he was eligible for an invalidity pension, and he was finally buried at
Arlington Military Cemetery, Virginia, in 1914.[113]

Soon after Fariola's arrest, Clarke's help on Fenian matters was requested by
the Irish police:

> SI [Sub Inspector] Rodolphus Harvey proceeds this evening to London for the
> purposes of procuring evidence respecting the case of William Harbuison [sic]
> and others charged with complicity in the Fenian conspiracy and to request
> that you will formally authorize Sergeant George Clarke of the Detective
> Department of the London Police, who on a former occasion assisted SI
> Hamilton in his enquiry respecting this case, to give his assistance to SI Harvey
> in endeavouring to obtain such further evidence as may be possible with refer-
> ence to it.[114]

Harbison was one of four Fenian representatives of the four provinces of
Ireland, who had been sent to London to confer with the Fenian leader,
Thomas Kelly, at a meeting that had taken place earlier in the year, probably on 10 February in Kelly's lodgings. The meeting had constituted its
participants as a Provisional Government for Ireland, and Harbison had been
arrested after the failed rising. The request for help indicates that Clarke had
also co-operated with Irish police on previous occasions. The date of the
Fenian meeting that involved Harbison is also close to the time when Clarke

had been making enquiries at residences in London where the Fenian leaders had rented rooms. As it turned out, whatever help Clarke gave to the Irish police, the investigations of Harbison were probably wasted; he never came to trial as he died beforehand in a Belfast prison cell on 9 September from an aortic aneurysm. However, there was some public suspicion that Harbison had been murdered in prison, and his funeral procession was reported as one of the largest demonstrations that had ever taken place in Belfast.[115]

It seems that this case was only the tip of the iceberg in the co-operation between Scotland Yard and the Irish police. Something of the scale of assistance given at this time (but sadly, nothing of the detail), can be measured by the Irish Government's payment of £1,060 16s 3d (equivalent to c. £48,000 today) in September 1867 'for expenses incurred by the Metropolitan Detective Police in connection with the Fenian Conspiracy'.[116] In the same month, the government's hopes for further Fenian arrests and convictions were raised and then dashed again over a few days. Following increased Fenian activity in Manchester, police vigilance was heightened there in early September. In the early hours of the morning of 11 September, a policeman patrolling near the Smithfield Market area of the city centre spotted four suspicious characters of whom two were arrested. One of these proved to be the Fenian leader Colonel Thomas Kelly; his companion was identified as another Fenian, Captain Timothy Deasy. Williamson was sent up to Manchester to keep an eye on proceedings, and was probably accompanied by Clarke. When Kelly and Deasy were brought before magistrates on 18 September, Williamson confirmed the men's identities and they were remanded in custody. As Kelly and Deasy travelled back to prison, the 'Black Maria' in which they were travelling was ambushed by about three-dozen Fenians, several armed with revolvers, in a rescue attempt planned by, amongst others, Ricard Burke. In the process of freeing Kelly and Deasy, the officer in charge of the van, Sergeant Charles Brett, was shot and killed. Several of the rescuers were arrested immediately, at or near the scene, but Kelly and Deasy successfully disappeared.[117] Their escape was promptly followed the next day by the issue of a reward notice and description of the two men. The section relevant to Kelly was as follows:

THREE HUNDRED POUNDS REWARD – Whereas two prisoners, who were charged at Manchester with being concerned in the Fenian conspiracy, were this day violently rescued from custody by an armed mob and escaped. Description of the prisoners:- Colonel Thomas J. Kelly, age 36, height 5 feet 6 inches, hair (cropped close), whiskers and beard brown, eyes hazel, flat nose, large nostrils, stout build, one tooth deficient next to double one on right top side, scar over right temple, small scar inside of right arm, large scar on inside of belly from an ulcerated wound; dress, brown mixture suit, coat (with pockets at sides), deerstalker hat …[118]

The telegraph wires must have been red hot between Manchester and Scotland Yard, as the cost of telegraphic messages flying backwards and forwards in the first few days after the rescue amounted to £123 17s.[119] With no immediate sightings of the two men, the rescue prompted widespread criticism that was not only directed at the Manchester Police. The Irish authorities, encouraged by Robert Anderson, had apparently sent a telegram to the Home Office, before the rescue, warning that an attempt might be made to free Kelly and Deasy, but the telegram was not addressed appropriately and was only received by the relevant Home Office official after Kelly and Deasy had been rescued. Scotland Yard's Detective Department also did not escape the flak as the Home Office felt that the men on the spot, including Williamson, should have reinforced the guard on the prison van on their own initiative.[120]

As the hunt for Kelly and Deasy continued, the police came in for criticism from civil servants, politicians and even from their 'own kind'; some detectives from G Division, Dublin, sent across to Manchester to help in the search reported back:

> ... English policeman, are not cheap at any price. I never met such thirsty fellows in my life ... They know as little how to discharge duty in connection with Fenianism as I do about translating Hebrew or marshalling troops to fight a battle, but of course a Dublin officer is only an officer from Dublin, and London leads the day ...[121]

Setting aside a natural rivalry between forces, this was still a damning indictment, which in fuller detail reached the desks of both the Irish chief secretary (Lord Mayo) and the Home Secretary (Gathorne Hardy who had replaced Spencer Walpole), and only reinforced their concerns about the capacity of the English police to deal with Fenian issues. Queen Victoria was also not amused and wrote to the Home Secretary: 'the government *ought* to take *some* very stringent measures ... to increase the police forces or to make the detectives more efficient.'[122]

While the search for Kelly and Deasy was intensive, numerous arrests were also made of men who were suspected of having participated in their rescue and in the murder of Sergeant Brett. By the end of October the Crown had selected five men (from almost thirty arrested) for immediate trial, against whom the evidence was felt to be particularly strong. The men were William Allen, Michael Larkin, Michael O'Brien, Edmund Condon and Thomas Maguire. All five were found guilty of murder by the jury and were sentenced to death. In an unprecedented development, reporters who had heard the evidence in court petitioned on behalf of Maguire's innocence. After a Home Office review of the case, Maguire received an unconditional pardon, and the death sentence received by Condon (an Irish-American who, with Ricard Burke, had been instrumental in the planning of the rescue of Kelly) was commuted. However, despite an Irish deputation storming into the Home Office in support of a reprieve for the three remaining men, none was granted. Allen, Larkin and O'Brien were executed in public at the New Bailey Prison, Salford, on 24 November at the hands of William Calcraft who, fearing Fenian reprisal, was nervous and bungled the execution; effectively, the men were strangled to death.[123] The three executed men have gone down in history as 'The Manchester Martyrs'. Kelly and Deasy were never re-arrested; intelligence from the British Consul in New York in August 1869 indicated that Kelly 'is now employed by the Post Office here, being in charge of Station F, a branch receiving office', and had been employed there for at least three months.[124] This rapid transition from leader of a large revolutionary republican group to working in a post office surely reinforces the maxim that reality is stranger than fiction! Nonetheless, Kelly did continue his links with Fenianism through the Irish republican movement in America.

Between the rescue in September and the end of November, concern in England and Ireland about the Fenian menace was inevitably heightened, and something approaching panic seems to have set in. There was increased suspicion that an alliance had been developed between English radicals and the Fenians, and warnings from the superintendent of the Dublin Metropolitan Police speculated that the Fenians 'are buying up arms in Birmingham and sending them to many parts of England, and it is spoken of by several that another Fenian rising is imminent'.[125] Arrangements were made in October to make additional arms available to the police by supplying a total of 174 Adams' revolver pistols across the twenty-nine principal police stations in the London Metropolitan area.[126] The safety of Queen Victoria came into question when the Mayor of Manchester sent a telegram to the Home Office on 14 October to alert them 'of the intention of Fenians to go to Scotland and seize the person of the Queen'. Somewhat to the queen's irritation, she was surrounded for several days at Balmoral by an increased police presence under the control of the long-serving Superintendent Walker (the same but somewhat older 'Inspector Stalker' who had been featured by Dickens in 1850). As Walker regularly telegraphed over the next few days, it was 'All quiet on Deeside; no strangers about'.[127]

Across England, 'Fenians' were being seen under virtually every stone. In Reading an enthusiastic local police force arrested James Queen, a hawker, and his stepson Peter Griffin on 10 November, following claims that Queen offered to administer the Fenian oath in a public house. 'There have been two detective officers in the town since Monday last [11 November], by order from the Home Office, and they have been engaged in making inquiries into the case. Nothing has been elicited to show that Queen is a Fenian or in any way identified with the movement.'[128] Clarke was undoubtedly one of the two detectives mentioned; Griffin was freed on 11 November and Queen on 13 November, with a warning.[129] However, if you turn over enough stones something significant will be found, and on 20 November Inspector Thomson, accompanied by an informer, arrested Ricard Burke and a companion, Joseph Casey, in Woburn Square, Bloomsbury, with the assistance of a local policeman, P.C. Fordham.[130] Both policemen were quickly rewarded for their 'gallant conduct'.[131]

The already eventful year of 1867 had still not ended and there were further developments to come, including an increase in the number of detectives based at Scotland Yard. Perhaps in response to Queen Victoria's earlier interjection about the detective force, Sir James Fergusson (Undersecretary of State at the Home Office) wrote to Mayne on 9 November to inform him that the Home Secretary 'is pleased to authorise the increase of the detective Police Force by the addition of one Inspector and three Sergeants'.[132] A few days earlier, on 1 November, Mayne had written to the Home Secretary, putting forward an unidentified sergeant for an unspecified new appointment: 'he is intelligent, trustworthy, and would I am confident prove himself worthy of the appointment if you think fit to select him.'[133] On 26 November 1867, Clarke (now 49 years old) was promoted to inspector (the only member of the detective team who was promoted at that time).

The principal consequence of the changes to the detective department was an increase in the number of detectives to fourteen; scarcely a radical step forward, but nonetheless a small response to recent criticisms and to the undoubted under-staffing of the detective function in the Metropolitan Police. Of the detective team that existed in 1864, seven were still present in November 1867; these were Chief Inspector Williamson; Inspectors Tanner, James Thomson and the newly promoted Clarke; and Sergeants Palmer, Druscovich and Mulvany. Amongst several new sergeants, the appointment of John Meiklejohn, from V Division (Wandsworth) was to prove particularly significant in the later career of Clarke, Druscovich and Palmer, and for the subsequent reputation of the entire detective department.[134]

With his promotion to inspector, Clarke's pay now rose to £200 per annum and provided him with the financial flexibility to move house. From about this time, he decided to rent a property at 20 Great College Street, Westminster, where he was to live for the rest of his life. It was within easy walking distance of Scotland Yard and had a pub a few doors away.

The Clerkenwell Explosion and Beyond

December 1867 – July 1868

Despite the successful arrest of Burke and the decision to increase the number of detectives, members of the government were still concerned about the perceived lack of efficacy of intelligence gathering and surveillance of the Fenians in England and the complacent and dismissive attitudes of Mayne; issues that Ireland's chief secretary Lord Mayo had first raised in August and September 1866. Prime Minister Lord Derby met privately with Chancellor of the Exchequer Benjamin Disraeli and Lord Mayo on 9 December 1867 'to discuss establishing a "separate and secret organization" to supplement the existing police'.[135] Home Secretary Gathorne Hardy was on holiday at the time and appears, like the Metropolitan Police commissioner, to have become aware of the proposals only after they were a fait accompli. Lieutenant-Colonel William Feilding, of the Coldstream Guards based in Ireland, had been identified as the ideal person to head this 'secret service department'. Feilding had been active in investigations into Fenianism in the army and had cultivated a number of spies and informants in England and Ireland to assist him in that task. After clarification of his role and responsibilities, Feilding arrived in London on the morning of 14 December, the day after a catastrophic event had taken place which 'graphically illustrated the dangers England faced and the incompetence of the London police'.[136]

Following the successful rescue of Kelly and Deasy in Manchester, it was perhaps not unreasonable to anticipate that a similar attempt could be made to free Ricard Burke. After his arrest, Burke and his colleague, Casey, were being held in the Clerkenwell House of Detention. At midday on 11 December the Home Office received a detailed tip-off from Ireland that a rescue was planned: 'The plan is to blow up the exercise walls by means of gunpowder – the hour between 3 and 4 p.m.; and the signal for "all right", a white ball thrown up outside when he is at exercise.'[137]

After its receipt at the Home Office, the information was passed quickly to the Metropolitan Police. From that point there are some significant discrepancies in the historical record with regard to the steps taken by the police.[138] Suffice it to say that whatever precise steps were taken, they were inadequate and misdirected. In what appears to have been farcical incompetence, the police took too literally the phrase 'to blow up' (contained in the warning message), suspecting that it was the intention of the Fenians to blow up the walls (from underground) using mines, whereas it materialised that their plans were instead 'to blow down' the walls using a gunpowder bomb! As a consequence, there was an insufficient police presence outside the prison walls to prevent the forthcoming events. On the afternoon of 12 December, a man was seen by one witness to wheel a gunpowder barrel to the prison wall and light a fuse. A white rubber ball was thrown over the wall and was picked up by a curious warder who pocketed it. Meanwhile, having seen the ball, Burke retreated to a corner of the exercise yard to await the blast, which never came because the fuse fizzled out. The barrel was wheeled away again. The following day, the bomb was set successfully, but arrangements had been made for Burke to exercise at a different time and he was not in the yard. At 3.45–3.50 p.m. on 13 December, the explosion blew down a length of the prison wall and demolished the fronts of many houses and shops in Corporation Row.[139] No prisoners escaped or died but at least six deaths occurred amongst members of the public as a direct consequence of the explosion, and no less than six more died through indirectly associated causes; 120 individuals were wounded. Once again, historical accounts of the event rarely agree on the final details of the damage caused.

Not surprisingly, criticism of the police came thick and fast, with Mayne and the detectives in particular being in the sights of the critics. Disraeli wrote to Lord Derby:

> It is my opinion that nothing effective can be done in any way in these dangers, if we don't get rid of Mayne. I have spoken to Hardy [Home Secretary] who says he 'wishes to God he would resign', but, surely, when even the safety of the State is at stake, there ought to be no false delicacy in such matters ... I think you ought to interfere.[140]

Derby told Disraeli:

> It is really lamentable that the peace of the metropolis, and its immunity from wilful devastation, should depend on a body of Police, who, as Detectives, are manifestly incompetent; and, under a chief who, whatever may be his other merits, has not the energy, nor, apparently, the skill to find out and employ men fitted for peculiar duties.[141]

Writing to the queen, Derby described the Metropolitan Police as 'overworked and dispirited' and 'especially deficient as a detective force'.[142] But, as others have pointed out, the disaster was not so much the result of poor detective work – it was poor everyday policing of the streets.[143] Ultimately, compare the political bluster of Derby and Disraeli with the actions taken by them. Having expressed their trenchant views within their own political circles, Mayne was allowed to continue until he died in post (despite at least one report that he had offered his resignation after the Clerkenwell explosion).[144] In equally contradictory style, those Scotland Yard detectives who had worked on the Fenian conspiracy were rewarded with substantial gratuities for their efforts.[145]

The day after the Clerkenwell explosion, Lieutenant-Colonel Feilding started his new posting at the Home Office as head of the new 'secret service department'. By Christmas, appointments to the 'department' included Captain Whelan, Robert Anderson and the temporary use of Irish Constabulary detectives. Beyond some initial successes in intelligence gathering, the successful recruitment of a long-term informer of American Fenian activity (Thomas Beach aka Henri Le Caron) and the establishment of Robert Anderson within the Home Office as an expert on Fenianism, the department added little value. This was not necessarily the fault of its members, but a combination of changing political imperatives, little or no co-operation with or from Scotland Yard, and (by March 1868) a significant weakening of the Fenian threat. The department was disbanded at the end of March 1868, leaving only Robert Anderson in place as an assistant on Irish Affairs within the Home Office.[146] Ultimately, it was left to the Metropolitan Police to pick up the pieces from Clerkenwell and to trace those responsible for the explosion. This involved not only the small number of detectives, but substantial numbers of police from other divisions. What follows is a brief summary of the investigation, of the arrests made and the subsequent trial; fuller accounts are available elsewhere.[147]

Immediately after the explosion had occurred, three people seen loitering near the Clerkenwell House of Detention were arrested. These were Anne Justice, Jeremiah Allen and Timothy Desmond. Justice had been visiting Casey in prison that day; Desmond came from an Irish community suspected of having strong Fenian connections and Allen claimed to be working for the police. On 20 December at Bow Street Police Court a self-confessed Fenian, James Vaughan, implicated himself and gave evidence which implicated four others – Nicholas English, Patrick Mullany, William Desmond and John O'Keefe – in the planning and execution of the bombing.[148] Describing one of the Bow Street Police Court scenes Percy Fitzgerald recorded that: 'As the authorities were now dealing with desperadoes, the novel spectacle was seen of policemen armed to the teeth with revolvers and cutlasses, for fear of a rescue.'[149]

In January 1868, Patrick Mullany decided to volunteer information to the police to save his own skin. The information he gave was damaging to his co-conspirators, but Mullany also added a new name to the list of suspects; that of a man from Glasgow, calling himself Jackson, but whose real name was Barrett. According to Mullany it was Barrett who had set off the explosion. By coincidence, a man named Willy Jackson had been arrested in a Glasgow street in mid-January following the discharge of a firearm, and was still being held by the Glasgow police, who had regarded him with sufficient suspicion to inform Scotland Yard. Williamson and some other officers from the detective department (probably including Clarke) travelled to Glasgow and returned with Jackson, who was subsequently identified as Michael Barrett. Individuals who had known Barrett before in London commented that he had changed his appearance between December 1867 and January 1868 by shaving off his whiskers, and some witnesses appeared to have difficulty in identifying him as a consequence. This created problems for the police who were seeking witnesses able to place Barrett in London in December, and at the scene of the bombing at Clerkenwell.

From the limited information of Clarke's involvement with the Clerkenwell inquiries, it appears that he helped to assemble identification evidence. He is known to have interviewed at least one witness, Thomas Kensley, who later gave evidence of Barrett's identity at the trial. Clarke also sent Detective Sergeant Sunerway (together with a Fenian informer) to Halstead, on 1 January 1868, to identify a man that the Essex Constabulary had arrested, whose description appeared to fit that of an individual wanted in connection with the bombing; it proved to be a false lead.[150] However, it seems that Clarke's main task at that time continued to be information gathering on Fenians and their plans. In late December 1867, Mayne had forwarded a report by Clarke and Williamson to Dublin Castle on the subject of 'Dr O'Leary'.[151] This was a reference to Dr Edmund O'Leary, the half-brother of Ellen O'Leary and the imprisoned *Irish People* editor John O'Leary. Edmund O'Leary had qualified as a doctor and had a London practice in Fetter Lane. The historical record now suggests that when the Fenians were penniless and on the run (as they had been after the failed rising), Edmund O'Leary acted as a courier of funds to Paris, including funds of his own that were never repaid.[152] The details that Clarke's report contained are unknown but, at the time, the Irish authorities commented that there was no evidence of importance against O'Leary and no warrant for his arrest.[153] In a different activity, correspondence from Mayne early in 1868 indicates that the police were, to some extent, intercepting mail to enhance their Fenian intelligence-gathering operation, and Clarke was involved in that process.[154]

When the time had come for the Old Bailey trial of those arrested for the Clerkenwell explosion, those in the dock on 20 April 1868 were charged with the wilful murder of Sarah Ann Hodgkinson, one of the victims of the explosion. They were Anne Justice, Timothy Desmond, William Desmond, Nicholas English, John O'Keefe and Michael Barrett, all of whom pleaded 'not guilty'.[155] Of those previously remanded, Mullany and Vaughan had turned 'Queen's Evidence' and appeared as witnesses for the prosecution. Clarke was not called to give evidence and had been sent by Mayne to Cheshire on other duties.

The Clerkenwell explosion trial lasted seven days and in view of the nature of the crime, and the subsequent public outrage it had created, was closely watched by politicians and public alike. Montagu Williams, who was counsel for Anne Justice and was known as 'the passionate defender of hopeless causes', has left some first-hand recollections of events during the seven days at the Old Bailey:

> To judge by the appearance of the prisoners, the Fenian movement must have been at a somewhat low ebb at that time. With the exception of Barrett, the accused seemed to be in a state of extreme poverty ... [Barrett was] a square-built fellow, scarcely five feet eight in height, and dressed like a well-to-do farmer ... A less murderous countenance than Barrett's, indeed I do not remember to have seen ... The only time I saw Barrett's face change was during the examination of the informers, and the look of disgust, scorn and hatred that he turned on these two miserable creatures was a thing to be remembered.[156]

Anne Justice was discharged on 23 April, when Lord Chief Justice Cockburn adjudged that the evidence against her was too slight to be sent to the jury and the prosecution case was also abandoned on the following day against O'Keefe, who was likewise discharged. As his female client left the dock, Montagu Williams recalled: 'She turned round to where Barrett was sitting, seized him by the hand, and with two large tears rolling down her cheeks, kissed him very gently on the forehead. Then she hurried away. This was not a very judicious proceeding perhaps – but how like a woman.'[157] On 27 April the jury members retired, taking two and a half hours to reach their verdict – a relatively long time for Victorian juries. On their return, the Desmonds and English were declared 'not guilty', and Barrett 'guilty'. Before sentencing, Barrett requested, and was granted, the opportunity to say a few words:

> I do not intend to occupy much of your Lordship's time, being fully conscious that any words of mine could in no way alter your Lordship's mind in this matter. Still, I cannot allow this opportunity to pass, as it is likely to be the only one I shall have on this side the grave, of endeavouring to place myself as I should like to stand before my fellow men. In doing so I may be compelled to expose the means that have been resorted to for the purpose of securing my conviction. I am not, however, going to adopt a whining tone or to ask for mercy; but yet I address your lordship as a humble individual whose career has been mercilessly assailed, and I wish to defend it, conscious as I am that I have never wilfully, maliciously or intentionally injured a human being that I am aware of ...[158]

Describing Mullany as 'that Prince of perjurers', Barrett saved his strongest words for the police. Referring to evidence given by a young witness, Thomas Wheeler, that it was Barrett who had lit the fuse of the bomb, Barrett stated that the witness had been intimidated by the police and that a 'positive' identification had been made only when: 'a wretch wearing the uniform [of a police officer] brought the boy back and held him by the shoulder until he was compelled to admit that he knew me.'[159] The police who had transported him from Glasgow to London were also targets for his criticism:

> I was hurried off to London where they knew I was alone and in their power. Their nervous haste, indeed has subjected me to the most flagrant injustice. I do not allude to the higher authorities in Glasgow, but I do to the mean, low, petty, truckling creatures who hang about police courts and who would not hesitate to have recourse to the most vile and heinous practices to benefit themselves, or even to gain a smile of approval from their superiors. They will now congratulate themselves on the success of their schemes.[160]

Finally, and anticipating the inevitable death sentence, he said 'I will now seek that other land, where I trust to obtain justice'. Barrett's 'few words' had lasted some thirty minutes and made a profound impression on those present, including Montagu Williams, who later wrote that 'I think I can safely say that there was not a dry eye in the court'.[161] Needless to say, as only one of the six initially accused had been found guilty, the mood of the politicians, the press and the public was also to blame the police, though from a different perspective than Barrett. It was not a good time to be a policeman.

Between sentence and execution, the case against Barrett was reviewed in depth by the principal trial judge, Lord Chief Justice Cockburn. Though the evidence that placed Barrett as lighting the fuse was regarded as less than satisfactory, Cockburn put little store in Barrett's alibi, and the evidence of his active involvement in the conspiracy to liberate Burke was regarded as sufficiently convincing that Cockburn finally reached the decision that the trial verdict was safe, and this view was submitted to the Home Secretary and accepted by him.[162] On 26 May 1868, outside Newgate, the death sentence was implemented and Barrett became the last person to be hung in public in the British Isles: 'Barrett mounted the steps with the most perfect firmness … he bore himself to the last with great fortitude … He died without making any confession of the crime of which he was convicted … Yet there was this peculiarity about him … that he never absolutely denied his guilt.'[163]

That Barrett helped plan Burke's rescue seems certain. However, he was certainly not alone in planning and carrying out the explosion, though he was the only one to be convicted. At the time of the trial, the person believed to have led the implementation of the plan to free Burke (a plan that was conceived by Burke himself) was James Murphy, the Fenian commander in Scotland who had escaped to France.[164] Various authors have suggested that the bomb itself was not set by Barrett but by Jeremiah O'Sullivan, who ran from the scene chased by police but escaped and eventually reached America.[165]

While large numbers of police were employed in tracing the perpetrators of the explosion, others were actively engaged in tasks to help reassure their political masters and the general public, who feared a Fenian campaign of terror. Substantial numbers of special constables were recruited and deployed in London to afford protection to life and property in their respective districts. Clarke is known to have visited Leeds around this time, either to identify Fenians attending pro-Fenian processions in the city or, perhaps, to investigate the Irishmen 'observed loitering in a suspicious manner near the New Gas Company's Works in Dewsbury-road Leeds'.[166] If you had an Irish or American accent, and didn't want to be taken into custody, now was not the time to stand anywhere potentially explosive.

The nervousness about Fenian intentions also led to checks of the sewers (as possible locations for bombs) beneath key buildings in central London. The searches, conducted by police and engineers under the guidance of the London Metropolitan Board of Works on 20 December 1867, revealed 'all correct' but demonstrated, on at least one occasion, the potential hazards for the men involved when their poor underground navigation or over-enthusiasm prompted concerns:

> Police Sergeant Reimers … accompanied by Police Constable Hilder and Corporal Bingham of the Royal Engineers report having carefully explored the sewer leading from the Thames Embankment to the River front of Somerset House, thence entered at Savoy Street and examined all side shores, coming out at Wellington Street, corner of Russell Street and entered again at Essex Street, passing under Wych Street and Drury Lane, coming out at Russell Street by Drury Lane Theatre. The party caused considerable anxiety to Mr. Lovick, of the Office of Works at Cannon Row, where we were equipped, as they received instructions only to explore the vicinity of Somerset House, and no directions were given that they were to proceed to Wych Street or Drury Lane. They were absent from 6.30 p.m. until 10.40 p.m.[167]

The superintendent's report of events above is dated and timed '20th December 1867 12 Midnight', enabling one to visualise a less-than-happy senior officer waiting in Scotland Yard to receive a late report from a less-than-sweet-smelling Reimers! However, the events do not seem to have had any adverse impact on his career, as Sergeant John William Reimers (born in Germany and by then a policeman for eight years) became a detective colleague of Clarke some eighteen months later.[168]

Once the Clerkenwell trial had finished, political and public concerns about the Fenians slowly started to quieten. Ricard Burke, Joseph Casey and a third man Henry Shaw (aka Mullady) were tried for treason-felony at the Old Bailey at the end of April. The case against Casey was withdrawn by the prosecution but both Burke and Shaw were found guilty; Burke was sentenced to fifteen years' penal servitude and Shaw to seven years. Amongst the witnesses for the prosecution were three Fenian informers, John Joseph Corydon, Godfrey Massey and John Devany, all of whom were soon to be 'paid-off' by the authorities for services rendered.[169]

Shortly before the Clerkenwell trial and Burke's trial, arrangements had been made for a royal visit to Ireland in mid-April by the Prince and Princess of Wales, to help ease tensions. The visit included an investiture in St Patrick's (Roman Catholic) cathedral, a Great Ball and (for the prince) an inescapable opportunity to attend the Punchestown Races on 16 April. The visit was regarded as a considerable success.[170] Williamson and four other (unnamed) detectives from Scotland Yard were sent out to Ireland for the races, apparently 'in case any of the swell mob from this side of the channel should seek a new field of operation', though it would be surprising if their remit was entirely restricted to this function.[171] In view of his extensive experience of policing English racecourses, and his working relationship with the Irish police, it is almost certain that Clarke would have been one of those detectives attending. If so, he would have been keen to return home in time to attend the wedding of his eldest son, George, to Louisa Beake at St Margaret's, Westminster, on Saturday 25 April. Louisa was the daughter of a former policeman employed by the Great Western Railway, and would prove to be a useful ally for Clarke towards the end of his career.

When the Prince of Wales was in Ireland he would probably not have known that his brother Alfred, the Duke of Edinburgh, had been shot and wounded in Australia on 12 March 1868. As commander of the Royal Navy frigate HMS *Galatea*, Alfred had started a round-the-world voyage in 1867. He was shot in the back at a beachfront suburb in Sydney while picnicking, a wound from which he recovered and later resumed command of his ship. The assailant was Dublin-born Henry James Farrell who was arrested at the scene and, despite probable insanity, was tried, found guilty and hanged on 21 April.[172] The Irish connection initially suggested that this was a Fenian plot and that there may have been accomplices. Thus, on 9 May, Clarke was sent to Liverpool to organise observation of the passengers arriving from Australia on the SS *Great Britain* to establish whether any Fenians might have been on board. Clarke reported to Mayne that there was no reason to suppose that any accomplice of Farrell was amongst the passengers. Clarke's task cannot have been an easy one as the ship could carry substantial numbers of passengers: in 1861, when carrying the first English cricket team to Australia, there were 544 passengers and 143 crew.[173]

By May 1867 the Fenian conspiracy had essentially ebbed away; senior Fenians were either in prison, had fled into exile in France or America or had simply had enough. For Clarke, however, his involvement with the Fenians continued a bit longer. On 11 July 1868 he emerged from his more recent 'behind-the-scenes' role to arrest two suspected Fenians at the tavern and eating house, His Lordships Larder in Cheapside, accompanied by Sergeants Sunerway and Meiklejohn. The two men arrested were James Williamson (aka Cooke) and John Blake, who were charged at Bow Street with treason-felony. After their arrest Clarke searched the residences of the two men, locating a loaded revolver at both properties, about a quarter hundredweight of ammunition at James Williamson's address and some Fenian documents hidden behind the fireplace. However, the main evidence against these men came from informers. Corydon identified James Williamson as Centre of the largest Fenian circle in London, who he had seen in the company of leading Fenians, including Kelly, Halpin, O'Donovan Rossa and thirty to forty others. Patrick Mullany also thought that Blake had been a Centre, but compromised this statement somewhat when saying that he 'believed that Blake wished to be a Fenian, but he had not got the necessary pluck'. Despite further evidence presented by the chief constable of the Irish Constabulary, the magistrate hearing the case, Mr Vaughan, freed Blake and gave the prosecution two days to obtain evidence of any specific act linking James Williamson to the conspiracy. This was not forthcoming and James Williamson was also released.[174] This failed prosecution essentially concluded Clarke's involvement with the Fenians during the 1865–68 conspiracy. Nevertheless, it was not the last time that he would have to deal with the impacts of Irish republicanism. He was drawn into two further major incidents in 1870, which would have a more successful outcome for the authorities, and continued to be called on from time to time until he retired, particularly when co-operation between the Irish police and London Metropolitan Police was required.

Undoubtedly, the challenges faced by the police at this time were essentially new to them, and it showed. As Phillip Smith concluded:

> … the Fenians challenged the police in a variety of ways, brought out deficiencies in the force and its leadership, and revealed their inexperience and lack of knowledge in dealing with urban terrorism … The police were not without some highly capable and intelligent men … Unfortunately, Commissioner Mayne did not take advice readily, and thus did not draw enough on the expertise his men gained in the streets … Criticism of the police properly fell on the head of the remote and aged Commissioner.[175]

During this period the detective department had to take on board nationwide information-gathering and surveillance operations of a nature and on a scale that they had never encountered before. They had to try to liaise effectively with police in Ireland and at the same time they had to sustain a detective capacity to deal with more routine criminal cases, both in London, and when called upon, in the provinces. It should not be forgotten that there were only ten detectives at Scotland Yard (until late November 1867) and each of them probably liked to see their families on occasion. Criticism of Mayne is appropriate, but it should not be forgotten that the Metropolitan Police was accountable to the government through the Home Office, and Mayne was poorly served by his political masters. If the government wanted a different approach from the police, politicians should have done more to deliver it. During the earlier part of his career as a commissioner, Mayne had delivered outstanding public service but had undoubtedly been allowed to stay in post too long. On at least one occasion (and probably more), by offering his resignation, Mayne had provided his political masters with an opportunity to bring in a new man at the top. That opportunity was not taken. Mayne was probably a difficult person to deal with, and also held firm viewpoints on issues. However, instead of 'grabbing the bull by the horns', the politicians criticised Mayne behind his back and established a separate 'secret service department'. Even then, the politicians failed to show any long-term commitment, dismantling the new department soon after its formation; though that, at least, was consistent with the prevailing attitude of the time, to renounce domestic intelligence-gathering as a political strategy.[176]

In May 1868, a Home Office Departmental Committee Report on the Metropolitan Police was issued, which included the following comments and recommendations:

> The detective police, having regard to their number, appear to the Committee to be very efficient for the detection of ordinary crime, but their numbers are wholly inadequate to the present requirements of the metropolis, and their constitution scarcely adapts them to cope with conspiracies and secret combinations ... the detective police should form a separate division under the immediate command of the head of police.[177]

The committee also commented on pay and expenses: 'The pay of the detective police is insufficient to attract very skilful men ...'[178] It took a year before any of these comments were acted on, by which time Mayne had worked himself into the grave. Fortunately for the government, the Fenian conspiracy ran out of steam, compromised by the posturing, arrogance and procrastination of its first leader, Stephens, and the recklessness of the second, Kelly; undermined by informers; combated effectively in the field by the military; and haunted by a determined, if not always effective, police presence.

From the incomplete jigsaw of Clarke's role in the Fenian conspiracy, it seems that his main responsibilities between 1865 and 1868 were to assemble information on the identities and descriptions of the principal Fenians and the locations in which they might be found; to undertake surveillance of Fenians and their associates in London and work with provincial police forces in this regard (including Manchester and Liverpool); and to liaise with the Irish police on Fenian matters. It is probable that this period of Clarke's career, more than any other, was responsible for the refinement of the skills that Superintendent Williamson later attributed to him: 'Clarke is a man of about as much shrewd common sense as any man in London, and is quite as able to track out anybody. It is his native gift.'[179]

The last three years had thrown up considerable new challenges for Clarke. His performance, and that of the Metropolitan Police, had not been free of errors. Yet in the view of his superiors he had shown sufficient ability as a detective to be promoted to inspector, and to take on greater responsibilities. Now, with the Fenian conspiracy on the back burner, he also had an opportunity to return to the basics of crime detection.

4

BACK TO BASICS

1868-71

In England's felon garb we're clad
And by her vengeance bound
Her concentrated hate we've had –
Her justice, never found
Her laws, accurs'd, have done their worst, -
In vain they still assail
To crush the hearts that beat for thee,
Our own loved Innisfail

Michael Davitt[1]

Suspicious Death at Lymm

After the political focus of much of George Clarke's work between 1865 and early 1868, the opportunity to return to crime detection must have provided a refreshing change or, at least, rather more variety. Although the Fenian cause lingered on and still expressed itself in poetry and the acquisition of arms, the focus of Clarke's cases in the next three years switched back to the criminal and social ills of the nation, including suspicious death and murder, burglary, bribery, betting, baby farming, abortion and arson. Life had already started to get back to 'normal' in April 1868 when, shortly before the Clerkenwell explosion trial was due to begin, Clarke headed northwards to Lymm, Cheshire, at the request of the commissioner to investigate his first suspicious death since being appointed inspector. He was asked, belatedly, to investigate the suspicious death of a rich widow, Mrs Elizabeth Brigham, whose son-in-law, Monsieur Henri Perreau, alleged had been accidentally shot. Perreau was the only witness to the events leading up to her death, and claimed that he had been showing his mother-in-law his new revolver at home one morning when it had accidentally discharged. He had handed the loaded gun to her at her request and, upon her returning it into his hand, it had gone off at such an angle that she had been shot in the head.

One immediate question is why Clarke was called in to investigate Mrs Brigham's death at all, as a verdict of accidental death had already been recorded by an inquest jury several days prior to his arrival. The clue probably lies within his recorded comments that 'there are various rumours afloat' and that two of Mrs Brigham's cousins had instructed a solicitor 'to act on their behalf'. It is probable that one of these individuals had contacted Scotland Yard, unhappy with the inquest verdict. The press also alluded to these issues: 'Rumour's busy tongue has thrown considerable doubt upon the purely accidental nature of the occurrence, and has attributed the death to interested motives; but the decision of the jury, after a patient and minute investigation, that it was a case of accidental death, will, of course, dispense these doubts.'[2] The cousins may have been concerned that the recently married Perreau might gain control of Mrs Brigham's estate (an impressive £40,000). Clarke's report suggests that he regarded this as a legitimate concern, Mrs Brigham 'being the only existing obstacle to Monsieur Perreau having absolute control over the property'. However, the report of the inquest proceedings suggest that the coroner thought otherwise, and that Perreau could not benefit under the existing will. The grounds for the coroner taking this view were that Mrs Brigham's estate was held in a trust, and her only daughter's inheritance would therefore not automatically become the property of her husband.[3]

Clarke's summary of the main points from the inquest were consistent with the contemporary newspaper reports of events, but greater details were available in these news reports and some are worth amplifying. In support of Perreau's evidence that Mrs Brigham's death had been accidental: 'Dr. Wright concurred in the opinion given by Dr. Bennett, and said that had the pistol gone off at the moment Mrs Brigham turned her head in the way described by Monsieur Perreau, it would have taken the direction described.'[4] However, in contradiction to this evidence, 'Mr Higham, gunsmith, Warrington, said he had had forty years experience as gunsmith, and did not think Mrs Brigham could fire the pistol in the way Monsieur Perreau described'. In his view the pistol at half-cock could not have gone off as it was in perfect order.[5] He would not swear, however, that it could not have happened as Perreau had told it. Finally, an assessment of Perreau's evidence provided by the coroner to the jury stated: 'It was not for him [the coroner] to say what the impression his [Perreau's] evidence might have made upon their minds, but his own impression was that he had given his evidence most truthfully … unless there was something in their minds to impress them to the contrary, they ought to receive his statement as an earnest of the truth, and not lightly reject his evidence.'[6] Taking these various comments into account, the jury had returned their verdict of 'accidental death', adding that they wished 'to record their strong conviction that Monsieur Perreau had exhibited great carelessness in the use of such a deadly weapon as had been produced before them that day'.[7]

Clarke, having made his own investigations as requested (though apparently without speaking directly to Perreau), had also decided that there were insufficient grounds to contest the inquest verdict. He returned to London midway through the Clerkenwell explosion trial to report back to Commissioner Mayne, who was still under siege from the criticisms of the press, the public and his political masters for the police-handling of the Fenian conspiracy. The absence of other police reports of the case in 1868 suggest that Mayne accepted Clarke's report and that no further action was taken. Clarke and Perreau would meet under different circumstances in 1876, however, and there would be a different outcome.

Change at the Top – A New Commissioner

On 26 December 1868 Sir Richard Mayne died while still in post as commissioner. Queen Victoria chose her words carefully when expressing: 'how grieved and concerned she is to hear of Sir R. Mayne's death. Not withstanding the attacks lately made upon him, Her Majesty believes him to have been a most efficient head of the Police, and to have discharged the duties of his important situation most ably and satisfactorily in very difficult times.'[8] John Meiklejohn, a detective sergeant at Scotland Yard at the time of Mayne's death, commented in 1890:

> The late Sir Richard Mayne was in every sense of the word a thorough and practical policeman. Under his mild and firmly effective way any lawbreaker from the horrible murderer to the contemptible pickpocket, had not a tithe of his present immunity, while neither the police nor the general public were subjected to the constant irritation inflicted upon them in the present day.[9]

Two days after Mayne died, Assistant Commissioner Labalmondière was appointed acting commissioner, during a short interregnum. For the Metropolitan Police, and particularly for those, like Clarke, who had worked closely with Sir Richard Mayne, it must have been a time of much speculation and uncertainty. On 13 February 1869 it was announced that Colonel Edmund Henderson would be the new commissioner, an unexpected appointment as far as the police were concerned. As Timothy Cavanagh, a serving police officer at the time, was later to record in his biography: 'How it happened that Colonel Labalmondière did not succeed Sir Richard in the commissionership I never heard. I only know that the whole of the Police were disappointed by his non-appointment.'[10]

Henderson had served in the Royal Engineers, rising to the rank of lieutenant-colonel. In 1850 he had become comptroller of the new convict settlement in Western Australia and, in 1863, was appointed to the Home Office as chairman of directors and surveyor general of prisons. Regardless of the views expressed by Cavanagh, it was undoubtedly appropriate for a new broom to be brought in; Henderson soon started sweeping. By the end of March he had made a start to help improve police morale by easing some of the pettier restrictions, including permitting his uniformed policemen to wear beards and moustaches and, somewhat later, to wear plain clothes when off duty.[11] By July 1869 he had also gained Home Office approval for the provision of recreation rooms at police stations, allowing smoking, games such as draughts and backgammon, and other recreational equipment including miniature billiard tables and boxing gloves.[12] Equally timely and promptly delivered were changes to the detective department.[13] Numbers of staff were increased from fifteen to twenty-seven, composed of a superintendent as head of the department, three chief inspectors, three inspectors and twenty sergeants. Williamson was promoted to superintendent, and Clarke to chief inspector, with his pay increasing to £250 per annum plus a £10 per annum allowance for plain clothes.[14] A few days later, and in a radical move, a divisional detective system was established in which a detective sergeant and a number of detective constables were permanently stationed in each division; a total of 20 sergeants and 160 constables.[15] Control of these detectives resided with the divisional superintendents rather than with the detective department at Scotland Yard, which remained a bone of contention over the coming years. Nonetheless, over a matter of days the number of detectives in the Metropolitan Police force had, on paper, increased from 15 to 207.

In the next days and months many personnel changes occurred in the department that must have taken some time to settle down. Inspector Richard Tanner finally retired on 3 July 1869 on the grounds of 'bodily infirmity' despite being only 38 years old.[16] He moved to Winchester to become landlord of the White Swan hotel, but died in 1873 from a stroke and heart disease. Chief Inspector James Thomson decided to further his career by returning to uniform and was promoted to superintendent of E Division (Holborn) on 6 July 1869.[17] These two changes created the situation where Clarke was now, on grounds of seniority, second only to Williamson within the department, and from this time onwards whenever Williamson was away Clarke became the acting senior officer. Nathaniel Druscovich and William Palmer were both promoted to the rank of inspector, followed in October 1870 by their further promotion to chief inspector. From which time, with Clarke, they filled these three senior posts until 1877.[18] Over the coming months John Mulvany and John Shore became inspectors. The other vacant detective posts at Scotland Yard were filled from recommendations made by divisional superintendents and, to a lesser extent, from external appointments. In the process the department added to its staff a greater linguistic ability (including John Reimers, the German-born sergeant who had lost his way in the London sewers in December 1867), to help deal with an influx of foreign criminals.[19] In the meantime, Clarke had already become acquainted with some of the challenges posed by foreign criminals.

Burglary and the Stratford Murder

Towards the end of 1868, the principal emphasis of Clarke's work switched to an outbreak of burglaries in some well-to-do areas on the fringes of London. One of the first of these, on 1 September, was at Copped Hall, a mansion in the Totteridge area near Barnet and previously the birthplace of Cardinal Henry Manning, the Roman Catholic Archbishop of Westminster.[20] Other burglaries took place in the Windsor area where various substantial properties had been targeted, including the residences of Equerry to the Queen Lord Bridport, and Sir Edward Sullivan, an Irish lawyer, MP and solicitor general for Ireland.[21] A common feature linked each of the robberies:

> When the robbery was discovered in the morning it seemed that the entry had been effected through the drawing-room window. A chisel appeared to have been thrust in the window, and a piece of wire inserted with a bent end, which caught the spring catch of the window , and thus the window catch being drawn back the window was opened. The shutter was opened by means of a hole being made by a chisel and the bolt of the shutter lifted-up. It was said by Inspector Clarke that this particular mode of entry is a novel introduction and was introduced from the Continent.[22]

Given the spate of burglaries at properties owned by wealthy and influential individuals, the investigation took a high priority within the detective department and Inspector Clarke, Detective Sergeants Druscovich and Meiklejohn were put on the case. Clarke and Druscovich soon arrested several foreigners suspected of the burglary at Copped Hall, who they brought before the magistrate at Barnet petty sessions on 5 October 1868. Evidence was presented

that holes cut in the drawing room and internal doors were exactly fitted by
the gimlet and chisel found on one of the prisoners, Joseph Bleiler. Another,
Auguste Blanche, was found in possession of an umbrella stolen from Copped
Hall. Clarke had also located a female acquaintance of the two men who
had pawned several items stolen in the Copped Hall and Windsor burgla-
ries.[23] On 17 October, acting on information received during their enquiries,
Druscovich arrested another Frenchman, Charles Maurien, at the Mogul
Music Hall, Drury Lane. Maurien was found to be carrying a gimlet and
wire and £60 in banknotes, taken from a robbery at a banker's residence in
Leatherhead, and had also been seen by witnesses loitering in Windsor Great
Park on the day when one of the Windsor properties was burgled. Bleiler and
Blanche were found guilty at the Hertford assizes of the burglary at Copped
Hall and were each sentenced to seven years' penal servitude. Maurien was
found guilty of the burglary at Windsor and received the same sentence at the
Reading assizes.[24] In addition to commendations and £5 rewards that Clarke
and Druscovich received from the judge at Hertford, they were also com-
mended and awarded £2 10s by Mr Justice Keating at Reading.[25]

Meiklejohn's memories present a rather different perspective and, if accurate, are revealing of certain tensions and jealousies in the detective department
at that time:

> A sergeant from the Yard was detailed to look into the matter. He spent much
> time examining the scenes of the various robberies and making local inquiries,
> which brought him no nearer his end, and all the while the burglars were coolly
> pursuing their avocation, now in one place, now in another … After some time
> I was ordered to his assistance … I set about looking for my men in London
> … I learned of the existence of a gang of French thieves in Soho, who, upon
> further inquiry, involving the expenditure of a good deal of loose cash upon
> informants, proved to be the very men I sought … With some little trouble I
> succeeded not only in arresting the lot, but in recovering a considerable amount
> of the proceeds of their robberies. Unfortunately, I knew no French, so officers
> who spoke that language fluently, had then to be brought into the case. Next
> morning on my appearance at the office I was informed that there was no
> necessity for my going to Barnet to testify against the men I had arrested, as two
> others had gone down. To complete the farce these two officers were highly
> commended for their clever capture of the thieves and awarded a gratuity of
> £5 each and I was left to whistle even for my out-of-pocket expenses … It was
> always thus.[26]

Although Meiklejohn's comments demonstrate an awareness of some of the
details of the case, and therefore have a ring of truth to them, his recollections
of his time as a detective also include some dubious claims which appear

to have no substance to them (e.g. that it was he who arrested the Fenian arms organiser Ricard Burke on 20 November 1867), and should therefore be interpreted with some caution.[27]

Being foreign wasn't a prerequisite for Victorian burglars, but for Clarke it must have appeared to be. On the night of 25 October 1869 he was called out to 9 Baker Street, Portman Square, concerning a burglary at the premises of Benjamin Lee, a jeweller and hair-worker, where property to a value of £500–600 had been stolen by burglars who had entered through a fanlight. Working together with Inspector Hinds of D Division (Marylebone), Clarke received information that encouraged them to place under surveillance individuals at 11 Gerrard Street, Soho. They then raided this address on 28 October and found, in rooms occupied by Frenchman Hippolyte Longuet: '82 duplicates [pawn-shop receipts], seven bracelets, 31 eardrops, nine hair rings, 19 brooches, nine necklets, two crosses, a key, 21 odd pieces of hair guards, silver coins, 10 pair ear-rings, one ear-ring, 16 watch-guards, seals, fish-slice, rings on keys, jewel cases, indecent photographs and other articles.'[28] Several of these were recognised as items taken from the jeweller's premises. Longuet stated that three other men had asked him to pawn the items for them on the morning after the robbery. Two of the men were known to the jeweller, as he had employed them to paint his premises during the previous summer. All three men were arrested within the next few days, with one being found in possession of a bag containing many items of jewellery, plus the tools of a burglar's trade: '23 skeleton keys, two centre-bits and stock, a keyhole saw, a gimlet, eight common keys and a file.'[29] At the Old Bailey the three burglars were found guilty and sentenced to five or seven years' penal servitude, depending on their previous record.[30] Longuet was found not guilty of burglary, but Clarke pursued charges against him of 'unlawful possession'. At a subsequent Old Bailey trial, Longuet was found guilty on that charge and sentenced to eighteen months' hard labour.[31] So within less than a month of the break-in, the burglars had been traced, tried, convicted and sent to prison; administering justice to the 'fence' had taken only two to three weeks longer.

The third major burglary case that Clarke worked on occurred in February 1871 in a middle-class neighbourhood in Stratford. The attempted burglary involved a style of entry that was favoured by the native English criminal, in which the burglar sought to gain entry to a property through a first-floor window, by climbing up the portico above the front door. Clarke's report describes the events:

13th February 1871
With reference to the attempted larceny at the residence of Mr Galloway, No. 2 Oxford Villas, Romford Road (K Division) and the attempt made on this gentleman's life by the thieves.

I beg to report that in conjunction with Sergeant Gibbs of this Department and Inspector Mason, and P.S. Briden (Detective) K Division, I have made enquiry and ascertained the subjoined particulars. The persons committing this outrage must have been in the neighbourhood for at least an hour and a half during which time they made two separate attempts to enter houses *viz.* at Mr Pedlar's, Romford Road, and Mr Paize's, 10 Vicarage Terrace, both houses being within a distance of three hundred yards from Mr Galloway's.

Martha Barker, servant to Mr Pedlar states that at 7.15 p.m. 9th Inst. she heard the gate bell ring and upon going to the front door saw a man who had one leg over the iron fence, and two other men were standing on the footway. She called out to the man saying 'You have no business there, go away'. At this time a constable came up and in his presence repeated that the men had no business there; she then shut the door. Shortly after, the bell again rang and upon answering it she saw [another] policeman who enquired if she knew the men, and she replied no. Upon examining these premises I find that the wire in connection with the bell runs along the iron fence and the man catching his foot in it caused the bell to ring, and was, when seen by Barker in the act of making off. I have seen the Constable spoken of, Edward Blackett 542K who states that on passing he saw three men standing on the footway. He said 'what are you doing here taking up the whole of the footway'. They replied they were only having a lark, upon which he told them to go away. This they did turning down Vicarage Lane. The P.C. denies seeing either Mr Pedlar's servant, or any other person on the force. I have however no doubt that this is untrue the statements being made to screen himself from having neglected his duty in not either satisfying himself who these men were or keeping some observation on them. He is further unable to give any description of the men and I place but little reliance upon what he says.

About 8.15 p.m. a man was seen by Miss Elizabeth Green of No. 4 Stratford Green to slide down the pillar of the portico in front of the residence of Mr Paize; two other men were also standing on the pavement; she thought the circumstance a very suspicious one and called the attention of a gentleman to it who happened to be passing. She gives a description of them and could identify them.

About 8.40 p.m. Miss Howlett niece of Mr Galloway saw a man on the front door step, and acquainted her uncle with the circumstance. He at once went to see what was the matter followed by his wife. Mrs Galloway states her husband ran out of the house and overtook a man about twenty yards distant whom he seized and accused of attempting to rob his house. Upon this two men crossed from the opposite side of the road, one of whom, struck the husband in the face. He fell and upon Mrs Galloway screaming out, a policeman came up and assisted Mr Galloway in-doors. She informed the P.C. her husband had been attacked by three men who ran down the road in the direction of Romford.

The P.C. endeavoured to find some trace of them but being unable to do so, went to West Ham police station and acquainted Inspector Mason with the particulars. Constables were at once despatched to the several Railway Stations and other places in the neighbourhood with a view of intercepting the persons guilty of the outrage but without success. P.C. Young 53K, who went to Mrs Galloways assistance states that he found Mr Galloway lying on the foot path, but the men had escaped and, after assisting to remove the gentleman into the house, went to West Ham Station and reported the circumstance to Inspector Mason by whose direction he then returned to Forest Gate Railway Station where upon his arrival at 9.56 p.m. he found the train had just left. Upon enquiry of the porter Henry Pickett he was informed that two men who seemed excited and appeared to have been in a scuffle had entered the station at the last minute and left by the train referred to. They both took third class tickets to Shoreditch. In consequence of there being no telegraph at the station no communications could be sent.

From the description given by the porter I have no doubt these were two of the men engaged in the three successive attempts at robbery on the night in question.

In addition to the persons whose names have been given as having seen these men, they were observed to run away from the neighbourhood of Mr Galloways house (after he had been stabbed) by William Nott, 7 William Cottages and Thomas Whitmarsh, 7 Back Barracks, Stratford, both of whom would be able to identify them. I beg to add that every exertion is being used to effect their apprehension. Mr Galloway was alive at a late hour yesterday, but was still unconscious and Mr Kennet his medical attendant informs me there is no hope that his life can be spared.[32]

Samuel Galloway died on 15 February without regaining consciousness and a '£100 Reward. Murder' poster containing a description of the three men was issued on 16 February. The reward was later increased to £250 by sums donated by residents of Stratford and other private individuals. A few days later Clarke reported the latest developments:

21st February 1871
I beg further to report … On the evening of 15th Inst. Sergeant Briden and P.C. Chapman Divisional Detectives K Division having been informed by a person (whom they introduced to me) that the murder was committed by three men who were known to the informant as 'Michael Campbell', 'James Bouger' alias 'Montague' alias 'May', and 'Charles Skinner' and who up to this time frequented the 'Seven Stars' and other Public Houses in the neighbourhood of Brick Lane, Spitalfields and further stated that about 4 p.m. 9th Inst. he saw the man 'Bouger' who said he was going with others to 'do a climb' (Portico

Larceny) and asked him (the informant) if he would lend him a knife for the purpose of pushing back the window fastenings, which he did not do.

The following day the informant again saw 'Bouger' who said 'we were damned near caught last night down below Stratford, a gentleman came out caught hold of me and accused me of trying to get in his house, but Campbell who is a good mate come up and struck the gentleman on the head with the Jemmy and we all run away. I struck across the fields and found myself at Forest Gate Railway Station.'

In consequence of this statement which I believed to be true, I used every exertion in conjunction with the Officers above named and Divisional Detective P.C. Foster H Division and yesterday P.C. Foster ascertained that Mrs Campbell the mother of the man 'Campbell' resided in some Court in the neighbourhood of Samuel Street, St Georges in the East; upon being informed of this I went to the Vestry Hall, St Georges and saw Mr Pritchard Inspector of Nuisances and induced him with Dr Reigate of the Parish to accompany me into some of the small Courts under the pretence of inspecting the houses. On going to No. 18 Waterloo Court, in a room upstairs I found a woman and two young men, one of whom answered the description which I had received of 'Campbell'. I then left and fetched P.C. Foster (who knew Campbell) who was waiting in the immediate neighbourhood with Inspector Mason K Division; upon going into the room he told me that he recognized 'Campbell' as the person alluded to by the informant.

I at once arrested him and conveyed him to Leman Street Police Station and thence to West Ham Station when I met Superintendent Worels, and it was arranged to call in 5 young men who were passing, for the purpose of placing the prisoner among them for identification.

On Mrs Galloway going into the room she at once recognized the prisoner 'Campbell' who (to the best of her belief) was the man who struck her husband. I then took in Miss E. Green who at once identified Campbell as the person who she saw on the Portico of the house of Mr Paize, 10 Vicarage Terrace, about half past 8 o'clock on the night of the attack on Mr Galloway. I then took in William Nott of 7 William Cottages who identified Campbell as one of three men whom he saw near the spot a few minutes before the attempted robbery took place, and subsequently ran away from Mr Galloway after he had fallen on the pavement.

I then took in P.C. 87 John Barnes K Division who identified Campbell as one of three men whom he saw near this spot on the night in question; he was then charged with being concerned with others with the Wilful Murder of Mr Galloway; he was this day taken before J. Spicer Esq. and Mr. Howard of the Town Hall Stratford and remanded to the Petty Sessions Ilford Saturday 25th Inst.

The other two men are still at large but the enquiry is being continued.[33]

St George's in the East, where Clarke arrested Campbell, was an infamous area in which the tenement rooms were usually filled with as many beds as could be fitted in.[34] The scene of the arrest would probably have graced any Dickensian description of crime and poverty in London's East End.

Four days later Clarke was able to report that a second man, 'Charles Skinner' who gave the name John Calbraith, was successfully apprehended, and had also been identified by several witnesses as one of the three men seen at the time that Samuel Galloway had been assaulted. The jury at the inquest on Samuel Galloway on 24 February recorded a verdict of wilful murder against Campbell, and wilful murder of the second degree against Calbraith.[35] Clarke also followed up the concerns that he had expressed about P.C. Edward Blackett and also a second P.C., John Barnes, reporting that: 'had the Constables performed their duty with any intelligence they would have arrested the men at the time, and I am of opinion that they now deny the facts to cover their negligence.'[36] As a consequence of Clarke's report, Blackett was dismissed without pay and Barnes was resigned compulsorily.[37]

At several magistrate's hearings the men arrested for Samuel Galloway's murder were remanded in custody and ultimately committed for trial at the Old Bailey on 5 April 1871. Montagu Williams appeared for Campbell and has left an account of the trial; he described Campbell as 'a very peculiar man in appearance, and several witnesses identified him by the mark or hole under his left eye', a distinctive feature for identification purposes. Williams also commented that: 'The principal witness to the murder was the dead man's wife, and anything more painful than her presence in the box has never come under my notice.'[38] As a consequence, Williams made a decision not to cross-examine Mrs Galloway, as he saw no benefit to be gained for his client. At the end of the prosecution evidence the judge, Mr Justice Lush, advised the jury that there was insufficient evidence to convict Calbraith of wilful murder and he was formally acquitted of that charge.

In his defence of Campbell, Williams pointed out that there must be something faulty on the part of the prosecution in not producing the constable (Blackett) who should have been the best qualified to speak to the identity of the prisoners. This weakness in the prosecution case did not in the end deflect the jury from returning a 'guilty' verdict against Campbell.[39] Before being sentenced to death Campbell admitted the offence but stated that he had not meant to kill Galloway. He was executed at Springfield Prison, Chelmsford, on 24 April 1871; the first execution behind closed doors at the prison. Thus, George Clarke has the dubious distinction of bringing to justice the last person to be hung in public at Chelmsford (Köhl) and the first to be executed under the new regime (Campbell).

Clarke and the Treasury prosecution team must have anticipated that the case for wilful murder against Calbraith was a weak one, as they had another charge up their sleeves. The day after the murder trial, Calbraith was back at the Old Bailey on a charge of 'breaking and entering'. He was found guilty and sentenced to twenty years' penal servitude.[40] Despite the circulation of a description of the third man to all police forces in the country, and the allocation of other police in London to help track him down, 'James Bouger' was never found.

Clarke added to his growing reputation by his handling of this case, not least in his uncompromising attitude in addressing the incompetence and attempted cover-up by two police constables. His efforts received reward; Henderson wrote to the Treasury recommending a £3 gratuity for Clarke and £2 for Inspector Mason. When the £250 reward was distributed, the informer, revealed as 'William Maxwell', received the government's £100, while the remaining £150 was distributed amongst the police team and witnesses, with Clarke receiving the largest individual amount of £30.[41]

Bribery

Two weeks after the death of Sir Richard Mayne, Clarke found himself handling a crime linked to a defence procurement contract. However, it had nothing to do with the purchase of sophisticated (or unsophisticated) Victorian weapons, or the latest version of an ironclad battleship; instead, it concerned a supply contract for 300 loads of elm timber for the Royal Navy at Portsmouth Dockyard.

On 15 January 1869, Antonio Brady, the registrar of contracts at the Admiralty, Somerset House, had been told by a potential contractor, Nicholas Maxwell, of an attempt to extract a bribe from him. Maxwell had been informed that he would only secure the timber-supply contract if he paid a £30 fee to a member of the Admiralty staff. The member of staff concerned was William Rumble, the Admiralty's 'Inspector of Machinery Afloat'. Antonio Brady promptly contacted Scotland Yard and sought the assistance of the detective department and the case was allocated to Clarke. The first task was to find out more about Rumble and to determine whether he alone was in a position to guarantee a contract or whether other Admiralty staff members were involved. A meeting between Maxwell and Rumble was arranged at Maxwell's office on 18 January, where Clarke listened from a side room. Rumble stated that he had an unnamed friend in the Admiralty who was in a position to influence the contractual arrangements. Clarke's next step was to maintain surveillance of Rumble and to identify any acquaintances.[42] Clarke and Detective Sergeant Sayer started to follow Rumble for part of each day. Fortunately, it did not take too long to make progress. On 20 January, at Waterloo Station, Clarke saw Rumble meet an unknown man at

10.30 a.m.: 'Rumble went up to him and commenced a conversation – they walked down the back stairs into York Street, and over Waterloo Bridge into Lancaster Place, and there they parted, and [the unknown man] went into Somerset House by the entrance in Lancaster Place.'[43]

Rumble's contact was quickly identified as James Gambier, a first-class clerk in the Admiralty storekeepers department, who was the first to know when a tender had been accepted and also had the responsibility of writing to the successful contractor. Thus, by delaying the issue of the formal contract letter Gambier could create a window of opportunity to extract a 'fee' from the successful contractors.

Clarke and Sayer maintained regular surveillance at Waterloo Station, and confirmed that Rumble and Gambier met there on at least eleven occasions. However, the police had no specific evidence linking Gambier to attempted bribery. A decision was therefore taken, with Maxwell's agreement, for the £30 'fee' that Rumble had asked for to be paid to him. Obtaining a £30 cheque from the Admiralty, Clarke cashed it into three traceable £10 Bank of England notes and, at a meeting at Maxwell's office on 2 February (at which Clarke again listened from the side room), Rumble was handed the money. By 3 February, Maxwell received confirmation that he was the successful contractor. The police had to wait only a short time for the banknotes to filter through the system; one was paid in to the Church of England Insurance Office by Gambier to cover his life insurance premium, and the other two were paid in by Rumble, one to a warehouseman and the other to a wine merchant.[44]

Armed with the information that Gambier had paid in one of the banknotes, and a warrant, Clarke arrested the two men at Waterloo Station on Wednesday 17 February. Both were taken to Bow Street Police Station and charged with having conspired to obtain £30 from Nicholas Maxwell by false and fraudulent pretences.[45] A search of the men revealed that both had pocket books, Gambier's proving particularly interesting, in the form of abbreviations and ciphers that were suggestive of other financial transactions of a similar kind. By the second magistrate's hearing, Clarke had found a means to translate at least part of the cipher in the pocket books, and it was said at the hearing that all the persons whose names were supposed to be identified by initials in Rumble's notebook had denied being party to any transactions involving the payment of any 'fee' to gain a contract. The suspects were committed for trial at the Old Bailey.[46]

Rumble's defence against the charges was that he had 'merely acted as an agent, and that he had no intention to commit a criminal act'. Gambier's defence counsel contended that 'although [Gambier] had acted indiscreetly and improperly in taking the money from Rumble for giving information relative to this contract he had not contemplated or been guilty of a criminal act'. The jury did not take long to disagree, bringing in a 'guilty' verdict against both men, who were each sentenced to eighteen months' hard labour.[47]

Something that did not appear in any of the hearings or newspaper accounts of the case was that Rumble had an interesting track record. In an unconnected case he had been previously charged, in 1864, with an offence relating to the fitting out of a gun-boat for later use by the Confederate States during the American Civil War. Originally named the *Seylla*, it had been sold by the Admiralty in 1863, ostensibly for the China trade, but in reality it had been bought by an agent acting for the Confederate States Navy. Rumble had been put on trial at the Queens Bench, Westminster, between December 1864 and February 1865. Charged with offences under the Foreign Enlistment Act which included the accusation that he had been actively involved in repairing and fitting out the ship at Sheerness, engaging crew and being on the ship on its testing voyage to Calais, on which occasion the Confederate flag was raised and the ship re-named as the CSS *Rappahannock*. (Ultimately, the ship did not go into active service as it was detained in port by the French authorities.) Though found 'not guilty' at this earlier trial, Rumble had nonetheless been punished subsequently by the Lords Commissioners of the Admiralty, who had reduced him to half-pay, giving him a motive for his subsequent crime.[48] It seems likely that Clarke and others must have been aware of that situation, and yet the newspapers did not refer to it in their coverage of Rumble's 1869 trial, perhaps because of the 'not guilty' verdict in 1864. Whether any reference to the CSS *Rappahannock* case was suppressed, to avoid further embarrassment to the British Government on the sensitive issue of breaches of neutrality during the American Civil War, might also have been a consideration. The '*Alabama* claims' by the United States ultimately led to substantial financial reparations being paid by Britain in 1872.[49]

Betting

In November 1868 a general election had brought in a change of government, with William Gladstone becoming prime minister at the head of a Liberal administration, and the appointment of Henry Bruce as Home Secretary. It is no coincidence that this change of government coincided with a greater involvement of the police in enforcing legislation to deal with perceived failures in the moral rectitude of the working man and woman. One of Bruce's main achievements in a historical context was the reform of the licensing laws, but in 1869 he also issued orders to the Metropolitan Police under their new commissioner to suppress betting houses.[50] Clarke was given the lead responsibility for this task. The following description of Clarke's involvement in the policing of betting houses covers the period from 1869 to 1877.

Legislation to reduce gambling had been strengthened by the Betting House Act of 1853 which 'outlawed betting houses, the exhibiting of lists and the promulgation of advertisements and circulars offering tips and advice'.[51] However, betting was still rife by 1869 not least because, despite the legislation, it had enjoyed virtual immunity from Home Office and police interference and prosecution.[52] Warnings about the moral dangers of betting were sounded regularly; one example coming from the Victorian philosopher and sociologist Herbert Spencer, who expressed the view that gambling was: '… essentially anti-social. A successful gambler receives financial and material benefit without "effort", and happiness at the expense of the "misery of the loser", combining to produce a "general deterioration of character and conduct".'[53] Gambling, particularly linked to horse racing, occurred in various forms and at various locations; the types that Clarke encountered included lotteries and cash betting on horses in individual races, with unregulated businesses operating in private houses, pubs, shops, clubs and through the post. The maximum penalty for someone convicted of running an illegal betting enterprise, within the meaning of the 1853 Betting Act, was a £100 fine or six months' imprisonment. These sentences certainly did not reflect the considerable effort and resources that were needed by the police to secure the evidence for a conviction.

Once an individual or group of individuals were suspected of running an illegal gambling operation, Clarke adopted the following general approach. Firstly, the property would be put under surveillance to observe whether the comings and goings were consistent with a betting operation taking place. Secondly, one or more detectives would enter the premises incognito and would place one or more cash bets or would buy a lottery ticket, as appropriate, and would also observe closely what was happening in the premises. If the betting business was operated by post, then bets would be submitted in the form of postal orders by at least one of the detectives, usually using their home address for replies. Thirdly, if the detectives were fortunate enough to have a winning bet or lottery ticket, then these would be cashed in to check whether the betting house was paying out on winning tickets or operating a scam in which they 'welshed' (defaulted) on the bets. Fourthly, if there was sufficient evidence that activities were illegal, then warrants were obtained from the appropriate police court magistrate (often Bow Street) and the betting premises were raided by the police, with the arrest of all individuals there who might be breaking the law, and the seizure of documents, betting slips, lottery tickets, tipsters circulars etc., all of which would need to be examined as a basis for assembling a case against the suspected offenders. When all the information suggested that a prosecution was justified, the case would be assembled in conjunction with the Treasury Solicitor, who always called on Harry Poland to lead the prosecution. In 1865 Poland had been appointed counsel to the Treasury and adviser to the Home Office in criminal matters and he held these offices for twenty-three years, earning the nickname 'the Sleuth Hound of the Treasury'. He was regarded as a lucid and forceful prosecutor, and scrupulously fair.[54] Poland's friend and colleague at the Bar, Montagu Williams (known to be a natty dresser), said of him:

> I don't suppose that there ever were two men so unlike one another – he, plodding, slow, unimpulsive, and most industrious … I was the reverse of Poland … He was very careless in his dress. He had a mind above that sort of thing, but his family hadn't, and times out of number his sister took him to task about his badly fitting clothes, and begged him to go to a proper tailor.[55]

The first gambling prosecution where Clarke and Poland worked together was the 'Deptford Spec'. On the night of Saturday 27 February 1869, Clarke and Detective Sergeant Palmer went to the Bedford Arms beerhouse, where numbered lottery tickets (printed with the name 'Deptford Spec') were being sold at 1s each for the Liverpool Grand National Steeplechase, which would be run later in March. The two men each bought one ticket; up to 60,000 tickets were available for sale, amounting to total takings of £3,000 for the organisers if all tickets were sold (worth c. £137,000 today).[56] After buying their tickets, Clarke and Palmer went up to the club room on the first floor to join the sixty to seventy people already there, awaiting the evening's entertainment. It is not hard to picture a scene of a dimly lit room, packed with working men, clutching their week's pay and determined to forget the labours of the previous week with the assistance of a few drinks and the chance to win a few pounds if they were lucky.

The 'entertainment' lasted at least three hours and consisted of the process of conducting a lottery. It started with the reading out of the numbers of the unsold tickets. The counterfoils of all the sold tickets were then placed in a 'wheel of fortune', together with a quantity of sand to stop the tickets sticking to each other, and tickets were drawn out individually until the numbers of selected tickets had been allocated against all the names of the individual horses expected to run at the Grand National. The cash prizes ranged from £500 for the first horse past the post, to much smaller sums for lower placings and non-runners. Having seen enough of the procedure by 9 p.m., Clarke left. Neither Clarke nor Palmer had a prize-winning ticket for the Grand National draw. However, on two other occasions in March Clarke bought tickets for a lottery based on the outcome of another major horse race, the City and Suburban Handicap, which he purchased at other outlets where Deptford Spec tickets were sold. After the results sheet for that race had been printed, Clarke found he had a winning ticket but, when he called to collect his £1 prize, he was refused payment as the ticket had ink on it.[57] It seems from later information (presented by a defence lawyer at the magistrate's hearing) that this unfortunate action on the part of the lottery organisers was taken in good faith: 'The ticket presented by Inspector Clarke was blotted with ink, and the private mark had thus been obliterated. Of course the defendants were not aware that they were dealing with as respectable an officer as Inspector Clarke, of the detective force, or they would not for a moment have suspected him!'[58]

By 19 April, Clarke's investigations had provided sufficient evidence for a case to be made, and various Deptford Spec ticket outlets were raided by Clarke with Detective Sergeants Sunerway and Palmer and uniformed police from R Division (Greenwich); six men were arrested and charged with 'establishing and maintaining offices for the purpose of conducting lotteries in contravention of the Lotteries Act and the Betting Act'. As this was the first case to be tackled since the Home Office crack-down, Poland sought to persuade the Bow Street magistrate Sir Thomas Henry that a trial at the Central Criminal Court would be appropriate. Poland also stressed that: 'The Government were determined to put down, not only lotteries but all those offices now carried on with a certain degree of secrecy, in contravention of the Betting Act.'[59]

After two magistrate's hearings at which Clarke was the principal witness for the prosecution, the six men were committed for trial at the Old Bailey. The men's defence lawyer had recognised that the Crown was determined to take the case to a higher court but stated:

> … in point of honour he was anxious to show that his clients, who had for years been engaged in transactions of very great magnitude, had acted with the most scrupulous good faith towards all the persons with whom they had dealt (Loud cheers.). Sir Thomas Henry observed that he could not allow any expression of feeling on the part of any persons in court. Order was at once restored …[60]

At the Old Bailey trial, the six accused had decided to plead 'guilty' and were released by the recorder after each had entered into their own recognisance of £100 to appear if subsequently called upon.[61]

The closing down of the Deptford Spec was effectively a 'show case' to send a message to the betting fraternity that the government was determined to close those schemes that fell outside the law, even though they had escaped legal sanction in the past because police investigations and prosecutions had not previously been implemented. The 'loud cheers' from the crowded court at Bow Street in support of the six Deptford Spec accused signalled that the actions that Clarke and his colleagues were now having to pursue for their Home Office masters were unpopular with the working man. However, this case was just the beginning for Clarke and his colleagues in the detective department. Newspaper accounts of betting prosecutions in London between

1869 and 1876 suggest that Clarke led at least two substantial betting investigations every year, each of which took up considerable time and resources and had to be fitted in around his many other responsibilities. After the Deptford Spec case he succeeded in shutting down at least three other lottery operations, including the 'East End Spec', the 'South London Art Union', and the 'Carshalton Circular Spec'.[62]

In addition to lotteries based on the outcome of horse races, which required no skill on the part of subscribers, Clarke also investigated those individuals who operated businesses in which cash bets were taken on individual horses selected by 'punters'. In the first of these, Clarke tackled The Racing, Telegram and Commission Agency, run by William Wright from 19 York Street; this agency advertised that it would take bets on commission through the post. On 2 June 1869 Clarke forwarded a postal order for £1 to the agency to back 'Cock of the Walk', at 10:1 to win in the Royal Hunt Cup at Ascot. His colleague Detective Sergeant Lansdowne backed 'See-Saw' in the same race at 8:1 to win. If the choice of horses was based on the men's undoubted experience of attending race meetings in the course of duty, they selected wisely. On the day of the race, in a large field of runners, See-Saw won, edging out Cock of the Walk by a neck, with both horses on closing odds of 100:30.[63]

Overall, William Wright was the principal loser when his premises were raided and he was arrested for 'keeping and using a betting house'. Despite arguing that no offence had been committed as 'persons did not resort to the house in question' (as all transactions were dealt with through the post), Wright was fined the maximum £100 at Bow Street Police Court.[64] Loath to lose his business, he gave notice of appeal which, together with some other similar appeals, was heard on 22 January 1870 at the Court of Queens Bench. Clarke was cited as the Crown respondent in the appeal. In what was clearly a test of the robustness of the betting house legislation, and its interpretation by the police and the courts, the judgement was given to the Crown, with the appeal judges concluding that 'all the cases belonged to that very class of cases which it was the object of the acts to suppress'.[65]

As with the example of lotteries, the test case against Wright's betting business and the failure of his appeal opened the door for further betting house prosecutions, whether they were based in houses, shops, pubs, clubs or conducted by post, and whether the operators were effectively bookmakers, tipsters or merely facilitated others to operate a bookmaking service on their premises. During the next six years, Clarke led prosecutions against at least ten further substantial betting operations.[66] By 1876, and probably earlier, he had become so well known to the betting 'trade' that he was no longer able to be the front-man in the initial covert enquiries at betting premises as he was too easily recognised. Even when making postal applications to place a bet, he began to adopt a pseudonym and a different address (e.g. 'Henry Lambert of 39 The Oval, Kennington'). As one of his detective colleagues, Sergeant (later Chief Inspector) George Greenham, was to say about him in 1877: 'I should think he was pretty notorious, not only in the force, but among the betting people themselves – he was constantly appearing at the police courts in such cases.'[67]

Some of the prosecutions opened the police and the courts to the criticism that there was 'one law for the rich and one for the poor'. The classic example was the 1870 prosecution of the 'Knightsbridge Exchange', a betting club. Clarke first paid a covert visit to the premises at 4 Chapel Place, Brompton, on 18 August 1869, and learned that the organisation was essentially a working-man's club in which members paid a 5s subscription to join; there were between 1,000 and 2,000 members. When he returned on 16 November with a membership card, he found that the yard at the premises contained a large assembly of people in which several bookmakers were accepting bets. There was then a gap of seven months before he returned overtly to the Exchange, on 20 June 1870, to inform the owners that they were breaking the law, and told them to close down their operations. When this request was ignored, the police raided the property in September and more than twenty men were arrested and brought before the courts.[68] The delay and greater delicacy shown before taking action in this case is interesting, and the likely explanation is that the Treasury Solicitor, the police and Home Office were considering whether there could be difficulties in securing a conviction, and also whether they might be creating a rod for their own backs by proceeding. The latter was certainly the case as the upper-class racing club, Tattersalls, was run along similar lines, albeit in more salubrious premises, and yet appears to have received no police investigation. When the case was heard at Bow Street, the owners of the Knightsbridge Exchange were represented by William Ballantine. He pointed out that: '… a strong feeling existed why one class of people should with impunity be permitted to keep open a betting club while another of more humble extraction should be prosecuted for doing exactly the same thing.'[69]

Notwithstanding these comments, eight of the defendants were fined for using the Brompton premises illegally as a betting house. *The Times* subsequently thundered in support of Ballantine's view, in its leader column:

> … He is quite right. Unless the public are entirely deluded, betting transactions at Tattersalls are open to at least as much reprehension on the score of gambling as any that were carried on at 'the Knightsbridge Exchange' … We will not say that a substantial distinction between the two cases does not exist. But it certainly ought to be rendered more manifest. If people must bet, it is no doubt better they should do so lawfully than unlawfully. But it is

impossible that the legality of a Betting Club can depend on the mere amount of the subscription, or on the exclusiveness of its members. That would simply be to say that poor men are to be heavily fined for practices which rich men may pursue with impunity.[70]

However, no prosecution of Tattersalls followed and the subject continued to be a running sore in the sporting columns over the next few years, as in the *Penny Illustrated Paper* in 1876:

> Now, though it has grown trite enough to ask what moral difference there can be in betting under the roof of Messrs. Tattersall's sacred establishment and in betting under any other roof, the injustice of dealing with this gambling evil cannot be too frequently protested against ... either the patrician supporters of the turf ought to set an example of self-abnegation and at least give up betting in public, or ... they surely ought to be made amenable to the same law which drags their poorer brethren ... off to prison, or inflicts upon them severe fines.[71]

Almost 120 years later, the historian Stefan Petrow concluded that 'the state seemed determined to wallow in hypocrisy ... It had no intention of making betting wholly illegal ... yet it had no intention of making betting wholly legal'.[72] In the meantime, the police, and Clarke in particular, were tasked with applying the law in this ambiguous situation. Clarke must have been acutely aware that those members of the lower classes who enjoyed a 'flutter' were not well served by the way in which the legislation was enforced, and it is probably this that prompted him in June 1874 to submit a report to Commissioner Henderson about betting stalls at Epsom racecourse. At this point, betting at racecourses was not suppressed, but Clarke had noticed that some landowners at Epsom had sub-let space to betting men 'of the lowest kind and what are commonly termed "welshers"'.[73] His concern was that these men could erect temporary stalls on sub-let land at the racecourse, take bets from working men and disappear with the takings before they had to pay out any winnings. He suggested that the landowners should be prosecuted and James Davis, the legal adviser to the Metropolitan Police, agreed. However, the legal opinion from Harry Poland demonstrates something of the philosophy underlying the hypocritical and moralistic stance of the Home Office to betting. The following sentences are particularly instructive:

> I am of opinion that they [the Epsom landowners] can be successfully prosecuted under the Betting Act 1853 but whether they should be prosecuted, appears to me to be a question that requires much consideration ... If the public find that they can bet with safety they are encouraged to bet, whereas if they find that they are cheated out of their money they are less likely to bet again ...[74]

So, Clarke's well-intentioned proposal did not get the support he hoped for and no further action was taken.

From the newspaper reports of gambling cases between 1869 and 1876, where Clarke was the principal investigating officer, at least thirty-eight people were found guilty of betting house and lottery offences, and the average fine received by these individuals was £49 (equivalent to about £2,200 today). However, from information published in 1877 it appears that this probably represents less than half of his overall achievement in suppressing betting crime. The Home Office-led campaign that Clarke had to implement was regarded at the time as successful; Superintendent Williamson in 1877 described Clarke's performance as one of 'great industry, energy and skill'.[75] Many businesses were closed down. However, others were set up overseas or in Scotland (which had been omitted from the 1853 Act, a loophole that was closed by the Betting Houses Act 1874).[76] In addition, some individuals also decided that they should devise more profitable, albeit fraudulent, betting schemes and it would be these men who would provide the criminal fraternity's nemesis for Clarke. Ultimately, Clarke's part in the effective suppression of betting houses and the public profile that came with it would prove to be his poisoned chalice; but he would not know that until 1877.

Offences Against Children

On 29 July 1869 the detective department at Scotland Yard received an anonymous letter, signed 'One Who Knows'. The contents related to abortion (which was illegal at that time) and infanticide, and made the following claims: 'A woman named Martin, residing at 33 Dean Street, Soho is in the habit of procuring abortion and boasts of having murdered 555 infants during the last 18 months … This woman is the greatest criminal in London; her house is a house where abortion and child murder is openly carried on!'[77] Inspector Druscovich was given charge of subsequent enquiries, keeping strict observation of Mrs Martin's movements, but failed to obtain sufficient evidence to warrant a prosecution. In September or thereabouts, press exposure caused Mrs Martin to move to Woking where she died suddenly on 29 November. In his concluding report, Druscovich commented: 'There is no doubt that the accusations against Mrs. Martin were well founded but it was impossible to obtain the necessary evidence in consequence of her extreme caution and the fact of the law holding both parties to transactions equally amenable.'[78] Here, Druscovich was referring to the fact that any abortionist, and any pregnant mother securing an abortion, would be held equally liable in law at that time. Any case taken to court would effectively require convincing evidence from a third party to secure a conviction.

At a time when effective birth control methods were not available, and where prostitution was rife, unwanted pregnancies and unwanted children were commonplace. The problem in 1869 was not a new one but that year seems to have marked a point at which the police started to take some action. For a pregnant woman in the mid-Victorian era who did not want to give birth or to keep their child, the options were stark. She could obtain an illegal abortion; murder the child; abandon the child at a workhouse or other refuge; or place the child with other women who, for a fee, would look after it. The term 'baby farming' came into popular usage in the second half of the 1860s to describe situations where women accepted payment in exchange for the care of children who were not their own, a process that was unregulated at the time.[79] Many women with unwanted pregnancies were often close to poverty themselves, and the majority were not able to provide sufficient funds for the adequate care of their child. However, despite the grim connotations that have become associated with the term 'baby farming', some unwanted and 'foster' children were successfully placed in environments where they appear to have been well treated. Clarke had an example of such a situation within his own extended family. His youngest sister-in-law, Louisa McGregor, had married an agricultural labourer, John Spicksley, but the couple do not appear to have been able to have children. Instead, in 1861, Louisa and her husband were looking after four 'nurse children'; sisters aged 8–13 years from a family in Brighton. How long the children stayed with Louisa and John is uncertain, but at least one of the sisters, Caroline Best, went on to become a governess in later life.

The criminal options to dispose of unwanted foetuses and children were abortion and murder. There were suspicions at the time that the individuals involved in both methods were the same, and the activities of midwives in particular came under considerable, and often undue, suspicion.[80] However, it is clear that there was a high level of infanticide (probably under-reported) amongst the murder victims of that period, and not only in London.[81] There is a chilling report of a visit paid by a Mrs Meredith to women in Brixton Prison:

Many of them [the women prisoners] killed more than one child. I discovered that there was a kind of sisterhood amongst them … I found a girl who had become a mother at sixteen, and who was taught to kill her child. She fully understands the art, and would, in my opinion, practise it again if she had an opportunity. In fact there are some women in the prison … who have quite a contempt for infant life, and who speak of their crime with a kind of triumph, being the subject of no shame whatever.[82]

Even allowing for an element of Victorian sensationalism in this report, other evidence suggests that unwanted children were murdered with the help of women with experience in such matters.[83]

By the time Clarke became involved in cases relevant to infanticide, baby farming and abortion, the Metropolitan Police had already made some progress. In the Brixton area a number of dead infants had been found in the streets in 1870, and Sergeant Richard Relf of W Division (Brixton) had been put on to the case. He had the good fortune to be able to connect the birth of a child in a 'lying-in establishment' (where some single mothers arranged to give birth) with the disposal of the infant from a baby farm run by Margaret Waters and her sister Sarah Ellis. When visiting the Waters and Ellis establishment, Relf found eleven emaciated and listless children (one of whom became known in the press as 'Little Emily'). Pilloried by the press, the two women were originally charged with manslaughter, later changed to murder. On 24 September at the Old Bailey, Waters was found guilty of murder and was subsequently hanged on 11 October 1870; her sister was acquitted of murder but found guilty of obtaining money by false pretences and sentenced to eighteen months' imprisonment.[84] Sergeant Relf received a gratuity of £20 for his 'exemplary conduct' and a testimony from the Reverend Oscar Thorpe (vicar of Christ Church, Camberwell, and Secretary of the Infant Life Protection Society), as well as a request by Thorpe to Commissioner Henderson that Relf should be solely employed in investigating such cases as he had done such a good job.[85]

Meanwhile, Druscovich had been making enquiries into Mary Hall of 6 Coldharbour Lane, Camberwell, who 'accommodates young ladies during their confinement and it is believed that occasionally, by a certain process, succeeds in bringing the children into the world still born'; this case was transferred to Relf, at Druscovich's suggestion. Although the Treasury abandoned a planned prosecution of Hall for murder because witnesses 'would have to confess to being guilty of the same dreadful crime', she was convicted of conspiracy and sentenced to two years' imprisonment and a £100 fine in December 1870.[86]

By 7 October 1870, Clarke was investigating other allegations relating to baby farming and infanticide, producing reports on that day on two different cases. The first of these related to his investigation of alleged baby farming by a Mrs Clarke, 44 Palmerston Street, Battersea Fields:

I beg to report that after making enquiries in the neighbourhood mentioned, I on Saturday last, went to Mrs. Clarke and asked her to let me see the children she had under her care. She replied, 'I have now in my charge five children and you are perfectly welcome to see them'. I was then shewn into a back room where I found them, and the particulars relating to whom are as follows:

Rosa Kettelty, age 10, Mercer Kettelty, age 7, Frank Kettelty, age 3½. These children were received by Mrs Clarke about the 5th Sept. 1869, from their Father, who is employed at Lloyds Newspaper Office, Fleet Street, and who pays

1 Chief Inspector George Clarke, 1877
(Cobb, *Critical Years at the Yard* [1956])

2 Sir Richard Mayne, Metropolitan Police
Commissioner 1829–68 (Mary Evans
Picture Library, Ref: 10082915)

Above, left to right
3 Superintendent Robert Walker (mounted) and A Division colleagues, including Eleazar Denning (foreground centre), at Epsom Races, 1864 (Metropolitan Police Historical Collection)

4 Superintendent Adolphus Frederick Williamson ('Picture Post Library' in Cobb, *Critical Years at the Yard* [1956])

5 Franz Müller *c.* 1864, murderer of Thomas Briggs

6 Earl of Cardigan (Mary Evans Picture Library, Ref: 10048834)

Above, left to right
7 James Stephens, leader of Irish Revolutionary Brotherhood until 1867

8 Sir Robert Anderson, Home Office expert on Fenians and later assistant commissioner of the London Metropolitan Police (H.L. Adam, *C.I.D. Behind the Scenes at Scotland Yard* [Sampson Low, Marston & Co. Ltd, 1930])

9 Fenians as portrayed after the Clerkenwell Explosion (Mary Evans Picture Library, Ref: 10024403)

10 Montagu Williams, barrister (Dilnot, *The Trial of the Detectives* [1928])

11 Sir Edmund Henderson, Metropolitan Police commissioner 1869–86 (Metropolitan Police Historical Collection)

12 Sir Harry Poland, barrister and Treasury counsel (Bowen-Rowlands, *Seventy-Two Years at the Bar* [1924])

13 Michael Davitt, Irish activist and MP (Mary Evans Picture Library, Ref: 10079194)

14 Shah of Persia Nasir-al-Din, 1873

15 The Tichborne Claimant Arthur Orton after his release from prison in 1884, with daughter, Theresa (Parliamentary Archives, Ref: PHO 11/3)

16 George Hammond Whalley, MP (Courtesy of Kjell Hoel)

17 William Henry Walters, fraudster and forger, at Pentonville Prison in 1880 (National Archives)

18 Charles Howard, aka Count von Howard, fraudster, at Pentonville Prison in 1876 (National Archives)

19 Charles Bravo (Getty Images, Ref: 3246501)

20 Florence Bravo (Getty Images, Ref: 3247033)

21 Harry Benson, fraudster, at Pentonville Prison in 1877 (National Archives)

22 William Kurr, fraudster ('The Great Detective Case', *Police News* [G. Purkess, Strand, London, *c.* 1877])

23 Charles Bale, at Pentonville Prison in 1877 (National Archives)

24 Frederick Kurr, at Pentonville Prison in 1877 (National Archives)

25 Inspector John Meiklejohn (Courtesy of Peter Meiklejohn)

26 Edward Froggatt, solicitor, at Pentonville Prison in 1880 (National Archives)

27 Sir George Lewis, solicitor (Mary Evans Picture Library, Ref: 10078949)

28 Sir Edward Clarke, barrister and MP (Mary Evans Picture Library, Ref: 10073125)

29 Emily Payne *née* Clarke, eldest daughter of George Clarke, with husband Henry and son Charles, 1883 (Author's own photograph)

30 Sir Richard Assheton Cross, Home Secretary 1874–80 and 1885–86 (Parliamentary Archives, Ref: PHO 11/1)

10/- per week for their support, such payments however not including the costs of their clothing and education.

Frederick K. Giles, 14 months old, received 16th Nov. 1869, from a woman giving the same name, but whose address she does not know, a weekly payment of 8/- is made by a gentleman signing himself K.L.M., Army and Navy Club.

Bertie Church, age 6 years, received from her Mother a Miss Church, of 127 High St., Chatham, when about a month old. This child was supported by its Grandfather, who resided at the above address, and was an artisan in Chatham Dockyard; about 12 months since, in consequence of his being thrown out of employment, the payments ceased; he informed Mrs. Clarke he was no longer in a position to pay for the maintenance, and suggested it should be taken to the Workhouse. Mrs. Clarke having become attached to the Child, did not assent to this, and has kept it under her care.

Mrs Clarke could have no intimation of my visit, for which she was entirely unprepared but I found the children decently clad, and to all appearances properly and sufficiently nourished.

The elder child Rosa Kettelty whom I questioned is a well-grown intelligent girl, and in reply to my questions said she had sufficient food and was kindly treated ... Mrs Clarke told me she had taken six children to nurse, as a means of support for the last eight years, and during that time had only lost one by death, which occurred two years since ...[87]

Clarke also spoke to the next-door neighbour and to Mrs Clarke's landlord (who lived opposite), both of whom gave positive accounts of Mrs Clarke and the way in which she treated the children. Thus it seems that Mrs Clarke (no relative of Chief Inspector Clarke as far as is known) was a good 'foster mother' to the children in her care, and that the information received against her was malicious or simply ill-informed.

The second report written on the same day was less comforting. This case had been referred to Scotland Yard by Sergeant Relf, and involved possible infanticide by Mrs Charlotte Davis, who operated as a midwife within a lying-in establishment. Clarke reported as follows:

I beg to report that I have made enquiry with reference to the alleged Child Murders and attempts to procure abortion.

Elizabeth Williams persists in asserting that her statements are true, and that when Betsy Harris was about to be confined, Mrs Davis told her to go down stairs to make some tea, and when she left the room she noticed that Mrs Davis locked the door. She did not go down stairs but remained on the landing, when she heard a child cry, and shortly after Mrs Davis opened the door, and said the child was dead. Miss Williams replied that she was surprised, as she heard it cry; she looked under the bed clothes and saw the dead body of a new born child quite naked and much discoloured. This girl is a common prostitute, and is at present in Westminster Hospital suffering from venereal disease.

Louise Foster, on my first visit said that her statement was an entire fabrication, and she was induced to make it by the girl Williams, for the purpose of revenge against Mrs. Davis for keeping her clothes, and further said that Williams was a wicked liar; but on my seeing her a second time she said the statement she had made to Sergeant Relf was true. This girl is a common prostitute and now resides at 7 Luckington Road, Battersea.

The girl called Betsy Harris has been seen; her name is Elizabeth Wigmore, and is now in the service of Captain George Popplewell, Headly Villas, Dagnalls Park, South Norwood. She states that she was taken to the house of Mrs Davies [sic] on the evening of the 13th May 1868 by her married sister Mrs Harris who then resided at 15 Colchester Street, Pimlico, for the purpose of being confined … she was confined early the following morning of a still born child. Mrs Davies gave a certificate to that effect, and she was told it was buried in Battersea Cemetery; she had provided proper clothing for the child. Mrs Davies had previously attended her sister in confinement. She further stated that there is no truth in the statement of Elizabeth Williams, and does not remember seeing her in Mrs Davies' house; that her present master and mistress are acquainted with her misfortune, and assisted her at the time (her sister having been in their service many years), and upon her recovery, also took her into their service; she appears to be a respectable, truthful girl … I respectfully beg to submit that the statements of Elizabeth Williams, and Louise Foster are not corroborated in any particular, and supposing the statements to be true as regards themselves, they are equally guilty, and their unsupported testimony could not be received as evidence.[88]

Though Clarke pursued one other potential witness, he failed to find her, and so with the conflicting statements received he concluded that 'there is no sufficient evidence upon which proceedings can be taken' against Mrs Davis.[89]

It is possible that there was some substance behind the allegations against Mrs Davis. However, it is equally possible that she was a victim of the vilification of groups of women, including midwives and child-carers that followed the Waters and Ellis case.[90] The police continued to receive information from various sources, not least from the Revd Oscar Thorpe, against women for being either baby farmers or midwives 'carrying on a murderous trade'. A modern assessment of the police response was that 'detectives investigated meticulously, invariably reporting the women to be clear of all suspicion of criminal activity'.[91] Clarke's final report of this kind, prompted by information from Thorpe in 1873, found no substantive grounds for the allegations made and commented with evident frustration: 'The Rev. Mr Thorpe … with his wife take a very active part in these matters, but they are unable to give one particulars of any cases in which enquiry can be made, and it appears to me that they are inclined to form very extreme opinions upon the subject ...'[92]

One of the more positive responses to the protestations of Thorpe and others in the Infant Life Protection Society occurred during 1871, when the government established a Select Committee on the Protection of Infant Life 'to inquire as to the best means of preventing the destruction of the lives of infants put out to nurse for hire by their parents'. The committee's recommendations were integrated into the Infant Life Protection Act 1872, which amongst other aspects required local authority registration for 'houses of persons retaining or receiving for hire two or more infants for the purpose of nursing'.[93] However, local authorities were erratic in putting the measures into practice, and ultimately failed to deal effectively and consistently with the issue.[94] One terrible consequence of this failure was the case of Amelia Dyer whose serial infanticide shocked the nation in 1896.[95]

After his enquiries into Mrs Davis had yielded no substantive evidence of infanticide, Clarke turned his focus towards abortionists. He reported on 28 December 1870, that observation had been maintained of a Dr William Harding who had been acquitted at the Old Bailey in June that year for the murder of Isabella Tewson, an actress who, the prosecution claimed, had died as a result of being treated by Harding with a noxious drug to procure abortion.[96] The judge in Harding's trial had concluded that there was insufficient evidence to support the charge and directed the jury to acquit him.[97] Clarke had not only arranged for observation to be made, he had also visited Harding. During their conversation, Harding had informed Clarke that he knew who the mother was of 'Little Emily' (one of the emaciated young children found in Waters' baby farming establishment) and had given Clarke the details; Emily was now being looked after at the Parish Schools, Lower Norwood. Perhaps the coincidence that Clarke himself had a young daughter of the same name, and indeed of the same stature, prompted him to ask the commissioner for approval (which was granted) to inform the parish authorities of the details of Little Emily's parentage.[98] Ultimately, Clarke's observation of Harding yielded no evidence to justify any action, though he did comment that:

> I have no doubt this man occasionally lends his professional assistance in cases of abortion but the operation would take place at the residence of the person undergoing it. No third person would be present and this being so the evidence of the woman being uncorroborated would not be admissible to support a prosecution, both the persons being equally guilty. Thus rendering it extremely difficult to bring to justice persons guilty of this class of offence.[99]

In 1871, by adopting a rather risky strategy, Clarke made a breakthrough by securing a conviction for the supply of abortion-inducing drugs. This case had a novel twist to it that could only have taken place in the Victorian era. Events were succinctly reported by the *British Medical Journal* on 1 July 1871 under the heading 'Mesmerism and Abortion':

> At the Lambeth Police Court, on the 22nd June, Charles de Badderley, described as a medical botanist, and Sarah, his wife, residing at Exeter Villas, Kennington, were brought up on remand, charged with selling various noxious drugs, knowing that the same were to be used in order to procure abortion ... The attention of the authorities having been drawn to an advertisement stating that 'the celebrated Madame de Badderley, clairvoyant, could be consulted daily at 4, Exeter Villas', they placed the matter in the hands of Inspector Clarke, of the Detective Department, for investigation. That officer employed a woman named Hansard to go to the address given, and, representing herself as the aunt of a young woman who had got into trouble, to ask for something which should induce a miscarriage. On the occasion of Mrs Hansard's first visit, the prisoner said she could say nothing until put into a state of clairvoyance by her husband. This was agreed to; and the male prisoner, having made several passes with his hands, declared Madame to be asleep. After some conversation, the female prisoner was recovered from her supposed clairvoyant state, and then gave Mrs Hansard some pills and herbs for the niece, charging half a guinea for them. A second visit was paid at which the same kind of formality was gone through, and more herbs given to Mrs Hansard, who again paid half a guinea. It was, however, stated by the female prisoner that, when in the mesmeric condition, she had discovered that the case was a very critical one, but that she could give some effective medicine for £5. Accordingly, Mrs Hansard took a £5 note, marked by Inspector Clarke, and paying it to the prisoners, received from them some powders and other medicine. On analysis, they were found to contain injurious and powerful drugs. Mr Ellison sent the case to trial at the Central Criminal Court, but consented to take bail of £150 for each.[100]

The drugs provided by the de Badderleys to Mrs Hansard included the known abortifacient, ergot of rye. However, as Mrs Hansard's pregnant niece was a fabrication, it was no surprise at the Old Bailey trial of the de Badderleys (for unlawfully supplying a noxious drug intended to procure miscarriage) that their defence counsel, Montagu Williams, contended that there was no case to go to the jury, as there was really no person in existence who intended to take the drug. Nevertheless, the prosecution team, led by Harry Poland, claimed that the intention by the de Badderleys to supply a drug for the purpose of causing miscarriage was the issue of importance, and the court overruled the defence counsel's objections. The de Badderleys were found guilty and both were sentenced to twelve months' imprisonment, but 'some strong observations were made as to the conduct of the police in laying the trap by which they had been caught'.[101] Though Clarke had found a mechanism to secure a conviction for the supply of abortion-inducing drugs, he appears not to have used that means again, though others did.[102]

Clarke's reports rarely betray any emotion, and usually consist of factual accounts of the cases that he had been working on. However, in some of the reports on his inquiries involving children, a few comments, particularly those which express frustration over the difficulty of obtaining adequate evidence against those involved in the crimes of abortion and infanticide, suggest that these were issues of particular importance to him. With five children of his own, and with his first grandchild, Fanny Clarke, having been born on 17 June 1870, it is perhaps not too surprising that signs of some emotion crept into his reporting of offences relating to young children. One must beware of reading too much into this, but he probably gained some satisfaction from finding a mechanism to secure a conviction of the de Badderleys, though he seems also to have decided, probably wisely, that he should not use that mechanism too often.

Irish Affairs

Though Fenian activity had dramatically reduced, it had not completely gone away. Irish opinion initiated a campaign for the recognition of the convicted Fenians as political prisoners, and sought their early release. With the change of government at the end of 1868, under William Gladstone a new political attitude started to emerge. During March 1869, forty-nine prisoners convicted of treason-felony in Ireland were freed though this did not include senior members of the movement such as Halpin, O'Donovan Rossa, O'Leary and Devoy.[103] Later that year the United States (US) Legation wrote to the government urging the release 'of all American citizens now confined in British prisons for political offences'.[104] As the privately expressed British view was that some of these were the most heinous of Fenians, the US Legation received a negative response, but the pressure for their release remained. Public meetings were held in Hyde Park in support of further amnesties, such as one on 24 October 1869, where 1,504 police were put on duty as a precaution.[105] Eventually, in January 1871, a conditional pardon was extended to many of the Fenian leaders, the condition being that they should immediately leave the UK and not return for periods of eleven to twenty years (depending on their individual cases). John O'Leary took exile in France, where he was joined in voluntary exile by his non-convicted sister, Ellen. Others, including O'Donovan Rossa and Devoy, travelled to the United States where they arrived in New York, on 19 January 1871, to find themselves being fêted by large welcoming crowds. On arrival, many of them joined and helped to

re-animate Clan na Gael, the most significant of the Irish revolutionary societies that emerged after the failure of the Fenian rising, and which had been
formed in the United States in 1867; Devoy would later become its leader.[106]

In September 1869, Clarke returned to Ireland, possibly for the first time
since April 1868; he was needed to provide evidence at the trial of Peter
Barrett (a letter carrier in London) for the attempted murder of Captain
Thomas Eyre Lambert.[107] On 11 July 1869, Lambert had been returning home
at 9.15 p.m. when he noticed a man nearby in the grounds. Approaching him,
the man raised a pistol and shot several times at Lambert. One ball struck
Lambert's watch, two shots hit him in the stomach and another hit him in the
temple, causing him to fall down, at which point the assailant ran off. A ball
was later removed from Lambert's temple by a doctor, and he survived because
he was wearing a hard hat at the time. Lambert claimed to have recognised
his assailant as Peter Barrett, the son of a respected tenant farmer on Lambert's
land who Lambert had evicted (apparently for no good reason) a few weeks
earlier.[108] After the alarm had been raised, Peter Barrett was arrested on a train
bound for Dublin. No gun was found on him. However: 'When the prisoner
was arrested the police in London were set in motion, and Inspector Clarke
discovered that the prisoner had resided in the house of a Mrs Starling and
upon his box being broken open and searched, this document [a receipt for a
hired gun] was found.'[109] Subsequent investigations by Clarke indicated that
Barrett had hired a pistol and bought eight ball cartridges on 9 July 1869 from
Thomas Wollams, a seller of surgical instruments and firearms in Tottenham
Court Road. Barrett had justified hiring the gun as he was taking care of a
house. On 10 July, Barrett had been given leave by the post office for five days
following receipt of a doctor's certificate for a knee injury, and he had then
travelled to Ireland by train.[110]

Clarke travelled to the trial in Galway in the company of Mrs Starling
and Mr Wollams. Barrett's defence counsel highlighted that Barrett was of
unblemished character and questioned whether Lambert could have seen
well enough in the dusk to be sure of his identification of Barrett. He also
pointed out that there had been other individuals in Lambert's house grounds
that day and claimed that the offence 'had been committed by … a band of
private assassins who now keep Ireland in terror'. The jury failed to reach a
verdict.[111] The rumour was that only one juror had held out against acquittal
and he was mobbed and pelted with stones and had to be escorted to his hotel
by police with fixed bayonets.[112] A second trial was originally planned to start
on 14 October, but this was delayed as the prosecution requested a change of
location on the basis that an impartial trial could not be held in Galway. The
second trial eventually started on 17 February 1870 at the Court of Queens
Bench, Dublin. Clarke, Walloms and Starling once more travelled to Ireland
to give evidence. Barrett was defended on this occasion by Isaac Butt, Irish

lawyer and politician, who was a strong supporter of Home Rule for Ireland. Once again the jury could not reach a verdict.[113]

A third trial was convened in Dublin on 23 June 1870 and Clarke and the other London-based witnesses travelled across yet again. Barrett was again defended by Butt who, on this occasion, was successful in unearthing some inconsistencies in Captain Lambert's evidence in relation to the timing of the attack, and raised further questions about the limited light levels and visibility at the time that Lambert was supposed to have identified Barrett. At this final trial, the jury took five minutes to reach a verdict of 'not guilty', which was greeted by cheers in the court, and Barrett was finally acquitted.[114] The trial never satisfactorily dealt with the issue of why Barrett had gone to Ireland at that time with a gun, and had tried to return to London with some rapidity. However, the case illustrates the tensions that existed in Ireland concerning tenant eviction and landlord-tenant relationships at that time; tensions that were later to lead to the creation of the Irish National Land League in 1879, as a mechanism to protect tenant farmers from the excesses and unfair demands of landlords. Only five weeks before Clarke travelled to Barrett's third trial, the man who would later be responsible for establishing the Land League, Michael Davitt, had been arrested by Clarke for gun-running.

On Saturday 14 May 1870, Clarke received a telegram at Scotland Yard informing him that a Birmingham arms dealer, John Wilson, had left the Midlands by train with two suspicious packages in his possession, possibly on his way to hand over the packages to the Fenian arms organiser, Michael Davitt. It was known that Davitt had replaced Ricard Burke in this role, but, though suspicion of Davitt's activities was not lacking, it was not till 1870 that sufficient evidence was obtained to justify his arrest.[115] The flow of arms to the Fenians was considerable and, ironically, assisted by government actions:

> During the year 1869 the illicit introduction of arms into Ireland became a matter of anxiety to the Irish Government. And such is the fatuity of Government methods and ways that this very time was chosen by the War Office to sell off scores of discarded rifles. The Fenians were thus enabled to purchase at 'knock-out' prices better arms than had ever been carried by British troops in actual warfare, and quantities of these were smuggled into Ireland for the use of the rebels.[116]

Despite, or perhaps because of, the unhelpful policy of selling off army surplus, the arrest and conviction of Davitt and the disruption of the Fenians' arms supply was a high priority. Thus, after receiving the telegram, Clarke took with him at least three detective sergeants, Lansdowne, Campbell and Foley, and headed for the Great Western Railway Station at Paddington, after first checking the adjacent underground station at Praed Street. Davitt was first spotted at Praed Street, and was followed as he made his way to the arrivals platform at Paddington station to meet the 10.40 p.m. train, which arrived ten minutes late. When Wilson emerged from a third-class carriage he was found to be carrying two heavy packages containing fifty revolvers, and was arrested by Foley. Davitt was arrested by Campbell on Clarke's signal. When questioned, Davitt would not give his name or address, but papers carried by Wilson gave the police sufficient information to locate the lodgings where Davitt had been staying under the name of 'Matthews'. When Davitt was searched by Clarke at Paddington, a large amount of money was found on him, about £152 in Irish and English banknotes (worth about £7,000 today). Clarke handed back some of the money to Davitt for use in his defence, and Davitt signed two receipts for the items returned; the receipts later being produced in court as evidence of his style of handwriting.[117]

On 17 May, Davitt and Wilson appeared before the magistrate Mr D'Eyncourt at Marylebone Police Court; Davitt was charged with loitering for unlawful purposes (later raised to 'treason-felony'). Harry Poland led the case for the prosecution, and was also in the prosecution team at the later Old Bailey trial. At his first court appearance, Davitt was described by *The Times* as:

> … a remarkably tall, powerful-looking man neat in his dress, and with a military bearing … His hair, short whiskers, and closely trimmed moustache are dark; his eyes are dark-blue, and his nose, mouth, and chin indicate great readiness and decision of character. He gave his age as 25, but appeared to be from three to five years older. The fact that he has lost his right fore-arm has, perhaps, better than any other mark, enabled the police to track him from place to place.[118]

Davitt had been born in County Mayo in 1846 soon after the first major failure of the Irish potato crop from potato blight; his family had been evicted by their landlord in 1850, and had travelled to Haslingden, Lancashire, where, as an 11-year-old he had lost part of his right arm after an accident while working at Victoria Mill. Subsequently employed at Haslingden post office, he had joined the IRB, quickly becoming a 'Centre' and leading a detachment of Fenians from Haslingden to take part in the abortive raid on Chester Castle. He had been appointed organising secretary and arms agent for the IRB for England in 1868 and spent the next two years organising arms shipments to Ireland.[119]

By 14 June 1870, the magistrate had heard sufficient evidence to commit both Davitt and Wilson for trial for treason-felony at the Old Bailey in July. Before the trial, Clarke was busy making enquiries to strengthen the case against Davitt and Wilson, including visiting Birmingham to identify witnesses able to establish a conclusive link between Davitt and Wilson, and to corroborate that Davitt had operated under several aliases. In addition, evidence was collated from Manchester, Leeds and Dublin which linked Davitt to the export of weapons and ammunition from England to Ireland. The Fenian informer, Joseph Corydon, was also dug out of 'retirement' to provide evidence of Davitt's Fenian associations and his involvement in the Chester Castle affair.[120] Between 14 June and the start of Davitt and Wilson's Old Bailey trial on 15 July, Clarke also fitted in two visits to Ireland, the first to give evidence at the third trial of Peter Barrett, the second, on 5 July, to Athlone to try to locate two individuals, 'John White' and 'Margaret Delmeyre', who appeared to have been the intended recipients of barrels of arms and ammunition sent from a Leeds warehouse rented by Davitt.[121] Clarke did not locate White, but found a 'Margaret Delamar' (sic) in Castlereagh, who was an elderly lady who 'knew nothing about the barrel, and made no claim to it'.[122] (Presumably the addresses used were those of innocent parties and the barrels were intercepted by Fenians en route.) Clarke also used his second visit to meet with Samuel Anderson, the Irish Crown solicitor, to get information and advice on the cases of Davitt and Wilson.[123]

The Old Bailey trial of Davitt and Wilson started on 15 July 1870, under Lord Chief Justice Cockburn, and lasted three days.[124] The prosecution, led by the attorney general, called witnesses from Birmingham who identified Wilson as an arms manufacturer and dealer, and provided evidence linking Wilson and Davitt. These were followed by detectives from Leeds who had identified Davitt as the man who had rented a warehouse used for arms storage and shipment. The Scotland Yard detectives involved in the arrests, including Clarke, were also called; Clarke providing information from his recent visit to Athlone. Corydon gave evidence of Davitt's Fenian connections and a handwriting expert, Charles Chabot (assisted by Davitt's signature on the receipts he had signed on the night of his arrest), confirmed that in his view it was Davitt's handwriting that was also found on a number of incriminating documents. Davitt's defence team called several witnesses from Haslingden, some who said that Davitt had been in Haslingden at the time of the abortive Chester Castle raid, and some who indicated that Davitt could easily have been mistaken for another one-armed Irishman, 'Burke'. After Cockburn's summing up, the jury retired for twenty minutes before returning 'guilty' verdicts against both men. Before sentence, Davitt delivered a dignified appeal to the judge:

> ... not for himself, but for Wilson, stating that if Wilson was guilty he (Davitt) was to blame for his guilt, and that Wilson never knew until he arrived at the Paddington Station that he (Davitt) was an Irishman or that his name was not Robert Jackson. He would cheerfully undergo any additional punishment if Wilson's wife and family could be saved from a workhouse, and he begged that his punishment, if the sentence against Wilson was irrevocable, might be added to his (Davitt's) sentence.[125]

Davitt and Wilson were sentenced to fifteen and seven years' penal servitude, respectively.

Michael Davitt's later life has been referred to by his most recent biographer, Carla King, as almost 'Mandela-like', and it is difficult to disagree. In 1878, shortly after his release on ticket of leave, he gave evidence to a government commission on penal reform, having already written a lengthy article on the subject.[126] In October 1879 the Irish National Land League was founded, largely by his efforts; Davitt became secretary and Charles Parnell, de facto leader of the Irish MPs in the House of Commons, was appointed chairman. As a consequence, 'in the course of the next fifty years a complete transfer of land ownership of Ireland was ... brought about'.[127] Davitt was re-arrested on three further occasions, in 1879, 1881 and 1882, for sedition or incitement (associated with his involvement with the Land League). As time progressed, his focus shifted from Irish Nationalism and land ownership to broader, socialist and humanitarian policies, probably reflecting his experiences as a youth in the cotton industry in Lancashire. Although a somewhat reluctant politician, he was elected MP for north-east Cork on 8 February 1893, resigning in 1899 in protest against the Boer War. He emerges from his writings as a man of vision and principle.[128] Davitt's time in prison clearly profoundly influenced his later attitudes and philosophy, and to some extent at least, he had Clarke to 'thank' for that – though for understandable reasons it is unlikely that he did.

The day after Davitt's trial concluded, the Franco-Prussian War started. Across the Channel, Napoleon III of France declared war on Prussia after years of tension between the combatants. By 2 September 1870 Napoleon III had surrendered after defeat at the Battle of Sedan, but in a bloodless coup on 4 September the French Second Empire was overthrown. A republic was established, led by a government, which continued to resist the German armies. Paris came under siege from 19 September 1870.[129] The British Government declared neutrality, and it was not long before the Scotland Yard Detective Department was engaged in helping to police it. On 6 September 1870, in a report counter-signed by Clarke, Detective Inspector James Pay reported that during his investigation of the alleged exportation of arms to France from Newhaven, he had been 'unable to ascertain that any war material had been sent through that port to France'.[130] Irish sympathies in the conflict lay with the French; a large spontaneous demonstration of popular support had already been held in Dublin on 19 July, and a national committee was formed on 7 September to provide medical aid and supplies to France by recruiting an Irish Ambulance Corps. Assembled from various parts of Ireland, the corps sailed to France on 8 October in a chartered ship, *La Fontaine*.[131]

On 24 September 1870, *The Times* reported that a London-based committee, with offices at 7 Bolt Court, Fleet Street, had also been formed to raise money and send out able-bodied young Irishmen to form an Irish National Ambulance Corps in France; *The Times* later reporting that 'upwards of 2000 athletic Irishmen had presented themselves'.[132] By the end of September, police enquiries had been initiated, as 7 Bolt Court was well known to police as a Fenian rendezvous. On 1 October, Inspector Brannan of Holborn Division reported that the 'Ambulance Corps' was a 'cover'; that the Fenians were attempting to raise an 'Irish Brigade'; and that as soon as the men landed in France they would be expected to take up arms for France and join the Foreign Legion.[133] If correct, this would be an offence against the Foreign Enlistment Act. On 3 October, P.C. James Haire went to 7 Bolt Street in plain clothes to investigate the recruitment process. He saw an Irish-American of military appearance in charge, and a clerk. He was told that only Irishmen could join and he noticed that about forty men applied during the hour that he was there.

On 5 October the solicitor general's office commented to the Home Office that 'there seems scarcely sufficient evidence that the enlistment is for other purposes than the formation of an ambulance corps', but their attitude was to change on receipt of a telegram from Frederick Bernal, the British Consul in Havre, which read: 'Thirteen men, Irish Ambulance Corps have applied Consulate. Required to bear arms – Refuse – Penniless – What shall I do?' An additional complication was a note received via the Foreign Office from the German Ambassador, Count Bernstadt, stating that 'He has reason to believe that enlistments of Irishmen for military service in France are being made in this country – requests urgent enquiries'.[134] By then, Clarke had already received his orders from the Home Office; he would be off on his travels again, this time to a country at war where he would be operating 'undercover':

> The main object of the Officer's [journey] is to obtain sufficient evidence to sustain a prosecution against the agents here who engaged these men …
> Then to return the men by the cheapest route. The men will not be aware that Mr Clarke is a Police Officer and he can therefore deal with them in whatever manner he may deem most advisable.[135]

Once again, the survival of Clarke's report allows him to tell the story:

> October 19th 1870
> With reference to the alleged infringement of the Foreign Enlistment Act, I beg to report that as directed I left London for Havre on Tuesday the 12th Inst. On my arrival at 4 p.m. on 13th I put myself in communication with Frederick Bernal Esq. H.M. Consul, who informed me that about 80 men arrived at that Port, on Friday the 7th Inst. by the 'John Bull' Steam Ship from London. Most

of these men called at the Consulate, and said they had been induced to leave home for the purpose of joining an Ambulance Corps. 21 of these went on to Caen the following day (Saturday) and 40 more on Sunday; 19 refusing to proceed any further, and remained at Havre in a destitute state till Monday when he paid their passage to Southampton.

I proceeded to Caen on Friday being furnished with a letter of introduction to C.G.Percival Esq.,Vice Consul at that place, and had an interview with him the following morning. He stated that a number of men from England had been lodged in the Barracks there for several days, but that most of them had returned to Havre. He accompanied me towards the Barracks and on the way we met several of the men, four of whom said they were penniless and begged to be sent back to England. I paid their fare to Havre and accompanied them there, the others about ten remained at Caen. On reaching Havre I found about 50 at that place; on questioning them they stated they had been engaged by Messrs. McDonald, Cotter, Cotter, O'Hagan and Carmandy, who had an office at Bolt Court, Fleet Street, London, to proceed to France for the purpose of joining an Ambulance Corps, and had each paid 8/- for their passage. They were accompanied on their journey by the two Cotters; on reaching Havre [they] were joined by O'Hagan, who took them to Caen and there lodged them in the Barracks. By this time they suspected all was not right, and asked O'Hagan, who had assumed the command as Colonel Dyers, for an explanation. He informed them they were not required for the Ambulance Corps, but to join an Irish Brigade and fight for France. This they refused to do, and demanded to be sent home. They were confined to Barracks under the charge of the two Cotters, who called themselves Captain and Ensign, and told them they would be required to take the Oath as Soldiers of France, and threatened to place them under arrest if they were not obedient. They remained in Barracks till the Friday still refusing to become Soldiers, when about 48 of them were marched down to the boat for Havre, escorted by Soldiers with loaded rifles, and fixed bayonets, accompanied by the two Cotters and O'Hagan. When on board they were given about 7d. each. These men remained at Havre until noon 17th when I engaged passages for them (52 in number) to London in the Steam Ship John Bull; Mr Bernal giving an Order to the Captain for the payment of their passage money. He also advanced me 453 francs for the purpose of providing them with food and lodgings during their stay in Havre, they being entirely destitute, and in a starving condition, having received but little food since they left London, some having sold the greater part of their clothing. They further complained of being cruelly deceived and badly treated by those who had engaged them; several had left wives and families quite destitute, being promised by McDonald and others, that they would receive pay at the rate of 25/- per week, with rations and an outfit – these promises induced them to leave their houses. McDonald and Carmandy went with them on their outward journey as far as Gravesend. I accompanied these men to London and provided them with food on the passage – their names, addresses, and statements are attached, and several are prepared to give evidence if required.

I beg to add that about 350 men said to form an Ambulance Corps arrived at Havre from Dublin on Wednesday 12th Inst., and were still there at the time of my leaving. A great number of these were about the streets in a drunken riotous state and on Saturday night broke out in open mutiny, refusing to obey those in command, and a guard of Soldiers was called out to quell the disturbance, and I was informed by some of the parties that only about 40 of their number were required as an Ambulance Corps, and that the others must either join the French Army or return home, and I am of opinion from the riotous demeanour of these men, should they remain at Havre serious consequences will follow.

I respectfully beg to state that I received every possible assistance and attention from F. Bernal Esq. at Havre, and C.G. Percival at Caen.[136]

The reference made in Clarke's report to an Ambulance Corps arriving from Dublin on 12 October was the ship *La Fontaine*. Several of the men from this ship did go on to serve in a medical assistance role. However:

Contrary to the original intentions of those who sent the Ambulance Corps to France, a number of the volunteers, including some Dundalk men, adopted a more active military role soon after their arrival … [including] those who joined the Foreign Legion: they enlisted in the 1st Compagne Irlandaise, Légion d'Étrangère. The Legion had its headquarters at Bourges, numbered 30,000 men, and was attached to the Army of the Loire.[137]

The men received rifle and machine-gun training and learnt how to operate as snipers and guerrilla fighters behind enemy lines. Whether any of the men from Dublin or London later participated in Irish Republican activities is not known.[138]

So Clarke returned home, having done what he could to return those men who had been potentially duped into fighting for France. He had obtained statements (including a full description of events from one of the volunteers, William Costello) implicating McDonald and others involved in the recruitment process.[139] On 21 October, the newly promoted Chief Inspector Druscovich arrested 'John McDonald', believed to be the principal recruiter for the Bolt Street recruits to the Irish Ambulance Corps, whose real name was Joseph Patrick McDonnell. He was brought up before Sir Thomas Henry at Bow Street on 21 and 28 October on charges under the Foreign Enlistment Act. At the second hearing Clarke's witness, William Costello, gave his evidence of events.[140] However, after the hearings, no trial appears to have taken place; the case against Joseph Patrick McDonnell was 'removed by *Certiorari*' (a writ from a superior court directing that a record of proceedings in a lower court be sent up for review) and it is possible that some legal or political mechanism was used to sweep the case under the carpet to avoid political embarrassment.[141] McDonnell had been involved with organisations associated with Irish nationalism since 1862, including the National Brotherhood of St Patrick and the Fenians; he had been detained under the suspension of *habeas corpus* but was probably freed in 1869. McDonnell had also been appointed by Karl Marx as the representative for Ireland on the General Council of the International Working Man's Association. In January 1872, at the latest, McDonnell was a free man, as newspaper reports for that month indicate that he attended the Association Council meeting.[142]

The Irish Ambulance Corps investigation, the monitoring of James Stephens in Paris and surveillance operations on foreign refugees seem to have been the closest that the Metropolitan Police got to covert operations during the time that Clarke was a detective.[143] Although Clarke had been sent to France on an 'undercover' mission, the object was for him to obtain evidence of criminal activity in the context of the Foreign Enlistment Act, rather than to play a political-espionage role. For Clarke, this appears to have been the last time that he was involved with Fenian investigations that reached court. There were subsequent occasions when his expertise on Irish matters was sought, but his involvement in these did not emerge as headline issues.[144] There was a resurgence of Irish terrorism in the 1880s, driven by a combination of Clan na Gael and the maverick, O'Donovan Rossa. By then, however, Clarke had long retired, though his friend and colleague 'Dolly' Williamson was still at Scotland Yard and in the front line of the policing of this next phase of Irish republicanism.[145]

Arson – London's Burning

At 12.55 a.m. on 20 September 1871, a fire was reported to Richard Gatehouse, the keeper of the fire escape opposite Shadwell church. The informant, a young man, said that a fire had just broken out at Sufferance Wharf on Wapping Wall and he assisted the fireman, William Padbury and Gatehouse, with the fire engine. When reaching the fire they found a wagon-load of straw ablaze on the ground floor, which had spread to the upper floor of the warehouse above. The fire took about an hour to put out, at which point the young man helped the firemen to return the equipment to Shadwell church, where he was given the standard reward of 'half a crown' (2*s* and 6*d*) for the call and his trouble, and he signed the receipt as 'W. Anthony'.[146]

After lobbying by insurance companies, a publicly funded fire service in London had been established after the passing of the Metropolitan Fire

Brigade Act in 1865. Alongside the Metropolitan Fire Brigade, the London Salvage Corps had started its operations in 1866; their responsibilities included salvage work after a fire had taken place.[147] One of the Salvage Corps employees, Thomas Meechan, had been investigating a number of fires of unknown cause, including one in July where the Holborn Fire Station had been called out by a man living at 2 Parker Street, Drury Lane. On the night of 26 September 1871, Meechan took the Shadwell fireman, Padbury, to Parker Street to see if the Holborn fire alert and the Wapping Wall alert might have been given by the same man. Using the ruse that they had lost the receipt that had been signed by the informant at Wapping, they knocked at the door and found the man that Padbury recognised as W. Anthony. However, Anthony said, 'You must be mistaken, I don't know where Wapping is, I was never up there'.[148]

Armed with this denial that Padbury knew to be false, Meechan and his superiors decided to call in the police. Clarke picks up the story:

> On 29th September, I received information about this fire at Wapping Wall, and next evening, Saturday, about 10 o'clock, I went with Meechan to the corner of Parker Street, near No. 2 – Meechan pointed out the prisoner to me as one of two men, and I went up to him and said 'Anthony, I want to speak to you about some money you received for calling fires' – He said 'What is it' – I said 'I will tell you directly,' and I took him to the corner of Long Acre – I then told him I was an Inspector of police, and should arrest him on a charge of wilfully setting fire to a wharf in Wapping Wall on the night of 19th September – He said 'I know nothing about it; I never was there' – He repeated that several times, and I took him to King David Lane Station [Shadwell], and charged him with the offence – After the charge was entered, the inspector asked him if he could read or write – he said 'No'; and then, after some hesitation said 'Only my name, I can write my name' – He did not write at the Station, he was not asked to do so. – He gave his name, William Anthony, Parker Street, Drury Lane, and said he was a blacksmith.[149]

Anthony appeared at the Thames Police Court on 2 October. In addition to Clarke's preliminary evidence, P.C. William Waller confirmed that he had seen Anthony opposite Shadwell church early in the morning of 20 September. Clarke also stated that there was evidence (from other signed reward receipts) that Anthony had called out the fire brigade at thirty-six fires, where the destruction of property amounted to £100,000 (equivalent to *c.* £4.5 million today).[150] Anthony was remanded in custody and by 17 October was suspected of having set fire to at least 109 buildings, houses, factories and other premises in London in the last two years: 'There was a large attendance of people whose premises had been destroyed and of others who were anxious to see a person accused of incendiarism on so very extensive a scale, merely for the purpose of the fee of half-a-crown ...'[151]

No doubt because of the seriousness of the case, Harry Poland had now taken over from Clarke the formal prosecution of Anthony, on behalf of the Treasury. At the 17 October hearing, witnesses had also been located who recalled seeing Anthony near the scene of the Wapping Wall fire before he had called out the fire brigade. Anthony, who represented himself, continued to deny the charges.[152]

On 7 November, additional detailed evidence emerged that Anthony had called out the fire engine and helped in the pumping at a fire at some workshops in Hampstead, and at a corn-chandlers workshop at Chalk Farm. By 29 November, Clarke's enquiries had unearthed a total of 150 probable fire setting offences, and he was engaged in the investigation of eighty-five others, or as Harry Poland said: 'Every day they obtained fresh information about the prisoner, who had in two years set fire to 150 places and caused immense losses. Inspector Clarke, the detective officer, had been engaged in the investigation of those cases for six weeks daily, and had not done with them yet.'[153] Anthony again claimed that all the witnesses were mistaken.

At his Old Bailey trial on 13 December 1871, Anthony defended himself against the indictment of setting fire to the warehouse at Wapping Wall. After some legal discussion the judge, Mr Justice Grove, also allowed witness evidence on the association of Anthony with other fires. Apart from the battery of witnesses from the police and fire services, Charles Chabot confirmed that the handwriting on thirteen different receipts signed 'W. Anthony' was the same. The jury recorded a 'guilty' verdict, and Anthony was sentenced to twelve years' penal servitude.[154] The *Pall Mall Gazette* was not happy: 'In the good old times arson was punishable with death, and now it is often visited with the punishment next in severity to hanging ... Where the crime has unquestionably been systematically carried on, it is surprising to find only twelve years' penal servitude awarded ...'[155]

The *Liverpool Mercury* focused on a more positive aspect, noting that whereas the fires from unknown causes in the metropolis had for some time numbered twenty-five or thirty per month they had, since the apprehension of the prisoner, dropped to three.[156] Police orders reported: 'Commendation and reward granted to a Detective Inspector – The Solicitor to the Treasury having highly eulogized the services of Chief Inspector Clarke, in connexion with the case of a man named Anthony ... the Secretary of State, on the recommendation of the Commissioner, has authorized a reward of £5 being paid to him for the skill displayed.'[157]

The huge variety of cases that Clarke tackled between 1868 and 1871 are vividly illustrative of the criminal and social environment of the time. The mental and physical pressures of the job must have been considerable, yet he seems to have thrived on the challenges as well as the increased responsibility that promotion to chief inspector brought. During these four years he had further demonstrated his ability to work with prosecution teams to assemble cases that would usually lead to convictions. He had also shown that he could be trusted to deal effectively with situations that were politically sensitive, such as the Irish Ambulance Corps, where a step in the wrong direction might have compromised Britain's position of neutrality between the combatants in the Franco-Prussian War. His investigations of gambling premises also delivered what his political masters wanted, though they would not have made him the most popular man in Britain. His relationship with the public, and with certain politicians, would also be tested in his next major case.

5

THE TICHBORNE CLAIMANT, THEFT AND FRAUD

1872-75

Poor old Roger Tichborne now,
Is on his trial again,
They will not rest contented,
They never will refrain;
From doing everything they can,
To strike the fatal blow.
If money can only do it now,
To prison he must go.

Anonymous[1]

Between March 1872 and April 1874, Clarke's life was dominated by the longest-running sensation of the Victorian age, the case of the Tichborne Claimant. This divided the British nation between those who enthusiastically supported a man who had returned from Australia to claim his inheritance, and those who considered his claims implausible and fraudulent. Matters were only resolved at great length, and at great cost, in the courts. To set Clarke's involvement into context, it is first necessary to provide some background information.[2]

The Tichborne Claimant

The Tichbornes were one of the oldest families in Hampshire, owning Tichborne House and its associated estate close to Alresford. On 5 January

1829, Roger Charles Doughty Tichborne was born in Paris, the first child of James Tichborne and his French wife Henriette. Roger's parents were far from compatible and he spent most of his early years in France, away from his father. He was educated in a French-speaking community dominated by a doting and over-attentive mother. At his father's insistence, Roger was sent to an English boarding school at the age of 15, but nonetheless only spoke English with a French accent. In 1848, Henriette purchased a commission for her son in the 6th Dragoon Guards, and he served for several years with his regiment, mainly in Ireland. When on leave, Roger stayed at Tichborne House and, after some time, developed a romantic attachment to his first cousin, Katherine Doughty, daughter of Sir Edward Doughty the ninth baronet. Katherine's parents were uncomfortable with the developing relationship and matters came to a head in February 1853 when Roger was forbidden to see Katherine by her father, although she managed to persuade him to sanction their marriage in three years' time on the understanding that she would be prepared to consider other potential suitors in the intervening period. Roger's reaction to this disappointment was to cash in his army commission and to travel to South America, arriving in Valparaiso, Chile, in June 1853. The continent was evolving as an increasingly important trade partner for British merchants, and also provided an array of animals and plants of interest to naturalists and to the hunting and shooting fraternity. In an apparently unrelated series of events, some three years previously a young cabin boy from Wapping, Arthur Orton, had also arrived at Valparaiso, had jumped ship there and spent time travelling in Chile before returning to Britain. In 1852, Arthur Orton immigrated to Australia.[3]

While in Chile, Roger Tichborne received news that his father had become the tenth baronet of Tichborne, following the death of Sir Edward Doughty. Roger was now next in line to inherit the title and the Tichborne estates but, for the moment, he continued his travels. In January 1854, he journeyed to Rio de Janiero via Buenos Aires, before deciding to seek a passage for Kingston, Jamaica, on board the *Bella*. The ship left harbour at Rio on 20 April 1854, and was never seen again. It was believed to have foundered in a storm with the loss of all hands and its only passenger, Roger Tichborne. On receiving the news, Henriette was distraught and refused to believe that Roger had perished. After receiving information some years later from an old sailor that crew members from a ship called the *Bella* had been heard of in Australia, she decided (after her husband's death in 1862) to place newspaper advertisements offering a reward for information on the whereabouts of her missing son. Nothing substantive was forthcoming, but Henriette then came across an advertisement placed by Arthur Cubitt, the Sydney-based owner of the 'Missing Friends Agency' and, with his help, her advertisement was circulated in the Australian press.[4]

Amongst those who read the advertisement in 1865 was the wife of William Gibbes, a lawyer in Wagga Wagga (a small town in New South Wales), who at the time was acting on behalf of a client, Tomas Castro, a butcher in the town who was in the process of being declared bankrupt. Mrs Gibbes had noticed that, despite his Spanish-sounding name, Castro spoke with an English accent and had also made passing references to a shipwreck and to some entitlement to property in England. Following discussion with his wife, Gibbes decided to speak to Castro about his identity. The outcome of their conversation was that Tomas Castro emerged into the limelight as the rediscovered 'Sir Roger Tichborne'. As he subsequently pursued his claims to the baronetcy and to the Tichborne estate he became universally known as the 'Tichborne Claimant'. The name he had used in Australia of 'Tomas Castro' he claimed to have adopted from a man he had met during his travels in Chile.[5]

Following correspondence with Henriette (by then the Dowager Lady Tichborne), and helped financially by her and Gibbes, the Claimant and his family set sail for England, eventually arriving on Christmas Day 1866. Though details were not to emerge until later, one of the first visits that the Claimant made shortly after arrival in London was to Wapping High Street, where he knocked at the door of a house that had been (but was no longer) the family home of the Ortons, and visited the Globe public house where, in conversation with the landlady and her mother (who felt she had recognised him), he denied being Arthur Orton. His next visit was to Alresford, near Tichborne House, where he stayed in the Swan public house under an assumed name, though he did tell the landlord that he was the long-lost Roger Tichborne but didn't wish the Tichborne family to know it until he had visited his mother. It was not until the 10 January 1867, in Paris, that the Claimant and Henriette came face to face; he was indisposed in bed, claiming seasickness as the cause but, despite his ailment, the Dowager Lady Tichborne immediately recognised her 'son'.[6]

The re-emergence of Sir Roger Tichborne was soon headline material in the national newspapers. Not surprisingly, after a period of thirteen years since Roger had sailed to South America, the Claimant was not recognised by all who had previously known him. Despite receiving Henriette's recognition, only one other member of the Tichborne family accepted his claim, though some friends of the family and former acquaintances, including the Guildford MP, Guildford Onslow, the Tichborne family doctor and the retired family solicitor, accepted him at face value, as did a number of family servants and former army colleagues. For some, the Claimant displayed knowledge of relevant events and of the Tichborne estate, which in their view could only have come from Roger Tichborne himself. For others, including most of the Tichborne family, the Claimant's physical appearance, the fact that he no longer had the ability to speak or write in his French native tongue and his lack of awareness of some key issues (including the contents of a sealed package that Roger had left behind at Tichborne House before leaving for South America) rendered him an implausible fraudster. Indeed, while the Roger Tichborne who had left England in 1853 had been lean, the individual who had returned in December 1866 was a hefty 18 stone, and continued to pile on the pounds over the coming years. There were also questions of how Roger Tichborne had reached Australia and why he had never bothered to contact his family until 1866. Though never satisfactorily dealing with the lack of contact, the Claimant explained that after the *Bella* had sunk, he and others had survived for several days in a lifeboat until they had been spotted by a passing ship, the *Osprey*, which had rescued the men and taken them to Melbourne.[7]

Over the following months and years, the Claimant and his supporters continued to build his case, while the Tichborne family and their agents sought evidence to contest his claims. In June 1867 the Claimant's solicitors initiated legal action to recover Sir Roger Tichborne's property and inheritance. Supporters provided some income but the legal process was painfully slow and Henriette, the Dowager Lady Tichborne, died in March 1868, removing the chance that she could provide her personal testimony in court. The case was further delayed by judicial permission in June 1868 for commissions to be dispatched to Chile and Australia to collect information from potential witnesses there; the idea also being that the Claimant himself and his legal team could travel and confront these witnesses. Although the Claimant travelled to Buenos Aires with his legal team, he chose not to travel with them to Chile, giving ill-health and possible threats to his life as reasons for his decision. On his return to London, his explanations did not satisfy his solicitor and many of his financial backers, who withdrew their support, effectively bankrupting him. New solicitors were appointed and they launched 'The Tichborne Bond' scheme, which raised sufficient money from his closest supporters and members of the public to provide the Claimant with funds to continue his case.

As early as March 1867, the Tichborne family had sent an agent to Australia to gather evidence on the background of 'Tomas Castro'. Several key witnesses were found, including one who recognised a photograph of the Claimant as someone she had known as 'Arthur Orton'; other witnesses claimed that 'Castro' had learnt his trade as a butcher in London, and another recalled that Orton had come from Wapping. The Tichborne family solicitors then hired Jonathan Whicher, Clarke's former Scotland Yard colleague who was now operating as a private detective. Whicher began making enquiries in Wapping, soon discovering that the Claimant had visited the area very shortly after his arrival in England in December 1866. Amongst other witnesses, Whicher located Arthur Orton's former sweetheart, Mary Loder, who identified the Claimant as Arthur Orton.[8]

The Claimant's case, by now a fully blown cause célèbre, finally came to court in 1871 as a civil action: Tichborne *v.* Lushington, at the Court of Common Pleas before a judge and jury. The 'Lushington' referred to was Colonel Franklin Lushington, the legal tenant of Tichborne House who, ironically, was a supporter of the Claimant's veracity from the knowledge that the Claimant had displayed when he had first visited the Tichborne estate. The Claimant's legal team consisted of William Ballantine and Hardinge Giffard. The opposing legal team was led by Solicitor General Sir John Coleridge and contained, amongst others, Henry Hawkins (later Lord Brampton). The critical issue in the case was whether the Claimant was indeed Sir Roger Tichborne or whether he was an impostor, previously known as Arthur Orton and Tomas (or Thomas) Castro. The Tichborne case lasted from 10 May 1871 to 6 March 1872. On the 102nd day, 4 March 1871, when the court had just learnt that Roger Tichborne had had a tattoo on his arm, while the Claimant did not, the jury foreman said that they did not need to hear further evidence. After legal discussion the judge decided that the jury's opinion represented a decision in favour of the Tichborne family, and that the Claimant had committed wilful and corrupt perjury during his examination. The judge then instructed the senior police officer present, Inspector Denning, to prosecute 'Thomas Castro', with bail of £10,000 being set. The Claimant was not in court at the time that proceedings concluded, and the police now needed to locate and arrest him. At this point, Denning called on his A Division colleagues, Superintendent Williamson and Chief Inspector George Clarke.[9]

Arrest and Trial of the Tichborne Claimant

1872–74

Inspector Eleazar Denning was a long-serving member of the executive branch of A Division, and had been the senior uniformed officer helping maintain order within and outside the courtroom during the Tichborne *v.* Lushington proceedings.[10] The Claimant was not difficult to track down as he had taken rooms at the Waterloo Hotel, and the three Scotland Yard officers arrived there during the evening of 6 March. Williamson read out the lengthy arrest warrant and the Claimant expressed surprise that he was being arrested in the name of Thomas Castro, a name which he refused to acknowledge. The charges included multiple charges of perjury: having falsely sworn that he was Roger Tichborne; that he had claimed to have seduced 'his' cousin Katherine, now married to Lord Radcliffe; and that he had also claimed not to be Arthur Orton.[11] An additional charge of forgery was later dropped.[12] The Claimant, described as calm and composed, was then taken in his brougham, accompanied by Williamson, to Newgate Prison; Clarke and Denning followed in a cab.[13] The Claimant had emerged as a popular hero during the civil trial, particularly amongst the working classes, and it was no surprise that a good-sized crowd had assembled at Newgate to greet him on arrival. Bail of £10,000 (equivalent to £460,000 today) was hard to find, and the Claimant remained in Newgate Prison until 26 April when securities were provided by supporters, including the MPs Guildford Onslow and George Whalley (the Liberal MP for Peterborough). Montagu Williams was on the team that acted for the Claimant in obtaining bail but not in the subsequent trial. In his reminiscences, Williams later commented: 'I always thank my stars for the escape that I had over the Tichborne case.'[14]

The Claimant's trial for perjury eventually started at the Court of the Queens Bench on 23 April 1873. Since the previous April, the Claimant and his supporters had been speaking at meetings round the country to maintain support and finance. In the process several of them, including the Claimant himself, Onslow and Whalley, had been charged and found guilty of contempt of court (for *sub judice* reasons), further enhancing the popular impression that the Claimant and his supporters were the oppressed victims in this saga.[15] The prosecution team for the Crown was led by Henry Hawkins, and, in view of the national importance of the case, three judges were appointed: Lord Chief Justice Cockburn being supported by two other distinguished judges, Justices Mellor and Lush. The Claimant's defence team was headed by Dr Edward Kenealy, an Irish-born lawyer who had previously been the counsel for the Fenian Ricard Burke, but had resigned from that position after the Clerkenwell explosion. Kenealy's performance did his client few favours:

> He was I think a conspicuous example of a clever man with all the external arts of the advocate, but hopelessly deficient in the most important quality of all – judgement ... He seems never to have understood that vituperation or even harsh treatment of a witness, unless it is clearly justified, does a case far more harm than good, and that it is most unwise to quarrel with the Judge unless you are confident that you have the sympathy of the jury with you.[16]

Both Clarke and Whicher were to find themselves facing the sharp edge of Kenealy's tongue during the trial's proceedings, though it did neither of them any significant harm.

Whicher's role in the case was clear-cut. He had been engaged to obtain evidence of the fraudulent nature of the Claimant and also attended the second trial in that capacity. Clarke's role is less well documented, but what is almost certain is that Clarke was regularly present throughout proceedings and worked behind the scenes with the Treasury Solicitors' office, helping to assess the accuracy of defence evidence presented in the second trial.[17] That he was a frequent attendee at the court (which was close to his home in Great College Street) is clear from the following extract from the *Bradford Observer's* atmospheric word sketch of court events:

> It is not so easy as it might be supposed to get a seat in Court for the Tichborne case, and a good look at Sir Roger. You must wind your way down to Westminster Hall, picking a dirty day for choice, and be at the great northern doors that open into Palace Yard by at least nine. They will be opened from within by about half-past. Then wedge yourself through, as if you were fighting your way into the pit of Drury Lane on Boxing night, wheel sharply to the right, and rush like a maniac up a flight of stone steps and against a heavy beetle-browed archway, over which is painted in big letters 'Queens Bench'. Plant yourselves resolutely against the double doors that here bar your way. They, too, will be opened at about a quarter to ten, and you have then only to race at full speed along a stone passage, to pass a set of swing doors, guarded jealously by tall constables of the A Division, then a second set similarly guarded, and so to find yourself in Court … I advise no one to attempt it whom cannot stand three-quarters an hour of very rough work indeed. For each seat in Court there are at least 50 combatants … An old gentleman who sits by you relieves the monotony … [the] cheery-looking inspector of police who stands by the door with his eye intently fixed on the defendant is Mr Denning, who is the nominated prosecutor, and that again, is Mr Whicher, and side-by-side with him is Inspector Clarke …[18]

As the trial progressed it became clear that one of Kenealy's strategies on behalf of his client was to undermine the credibility of the evidence assembled by Whicher.[19] The same was equally true for Clarke's involvement in the case. On 20 May 1873, Mrs Mina Jury gave evidence that the Claimant was Arthur Orton; information that came from her family's association with the Ortons, as her brother George had married one of Arthur Orton's sisters. In cross-examination, Kenealy asked her whether she knew Clarke. She replied, 'Yes, he is a detective'. Kenealy then followed this with a question asking how much money she had been promised to give evidence. The feisty Mrs Jury replied, 'I do not suppose you come here for nothing any more than me', a response that was greeted by cheers within the crowded courtroom.[20] On 27 May, while questioning a prosecution witness from Wapping who, like Mina Jury, had recognised the Claimant as Orton, Kenealy again sought to undermine the integrity of Whicher and Clarke, as he did repeatedly throughout the trial.[21]

By mid-August the prosecution had completed their evidence. It was now the turn of the defence to make their case. Between 8 and 17 October Kenealy introduced two new witnesses, relevant to events in Rio de Janeiro and to the Claimant's contention that he had been rescued after the sinking of the *Bella*. The first of these, Captain James Brown, claimed that he had been in Rio in 1854 working as a shipping clerk. He told the court that he had met a man called Roger Tichborne and, after drinking together, they had shared a room at Brown's lodgings where Brown had noted several physical marks on Tichborne's left side and on his arm, which the Claimant also possessed. He had also seen the *Osprey* in Rio harbour at that time. During cross-examination it emerged that some of the detail of Brown's time at Rio, such as the ships in port at that time, appeared to be false.[22] However, Brown's testimony was followed by sensational new evidence given by the second witness, Jean Luie.

Luie appeared in court on 14 October, presenting himself as the steward of the *Osprey*. He stated that the ship had called in to Rio in 1854 during a voyage from Staten Island, New York, to Melbourne. After leaving Rio in April 1854, Luie claimed that the *Osprey* had come across a sharp-sterned lifeboat containing six survivors from the *Bella*, four of whom were in a delirious condition. One young man, who remained delirious during the entire three-month voyage to Melbourne, had been looked after by Luie; his name was Roger and, because Luie had washed him regularly, he had noticed an olive-coloured mark above the young man's hip (a mark which the Claimant was also known to possess). Luie claimed that it was not until the summer of 1873, when he arrived in England, that he had heard about the Tichborne case. He had then made himself known to one of the Claimant's supporters, George Whalley, and had been introduced to the Claimant who he recognised, in physical appearance and voice, as the man he had looked after in 1854. The evidence given by Luie was a serious blow to the prosecution and, on 16 October, Henry Hawkins asked the court for further time to cross-examine Luie, as the witness had been sprung on him at very short notice. The Lord Chief Justice agreed to Hawkins' request.[23]

It is highly likely that the Treasury Solicitor's office called on Clarke, who had been present in court throughout Luie's appearance, to assist them in investigating aspects of Luie's evidence, as well as sending a barrister to America to investigate Luie's claims.[24] Clarke's familiarity with Staten Island harbour and the record-keeping there for ships arrivals and departures (from time spent in New York in 1864 prior to his arrest of Franz Müller) may have come in useful.

After Kenealy had concluded the defence evidence, Hawkins introduced several prosecution witnesses to give evidence in reply. Two of these, Captains Oates and Hoskins, had been in Rio at the time that Roger Tichborne was there and denied any knowledge of Captain Brown and several people that Brown had mentioned. Witnesses also indicated that the *Bella*'s lifeboats had been square-sterned, rather than sharp-sterned as described by Luie.[25]

On 31 October Hawkins sought, and obtained, a prolonged adjournment in the trial proceedings 'to enable him to adduce further evidence to contradict the witness Luie' and to allow sufficient time for witnesses to arrive from America. The trial did not recommence until 27 November.[26]

During the first two days after the adjournment several prosecution witnesses from America were called by Hawkins, and their evidence raised serious doubts about Luie's version of events. The *Osprey* had apparently not been at Staten Island when Luie had said, and the crew list of the *Osprey* did not have Luie's name on it.[27] But the real fireworks were saved for the end of the hearing on 28 November when the assistant Treasury Solicitor, Pollard, made a clumsy attempt to stop Luie leaving the court, apparently to enable a visitor in the court to make an identification of him. At about this time an office clerk had come forward to the police, having seen a photograph of Luie in a shop window; the clerk had recognised Luie as a man that he knew as 'Sorensen', who was believed to have committed a fraud in Britain earlier in the year.[28] On the following morning, in what *The Times* described as 'the most exciting day which has yet occurred in the course of the trial', Kenealy complained vigorously at the previous evening's events, which he described as a contempt of court and an attempt to poison the jury's minds against the witness Luie. He was to regret his actions, as they opened the door for the prosecution to produce new witnesses who declared that they knew Luie as 'Captain Sorensen', and that he had been in England in March 1873, several months before the date stated in his initial evidence.[29] As a result, Lord Chief Justice Cockburn held Luie for a potential perjury charge. Although Luie was granted bail, all the sureties were not forthcoming and he was taken to Holloway Prison.

By what precise route Clarke discovered Luie's true identity is unclear, but it proved not to be either 'Jean Luie' or 'Captain Sorensen'. Like so many members of the criminal fraternity, Luie had proved to be adept at the use of aliases in an attempt to hide his past. By 4 December, Clarke had identified that 'Luie' had been a resident of Chatham Prison, where he was known as 'John Lundgren' and had been serving a sentence of seven years' penal servitude until he had been released on ticket of leave on 25 March 1873.[30] By 8 December, Clarke had assembled a battery of identification witnesses who appeared at the trial of the Claimant. 'In anticipation of the revelations respecting the antecedents of the witness Jean Luie, the court was crowded to excess.'[31] The witnesses from Chatham Prison identified Luie as John Lundgren. A Bristol policeman identified him as Charles Lundgren (who had been arrested and sentenced to five years' penal servitude between 1862 and 1867) and some Bristol-based former employers of Luie identified him as Carl Lundgren. Much laughter was heard in court when it was learnt that Luie had been married to a woman who now called herself Mrs Hawkins, and that

her maiden name was Cockburn (actually Coulburn).[32] Later events demonstrated that Luie had also bigamously married a second wife in the name of
'John Smith', and had briefly been imprisoned for assaulting her.[33] Following
this evidence, the Claimant's defence team were given a day's adjournment
to consider their position. It was also decided to provide a medical examination of Luie and compare this with the medical records at Chatham Prison
of John Lundgren. When the two proved identical, the court formally committed Luie to prison on a charge of perjury. Clarke took Luie into custody
and also searched his lodgings, removing several letters and papers that were
later produced in court.[34] From that point, the proceedings in the trial of the
Tichborne Claimant and the trial of 'Jean Luie' became separate events but
remained intimately linked.

At the trial of the Claimant, Kenealy was presenting his closing summary
for the Claimant's defence and commented that no matter what crimes might
be proved against Luie, he would uphold Luie's evidence as true and that
no subsequent criminality could destroy its truth. When he also claimed that
Captain Brown's evidence in favour of the Claimant was also 'confirmed', the
jury burst into laughter.[35] Surely things couldn't get worse for Kenealy and
the Claimant? But they did, and Clarke had a large hand in it.

On Saturday 13 December 1873, Clarke transported Luie from Holloway
Prison to Bow Street Police Court for the first magistrate's hearing of the
charge of perjury against the prisoner. Luie, having forfeited his ticket-of-
leave licence, was then remanded in custody and taken by Clarke to the
Clerkenwell House of Detention. During these journeys to and from prison,
Luie apparently spoke freely to Clarke about his situation. Details of this con-
versation emerged at the next Bow Street hearing on 8 January 1874 when
Luie arrived at court manacled and close-shaven, as he had been moved to the
convict prison at Millbank to complete his previous penal servitude sentence.
Clarke was the principal witness, and the evidence of his conversations with
Luie was explosive:

> I took the prisoner from this court to the House of Detention on 13th
> December. I had some conversation with him. I had first some conversation
> with him in the cab from Holloway Prison. He asked me what he had better
> do in the matter. I said 'You are old enough to advise yourself'. He said noth-
> ing more particularly to me, but after leaving this court he said 'I wish you
> would advise me; you know more of the matter than I do'. I said 'I can't advise
> you'. He said 'I was first spoken to about the matter in the spring of the year at
> Brussels by Mr. Whalley who was stopping there with his daughter. I got into
> conversation with him and he said there was a trial pending in this country,
> which made him ashamed of his country, and seeing that I was a sailor he said
> he had never been able to find any of the crew of a shipwrecked vessel, which

it was important he should do. I said to him, I don't think that would be very difficult as I have been a sailor myself. But nothing was arranged particularly at this interview.' The prisoner further said 'I first went to Poets-corner [location of the Claimant's residence] about the 4th or 5th of July. I met a man there with something the matter with his eye.' The prisoner afterwards stated this was Baigent [Francis Baigent; old friend of the Tichborne family and a Claimant supporter]. Baigent asked him who he was, and he replied 'I am Jean Luie'. Baigent said 'I know all about it'. But nothing further was done that day. On Monday the 7th, Baigent said it was all arranged, and that he [The Claimant] knew he was coming. He [Luie] then continued, 'I showed my fingers to the little black fellow, Bogle [old family servant of the Tichborne's and a Claimant supporter], who ran into the inner room, I believe, to tell Sir Roger. Sir Roger [the Claimant] came out to me and said, if you are the man who saved me, your fingers are crooked.'

I afterwards saw the prisoner Luie the same day in the House of Detention by his own request and he then said. – 'If I thought they would not prosecute me I would tell all particulars'. I replied that I could make him no promise, but if he wished to make a statement I would rather he did it through the solicitors. Luie then said 'Very well, let them come on Monday'. This was on the Saturday. I left him then. On Monday, the 15th, I went with Mr Pollard [assistant Treasury Solicitor] to the House of Detention, and there saw the prisoner. The warder then said to him 'This is Mr Pollard and Mr Clarke, do you wish to see them?' Luie then led me to a corner of the room and said, 'I will not now. I have been advised to hold my tongue' … On the way here he said 'Since you last saw me I have had a visit from Captain Nicholson [nephew of George Whalley]. He brought me a letter from Mr. Whalley, saying that he could get me remanded from time to time, and that I should not go to the convict prison and that he had given £5 to Harding [Claimant's servant] to keep me … I should not have got into trouble had it not been for the folly of Dr Kenealy, who forced Mr Hawkins to call the rebutting evidence. It is not all my fault. I begged of them scores of times not to put me in the witness-box. Mr Onslow is a very violent man, and would not listen to me. He gave me a book of evidence given at the last trial, and marked the different passages in it which I had to learn at night time and had frequently to sit up all night. He told me about the brown mark on the side, and frequently made a drawing with his finger to show me the shape and size of it, and placed his hand on my side to show the position.' … The prisoner said 'that he never intended originally to give evidence.' He expected to have made some money without, but they forced him to do it, and he was never allowed out by himself. One or the other of them was always with him … He said 'I should have been put in the box earlier, only I could not learn my story correctly'.[36]

The response to Clarke's account of events, by supporters of the Claimant and Luie, was immediate. In a letter published in *The Times* on 12 January 1874, George Whalley, referred to the 'extraordinary statement of Detective Officer Clarke as to what Luie has, he alleges, confessed to him, and which, so far as I am concerned and also in other respects within my own knowledge is an absolute fiction'. Whalley then, displaying arrogance, folly or an ignorance of legal procedure (or probably a combination of all three), attended the next Bow Street hearing of Luie's case on 15 January and asked to address the court. This was refused and he was told to pass any relevant information to Luie's solicitor. Two days later, when Clarke was cross-examined, 'the small attorney's box was literally besieged by friends of the Claimant including Mr Whalley'.[37] Undeterred in his attempt to negate the effect of Clarke's evidence, Whalley then wrote further letters to the press including one published in the *Daily News* on 21 January which stated:

> As the statements of Detective Clarke of what Jean Luie has told him – though denied, as it seems by Luie himself – may materially prejudice the trial, I consider that I am called upon to state that nothing that has occurred in relation to this man [Luie] that affects my belief that his evidence as to the *Osprey* is substantially true.[38]

Hearing of these letters, Lord Chief Justice Cockburn demanded that Whalley should appear at the Court of Queens Bench to answer a charge of contempt of court. Whalley was fined £250, which he refused to pay and, as a consequence, he was arrested and removed to Holloway Prison.[39]

By now, the Claimant's trial was proceeding to its conclusion. Henry Hawkins made reference to the detectives during his final statement for the prosecution:

> But as to Whicher and Clarke; I quite agree that you may have detectives who grossly deceive you, and you may also have men of all ranks and classes who will invent a story to deceive you. But Whicher and Clarke belong to a highly respectable body of men, and I challenge any one to point to a single thing, from the time when this Defendant first set foot in England till now, that Whicher, or Clarke, or Mackenzie [the agent sent by the Tichborne family to Australia in 1867] has done that has not been done in the strict discharge of the duties they had to perform. They have simply been employed in the detection of crime, and because they have discharged their duty, are they to be branded as perjurers? I shall say no more about them. You have heard a great deal about them, but hard words do not injure anybody's character, and I say there has been no foundation for the attacks upon them.[40]

The trial finally ended on 28 February 1874. The jury took only thirty minutes to reach a guilty verdict on the counts of perjury, and to conclude that the Claimant was not Roger Charles Doughty Tichborne, that he did not seduce Miss Katherine Doughty (Lady Radcliffe), and that he was Arthur Orton. He was sentenced to two consecutive terms of seven years' penal servitude.[41]

Clarke's involvement had been highly significant in undermining aspects of the pro-Claimant evidence, particularly that of 'Luie', and he had also exposed the incompetence of some of the Claimant's supporters and legal team. Henry Hawkins commented later that:

> Luie's story of picking him up in the boat must have amused him [the Claimant] greatly. If he was amused at the ease with which fools can be humbugged, he must also have been astounded at the awful villainy of those who, perfect strangers to him, had perjured themselves for the sake of notoriety.[42]

Ultimately, the Claimant had only himself to blame for the end result of the charade that he had persisted with (and continued to persist with throughout most of his life). Nonetheless:

> Whatever crime the Claimant was guilty of, whatever view one may take of his moral obliquities, and of his mean, cruel and disgraceful lies told over a series of years to support a long-drawn-out fraud, we must not deny him some share of the virtue, which, according to Dr Johnson is the most important of all – courage.[43]

Clarke's responsibilities did not end when Arthur Orton was transferred to prison. He was still employed on the Luie perjury case which came to trial at the Old Bailey on 9 April 1874. A month prior to that, Clarke had also arrested Captain James Brown on a similar charge.[44] At his trial Luie was charged under his real name of Carl Peter Lundgren; it had now been established that he was a native of Gothenberg. He had been a ship's master and, in 1853, at the time that Luie had stated that he was on board the *Osprey*, he had been employed in Hull. Though Luie was legally represented at the beginning of his trial, his counsel had withdrawn by the time the defence were required to put their case, and his supporters were noticeable by their absence. There was one exception, the ever-present George Whalley, who offered himself as a witness for Luie, but was prevented by the judge from presenting his hearsay evidence. When summing up, the judge blamed Luie's so-called friends for his lack of representation, and criticised Whalley for 'tendering himself as a useless and futile witness'. The jury returned a unanimous 'guilty' verdict on the grounds of perjury. A charge of bigamy was not proceeded with, but was left on the books. Captain Brown was tried immediately after Luie, with a new jury, and also found guilty of perjury – the jury not finding it necessary to retire to consider their verdict. Luie was sentenced to seven years' penal servitude and Brown to five years.[45]

After the Claimant had been imprisoned, his popularity continued as his supporters transferred their efforts to securing his release. Others jumped on the bandwagon that the Claimant's cause provided for their own radical political purposes.[46] From 1875 onwards, there was a regular meeting at Hyde Park on Easter Monday in support of the Claimant's cause. For these events, large numbers of police were put on standby and detectives attended to observe proceedings.[47] By 1877 John de Morgan, a notorious radical of the time, had become involved in the Claimant's cause. De Morgan was an Irish nationalist who, after arriving in London, had achieved success in leading a movement against the enclosure of common lands and, in 1875 and 1876, had taken direct action against the attempted enclosure of part of Hackney Downs and Plumstead Common. De Morgan had given notice to the Home Office that he planned to organise a march on the Houses of Parliament on 17 April to present a petition in favour of the Claimant's release.[48] Clarke, as the Scotland Yard expert on Tichborne-related matters, was asked to assess the significance of the threat. On 1 February 1877 Clarke reported that de Morgan: '... appears to be so elated by the notoriety he gained in getting up meetings for the preservation of Commons and Open Spaces, and is so eager to keep up his name before the public that I believe there is nothing too rash or too ridiculous for him to attempt.'[49] On the 17 April, there was a significant police presence, but no disorder.

This was the last time that Clarke was involved in matters relating to the Claimant. The Claimant himself was released from Pentonville Prison on 11 October 1884 on ticket of leave, continuing to insist that he was Sir Roger Tichborne until 1895, by which time he was destitute and had accepted an offer from *The People* to publish his 'confession', later retracting it. He died on 1 April 1898, an appropriate date for a man who had managed to hoodwink thousands of people, including his 'mother'. About 5,000 people attended his funeral.[50]

Theft at Gray's Inn

While the Tichborne case and betting prosecutions were the dominant features in Clarke's working life between 1872 and 1875, these were far from being the only responsibilities that he had. In 1873, for example, His Imperial Majesty the Shah of Persia Nasir-al-Din paid his first visit to Britain, and wherever the shah went, Clarke was on his heels guarding his precious gems. Preparing for this important visit, Commissioner Henderson had assembled the latest statistics on the Metropolitan Police force, which had expanded considerably over the past few years. The shah was informed that 'the streets of London patrolled by the Police would reach, in a straight line from London to Teheran, and thence to Point de Galle in Ceylon, 6,612 miles'.[51] In 1873 the estimated population of London was almost 4 million; the numbers of police in the City and the Metropolitan areas were 785 and 9,927 (449 and 14 per square mile), respectively. There were about 1,400 horse-drawn omnibuses, 8,108 hackney carriages and 25,000 horses on the streets.[52] Indeed, since Clarke had joined the force in 1840 the population in London had doubled and the manpower levels in the Metropolitan Police had increased by a slightly greater factor (2.3 fold). Yet despite this overall increase and the 1869 enlargement of the detective department, Clarke was still expected to tackle a very diverse range of criminal investigations; including theft, murder in international waters, guarding visiting dignitaries and witness abductions. Clarke also provided cover for Superintendent Williamson when he was absent on business or leave.

On 7 May 1872 Clarke was brought in at a late stage to investigate a number of thefts from lawyers' offices at Gray's Inn Square. Three separate burglaries and thefts had occurred at night at the offices of Messrs Denton, Hall and Barker during the previous year and had remained unsolved. The earlier burglaries had involved the theft of money, but the most recent had involved several valuable parchment deeds. This theft had been followed by the receipt of a letter, signed 'C.M.H.', offering to return the stolen deeds if £7 was paid. The writer used the post office in Judd Street as a poste restante address for reply. In February 1872, the nearby legal firm of Messrs Stuart and Massey had discovered that a locked iron box containing important documents had also been stolen. Mr Massey had placed a £20 reward notice in the newspapers for the return of the box and its contents. He subsequently received a letter from 'W.H.' (replies to the Gray's Inn Road post office) asking if a reward would be given for the documents alone. After a prolonged correspondence, a £20 reward was paid using numbered banknotes, and the documents had been returned by a woman to the hall porter's office at Gray's Inn Square. The head porter, John Andrews, had been expecting such a delivery and called uniformed colleagues William Comley and P.C. David Edwards (posted at Gray's Inn) to follow the woman. Taking the lead, Edwards asked Comley to hold back and follow at a distance, while he went in front. However, Edwards soon reported that he had lost sight of the woman, and the two men returned empty handed. Meanwhile, a watch had been put on the two post offices and, on 3 May, an E Division detective saw a woman collect a letter addressed to 'C.M.H.' at Judd Street. She was arrested and taken to Bow Street Police Station where she was recognised as Sarah Edwards, the wife of P.C. Edwards.[53]

This apparent connection between the robberies and a serving officer drew a senior Scotland Yard officer on to the case. Clarke travelled to Bow Street Police Station on 9 May to collect P.C. Edwards and went from there to search the two rooms that Edwards and his wife rented. Finding examples of handwriting and stationery that corresponded with those in the letters sent to Gray's Inn by 'C.M.H.' and 'W.H.', Clarke arrested Edwards and his wife. Later in the day Clarke also travelled to Walworth and arrested Sarah Edwards' mother, Elizabeth Hopkins. In an identification parade, Hopkins was identified as the woman who had returned the stolen items by the Gray's Inn Square hall porter, Andrews, and his colleague Comley.[54] After several Bow Street Police Court hearings in front of the magistrate, Mr Flowers, the three prisoners were sent for trial at the Old Bailey. By then witnesses had been identified who could confirm that Sarah Edwards had collected mail for 'C.M.H' and 'W.H.' at the two post offices. The stationery used by 'C.M.H.' was also confirmed as the same as that found at Edwards' lodgings, both items having the same watermark.[55]

At the Old Bailey, the indictments were split between two trials. In the first, all three prisoners were indicted for stealing property from Mr Massey. Once again, Charles Chabot was called as a prosecution witness to confirm that Edwards' handwriting was the same as that found on the letters written by 'W.H.' and 'C.M.H.' In Edwards' case the handwriting evidence was almost the only direct evidence linking him to the theft of documents from Mr Massey. However, as the local and trusted police officer at Gray's Inn Square, he had easy access to the offices that had been burgled, and his recruitment of family members to assist in the crimes added additional circumstantial evidence. He was found 'guilty' as charged. His mother-in-law, Elizabeth Hopkins, was found guilty of receiving, and sentenced to twelve months' imprisonment. The jury acquitted Sarah Edwards on the advice of the common serjeant that 'it was to be presumed she was acting under the influence of her husband'. Thus the andro-centric Victorian viewpoint that a married woman had no independent thought or existence beyond that of her husband ensured that Sarah Edwards avoided prison. One assumes that, in the circumstances, she did not object too strongly to this. On the second indictment for stealing from Mr Hall, David Edwards decided to plead guilty and was sentenced to two consecutive terms of five years' penal servitude for the offences.[56]

In their later years, several senior lawyers of the mid-Victorian era became increasingly critical of handwriting experts, Montagu Williams being one of them: 'I never was much of a believer in experts in handwriting. I have examined and more frequently cross-examined, Chabot, Nethercliffe, and all the experts of the day, and have nearly always caught them tripping. In fact, in my opinion they are utterly unreliable.'[57] Nonetheless, Clarke had once more helped secure a conviction and he was 'highly commended by the Common Serjeant ... for the intelligence and judgement shewn'.[58]

The General Society for Assurance against Losses on the Turf

At 2 a.m. on the morning of 15 February 1874, four men armed with revolvers attempted to break into Stannard's Mill at Nayland near Colchester, only to find that the mill was occupied by Mr Stannard, his two sons and foreman. There was a skirmish, during which one of the burglars was arrested at the spot, but the others escaped and were believed to have headed to London. In view of the seriousness of the attempted armed robbery and the London connection, Scotland Yard was drawn into the enquiries; Inspector Pay of the detective department was given charge of the case.[59] During Pay's investigations, information emerged to suggest that the burglary had been planned at The Grapes, at Red Lion Square, Holborn. The youthful publican there, William Henry Walters, had been known to Clarke since 1871 as a betting man and he had already arrested Walters twice for betting offences.[60] Walters had previously offered to act as an informant and, with Williamson's agreement, Clarke sent Walters an unsigned letter to arrange a meeting. The letter was to assume great significance later:

> Westminster April 4, 1874
> Sir, I should be glad if you could make it convenient to call at my house from eight to nine p.m. this day. Very important. Don't show this or bring anyone with you. If you cannot come I will be at Charing Cross Station at twelve noon tomorrow.[61]

The lack of detail in the letter indicates that the two men had met previously, that Walters would have known who had sent the letter and knew where Clarke lived. In 1874 Walters proved to have no useful information on the Stannard's Mill case, but Clarke would soon be pursuing Walters for other reasons: a fraudulent betting scheme which went beyond anything that Clarke had encountered before.

Towards the end of 1874, large advertisements started appearing in national and provincial newspapers in Russia and several European countries for a 'General Society for Assurance against Losses on the Turf'. The advertisements promoted the idea that the way to make money on horse racing was to bet on runners at the smaller race meetings in Britain, and that investors would be guaranteed a high return if they placed their bets through the Society offices. The advertisements claimed that the system was guaranteed to beat the book and promised to pay £1,000 to anyone who could prove that an investor in the Society had incurred any loss. The advertisements also highlighted that the Society had a substantial number of influential and titled office holders as directors. Individuals were invited to send their remittances to named offices in London: William Osborne and Co., Sidney

Clarke and Co. and S. Montague and Co. However, the originators of the scheme had no intention of fulfilling their promises by returning any 'winnings', because the offices were a front for a fraudulent operation that relied on significant ignorance of the British horse-racing scene and hence was focused on gullible foreigners.

The Society started to receive money from overseas clients in October. During December, some of the 'directors' of the Society raised their concerns; they claimed to have known nothing of their apparent involvement in the scheme. By late December the post office had also become suspicious of the three offices, which were usually unmanned. As a consequence postal deliveries were stopped and the police were alerted. The *Daily Telegraph*, suspecting fraud, commented in a December editorial: '... is it not high time for the Metropolitan Police to make active enquiries respecting Mr William Osborne?'[62]

As the Scotland Yard expert on betting cases, Clarke was the obvious choice to lead the enquiries. How soon he was involved is not entirely clear, but by 11 February Clarke had arrested William Henry Walters, 24, and Edward Murray, 30 (aka Edwin Murray).[63] The initial charge on the arrest warrant was not for committing fraud, but for assaulting Daniel Portch, a friend of Captain Henry Berkeley who was one of the named directors of the Society. During several magistrate's hearings at Clerkenwell Police Court in February and March 1875, the link between the assault charge and the 'turf fraud' became clear.

As investigations got underway, it emerged that Captain Berkeley (a member of the betting club Tattersalls) and William Walters had been previously known to each other through horse-racing connections. Indeed, Walters had come to Berkeley's aid with a loan to help him recover his membership of Tattersalls after Berkeley had been thrown out for defaulting on bets. In all probability, Berkeley had knowingly agreed to participate as a director in the turf fraud, but had felt obliged to deny this (albeit belatedly) when the *Daily Telegraph* started to expose the fraud in December 1874. If so, what followed later was effectively a falling out between thieves.

Berkeley, after publicly denying that he had any involvement with the Society, had written to Walters seeking compensation for the 'injuries he had sustained' by his apparent association with the fraud. In response, Walters had sent Berkeley some letters which he had unwisely signed, in his own handwriting, as 'W. Osborne'. Berkeley decided to use these letters against Walters to try to negotiate financial compensation, suspecting that Walters must have raised substantial sums of money from the fraud. Certainly Walters was already living in style, having rented a large property, and was seen driving around in a carriage and pair; the carriage having armorial bearings and the motto *Qualis ab incepto* ('the same as from the beginning') – rather apt for a villain who started young and continued in the same vein.[64]

When attempts to obtain financial compensation from Walters had not achieved resolution, Berkeley, together with two of his friends, Manning and Portch, fixed a meeting with Walters through Walters' partner in crime, Murray. Murray took them to a property in the Holloway Road where they found Walters and a man named Kerr. Berkeley later gave an account in court of what followed:

> Portch began reading the letters, upon which Walters said those were the ones he had wanted. The door was then opened by Kerr, and four or five 'roughs' came in, from the upper part of the house and seized Portch, threw him down on his back on a sofa, and after seizing him by the throat, took the letters from him. Portch was a stout man and he became very black in the face. The door had been previously locked on the inside by Kerr. Witness [Berkeley] was pushed back in a chair. After the papers had been taken from Portch it was suggested that Walters should go out and see if they were those he had wanted. He went out and, returning, said they were 'all right'. Manning was seized and some papers were taken from him and thrown into the fire. Witness was searched by Murray who took from him a batch of documents and threw them into the fire. Before that he had asked witness if any of the papers referred to Walters. Witness said they did, and it was then Murray took them and threw them on the fire. One was a legal document, which witness, by the advice of his solicitor, had submitted to Mr. Montagu Williams. Then they made witness sit down and sign a paper which Walters had dictated. In that, witness was made to apologize for stating that he had any papers seized by Walters relating to betting transactions either in London or elsewhere. Immediately after witness had signed the document, the men who had come from upstairs, with Walters and Kerr, left the place. Walters had previously said that theirs 'was a very hot mob' and that he had done better jobs than that in America. Murray pulled out a handful of notes and said to witness he had better have a 'fiver'. Witness declined, upon which Manning signified to him that he had better take it. Witness afterwards went with Portch and Manning to consult his solicitor.[65]

These events had led to the arrest of Walters and Murray by Clarke, on a charge of assault. There were four other men named in the arrest warrant but Clarke had not been able to locate them.[66] One of these was Kerr who, though not yet arrested, soon had a representative in court watching the case on his behalf. By 2 March the Home Office was showing close interest and confirmed that the Treasury Solicitor would take over the prosecution which now included an additional charge of conspiracy to defraud.[67] After due deliberation, the Clerkenwell magistrate informed the court that he felt that the case for assault had not been 'made', probably because suspicion was attached to aspects of the evidence given by Berkeley and Portch. Anticipating these events, Clarke and a colleague were waiting outside the court when Walters and Murray were released, and the two men were re-arrested, this time on a warrant issued in the City charging them with defrauding persons in France, Germany and Russia.[68]

On Saturday 6 March, Clarke and Harry Poland were rushing from one courtroom to another. For part of the day they were at Lambeth Police Court presenting prosecution evidence in a betting house case in Southwark. The rest of the day was spent at the Mansion House, before the lord mayor. By now Scotland Yard had assembled evidence of the turf fraud against Walters and Murray which Clarke presented. At least four detectives from the detective department were working on the case, including those with foreign language skills such as George Greenham. Several witnesses were called who had let office accommodation to Walters and Murray, with one female witness stating that she thought that at least seven men had been involved to her knowledge. The prisoners were remanded without bail. At later hearings during March and April, Berkeley was again called to give evidence, as were other 'directors' who had been listed on the advertisements, all of whom denied knowledge of, or involvement in, the scheme. Representatives of the postal authorities and parcels agency who had delivered items to the suspect offices were also called. Fifty-eight packages that had been detained in December 1874 were opened in court; all were found to be from Russia and contained remittances of money. By the conclusion of the prosecution evidence the Treasury authorities estimated that upwards of £16,000 had been received from abroad in response to the advertisements.[69]

On 11 April Clarke received a visit at his home from a London-based accountant, Mr Frederick Andrews, who informed Clarke that a business colleague in Shanklin, Mr George Yonge, could give some information about the turf fraud. Waiving Andrews' offer of travel expenses, Clarke decided to travel down to see Yonge the following day, after first clearing the visit with Superintendent Williamson. Arriving in the evening, Clarke interviewed Yonge and also breakfasted with him the following day before returning to London. Yonge was a cripple, apparently from injuries received in a railway accident, and could only walk small distances with the aid of two sticks; though being of slight build he was frequently carried about by his manservant. During their discussions, Yonge admitted that he had been indirectly involved with Walters and Murray, having translated a prospectus for them but, as he was a cripple, he would appreciate Clarke's help to make it unnecessary for him to have to travel to court, adding that he could provide Clarke with £100 if that would help. Spurning the offer of money, Clarke returned to London and reported to Williamson that he had seen Yonge, who he regarded as an 'infernal scoundrel', but who might be able to help in the Walters and Murray case.[70]

On 27 April the lord mayor, having heard sufficient details from both the prosecution and the defence representatives, committed Walters and Murray for trial at the Old Bailey and they were remanded in custody. Much to Clarke's concern, on 5 May an application was made for bail, which was granted.[71] As Clarke had feared, when their trial date arrived there was no sign of Walters and Murray.[72] It later became known that they had absconded to America where their fraudulent skills and gangster-like propensities made sure that they could earn a living. Murray returned to Britain in 1876 and was soon back in prison. Precisely when Walters returned is not clear. However, when he did return he had added forgery to his other criminal attributes. As one of Clarke's colleagues was to comment in 1894:

> Probably there has been no criminal in the last quarter of a century who has given the detective police – not only those of the metropolitan force and of the City of London, but also those of the provinces and Ireland – so much work to do as the notorious forger, William Walters, the king of a very dangerous gang of 'cheque raisers' … The members of the 'mob' regarded him as a genius and looked up to him as their leader.[73]

Nonetheless, even criminal geniuses can get caught and Walters was tried at the Old Bailey in March 1880, pleading 'guilty' to forging and uttering a cheque and was sentenced to twenty years' penal servitude.[74]

What became apparent with hindsight was that Walters and Murray were essentially the 'front men' for the gang involved in the 1874 Society turf fraud case. There were at least two others behind the scenes who were responsible for the design and implementation of the fraudulent scheme. One was Kerr, who avoided arrest and who would emerge in another turf fraud in 1876 as 'William Kurr'. The other was Kurr's partner in this and other ventures, Mr G.H.Yonge, the physically crippled but mentally alert Isle of Wight resident who had been so keen to talk to Clarke, and whose real name was Harry Benson. Unknowingly, by walking through Mr Yonge's front door in Shanklin, Clarke had met his nemesis – but he was not to realise that for some time yet.

6

SUICIDE, ACCIDENTAL DEATH OR MURDER?

1876–77

When lovely woman stoops to folly
And finds her husband in the way,
What charm can soothe her melancholy
What art can turn him into clay?

The only means her aim to cover,
And save herself from prison locks.
And repossess her ancient lover
Are Burgundy and Mrs Cox!

Anonymous[1]

Clarke's first major case in 1876 did not appear until March. Before then he had held the fort at Scotland Yard while Superintendent Williamson was overseas, investigating mutiny and murder on the British merchant ship *Lennie*.[2] In February the hazards of the job were highlighted by the unexpected death of Detective Inspector Davey, who had been sent to Naples to extradite a prisoner. While in Italy, Davey had gone down 'with an attack of a malarious fever' but had insisted on returning to Britain with his prisoner. On arrival he had collapsed and died; his prisoner escaped but was later re-arrested by Detective Sergeant Greenham.[3] Davey's position was promptly filled by John Meiklejohn, who had previously been overlooked for promotion in 1875.[4] Meiklejohn's replacement as detective sergeant was German-born Charles von Tornow; 'blessed with a rare amount of courage, daring, and resourcefulness', he would work closely with Clarke during the next two years.[5]

A Curious Case of Conspiracy to Murder

At the end of March, Clarke's attention was alerted to some correspondence from the post office 'dead letter office' that contained intriguing references to death by poison. The letter, addressed to 'M.Q.', had been written on 23 February 1876 and was delivered to the Junction Road post office in Kentish Town. It had remained uncollected for a month and had been transferred to the dead letter office, where it was read by a clerk who reported its contents to his superiors. It had then been forwarded to Scotland Yard.

No one reading the lengthy letter could doubt that the writer (who signed himself 'W.K.V.', from 59 Euston Road) was responding to an individual who intended to poison someone with chloral in a manner that would not cause undue suspicion. Extracts included:

> I must say there is a risk of discovery with whatever mode of death … The peculiarity of my suggestion is that although the actual cause of death is found out, and that a narcotic, yet the verdict will be the most lenient – *viz.*, 'by misadventure,' or as it is phrased sometimes more specifically, 'the deceased was in the habit of taking chloral, and died from an overdose incautiously administered by himself' … The cases of the poisoners Pritchard and Palmer, both doctors, were ingenious, yet they were detected. They lived before these chloral times …[6]

Fortunately, the letter contained sufficient clues to discover the writer: 'I write this letter at 52, Brady-street, Bethnal-green where I am since yesterday doing full duty for Surgeon Mainwaring. We have a surgery here, and I have access to the drugs, bottles and labels …'[7]

When Clarke had located the surgeon, the author was identified from his handwriting as one of Mainwaring's locums, William Kingston Vance. However, the identity of the intended recipient was unknown. Here Clarke had some good luck, as the post office authorities told him that they had received a letter from a 'William Quarll' asking for poste restante letters addressed to 'M.Q.' and 'Q.W.' to be returned to Junction Road post office for collection. The authorities did as requested and Clarke arranged for the post office to be kept under surveillance. When a woman arrived to collect the letter she was followed to her lodgings in Camden Town by Detective Sergeants Manton and Robson. She was identified as Ellen Snee, a married woman whose husband, Frederick, was often overseas. By keeping Snee under surveillance, the connection was established between her and Vance when she purchased a money order in the name of 'W. Quarll', made payable to 'William K. Vance', at a Camden Town post office. By 21 April, Clarke had sufficient information to obtain warrants for the arrest of both Vance and Snee on charges of conspiracy to commit murder.

Vance was arrested at 59 Euston Road, and 'came quietly', obligingly providing Clarke with a copy of an advertisement in the *Daily Telegraph* which had prompted the correspondence: 'To medical men in need of money, or to students well up in chymistry [sic] and anatomy. A gentleman engaged in an interesting experiment is willing to give liberal remuneration for professional assistance, Q.W., Post office, Junction-road, Kentish-town, N.W.'[8] Having replied to the advertisement, Vance had then received a letter, which had later caused him to write his uncollected response. The letter read as follows:

> I am tired of my life. I could do a great deal of good to a person I am interested in by leaving the world just now, and, one way or another, I am resolved to do so, but if possible I should prefer not to wound the feelings of the person who will gain most by my death, by allowing it to be supposed voluntary. Besides, the most merciful verdict of a coroner's jury would be sufficient to invalidate my will. Now, although I have some acquaintance with medicine and chymistry [sic], I know of no drug or combination of drugs which would do this for me without risk of discovery. It is possible you may … I am willing to allow time for experiments, and have no objection to a personal interview. I will give any assurance of bona fides that may be thought necessary. I only request that this communication be considered strictly private.[9]

Vance had never met his curiously suicidal correspondent, and was indeed surprised to discover that a woman was involved. His lodgings were searched by Clarke and a large quantity of drugs were removed. These were sent for analysis to Dr Thomas Bond, lecturer on forensic medicine at Westminster Hospital (later to become known for his forensic association with the Jack the Ripper murders and as one of the first individuals to attempt offender profiling). The detectives then travelled to Camden Town to arrest Ellen Snee, who was 'a good deal alarmed and surprised'.[10]

Snee and Vance appeared at Bow Street Police Court on three occasions between 21 April and 5 May, during which time Clarke and his colleagues were adding to the evidence against the two prisoners. Five more letters relevant to the case were found at the Kentish Town post office; Snee's landlady described her as 'a person who was suffering', and one of the bottles removed from Vance's house was found to contain chloral, a drug that Thomas Bond confirmed would provide a death whose symptoms would appear similar to natural causes. At the end of the hearing on 5 May the prisoners were committed for trial at the Old Bailey, both being charged with conspiracy to murder Ellen Snee; Vance additionally being charged with unlawfully encouraging Snee to commit self-murder.[11] (It was only in 1961 that the Suicide Act decriminalised suicide in England and Wales.)

This strange case, which 'excited much interest', came to trial on 31 May. Clarke was the first prosecution witness to appear, adding to his previous evidence by stating that an impression of the name 'William Quarll' had been found in Ellen Snee's diary. Snee's landlady informed the court that her tenant often suffered much pain and had three cats, one of which had recently been sick, the implication being that it had been used as a 'guinea-pig' to evaluate the effect of chloral. Snee's defence counsel contended that an attempt to commit suicide was not an attempt to commit murder, but was overruled. The jury retired for thirty minutes before reaching a 'guilty' verdict, but recommended both prisoners to mercy – Vance on the basis of his previously good character, and Snee because of the frequent absence of her husband. Snee received six months' imprisonment and Vance eighteen months, though the judge showed some regret that the relevant statute did not allow him to sentence Vance to ten years' penal servitude.[12] By 1881 William Vance had resumed his medical career; however, Ellen Snee had already achieved her objective of an early death. She died on 18 April 1880, not from chloral poisoning, but from tuberculosis.

The Balham Mystery

Before Clarke had completed the Vance and Snee inquiry, another poisoning case landed on his desk on 1 May 1876. The coincidence of the two events occurring within weeks of one another was noted in *The Times* on 18 May: 'The investigations have been made by one of the most experienced detectives, Inspector G. Clarke, under Superintendent Williamson … they have come to the conclusion that there is no reason to suppose that there is any … connexion.'[13] The second case was nevertheless to become the public sensation of 1876.

On the morning of 21 April 1876 Charles Bravo, a barrister in his thirties, had died at his home, the Priory in Balham. It was an unexplained death (though as far as his wife was concerned, a suspected suicide). A post-mortem was undertaken and the inquest took place at the Priory. Neither the coroner nor Bravo's family or friends took any early action to notify the police or the press. However, the police were brought in when the inquest jury returned an open verdict on 28 April, 'that the deceased died from the effects of a poison – antimony – but we have not sufficient evidence under what circumstances it came into his body'.[14] Certain members of Bravo's family, including his stepfather Joseph Bravo and a work colleague Carlyle Willoughby, were convinced that Bravo was not a person likely to commit suicide. On Monday 1 May Willoughby contacted Scotland Yard, and the detective department was asked to investigate.[15] That same day Superintendent Williamson passed the case to Clarke. Though still busy with the Vance and Snee inquiry, Clarke immediately headed off to Balham ten days after Bravo had died, to a 'crime' scene that had not been preserved:

11 May 1876

I beg to report that as directed, assisted by Sergeant Andrews, I have made enquiry and find that Mr. Charles Delaney [sic] Turner took the name of Bravo on the marriage of his mother with a Mr. Bravo of 2 Palace Green Kensington several years ago. He was a barrister having chambers at 1 East Court, Temple and about October last formed the acquaintance of a Mrs. [Florence] Ricardo, widow of Captain Ricardo of the Guards, and residing at the Priory Balham and they were married on 7th December. They continued to reside at the Priory and are said to have lived very happily together.

On Tuesday the 18th ult. Mr. Bravo returned from the City in the afternoon, and went out riding. On his return between six and seven o/c he complained that the pony had run away with him, and said he felt shaken, and had a hot bath, and at ½ past 7 dined with Mrs. Bravo and her lady companion a Mrs. Cox.

The household consisted of Mrs. Hunt (cook), Mary Ann Keeber (housemaid), Elizabeth Evans (housemaid), Edward Smith (footman) and a butler named Rowe.

The dinner consisted of soup, filleted soles, roast lamb, and poached eggs on toast. Mr. Bravo only partook of the lamb and eggs, and drank 3 or 4 glasses of Burgundy. Both ladies partook of the lamb, and Mrs Cox of the poached eggs, but neither of them drank any of the Burgundy. Dinner was finished about ½ past 8 and they all retired to a room called the 'Morning Room' where they remained till shortly before nine, when at Mr. Bravo's request, Mrs. Bravo retired to her bedroom, she having been somewhat unwell, and they wished each other 'good night'. Mrs. Cox accompanied her.

Mr. Bravo remained in the morning room till about ¼ past 9, when he retired to his bedroom (separate from Mrs. Bravo's). Shortly after he had gone upstairs he called to the housemaid to bring him some hot water, and before getting it she told Mrs. Cox that he was ill and what he wanted. On her return with the hot water she found Mrs. Cox in his room, who at once told her to get some mustard, which she did, some of which was given Mr. Bravo to drink, and his hands and feet were placed in mustard and water. He became very sick and Mrs. Cox sent for Dr. Moore of Balham, and Dr. Harrison of Streatham Hill, but before their arrival he had become unconscious. Dr. Moore arrived about ½ past 10 and was quickly followed by Dr. Harrison. By this time Mrs. Bravo had become aware of her husband's illness, and she sent for Dr. Royes Bell of 44 Harley Street, Cavendish Square (a cousin of Mr. Bravo's) at the request of Drs. Harrison and Moore. He arrived about ½ past 2 a.m. bringing with him

Dr. Johnson of No. 11 Saville Row, and it was shortly after this that Mrs. Cox communicated to Drs. Johnson and Bell that Mr. Bravo had told her he had taken poison. Strong measures were then used and he became conscious about ½ past 4 and continued so during the two following days. On Wednesday afternoon he dictated his will which was written by Dr. Bell, in which he devised <u>everything</u> to his wife, and which was attested by Rowe the butler.

On Thursday morning he became worse and Sir William Gull [Physician to Queen Victoria] was sent for who arrived in the afternoon. He remained two or three hours in consultation with Drs. Johnson and Bell.

Mr. Bravo died at ½ past 5 on Friday morning the 21st ult.; a post-mortem examination was made by Dr. Payne of 6 Saville Row and the stomach and vomit analyzed by Professor Redwood of the Pharmaceutical Hall, Bloomsbury Square, who found the whole to contain about 140 grains of Antimony of which Mr. Bravo undoubtedly died.

An inquest was held on the body on Tuesday 25th ult. by Mr. Carter, the Coroner, and adjourned to Friday 28th ult., and after the several witnesses had been examined the Jury returned a verdict, that the deceased died of Antimony, but by whom administered there was no evidence to show. The body was buried at Norwood Cemetery on Saturday the 29th ult..

The butler – Rowe – states that on the Tuesday in question he brought a bottle of Burgundy from the cellar (of which he had the key) and decanted it, leaving it on the sideboard in the dining room until it was required for dinner; he waited at table during dinner, and Mr. Bravo took three or four glasses of Burgundy and the ladies took sherry. Mr. Bravo seemed in his usual spirits during dinner, and all passed off in the most pleasant way. Shortly after dinner he had occasion to go to the morning room to speak to Mr. Bravo about a letter and he then appeared to be in pleasant conversation with the two ladies, and he saw nothing more of Mr. Bravo until he was summoned to his bedroom by the housemaid Keeber. He says it was a large bottle of Burgundy that he decanted, and that not consumed by Mr. Bravo was left in the decanter on the sideboard in the dining room and he believes it was drunk by the medical gentlemen during the night but of this he is not at all sure; he decanted another bottle in the same decanter on the Wednesday and this fact is confirmed by his cellar book.

Mrs. Cox states that … After dinner they retired to the morning room and remained in pleasant conversation until Mrs. Bravo and herself withdrew to the bedroom. In about half an hour Mr. Bravo came in and bid his wife good night and at this time he did not appear to be ill. About a quarter of an hour after this, the housemaid Keeber made a communication to her as stated and in consequence she went to his room. He then appeared ill and said 'I have taken poison don't tell Florence', meaning his wife … Dr. Moore arrived first and was shortly followed by Dr. Harrison but she said nothing to these gentlemen about Mr. Bravo having taken poison until after the arrival of Drs. Johnson and Bell and she accounts for this by saying she hoped he would get better and that no one would know anything about it. She continued to attend upon him until his death.

On Thursday after the arrival of Sir William Gull, she was in the room alone with Mr. Bravo, when he said 'why did you tell anyone I had poisoned myself, does Flo know?' On the Thursday afternoon she went to Dr. Gully who resides near, at the request of Mrs Bravo to ask his advice. He advised mustard poultice on the back, cold bandage to the belly, and a mild dose of Arsenicum.

Mrs. Cox is a widow with three children, and formerly resided at Jamaica, where she knew Mr. Bravo Senior [Joseph Bravo] and has been friendly with him up to the present time. She states that there was no Antimony in the house to her knowledge and believes that he took it himself.

I saw Mrs. [Florence] Bravo at 38 Brunswick Terrace, Brighton on Tuesday 9th inst.; she states that on the Tuesday in question she saw nothing unusual in the manner of Mr. Bravo, either at dinner or when he came into her room to bid her good night. There was no Antimony in the house to her knowledge, and she cannot account for the possession of it by Mr. Bravo or any other person. He was much beloved by the servants and everyone about him, and she is not aware that he had a single enemy. She does not suspect any person and expresses her strong belief that he committed suicide from the fact that he was much pressed for money, by a woman he formerly kept, and by whom he had a child, but she declares she does not know her name and address.

She says that occasionally he was excitable and generally quick-tempered. About three weeks before this event she (Mrs Bravo) complained of his mother interfering in their domestic affairs; he then struck her and threatened to cut his throat, which she prevented him from doing, and that on the day in question he received an angry letter from his father respecting money matters, and this seemed to excite him very much. She also says that he had no private means of his own and that she had a fortune of £3,500 a year. She expressed her disagreement with the verdict of the Coroner's Jury and thinks it ought to be one of '*Felo de se*' [suicide]. She appears to have a great aversion to his family especially his mother. I was shown his diary and cheque book but they throw no light on the matter.

I may here add that from subsequent inquiries I find there is no foundation to her statement as to his being pressed for money or that there was anything in his father's letter to cause him any uneasiness, and there is nothing to account for his being in a state of mind to commit suicide.

She further states that on the Thursday evening after the Doctors had said there was no hope of her husband getting better she sent her companion to Dr. Gully of Crewell Lodge (close by), an old friend, and in whose skill she had great faith, and that he advised, as stated by Mrs. Cox, and that she had not spoken to or had any communication with Dr. Gully since her marriage. She also says that prior to her marriage Mr. Bravo told her he had been living with a woman, and on the night before his death requested her to look after the child.

Mr. [William] Campbell, Mrs Bravo's brother, now residing at Buscot, Berks., says that he arrived accompanied by his mother, on Thursday afternoon, and in the evening after Sir William Gull had left Mr. Bravo's bedroom he went in, (having been on the most intimate terms with Mr Bravo) when he (Mr. B.) said 'Willy, old fellow, kiss me. I have told Sir William I have taken laudanum but he don't believe me. I have told him the truth.' And that later in the evening he (Mr. Campbell) had a conversation with Mr. Bravo Senior when he said he believed his son had taken the poison himself. This last sentence is denied by Mr. Bravo Senior.

I have seen Sir William Gull and attach a copy of his letter to Lord Francis Hervey as to what took place. Sir William says he has nothing to add to that except that it would be impossible for any person to have sat down to dinner with that quantity of poison in his stomach, and that he must have taken it during dinner or very shortly afterwards. Dr. Johnson confirms Sir William in every particular, but adds that after the questions put by Sir William [to Charles Bravo, asking what he had taken] he (Dr. Johnson) added 'do consider that some person may be suspected after your death of having poisoned you', to which he replied 'I am aware of that. I can tell you nothing more. I have told you the truth.'

Dr. Bell states that he is a cousin of the deceased and was with him most of the time after his arrival till his death, and from the conversation that he had with him, he appeared to be totally unconscious of having taken any poison other than laudanum. He adds that when Mrs. Cox informed him that Mr. Bravo had admitted taking poison he felt utterly astonished that she had not told Drs. Moore and Harrison on their arrival as she did not do.

I may here add that had she done so and active measures had been adopted to take it from him his life might have been saved (and give this as the opinion of the medical gentlemen with whom I have had conversation).

Drs. Moore and Harrison have nothing to state beyond being called to attend when they found the deceased unconscious, in which state he remained until after the arrival of Drs. Johnson and Bell.

I yesterday saw Dr. Gully at his residence Crewell Lodge, Balham. He is about 68 years of age and states that he has known Mrs. Bravo and her family for many years but had become more intimate with her after the death of her first husband Captain Ricardo. He travelled with her on the continent – resided near her at Streatham and was a constant visitor at her house. He was opposed to her marriage with Mr. Bravo after so short an acquaintance, but when it was decided upon he discontinued his visits and has not spoken to her since last October but shortly before her marriage he wrote to wish her every happiness. In the early part of April he met Mrs Cox at Balham Railway Station and inquired after the welfare of Mrs. and Mr. Bravo, and he then learnt from her generally that Mrs. Bravo was somewhat unhappy in consequence of the interference with their domestic affairs of Mr. Bravo's mother.

He again met Mrs. Cox at the same station on 12th April and rode with her to Victoria Station, where Mr. and Mrs. Bravo were again the subject of conversation but he does not remember anything particular being said.

On the morning of Wednesday 19th April Mrs Cox called upon him and informed him of Mr. Bravo's illness and after enquiring the symptoms he advised the mustard poultices, cold bandage, and the mild dose of Arsenicum as has been stated. He further says that the unconscious state of Mr. Bravo would not be produced by poisoning by antimony and could only have been produced by a narcotic such as chloroform or laudanum.

I would here draw attention to the fact that Dr. Gully's statement as to the visit of Mrs. Cox on Wednesday morning is a direct contradiction of Mrs. Bravo's and Mrs. Cox (*viz*) that it did not take place until Thursday evening after the medical gentlemen had said there was no hope of his getting any better.

Dr. Gully is a Hydropath and for many years has had an establishment at Malvern but has now retired.

I have to add that during the enquiry I find that Mrs. Bravo and her family hold very strong opinion that Mr. Bravo committed suicide and appear most anxious that this should be shewn but can give me no facts to support these opinions other than those already stated. Should he have committed suicide he must have taken the poison after Mrs. Bravo and Mrs. Cox left the morning room at about 9 o'clock but nothing has been found either in the morning room or bedroom containing poison.

This fact may be accounted for by the confusion which prevailed during the early part of Tuesday night when glasses etc. would be used probably several times and no particular search was made until after the communication made by Mrs. Cox. On the other hand Mr. Bravo's friends and acquaintances entertain equally strong opinions that he did not commit suicide and support their opinion by saying that he had nothing to cause him the slightest uneasiness, that he was of a cheerful disposition and in no way pressed for money and that he was a most truthful and honourable gentleman and would certainly not have denied or equivocated in any way had he taken the poison himself, and they strongly suspect that the poison was administered in the wine he had for dinner.

I wish to particularly call attention to the butler's statement as to his having brought the wine from the cellar and decanted it that afternoon and leaving it on the side board where what remained after dinner was again placed and he is unable to say what became of it; further, his belief is that it was consumed by the medical gentlemen during the Tuesday night. I have questioned each medical gentleman upon this point and they state most emphatically that they did not drink any Burgundy on Tuesday night and I am unable to gather what became of it.

Enquiries are still being continued to ascertain where the poison was purchased and other particulars and a further report will be submitted.[16]

The death of Charles Bravo was indeed a mystery, although the cause of death appeared clear-cut – he had swallowed poison. However, the means by which it had been administered was not known. Antimony is a corrosive poison quite different in its effect and mode of action from the narcotic laudanum, the only 'medicine' which Bravo had admitted taking in a small quantity to ease toothache. No evidence of the source of the antimony that had killed Bravo had been found at the house. It could not have been in the food at dinner as the dishes were shared with others who showed no signs of poisoning. The burgundy drunk by Bravo at dinner could have been a vehicle for the poison; however, the wine that remained undrunk had disappeared. According to the butler it could have been finished by the visiting doctors but they had denied that they had consumed any. Even if they (or the servants) had drunk some burgundy, no one else amongst the household members or visitors had shown signs of antimony poisoning.

In terms of motive, there was scope for further investigation. There were strong differences of opinion on whether or not Bravo was likely to have committed suicide. His wife and her companion, Mrs Cox, expressed the view that suicide was the most likely cause of death, while his friends held a contrary view. Mrs Cox told Clarke that Bravo had declared to her that he had taken poison and had asked her not to tell his wife, but she also had not told the doctors of this immediately upon their arrival. Though the recently married couple had created the perception that they were living happily together, Florence Bravo had told Clarke that her husband was excitable, had hit her and had threatened to cut his own throat. In addition, Clarke had heard sufficient testimony from Florence Bravo for him to conclude that she did not get on with her husband's mother. Clarke had discounted her suggestion that Charles Bravo was pressed for money. Nonetheless, Florence Bravo had been insistent that her husband should receive the best medical treatment and had been personally responsible for calling out several of the doctors, including Sir William Gull, a friend of her father's. Overall, Clarke's report suggests that he had reservations about the information relayed by both Mrs Cox and Florence Bravo. His enquiries had also prompted him to visit Dr James Gully, a well known and respected Victorian proponent of the medical techniques of hydrotherapy and homeopathy, an intimate acquaintance of Florence Bravo. Indeed more would emerge later about the extent of the 'intimacy'.

The delay between the evening of 18 April, when Bravo first became ill, and 1 May undoubtedly made Clarke's attempts to locate the source of the antimony poison much more difficult. Having found no evidence at the house itself, a Metropolitan Police 'Special Enquiry' was sent out to all divisions on 10 May, asking for urgent enquiries to be made at all chemists and druggists who might have sold a relatively large quantity of antimony on 18 April or shortly before; however, no substantive information was obtained.[17] The first newspaper report of Bravo's death and the inquest verdict only appeared on 9 May 1876, though the paucity of news on the case was soon to change dramatically.[18]

On 24 May Clarke provided his second report, belatedly mentioning that on his first visit to the Priory he had searched the house and gardens and had sent away any suspicious bottles and their contents for chemical analysis. Clarke also reported interviews with George Younger, a helper in the stables, who had prepared the cob that Charles Bravo had ridden on 18 April. George Griffiths, the former coachman at the Priory, denied that he had overheard an conversation between Florence Ricardo and Dr Gully in which Gully had apparently said, concerning her then-impending marriage to Charles Bravo, 'if you do marry him he won't live long'. Clarke's second report continued:

> I would mention that the wildest rumours are afloat in the neighbourhood of Balham respecting this matter, which no doubt arise from the mysterious nature of the occurrence. I have made enquiry respecting most of them but they afford no information.
>
> A number of letters have been received (many of them anonymous) suggesting that the poison was administered to Mr. Bravo by Mrs. Bravo or Mrs. Cox, or both, and supplied by Dr. Gully for the purpose of getting rid of him to enable Mrs Bravo and Dr. Gully to get married, but after careful enquiry I can find no evidence to support these suggestions. Dr Gully is a married man but living apart from his wife. These suggestions are proffered through the close intimacy known to exist between Dr. Gully and Mrs. Bravo during her widowhood; they are known to have travelled together on the continent, where they stayed at the same Hotels, and when at Streatham and Balham, he had a key of her premises, and their conduct, altogether, was the cause of a deal of scandal, and they were treated very coolly by the other residents.
>
> I have again seen Dr. Gully, and he solemnly declares that he has never seen Mrs. Bravo, or held any communication with her since her marriage, and has only seen Mrs. Cox on the two occasions mentioned in my former report, and after careful enquiry of the servants and neighbours, I cannot find that he has done so.
>
> I beg respectfully to again draw attention to what took place on the evening of the 18th ult. They having commenced dinner at half past seven, it may reasonably be assumed that the greater part of the wine was drunk by a quarter

past eight. The sickness did not occur until about a quarter to ten – certainly not before half past nine – and it is the opinion of many medical Gentlemen that if the poison was taken in the wine, during dinner, it must have shewn itself before that time. Some are of opinion that if taken on a full stomach, it might not have shewn itself before, but all say that an hour and half is quite an outside time, and that it generally operates in about fifteen or twenty minutes.

I cannot ascertain that he took anything after dinner until he entered his bedroom ... indeed the evidence of the servants shew that he did not – and if this can be relied upon (and I believe it) he must have taken the poison after he retired to his room, but whether it was with his own knowledge, or whether placed there secretly by some other person, I refrain from giving an opinion. The poison could only have been placed there, by some other person, in the water bottle or glass upon the chance of his drinking it, and I would here remark upon the behaviour of Mr. Bravo after he was seized with illness. He first calls for hot water, which would indicate a knowledge that he had taken poison, and during his two day's illness I cannot find that he expressed any surprise as to it, or asked any question how it could have been brought about. He said he had taken laudanum, but I cannot find that he had done so – it could only have been a very small quantity – and I cannot but believe that he knew laudanum was not causing his illness. His friends are still strongly of opinion that he did not commit suicide, and aver that he had no cause to induce him to do so, but in making these enquiries, it appears to me that his marriage was not altogether a happy one, although it does not appear that he complained.

Both Mrs. Bravo and Mrs. Cox are much given to drink and Mrs. Bravo admits to me, that on several occasions when he attempted to make any change in their domestic arrangements, she reminded him that she found the money and does not appear to have had that sympathy and love for him that he might have expected, and she certainly shews no grief at his death.[19]

Clarke's investigations had not yet proved successful in identifying the source of the poison. Instead, he had focused his attention on the time at which Bravo had ingested the poison and the likelihood that he had swallowed it in his bedroom rather than at the dinner table. In addition, Bravo also appeared to be well aware that he had taken a poisonous substance and was likely to die. Clarke was beginning to give some greater credence (than in his first report) to the possibility that Bravo may have poisoned himself but he nonetheless continued to consider all options.

On 17 May the Home Office, noting the increasing public interest in the case and the strong views of Joseph Bravo and others, had directed the solicitor to the Treasury to take charge of the enquiry. At 11.15 a.m. on 18 May, Clarke had visited the Treasury to receive his instructions.[20] On the same day *The Times* commented that the first inquest had been procedurally unsatisfactory and that a further inquest was needed. The *Daily Telegraph* had also initiated a campaign in favour of a new inquest. The Home Secretary, Richard Cross, was questioned in the House of Commons about the situation. He replied:

> So far as the inquest and the Coroner's verdict are concerned, the House knows that I have no power over the Coroner. All I can say is that, from the facts I have stated, I, for one, am entirely dissatisfied with the way in which the inquest was carried on; and after much consideration I have thought it best to place the whole of the papers in the hands of the Law Officers of the Crown who will advise me … whether any and what further steps ought to be taken.[21]

On 26 June 1876 at the Court of Queens Bench, the coroner, Mr W. Carter, was felt to have performed his duties in a perfunctory and unsatisfactory manner and a panel of judges, including Lord Chief Justice Cockburn, quashed the verdict of the first inquest and confirmed that a second inquest with a new jury would be required.[22] This eventually started on 22 July 1876.

Still pursuing enquiries, on 29 May, Clarke was told that a substantial quantity of antimony, in the form of tartar emetic, had been sold in the middle of April in Abingdon, some 15 miles from the family estate of the Campbells (the parents of Florence Bravo), at Buscot. Detective Sergeant Walter Andrews was sent to Abingdon to investigate, but found no link with the death of Charles Bravo and concluded that the statement had been made with a view to obtain a £500 reward that had been offered by Joseph Bravo for information leading to the identification of the source of the antimony that had poisoned his stepson.[23]

On 31 May Clarke was instructed by the solicitor to the Treasury to provide more detail of what Mrs Cox was doing on 18 April (the day of the poisoning), to enquire further about the fate of the missing burgundy bottles and to provide more information on a meeting that Clarke had had with a Dr Dill in Brighton (who had been a medical adviser and confidant to Florence Bravo).[24] Clarke reported back on 5 June confirming that, on 18 April, Mrs Cox had travelled to Worthing to rent a property on behalf of Mrs Bravo, who was convalescing from a miscarriage that had occurred earlier in April. Mrs Cox had returned from Worthing the same day, just in time for dinner. However, during his latest interview with Mrs Cox, she had been much more revealing about the relationship between Florence and Charles Bravo:

> Mrs. Cox also states that on the night of the 18th before Mr. Bravo retired to his room, he came into his wife's room and said in French 'You have drunk one bottle of wine today; I hoped that would be sufficient but you have sent for another'. Mrs. Bravo made no answer and he seemed very much annoyed, and

went to his room. He had passed the housemaid (Keeber) on the stairs with a bottle of wine and which she had fetched from the cellaret in the dining room by the directions of Mrs. Bravo.

Mary Ann Keeber further states that when she saw Mr. Bravo on the stairs (as mentioned in her previous statement) she was then taking a bottle of sherry to her mistress.

Mrs. Cox also states that on their way to London that morning [18 April] Mr. and Mrs. Bravo had some unpleasant words and Mr. Bravo ordered the Coachman to turn back, but in a few minutes was prevailed on by his wife to continue the journey, but he said 'you will see what I will do when I get home'. She only knows this from what Mrs. Bravo has told her.

Edward Smith (Footman) states that the carriage was turned round and went a short distance towards home, when they were a little on the London side of Clapham Common but he thought it was owing to the weather as it came on to snow. The carriage was open when they started but at this time he closed it. The Coachman (Parton) says he does not remember having turned round on that occasion.

Mrs. [Cox] further states that on Good Friday [14 April], Mr. and Mrs. Bravo had a desperate quarrel; he said he despised himself for having married her and would not live with her but leave the house at once. Mrs. Cox followed him to his room and begged of him to consider his wife's feelings, when he said 'She can go to Dr. Gully'.

She also says that on one evening (previous to the Good Friday) he did actually leave the house during a quarrel but she (Mrs. Cox) followed him and prevailed on him to return, and that they frequently quarrelled owing to Mrs. Bravo giving way to drink and (as he thought) extravagance; he was very much opposed to going to Worthing on these grounds.

She states as her reason for not mentioning this to me on my other visits, that she was anxious not to expose the unpleasantness between them, as at times they appeared very affectionate to each other.[25]

Clarke then described Mrs Cox's background and how she had become acquainted with, and employed by, Florence Bravo, before moving on to report on the other tasks given to him by the Treasury, namely Dr Dill, and the wine bottles:

I also again saw Dr Dill who states that the communication made to him by Mrs. Bravo was after the death of her husband, when she said he was very persistent in that line of conduct. He further states that Mr. Bravo called upon him after his marriage and bitterly complained of his wife's drinking propensity and begged that he would see her and endeavour to pursuade her to refrain from it, as he knew he had great influence over her. Dr. Dill promised to do this and said he knew she drank a great deal more than was good for her, and should be stopped. He said that he had spoken to her about this and her behaviour with Dr. Gully, at the request of Mr. Campbell, her father, last autumn, before her marriage, and that on Saturday last she was in a most excited state and for the time had lost her reason, partly arising from drink and excitement consequent upon this enquiry.

On enquiry at Messrs. Todd Heatly's, I am informed that the wine was ordered on the 27th April by Mrs. Cox and the order was executed the same day. The wine was taken by Thomas Horley who states that he brought back two dozen bottles – sherry and claret, but believes there were no Burgundy bottles with them. On his return they were put in the cellar with thousands of others and it is now impossible to find them.[26]

These interviews added no fresh light on the key aspects of the case: the source of the poison or the manner in which it might have been administered. In this regard the police investigations got no further. Suicide, murder or even accidental death therefore remained possibilities, as there was no forensic evidence that pointed specifically to any one of these options. The chance of tracing any missing burgundy bottles that might have contained residues of any antimony-contaminated wine had now finally disappeared too. However, the information gleaned from Mrs Cox (if accurate) suggested that, after only four months, the Bravos' marriage was far from happy. Indeed, her information suggested that the deteriorating relationship between Florence and Charles Bravo could have reached a point where either partner might contemplate suicide or murder. What is not mentioned in Clarke's reports, but did emerge at the second inquest, was that Mrs Cox might have her own motive to murder Charles Bravo, as Bravo had expressed the view that Florence no longer needed a female companion now that she had a husband and Mrs Cox's employment at the Priory was therefore under threat.

Clarke's report is also intriguing in its reference to his conversation with Dr Dill, and the phrase: 'he [Charles Bravo] was very persistent in that line of conduct.' The precise context of that phrase has been variously interpreted by different commentators to have been a reference either to the possibility that Bravo had persisted with sexual intercourse despite having a venereal disease (of which no confirmatory evidence was given by post-mortem evidence); or that he regularly sodomised his wife; or that he was suspected of adding low doses of antimony to her wine and sherry to induce vomiting as a means of discouraging her from drinking.[27] This matter was not resolved, as Dr Dill was not called to attend the second inquest, presumably because of issues of doctor-patient confidentiality.

By now the case was proving fascinating to the British press and public; with a dramatic 'cast' consisting of a beautiful widow (Florence), a former and much older lover (Dr Gully), a mysterious ladies' companion (Mrs Cox) and a husband who, prior to his marriage, had maintained another woman and fathered her child (Charles Bravo). As the second inquest got underway at the Bedford Hotel, Balham, the 'disgusting public exhibition', as *The Times* was later to call it, was about to start. For more than a month, public attention was wholly absorbed in the proceedings.[28]

The inquest lasted from 11 July to 12 August under the control (or lack of control) of the coroner, Mr Carter. The Crown was represented by Attorney General Sir John Holker (known as 'Sleepy Jack' to his colleagues), Mr John Gorst and the ubiquitous Harry Poland. Mrs Florence Bravo, Mrs Jane Cox, Dr James Gully and Mr Joseph Bravo were each independently represented in court by leading solicitors or counsels who were given the opportunity during the proceedings to cross-examine witnesses.[29] One of the most strident and effective of these was the solicitor George Lewis (representing Joseph Bravo) who, though not a barrister, had the authority to cross-examine witnesses in a coroner's court and grasped the chance to demonstrate his interrogation skills with great vigour.[30] Clarke attended the inquest but was not required to give evidence. As the precise cause and mechanism of death had not been formally confirmed no one was on trial, and there had been insufficient evidence to arrest anyone. Thus Clarke's role in the proceedings was effectively as an observer, collecting any new evidence and following up any new leads that might emerge during the witness examinations.

For the new jury, events started with a gruesome visit to observe the exhumed body of Charles Bravo before returning to the crowded room at the Bedford Hotel. On the second day, the coroner comfortingly informed the tightly packed participants and spectators that a surveyor had checked the beams supporting the floor and had said that there was no danger of the floor collapsing from the great weight of the crowd. On the ninth day, potential new evidence emerged when the former coachman at the Priory, George Griffiths, stated that it had been his habit to purchase tartar emetic as a treatment for his horses, a technique that he had learnt from a book entitled *Every Man His Own Farrier*, and he had used this antimony-based product during his time at the Priory (though none had been found during Clarke's searches). As a result, Clarke sent Detective Sergeant Roots with Griffiths to Stroud Park in Kent, where Griffiths was now employed, to retrieve the book and any tartar emetic that he might still have (none was found).[31] Griffiths was subsequently recalled for further cross-examination but the incident threw more heat than light on the proceedings.

On the thirteenth day there was a great stir when Mrs Cox was called. This rose to a crescendo in the Bedford Hotel, and more widely in prurient Victorian society when, under cross-examination by George Lewis, Mrs Cox admitted that she had been told by her mistress that she had had a 'criminal intimacy' (had committed adultery) with Dr Gully, who was still married though long separated from his much older wife. Mrs Cox was followed to the witness stand by Florence Bravo, who received a merciless cross-examination from George Lewis. This eventually caused Florence to 'appeal to the Coroner and to the jury as men and Britons to protect me'; an emotional outburst that prompted the spectators in court to stamp their feet in applause and sympathy.[32] James Gully gave evidence on the twenty-second and penultimate day, having expressed a wish to be examined, though Clarke had earlier reported to the solicitor to the Treasury that 'I see no reason to attach the slightest suspicion to Dr. Gully'.[33]

When the time arrived for the coroner to sum up, he did a more adequate job than at the first inquest. After two and a half hours the jury issued their verdict: 'We find that Mr. Charles Delauney Turner Bravo did not commit suicide: that he did not meet with his death by misadventure, but that he was wilfully murdered by the administration of tartar emetic, but that there is not sufficient evidence to fix the guilt on any person or persons.'[34] This went down well with the public but not with a contributor to the *British Medical Journal*:

> The verdict of the last jury has been eminently satisfactory to a large number
> of the public, consisting chiefly, if not entirely, of those persons who, without
> waiting to hear the evidence, had come to the same conclusion at which the
> jury arrived. For my own part, having read the evidence daily in the *Times*'
> reports, I had come to think that, on the whole an open verdict would be the
> proper one ...[35]

Clarke effectively concurred: 'I would respectfully call the Commissioner's attention to the fact that during this long enquiry nothing has been elicited to shew by what means the deceased met with his death other than is contained in my former reports.'[36]

Though the police efforts to obtain sufficient evidence for any arrest appeared to have been exhausted, the inquest verdict obliged them to do something so, on 14 August 1876, a reward poster was issued offering £250 for information leading to the arrest and conviction of the murderer or murderers.[37] No substantive new evidence was forthcoming, and the 'Balham Mystery' was never solved. Florence Bravo, shunned by society, retreated to Southsea and died of causes related to excessive drinking in September 1878, while James Gully, ostracised by some of his family and friends, died in Malvern in March 1883 from cancer. The resilient Mrs Cox immigrated to Jamaica, later returning to London where she died aged 90 in 1917.[38]

The sensational events of 1876 have attracted a number of individuals to present their own solutions to the 'Balham Mystery'. Of those directly involved in the case, George Lewis is reported to have said: 'Had I been able to do so, I should at once have relieved both Dr Gully and Mrs Bravo from any suggestion that they in any way participated in the crime. I then – and still do – believe them: Not Guilty.'[39] Lewis' suspicions focused on Mrs Cox, who he saw as a schemer and opportunist, and in every way the most likely suspect. The more measured views of the Treasury counsel, Harry Poland, were:

> I am not entitled to give any opinion – for publication. But it is certain that someone in the house poisoned Bravo. It might have been a servant. But if so what was the motive? It might have been Mrs. Cox, who certainly knew that her situation was in jeopardy, but that is a slight motive for murder. It might have been Mrs. Bravo, but would even a revival of her affection for Dr. Gully provide a sufficient motive for such a crime? Then remember that she summoned Sir William Gull, one of the greatest doctors of the day. Her conduct generally was consistent with innocence ... Of course I have my own opinion; but what I think is one thing, and legal proof is another: anyway we lacked the evidence to prosecute ...[40]

Amongst several books on the subject, *The Bravo Mystery and Other Cases* dismisses misadventure and suicide and suggests that only Florence Bravo or Mrs Cox could have committed the crime; *Death at the Priory* lays the murder of Charles Bravo's death at the door of Florence Bravo, with the complicity of Mrs Cox.[41] In contrast, in *How Charles Bravo died*, the perceived culprit is Charles Bravo himself, accidentally consuming tartar emetic (purchased to control his wife's drinking habits) instead of Epsom salts and, after realising his mistake, feeling compelled to remain silent about the poison he had consumed as he lay dying.[42] Of course, unlike Clarke and the Treasury legal team, those who have assembled these versions of events have the luxury of not being required to present their evidence to the rigour of legal process.

With no new evidence forthcoming, it was time for Clarke to move on. The Bravo inquest adjourned from Wednesday 9 August until its final day on 12 August. He found time on the Thursday to attend the wedding of his eldest daughter, Emily, to Henry Stableforth Payne, the son of a tailor from Tufton Street, Westminster. The wedding took place on a pleasantly warm day in the splendid baroque church of St John Evangelist in Smith Square, Westminster. The newlyweds spent their honeymoon at Boston, Lincolnshire, at the home of a family friend of the Paynes, William Norfolk, who would provide valuable assistance to Clarke in 1877. Clarke then returned to Balham for the last day of the Bravo inquest on 12 August but, by mid-August, having had little time to draw breath, he was engaged in not just one but two new investigations.

'Count von Howard'

On 25 August Clarke arrived in Hamburg carrying an extradition warrant for the arrest of 'Charles Howard' (also known as Count von Howard of Eisenach, amongst other aliases), on a charge of obtaining £380 by false and fraudulent pretences. By 27 August Clarke was back in England with the prisoner and a sealed portmanteau containing documents and other items that had been found in Howard's rooms when he had been arrested by German police in February 1876.[43]

Back in January of 1875, John Harvey of 13 Upper Thames Street, City of London, had received a 'private and confidential' letter from 'F.C. Judford', a person not known to him. The letter stated that a 'Mr. Richard Harvey' had died in July 1870 and that, although an earlier will had been proved, a more recent will had been found in which John Harvey was a beneficiary and stood to receive a legacy of £40,000 plus approximately £10,000 from a freehold property. The writer said that the most recent will was genuine and was in the hands of a person in humble circumstances. The will would be released if Harvey would agree to pay a small commission to the will holder. After an exchange of correspondence, Judford reported that a 'hitch' had arisen in negotiations, as the will holder had placed the will at a bank for safe keeping but, unfortunately, had got into debt with the bank, owing £380, and the bank would not release the will until this amount was paid. However, if Harvey sent £380 to Judford, this would ensure that the bank would release the will. Harvey duly sent the money in instalments during June 1875, and Judford acknowledged the payments. Harvey's subsequent letters received no reply and were returned to him by the post office 'dead letter office'. Thus, Harvey had invested £380 and had not received the promised will.[44]

Count von Howard had been living at the Hotel de Rautenkrantz in Eisenach since November 1875. Together with a woman who passed as his wife, he occupied three rooms, a bedroom, a sitting room and a study. On arrival, he had brought several portmanteaus with him that were always locked and kept in the study, where he spent long hours working. He was also a regular customer at the post office, where he sent and collected substantial quantities of post. After receipt of information from England (prompted by John Harvey contacting the police), Howard was arrested under suspicion of being 'F.C. Judford'. Precisely how the connection between Judford and Howard was made is unclear, though his working practices probably made him stand out from the usual hotel guest. A protracted series of court appearances in Germany had filled the time between Howard's arrest in February and Clarke's journey to Hamburg in August. Though Howard had some success in the German courtroom, it only postponed the court's final decision that he should face trial in England.

When Clarke returned from Hamburg on 28 August with his prisoner he brought him to the Mansion House, where the Treasury prosecution team were assembled with Harry Poland ready to open the case for the prosecution. In front of Alderman Sir Robert Carden (a former lord mayor of London), Poland described the case as a 'fraud of the most remarkable character, which had been carried out with extraordinary ingenuity'. Howard, described as well dressed, aged 48 and of no occupation, presented himself as a relation of the chancellor of the German empire (Bismarck) which, he was later to claim, 'ought of itself to have shielded him from such a charge'. Clarke gave evidence of Howard's arrest, and Howard was remanded in custody in Newgate Prison.

There were several hearings at the Mansion House, between 28 August and 10 October, before Alderman Carden committed the prisoner for trial at the Old Bailey. Clarke's principal job during September, together with Detective Sergeant von Tornow and the Treasury team, was to disentangle the contents of the portmanteau, identify and contact potential key witnesses and build the case against Howard. As the hearings progressed it emerged that Howard had been born in America, and that he had worked in the War Office in London between 1855 and 1858 in the name of Temple Bouverie Cleveland Willmott. The portmanteau contained numerous documents, suggesting that Howard had corresponded with up to 100 individuals on the subject of wills, including John Harvey. In addition, a Captain Henry Williams of Pilton House, Barnstaple (and previously an MP of that borough), emerged to give evidence that he had been in correspondence of a similar nature, but with someone named 'Tent' rather than 'Judford'. It was noted that the handwriting of 'Howard', 'Tent' and 'Judford' were remarkably similar.[45] Howard's counsel pursued the course that, if the offence had been committed at all, it was committed in Germany and not in this country.[46] That argument was dismissed by Alderman Carden on the basis that the German authorities had seen fit to send Howard to England for trial. In addition, Harvey had received at least one letter from Judford which bore a British stamp and had been posted in Britain.[47]

At the Old Bailey on 25 October, a plea of 'not guilty' was entered by the court on Howard's behalf, after he refused to plead. The prosecution had assembled a team of witnesses from Britain and Germany, the majority of whom had appeared at the Mansion House hearings. One who had not was Charles Chabot, called once more to identify the handwriting on various items of correspondence. In addition, there were several new witnesses who identified Howard as an individual they knew under different aliases. Howard's defence counsel called no witnesses and persisted with the legal argument that there was no evidence that Howard had been in Britain since July 1875, commenting also that the handwriting evidence was unreliable and that the style of some of the letters quoted in evidence was not consistent with them having been written by a single person. This last point may have caused some amusement in court, bearing in mind the multiple identities that Howard had assumed.[48]

The jury consulted only briefly before returning a 'guilty' verdict. Prior to sentencing, Clarke stated that there was considerable evidence from the 1,000 or so letters and papers in the portmanteau that there were many other fraud victims (some of whom had now complained to Scotland Yard), and that Howard had been getting large sums of money in that way for at least ten years. Indeed, from each victim, Howard had acquired a sum in excess of Clarke's annual salary of £276. Recognising Howard as an accomplished swindler, Mr Justice Lush delivered the maximum sentence for the offence, five years' penal servitude.[49] Once again, a case in which Clarke had played a significant part was featured in *The Times* leader columns, describing Howard's activities as 'a crowning act of roguery, strange enough in some of its details, and strangest, perhaps, of all in its partial success'.[50]

The Austrian Tragedy – The Re-appearance of 'Henri Perreau'

Shortly before his journey to Hamburg to arrest Howard, Clarke received a letter from Jonathan Oldfield, who Clarke had met in April 1868 when investigating the death of Mrs Elizabeth Brigham.[51] Oldfield's letter stated that Mrs Brigham's son-in-law, Henri Perreau, had changed his name to 'de Tourville' and had remarried following the early death of his first wife. Now his second wife had died in a 'strange tragedy' in Austria in July 1876. Suspicious of these events, Oldfield wrote:

> From the previous enquiries made by you, no doubt you will feel an interest in this matter and no doubt you will see the propriety of at once placing yourself in communication with the relatives of the second wife and ascertain whether he is the same person and if it turns out that he is you will then know what course to take.[52]

Oldfield, who had been a trustee of Mrs Brigham's estate, was by now well versed in matters concerning de Tourville, as the latter had taken legal action against Oldfield in June 1872 concerning the income generated by the late Mrs Brigham's investments.[53]

Having obtained approval to make enquiries about Perreau, Clarke reported back on 21 August:

> I beg to report that about the latter end of 1867 a Monsieur Henri Perreau married (supposed on the Continent) a young lady named Henrietta Felicia

Helen Elizabeth Brigham, the daughter of Mrs Elizabeth Brigham, Foxley Hall, Lymm, Cheshire. On the 11th April 1868, the latter was shot in the breakfast room at Foxley Hall, under very suspicious circumstances and, by direction of the late Sir Richard Mayne I made enquiries into the case … Shortly after, Monsieur Perreau (who had changed his name to De Tourville) and his wife took up their residence at 16 Craven Hill, Bayswater, and on the 27th July 1869, Madame de Tourville gave birth to a son who was registered as William Perreau de Tourville; this child is supposed to be now alive.

On the 30th June 1871, Madame de Tourville died at the same address, according to the Register, of 'Phthisis Pulmonalis' [tuberculosis] of some years standing, and by her death her husband is believed to have come into possession of a large fortune said to be about £40,000.

On the 11th November 1875, De Tourville was again married at the church of the Holy Trinity, Westbourne Terrace, to Madeline Pike (commonly known as Madeline Miller) of 6 Southwick Crescent, widow of Charles Frederick Pike Esq. and daughter of the late Captain William Miller R.N. and who had a fortune of £70,000, and by a will made shortly after the marriage the greater part of this was left to the husband. They left England to travel on the Continent and on the 6th July last were staying at the Hotel von Kammerzofe, Trafoi, in Austria on the confines of the Tyrol when the occurrence happened as stated in the newspaper extracts.

I have seen the maid, Sarah Clappinson, who was travelling with Monsieur and Madame de Tourville at the time, and who is at present at No. 6 Southwick Terrace. She states that about 9 a.m. on the 6th July last, her Master and Mistress left the Inn mentioned in a carriage to view the scenery in the neighbourhood and about 6½ p.m. her master returned alone, and said that Madame had met with an accident by falling over a precipice, and was killed, but she – Clappinson – never saw the body, as her master stated it was lying some distance away. Two days afterwards two gentlemen whom she believes to have been Police Officials, called and took her statement, and during the enquiry which succeeded into the cause of her mistress's death, her master was kept under surveillance of the Police at the Hotel. After the funeral De Tourville returned to London – having first sent her home – and continued to reside at 16 Craven Hill, until Saturday last, when he left for Austria, supposed for the purpose of removing the body to another resting place.

I have also seen Mr. Thomas Frank Wilding, 5 Lime Street Square, who informed me that he had known the late Madame de Tourville for many years, that he was a trustee under the marriage settlement, and executor under the subsequent will. At the latter end of July he received a letter from Monsieur De Tourville, dated from Paris, detailing the circumstances of his wife's death, and stating he was in Paris for the purpose of obtaining a copper coffin in which to deposit the body, also inviting him to attend the funeral, but he declined to do so. In the early part of last week De Tourville called upon him and gave him an account of the accident. Mr. Wilding considered the circumstances most suspicious, but at present is quite at a loss to know what steps to take in the matter.

I have seen Mr. Freshfield, Solicitor, Bank Buildings, who said he was Mrs. De Tourville's solicitor previous to her marriage, and drew the settlements, and made the will, but at present he has no instructions from any person to take any steps in the matter. He is strongly of opinion that further enquiry should be made, and suggests that a communication should be made to the authorities where the occurrence took place.

There are two sisters of Madame de Tourville, who each take £10,000 under the will *viz*. Mrs Cox at present at Port Natal, and Mrs. Thompson of Gravesend, and they have been informed of their sister's death by Mr. Wilding.[54]

Clarke's reports of 24 April 1868 and of 21 August 1876 are contemporary to the events he was investigating and are entirely consistent with other sources of primary information from the same period. Unfortunately, the same cannot be said of several accounts of the 'de Tourville' case that emerged in the 'true-crime' literature between 1890 and 1930. In these accounts, the predominant (but not the only) errors are that Druscovich was the investigating officer and that the name of the woman shot in 1868 was a 'Mrs Ramsden'.[55]

Perreau had become a naturalised British citizen on 13 June 1871, in the name of 'Henri Dieudonnée Perreau de Tourville'.[56] He had increasingly moved in high society and had been presented to His Royal Highness the Prince of Wales, and called to the degree of the Utter Bar in November 1871, permitting him to practise as a barrister. The legal knowledge that he acquired he had immediately used in trying to gain greater access to the estates of both his late mother-in-law and his late first wife.[57]

Of the people who Clarke had contacted about Madeline de Tourville, at least two of them were suspicious of the circumstances of her death. Establishing what had happened in Austria was clearly important. Fortuitously, the Foreign Secretary had received a confidential letter from an English solicitor, John Jennings, who had been travelling in the Tyrol soon after Madeline de Tourville had died. The letter was passed on to Scotland Yard for information:

My Lord

I have just returned from a tour of some weeks in the Tyrol and find that no account of the dreadful and mysterious death of an English lady on the Stelvio Pass has been seen in the papers. This coupled with the fact that no friends or relations of the parties appeared at the trial or at the funeral has strengthened the suspicion of foul play. I deem it my duty to lay the following facts stated to me by eye witnesses at Trafoi before your Lordship in the hope that you may deem it right to cause further enquiry to be made. A gentleman styling himself as Henry Dieudonnée de Tourville with his wife (an English lady) and their maid had been travelling from Innsbrüch with a Voiturier and arrived on Saturday evening the 15 July at Spondinig where they passed the night at the small Inn. On Sunday morning another carriage was ordered to drive to the highest point on the Stelvio Road. The maid was left at Spondinig – supper having been ordered for their expected return at 8 in the evening – nothing unusual was remarked. The couple arrived at Trafoi and dined. They then continued their drive to Franzenshöhe five miles further, pulled up there, took some wine and drove on nearly to the top of the pass, not stopping again at Franzenshöhe on the return journey. About two miles before regaining Trafoi they alighted, the gentleman telling the driver that they would go down on foot to Trafoi and that he was to await them there at about 6 o'clock; the gentleman arrived alone and met the landlord who was standing outside his Inn. The latter at once asked where the lady was – de Tourville replied quite calmly 'she has fallen on the road and (pointing to the temple) is bleeding'. He then went into the salle à manger and ordered a bottle of wine and while drinking it narrated to a woman of the house that he had been a widower, that he had been remarried about 8 months, with other particulars. The landlord had in the meantime despatched two men in search of the lady but not until half an hour had elapsed did de Tourville request that his carriage might be prepared and 4 strong men sent with him to bring down his wife. The men previously despatched by the landlord did not find her and on the arrival of the whole party the lady's hat was found with blood on it a few yards from the road but the lady could not be seen and was at length discovered lifeless several hundred yards down a slope out of sight of the road, while on the grass was a narrow track as if some heavy body had been dragged downwards – a piece of an umbrella was also found a little lower than the road and was admitted by de Tourville to be part of the one which he had in his hand when he first came down to Trafoi. An earring was subsequently found just by the road, but several valuable rings which the lady had on her fingers were untouched. De Tourville was arrested and confined in a room at Spondinig for 8 days while undergoing examination by the police authorities from [illegible] and Botzen. To the latter he alleged what he had not previously stated, that his wife had attempted to destroy herself and that after he had left her she must have thrown herself down to the spot where the corpse was lying. I have myself inspected the place and agree with all the people in the neighbourhood in believing it impossible that:

1st She could have fallen from the road to any distance on a descent so little precipitous, and

2nd That after receiving such a wound as is indicated by the blood on her hat which I have carefully examined, she could alone have reached the spot where she lay dead. I have seen the lady's dress and her boots which bear distinct marks of having been scratched and torn behind as if the wearer had been dragged on her back. In spite of these facts the Austrian authorities have set M. de Tourville free. There are ugly rumours afloat as to money having been paid by him to the officials at Botzen, and though this wants confirmation, the prevalence of the report among the natives, shews that such a proceeding is not deemed improbable.

M. de Tourville said his wife was labouring under monomania but this rests on his evidence only, the Commissioner having liberated him without requiring any testimony from England as to her state of mind. The lady is said to have had considerable property, and there is a general conviction in that part of the Tyrol that she has been the victim of foul play. De Tourville gives her name as Madeline Miller and states that she was 47 years of age. Those who saw her describe her to have been a tall fine looking woman inclined to corpulence. The lady has been buried in the Cemetery at Meran. Her late address I could not learn but the maid stated her mistress lived in one of the best parts of London and was the owner of large houses.

I need scarcely ask your lordship to regard my letter as strictly confidential. My information has been obtained principally from the pastor of the parish, the postmaster and an officer of Austrian Customs who was present when the body was found. I make this statement in the interests of humanity only, the parties being quite unknown to me.

John Rogers Jennings.[58]

This information seemed to come from a trustworthy source and added further to the suspicions surrounding Madeline de Tourville's death. However, as her death had occurred in Austrian territory, any criminal proceedings would require the Austrian authorities to review the case. If de Tourville was required again to face justice in Austria that would first require his extradition from Britain.

By early September the Austrian consulate had been informed of Clarke's enquiries. In response, the Austrian Consul General had asked Scotland Yard to provide him with some further information. Clarke replied on 22 September, including further background to his 1868 Lymm investigation, as well as details of Madeline de Tourville's will, and reports of recent interviews with some of her friends and associates.[59] His report also included a surprising re-evaluation of his 1868 investigation, and the suspicions he had of 'Perreau', which he now claimed he would have pursued further if the coroner's inquest had not already returned a verdict of accidental death on Mrs Brigham:

Had this verdict not been returned I certainly should have felt it my duty to prefer a charge of murder against Perreau, as I found many of the circumstances attending Mrs. Brigham's death most suspicious. The circumstances were:

Perreau who was a Frenchman by birth was believed to be an adventurer, he had no estate or means of his own; he had not introduced his young wife to any of his family nor had they learned anything of his previous history, and by the death of his mother-in-law, he came into possession through his wife (herself of weak intellect) of a fortune of £40,000.

The fact that Perreau had but a short time previous to Mrs. Brigham's death, purchased the revolver in London, without any apparent reason or having any use for such an article.

That he should have found it necessary to place a ball cartridge in the weapon, merely to explain its action.

That the ball struck her on the side of the head, taking a slanting direction, as if fired from behind, and not in the front of the head, as might have been expected, and it was the opinion of myself, and other competent persons with whom I consulted, that it was physically impossible for the wound to have been inflicted in the way described by Perreau.[60]

Clarke's report then added information about de Tourville's second wife, obtained from the trustees of her will, friends and associates:

… She leaves legacies of £10,000 to each of her two sisters, and other legacies amounting in total to £5,000; the remainder £35,000 she left to her husband of which he now takes possession, she being dead … It is believed by the executors Messrs. Wilding and Robertson that de Tourville as the husband of the deceased lady would have a full knowledge of the will, but no direct evidence can be obtained to shew this fact … I have seen Miss Scott of 42, Addison Road Kensington; she states that she has known the late Mrs. de Tourville for many years, and receives a legacy of £1000 under her will. About the later end of May last, she was told by the Chevalier de Guillenan (Secretary to the Portugese Embassy 12, Gloucester Place Portman Square) that that gentleman had heard, that Mrs. de Tourville was unhappy and likely to commit suicide, in consequence of being threatened to be called as a witness in a divorce case about to be instituted by the wife of Mr. Warwick Hunt. Miss Scott accordingly wrote to Madame de Tourville at the Grand Hotel Paris … telling her about the rumour she had heard; about the 5th June Miss Scott received a reply from Madame de Tourvillle in her handwriting stating that it was untrue, and that she was about the last person in the world to commit suicide, but if Miss Scott were to hear of her death, she might be certain she had been murdered. Miss Scott shewed this letter to Mr. Warwick Hunt and it was then destroyed.

I have also seen Mr. Hunt, who is a clerk in the War Office; he states that he saw the letter spoken of by Miss Scott, and he confirms her statements as to the contents; he further states that there were no grounds for the statement that Mrs. de Tourville would have been called as a witness in his divorce case.

I have further seen Mr. Brown solicitor to Mrs. Hunt 11, Pall Mall who states that Madame de Tourville had no knowledge of any of the circumstances relating to the divorce case and could not have been called as a witness.

I have lastly seen Monsieur de Guillenan; he informs me that the rumour of Madame de Tourville being wanted as a witness in the Hunt divorce case originated with Monsieur de Tourville.

The inquiries in this matter are being continued and any further information obtained will be submitted.[61]

Apart from revealing that Clarke had previous suspicions about Perreau at the time of the death of Mrs Brigham (which we will return to later), he had now confirmed the very substantial sum that de Tourville would gain from the death of his second wife. From a close friend of de Tourville's wife, Miss Scott, Clarke had also heard that her death was unlikely to have occurred as a result of suicide.

By 25 September the press had started to publish articles linking the death of Madeline de Tourville with the earlier death of Mrs Brigham.[62] Concerned by this, de Tourville's solicitors wrote a letter to the *Standard* (that was also published in other newspapers) to present their client's version of events.[63] Despite this attempt to dampen press interest, the Austrian authorities decided on 11 October that there was now sufficient information to re-examine the death of Madeline de Tourville and they wrote to Commissioner Henderson requesting de Tourville's arrest so that a case for his extradition could be heard.[64] The arrest was not made until 28 October, probably because of delays in obtaining the extradition warrant and because Clarke was busy running the detective department in Williamson's absence, as well as engaged in the Old Bailey trial of Charles Howard.[65] However, on the evening of 28 October, assisted by Detective Sergeants Greenham and von Tornow, Clarke arrested de Tourville at his home.[66]

There was some confusion whether the Austrian authorities or the Treasury legal team would take the lead in the prosecution, and de Tourville's solicitors seized the opportunity to assemble a strong team for the defence by appointing Harry Poland as lead counsel, together with Montagu Williams, thereby depriving the Treasury team of their usual 'Sleuth Hound'. Both were present at Bow Street Police Court on the following Monday when Clarke brought de Tourville before the magistrate, Mr Vaughan, on an extradition warrant charging him with the wilful murder of his second wife. Williams later described his client's appearance: 'The accused was a man who might be any age between forty and sixty, and his hair, moustache and other hirsute appendages were of a glossy blackness that was suggestive of meretricious applications. He was somewhat showily dressed, and had on an open-worked shirt, decorated with handsome studs. Altogether, de Tourville was certainly not a very prepossessing–looking person.'[67] De Tourville appeared at Bow Street on several occasions between 30 October and 6 December 1876 before the magistrate's decision was made. The courtroom was always crowded, patronised particularly by female friends of the late Madeline de Tourville.

At the first hearing Clarke gave evidence of the arrest and read the warrant which, the magistrate noted, required some further signatures from the Austrian Embassy to be regularised. Mr Jennings and Miss Scott were brought forward as prosecution witnesses. Not surprisingly, Poland objected to the hearsay evidence of Jennings being presented, an objection which the magistrate allowed. Miss Scott, on the two occasions she was called, indicated that her friend was most unlikely to have committed suicide, and that de Tourville had changed his story about the cause of his wife's death: he had first told Miss Scott that she had fallen accidentally, only later had he said that Madeline had attempted to commit suicide by jumping down the mountainside. At the end of proceedings de Tourville was remanded in custody and was taken by Clarke to the Clerkenwell House of Detention.[68]

On 4 November Poland sought de Tourville's release on technical grounds: firstly, the Austrian warrant described the prisoner as a native of France, whereas he was in fact a naturalised British citizen; secondly, that it was a rule with governments never to give up their own subjects for extradition. Fortunately for Clarke and the Treasury team, the magistrate did not accept Poland's arguments.[69] On 4 November and in subsequent hearings, translated written depositions from Austrian witnesses were read in court. These included statements from the driver who had taken de Tourville and his wife on to the Stelvio Pass on 17 July 1876, the owners and staff of the inns in Spondinig and Trafoi where de Tourville and his wife had stayed, as well as from witnesses who had been involved in the search for Madeline de Tourville's body. Their statements broadly concurred with the information contained in the letter from John Jennings, and confirmed that there was considerable suspicion of de Tourville's actions. The evidence of Frederick Hoffer, the manager of the inn at Trafoi, was one example:

> De Tourville returned and told witness his wife had fallen. He did not seem at all excited and witness did not think the fall was serious … At halfpast 8 or a quarter to 9, Zoller and Asper returned and said the lady was dead. Everybody said she could not have fallen where she was found and that she must have been murdered and dragged down … the circumstance of the stripe in the grass being so narrow that it could only be caused by dragging a body, and the fact that from the nature of the ground it was very improbable anybody could have fallen so far. Witness tried whether stones would roll so far but they would not … It was also suspicious that he should ask for four men to go and fetch his wife when, if she had not been dead, two would have been sufficient to assist her.[70]

After his wife's body had been found, de Tourville had been moved to a hotel in Spondinig and had been kept under guard between 18 and 22 July, while witness depositions were collected by the Austrian police authorities. De Tourville had then appeared before a district judge, when the decision was made to release him with no further charge. Adolph Schmidt, an interpreter at that event, reported that the proceedings in Austria had been to some extent unsatisfactory: 'De Tourville's statement before the Judge was not taken down at all; but after hearing it, the Judge said "I have heard enough", and then discharged de Tourville.'[71]

At Bow Street on 6 December the magistrate's hearings ended. The maid, Sarah Clappinson, denied that she had ever told anyone that 'of course he killed her'.[72] Despite Poland's objection the written reports by Austrian doctors on Madeline de Tourville's injuries were interpreted for the court by Dr Thomas Bond, who stated that the injuries could not have been caused by a fall but were consistent with her receiving several severe blows to the face and head.[73] Poland, in his defence statement, observed that:

> ... this was a case altogether unprecedented in its character and importance. It was asked that a British subject, amenable to the British law, should be given up as a fugitive criminal after the offence of which he was now accused had been investigated by the judicial authorities of the district in which it was said to have occurred, and the accused had been honourably acquitted.[74]

Nonetheless, the magistrate concluded that it was his duty to commit de Tourville for trial in Austria. Arrangements were then put in place for de Tourville to be handed over to the Austrian authorities at their consulate in Hamburg. Several days later than planned, because of bad weather and the frozen state of the river at Hamburg, Clarke left England with his prisoner on 2 January 1877 and handed de Tourville over to the Austrians.[75]

That was not the end of the matter for Clarke, as he was asked to attend de Tourville's trial in Austria in June 1877 on behalf of the Home Office and the solicitors of Madeline de Tourville. Accompanied by his colleague and interpreter, Detective Sergeant von Tornow, he left England on 15 June 1877 for Botzen, where the trial started on 18 July. The trial's procedures received some criticism from the British press: 'In accordance with Austrian law and practice which accords very ill with English notions of justice and fair play, every section of the prisoner's life has been carefully raked up. The tragedy at Foxley Hall has been minutely gone through, with as much formality as though the prisoner was being tried for the wilful murder of Mrs. Brigham.'[76] This was reinforced during proceedings on 21 June when Clarke was called to give evidence: 'The event of the sitting in the afternoon was the evidence of George Clarke the detective officer ... He brought with him a piece of bone from that portion of the skull of Mrs. Brigham where the bullet had entered.'[77]

There then followed a court discussion with three doctors, in which one suggested that the injury could have been inflicted in the way that de Tourville had described in 1868, while two others declared that de Tourville's description was inconsistent with the location of the bullet holes in the skull. Clarke then revealed information that had not been previously presented, implying that de Tourville may also have attempted to murder his son:

> A long discussion occurred about the fire in de Tourville's house in London in 1871. The police report of the time said that both de Tourville and his son were in great danger and were saved by a policeman ... According to Clarke's account Tourville never took any trouble about the child, and it was almost stifled when he brought it down. He expressed the suspicion that the fire had not originated accidentally, and the opinion of the Fire Brigade was the same. In reply to the question what motive Tourville could have had for acting so, an opinion was expressed that he wanted to get rid of the child. In cross examination the counsel for the defendant asked whether eye-witnesses had not said that Tourville risked his own life to save that of the child. Clarke replied that 'he could not but come to this conclusion'. The counsel for the defence declared himself satisfied with this admission ...[78]

The remainder of the trial focused on the events in the Tyrol. Other witnesses from Britain included Miss Scott, Sarah Clappinson and Mr Turner (de Tourville's solicitor, who appeared for the defence). Clappinson's evidence continued to be supportive of the defendant. Amongst the information presented by de Tourville and his defence team was that he had no knowledge of his wife's will prior to her death; his apparently indifferent behaviour at Trafoi after his wife had fallen had arisen through a combination of heart disease and the physical exertions he had made to climb down to her; his imperfect understanding of German was responsible for any inconsistency in his responses to questions at the time; and the fact he had initially claimed that she had fallen accidentally was because he did not want to stain her memory with the possibility that she had committed suicide. His friend de Guillenan gave evidence which essentially consisted of the view that de Tourville 'was incapable of such a deed'.[79]

The medical experts concluded that Madeline de Tourville's injuries were not consistent with a suicide attempt. The district judge who had conducted the first inquiry in July 1876 acknowledged that he may have made some mistakes which showed a partiality for the accused. An Austrian police sergeant denied that de Tourville had tried to bribe the police in 1876 but confirmed that he had given some money as a 'present' when he had been discharged;

however, the money had been distributed amongst the poor.[80] Finally, on 2 July, when asked to consider their verdict, the jury returned an 11:1 majority 'guilty' verdict, and de Tourville was sentenced to be hanged.[81]

British press reaction was mixed. The *Warrington Guardian*, expressing perceptions linked to the 1868 death of Mrs Brigham, wrote in its leader section: 'It is perhaps, a hard thing to say, but it is nevertheless true, that the passing of sentence of death on Henri de Tourville was heard of with a feeling of relief. The general impression about the man was that he was so dangerous it was perilous he should be at large.'[82] In contrast, *Lloyds Weekly Newspaper* focused on the conduct of the trial:

> The procedure by which this conviction has been obtained resembles, in the main, that of France, and has consequently, many features that are repugnant to our sense of justice. In the first place, every act of De Tourville's life that could tell against him, every suggestion that could be raised to his prejudice, has been used in order to bring him to the gallows ... The prisoner has appealed, and it is to be hoped that a more judicial spirit will preside over the higher court of justice than that which was apparent at the trial.[83]

De Tourville's appeal was rejected by the Supreme Court in Vienna, but the sentence of death was later commuted by Emperor Franz Joseph I to eighteen years' penal servitude, to be served in the fortress of Gradiska. By December 1877, de Tourville's wax image was on display at Madame Tussauds. He died in prison from influenza on 27 January 1890 and, in his will, left everything in trust for his son.[84] The death of his murdered wife, Madeline, is commemorated by a small plaque near the location of her death on the Stelvio Pass, just above Weisse Knott.[85]

Despite some press concerns over the Austrian trial proceedings, de Tourville's conviction for the murder of his wife seems as robust as any other Victorian murder conviction, in which the forensic tools available to the police were very limited. Likewise, Mrs Brigham's death was probably a deliberate act on de Tourville's part. He may have attempted to murder his son in a fire in 1871, but did not succeed. Indeed, he seems to have been responsible for rescuing him (albeit at the last minute), despite the fact that, if his son had died, he would at last have got his hands on the capital and income from his first wife's estate.[86] If de Tourville had been arrested and tried in a timely fashion for the murder of his mother-in-law, then Madeline Miller would not have died. A key question therefore remains: why did George Clarke not initially pursue the suspicions of de Tourville that he claimed (in 1876) to have had during April 1868?

A number of issues may have affected the 1868 decision not to proceed with further enquiries against de Tourville. In one account of the case, the author

Charles Kingston suggested that the investigating officer from Scotland Yard was probably bribed by de Tourville (albeit that Kingston claimed incorrectly that Druscovich was in charge of the inquiry).[87] This cannot be ruled out but, as Clarke's enquiries into Mrs Brigham's death only started *after* an inquest jury had already returned an 'accidental death' verdict, the principal targets for any such bribery would have been the coroner, key witnesses and/or the inquest jury. Undoubtedly, the fact that an inquest had already reached a verdict of accidental death before Clarke arrived on the scene influenced the decision of whether or not to pursue further inquiries. Inquest verdicts were not easily overturned. For example, although the first Bravo inquest verdict had been discounted, it had taken a legal review in a higher court to overturn it. Clarke's 1868 report on Mrs Brigham's death had not contained any evidence that had not already been considered at the inquest on Mrs Brigham. In addition, as Clarke was investigating a case outside the Metropolitan Police area, he would have required the agreement of the Cheshire Constabulary to pursue matters further. It is also relevant to consider what other priorities the Metropolitan Police had at that time. In April 1868, Commissioner Mayne and the detective department were nervously awaiting the outcome of the Clerkenwell trial. Their principal focus for the previous two years had been the policing of the Fenian conspiracy and, after the Clerkenwell explosion, it would not be surprising if the pressure that the detective department was facing, from politicians, press and public, meant that other cases received less attention.

With the benefit of hindsight, Clarke was wrong to advise Mayne in April 1868 that there was no basis for further enquiries. However, when Clarke reported in 1876 that he had suspected de Tourville's evidence in the shooting of his mother-in-law, nothing in the surviving Scotland Yard documentation suggest that Clarke was regarded by his superiors as in any way culpable. Indeed, Clarke probably had renewed motivation to ensure that de Tourville was not allowed to commit any further murders, and his superiors let him get on with it.

The Gathering Storm

As 1876 moved toward its conclusion, the detective department was under pressure. It had been a testing year for Clarke and for the department. It is not unreasonable to assume that the British public found it difficult to understand why the police had failed to solve the 'murder' of Charles Bravo when it was so obviously (depending on your personal prejudice) Mrs Cox, or Florence Bravo, or Dr Gully, or any combination of all three. Equally, the gossips discussing Madeline de Tourville's death and that of Mrs Brigham cannot have failed to ask themselves why the police hadn't prevented the former by conducting a 'proper investigation' of the latter. In addition, a high-profile art theft had occurred, when the portrait by Gainsborough of the Duchess of Devonshire was stolen on 26 May. Despite the efforts of Inspector Meiklejohn and Sergeant Reimers, no significant progress had been made by Scotland Yard in recovering the picture. (In 1901 Adam Worth, 'the Napoleon of crime', struck a deal with Agnews, the art dealers, to return the painting.[88]) Worse was to come. At the end of September, the department were alerted by a solicitor, Michael Abrahams, that another 'turf fraud' was underway.[89] However this fraud, the subject of the next chapter, would have an impact much greater than the fraudsters themselves had contemplated.

It was not until August 1877 that it became known that Clarke had sought to retire from the police during 1876; scarcely surprising for a man aged 58, with thirty-six years' service in an occupation in which few stayed as long as he had.[90] What persuaded him to continue is not certain. As he enjoyed some time with his family and friends between Christmas and New Year, and had time to reflect, he must have hoped that 1877 would be easier than the year that he had just emerged from. Unfortunately for him, it would be much more difficult.

7

THE GREAT TURF SWINDLE AND POLICE CORRUPTION

1876–77

I read with regret in the news of the day
That detectives are all in our criminals pay,
And the wages they get are so awfully high
It must cost a small fortune their silence to buy.
I've a robbery planned and I'm ready to start,
But I want to know first with how much I must part.
No longer the course of my scheme to retard
I will send for the Tariff of Fees to 'the Yard'.[1]

The Great Turf Swindle

In late September 1876 Michael Abrahams, solicitor of the London firm of Abrahams and Roffey, arrived at Scotland Yard for a meeting with Superintendent Williamson. He was representing a French client, Comtesse Marie Cécile de Goncourt, who suspected, somewhat belatedly, that she had become the victim of a fraudulent enterprise operated from London.[2] In late August the comtesse had received in the post a copy of 5 August edition of an English sporting newspaper, *The Sport and Racing Chronicle*, together with a covering letter and a translation, in French, of one of the editorial articles. This particular article expressed sympathy for a commission agent, Andrew Montgomery, who had been so successful in selecting winning horses at British race tracks that bookmakers had closed ranks to limit their losses and had decided to accept Mr Montgomery's bets only at much shorter odds than those available to the general public. Deploring this action on the part of the bookmakers, the article went on to suggest that Montgomery's only option would be to employ agents outside Britain who could place bets on his behalf. Commission would be paid to the agents, and they would have the opportunity to invest some of their own money on his horse-racing selections. An accompanying letter, also in French, invited the recipient to become one of Mr Montgomery's agents; offered to provide references if required; promised 5 per cent commission, probably amounting to 5,000–6,000 francs a week (about £200–300); and assured the comtesse that all communications would remain strictly private and confidential.[3]

The comtesse responded positively to the invitation. Within a few days she received the numerical codes for horses that Montgomery had selected from a bookmaker's list, against which bets should be placed, together with several cheques drawn on the Royal Bank of London, already signed by one George Simpson. The considerate Montgomery had also provided the names and addresses of two 'sworn bookmakers', Charles Jackson and Jacob Francis, to whom the bets and signed cheques should be submitted. All the comtesse had to do was post them to the bookmakers. Within a few days, sizeable cheques were received by the comtesse from the bookmakers, as the selected horses had apparently won. She duly forwarded these to Mr Montgomery from whom she received the promised commission for her services in the form of another Royal Bank of London cheque, together with a reminder that, because of British banking regulations, a certain time had to elapse between the issue date of a cheque and its presentation for payment. Convinced by the smooth operation of the scheme, and the very solicitous and encouraging correspondence she received from Mr Montgomery, the comtesse decided to invest some of her own money. Guided by correspondence from Mr Montgomery, she invested a total of £10,000 and was considering a further £20,000 investment. However, she needed to obtain the additional money from her bankers. Suspecting that the scheme was fraudulent, they convinced her to leave the £20,000 where it was, and to contact her notary, Monsieur Chavances, with some speed. It was Chavances who had contacted Abrahams and Roffey.[4]

Abrahams had probably done some homework before he arrived at Scotland Yard but, even if he hadn't, it would not have taken too long for the detective department to establish that there was no such sporting newspaper as *The Sport and Racing Chronicle*; no such bank as the Royal Bank of London; no such profession as a 'sworn bookmaker' and indeed, no known bookmakers with the names Charles Jackson or Jacob Francis. The scheme was another fraudulent betting operation and, unless the police were able to act promptly to locate the fraudsters and recover the money, the Comtesse de Goncourt (and some other French citizens who had also succumbed to the scheme's plausibility) would have learnt the hard way that there is no such thing as a sure bet. Once the nature of the fraud was fully recognised, the comtesse and her legal representatives proved relentless in their determination to ensure that the culprits were arrested and her money recovered.

Clarke would have been the natural choice to lead the Scotland Yard inquiries. However, because many of the documents involved in the case were in French and because he was busy with the de Tourville and Charles Howard cases, Superintendent Williamson allocated the new turf fraud investigations to Chief Inspector Druscovich. When Williamson went on holiday for a month from 28 September, Clarke, as usual, was left in charge of the department as the investigation got going.[5] After a conversation with Abrahams, Druscovich visited the London addresses that the French contacts had provided, including some rooms at 8 Northumberland Street (near Scotland Yard) which had been used as the gang's headquarters. He found that the tenants had disappeared. However, the landlords provided descriptions of several men who had occupied the rented accommodation. From the descriptions given, it appeared that there were at least five men involved (in fact there were only four), several of whom were using aliases. Warrants were therefore obtained for the arrest of the 'five' individuals on a charge of obtaining £10,000 by fraudulent conspiracy; the wanted men were initially recorded as 'Andrew Montgomery', 'Jacob Francis' and 'Charles Jackson' (the three mentioned in the correspondence with the Comtesse de Goncourt), plus 'Thomas Ellerton' and 'Richard Gregory'. Visits to London money changers on 28 September yielded the information that one company, Reinhardt's, had changed about £13,000 of francs into Bank of England notes over the last few weeks, for a man calling himself 'Richard Gregory'. As the notes were numbered, and the numbers had been recorded by Reinhardt's, Druscovich asked for transactions with these notes to be stopped, but there was some delay in implementing this.[6]

On 3 October news was received from the Bank of England that most of the notes had been paid in by a Glasgow firm and Druscovich wrote a letter on the same day to the Glasgow police, asking for their help in tracing the individual who had paid the notes in; the letter was countersigned by Clarke as the officer in charge. Druscovich travelled up to Glasgow overnight on 4 October and was told that the Glasgow transactions had been traced to a man called Coster, whose description fitted that of the 'bookmaker' Jacob Francis – as later published on 8 November: '35 years of age, 5ft. 4in. or 5in. high, sallow complexion, black moustache, very thin round the waist, now growing whiskers, has cut on side of left eye, wears diamond studs and rings, pretends to be lame, and carries two sticks, dark complexion, supposed to be a Frenchman, but speaks English well.'[7]

Coster/Francis had successfully exchanged £10,000 numbered Bank of England notes for the equivalent amount in £100 Clydesdale banknotes (un-numbered, as was Scottish practice). In 'laundering' the money in this way, the fraudsters hoped to reduce the risk of being tracked down; however, Clydesdale banknotes were relatively unfamiliar outside their area, and police forces around the country were alerted to report any transactions involving such currency.

Enquiries were made at the London railway termini for any information about the movements of a man fitting the description of 'Jacob Francis'. One cabman at St Pancras remembered collecting a fare answering Francis' description on the morning of 4 October, but could not remember the destination though it was somewhere in Stoke Newington. The cabman's horse had gone lame during the journey and the passenger had transferred to another cab. Despite a £2 reward being offered to track down the second cabman, no further information was obtained by Detective Sergeant von Tornow, the officer dealing with this task.[8] Abrahams, concerned at what he saw as slow progress in the investigations, decided to employ some private investigators to help in the search for the fraudsters.

On 25 October, Chief Constable of Leeds William Henderson wrote to Superintendent Williamson (still on leave) to point out that a £100 Clydesdale banknote had been changed in Leeds by a man called Meiklejohn. The letter should have arrived in the detective department on 26 October, when Clarke was attending the Old Bailey trial of Charles Howard, and Druscovich was in charge of the office. However, Williamson did not discover the existence of this letter until the end of December, when the Leeds chief constable visited him in London. When Druscovich was asked by Williamson about the letter, he claimed to know nothing about it. By that time in the investigation, missing correspondence in the office was being regarded as a cause for suspicion rather than merely an item lost by the postal service.[9]

Williamson returned to the office from his holiday on 28 October and, having received the offer of a £1,000 reward from Abrahams, publicly issued the descriptions of the five men believed to be involved in the fraud. There was an immediate and positive response. The postmaster at Shanklin, Isle of Wight, recognised the description of 'Jacob Francis' as consistent with that of Mr G.H. Yonge, the recent resident of Rose Bank, Shanklin. In addition, the postmaster had noticed that a girl in Shanklin, who had developed a relationship with Yonge's manservant, Pierre Ponchon, had been sending letters to Ponchon addressed to the Queen's Hotel, Bridge of Allan – a spa town in Scotland. This news coincided with the discovery in Edinburgh on 9 November of the printer of the 'Royal Bank of London' cheques.[10] These leads directed the hunt to Scotland, and the search was now on for Mr Yonge and the other fraudsters.

Druscovich headed north to Scotland, arriving at Bridge of Allan on the 11 November. He just missed the suspected fraudsters, two of whom had been staying there but had left somewhat hastily after receiving a telegram. They had paid their bill with a £100 Clydesdale banknote. One fitted the description of Mr Yonge, the other had signed in as Mr W. Gifford. It later emerged that the two men had established an account at the Clydesdale Bank in Alloa, using some of the £100 Clydesdale banknotes. However, they had not been alone during their stay at the Queen's Hotel. They had been seen at dinner in the company of three known policemen, including one from Edinburgh and one from Glasgow; the third policeman was Inspector Meiklejohn.[11]

When Druscovich returned from Scotland on 18 November he brought with him some items of correspondence that had been addressed to Mr Gifford, in one of which, the writer had revealed:

> There is very strong particulars from Edinburgh, which I suppose you know; they have the address at the shop there. It is also known that you were in Edinburgh a day or two ago. Perhaps you had better see me – things begin to look fishy. News may be given to Isle of Wight, where Shanks is. You know best. Wired from Edinburgh that plates have been seized. A letter from Shanklin saying that one of the men well known there, D. goes to Isle of Wight tomorrow. Send this back.
>
>   W. Brown, who was with you at the 'Daniel Lambert'.[12]

The second item of correspondence consisted of a piece of blotting paper with the words: 'Keep the lame man out of the way.'[13] Both messages were clearly intended to provide Gifford with information that would assist him and Yonge in evading arrest. When Superintendent Williamson was shown the correspondence by Druscovich, he did not recognise the handwriting on the blotting paper. However, he was well acquainted with the handwriting on the letter: it was that of Chief Inspector William Palmer of Scotland Yard.

The record of what Superintendent Williamson did next is not complete. Meiklejohn's name had now cropped up twice in police enquiries (though in November, Williamson was still unaware that Meiklejohn had been linked to a Clydesdale banknote transaction in Leeds). Williamson accordingly wrote to Meiklejohn on 15 November asking him to explain why he had been in the company of two wanted men at Bridge of Allan, between 4 and 6 November. Meiklejohn's response was that he had arranged a meeting there with two Scottish policemen who were helping him with enquiries about a stolen portmanteau. He claimed that he had unexpectedly met Yonge, whom he had known since 1875 when Yonge had given him some useful information. While he was at the Queen's Hotel, Yonge had introduced him to his companion, Gifford, and they had dined together.[14]

Precisely what transpired between Superintendent Williamson and Chief Inspector Palmer at that time is unknown. However, faced with evidence of corruption in the detective department, Williamson undoubtedly informed his superiors, and probably discussed the issue with his trusted lieutenant, Clarke. By 21 November the permanent secretary at the Home Office was in correspondence with Commissioner Henderson, commenting that it shows 'great discredit on the police I fear', but there was uncertainty about what action should be taken: 'No doubt they would say we should have had our man had it not been for the treachery of one of the detectives, and that is true. But whether that is a ground for the Government taking up the case is very doubtful.'[15]

Correspondence was also taking place between the commissioner's office and the Procurator Fiscal to establish the extent of any corruption involving Scotland Yard officers and the Scottish police: 'If I can get a photograph of Meiklejohn it will be sent to you ... The prosecution of the Turf Swindlers is now in the hands of the Treasury Solicitor and Meiklejohn is I understand to be summoned as a witness. Any further information you can gather will be very useful.'[16] However, despite this initial flurry of activity, it was to be some months before substantive action was taken to address the issue of police corruption.

Meanwhile, the task of catching the fraudsters was even higher on the agenda. The information from the Shanklin postmaster, and from Bridge of Allan, had suggested that Yonge was one of the leaders of the fraud. Further than that, the police had obtained sufficient information from the Isle of Wight to realise that Yonge was, in reality, Harry Benson, a young man who had pleaded guilty at the Old Bailey in 1872 to obtaining £1,000 by false pretences from the Lord Mayor of London. In addition, his crippling injuries had not been sustained, as was previously thought, from a railway accident, but had occurred during a fire in his cell in Newgate, probably lit in a deliberate attempt to commit suicide.[17]

Thus, by mid-November 1876, the identity and history of one of the probable fraudsters had been established. A new 'reward' notice for the suspected five men was issued late in November, incorporating a photograph of a bearded Benson and a list of the aliases believed to have been used by him (including Andrew Montgomery, Montagu Posno, Montagu Coster, George Henry Yonge, Henry Young, Count de Montagu and Count de Mentargo).[18] The identities of the remaining members of the gang were not publicly known at that time, but emerged over the coming months. Only the men's 'real' names will be used in the following account. Apart from Harry Benson, the Comtesse de Goncourt fraudsters eventually proved to be William Kurr (aka William Gifford, William Giffard and William Kerr); his younger brother Frederick Kurr (aka Charles Collinge, Andrew Montgomery and Thomas Ellerton) and William Kurr's school friend Charles Bale (aka William Bale, Thomas Henry Taylor, Richard Gregory, Charles Jackson and 'Jerry the Greengrocer'). In early November 1876, William Kurr had also engaged an old acquaintance, Edwin Murray (aka Edward Murray, Henry Monroe and Henry Wells), from the 1875 'General Society for Assurance against Losses on the Turf', to help cash the Clydesdale notes.[19]

After Williamson had returned from his October holiday, Clarke had been concentrating on the extradition proceedings against Henri de Tourville. The turf fraud case remained under the charge of Druscovich and Williamson. However, on Saturday 25 November Clarke received a visit at Scotland Yard from John Savory, a solicitor's clerk who had information about Clydesdale banknotes. Savory had been one of the guarantors for Edwin Murray's bail in 1875 and had lost money when Murray absconded. He told Clarke that he had recently been approached by Murray who had suggested he could pay Savory all the money he owed him, and more, if he would help cash some Clydesdale notes. Savory had arranged to meet Murray on 27 November, near St Martin's church in the Strand. When the two men met, Savory gave a pre-arranged signal and Detective Sergeants Littlechild and Robson moved in to arrest Murray. Clarke, who was too well known to Murray from their earlier encounters in 1875, had been standing out of sight in Charing Cross Station. Later in the day, Clarke went to search Murray's lodgings with Littlechild and Robson. Murray was then taken to Marlborough Street Police Station and charged with obtaining £10,000 by fraud from the Comtesse de Goncourt. He was represented in court by a solicitor, Edward Froggatt, who also became a central character in subsequent events.[20]

Within a week further progress had been made. Williamson had arranged for descriptions of the wanted men to be sent to some European police forces in case any of the men left Britain. By then, William Kurr had put Benson on a boat to Boulogne with Frederick Kurr and Bale. On arrival, the three men split up and arranged to meet up later in Rotterdam. Meanwhile, William Kurr remained in the UK. On 2 December, Williamson received a telegram from the Rotterdam police saying that three men matching the descriptions of three of the fraudsters had been arrested. The men had contributed substantially to their own detection. Suspicions had been aroused when Bale and Frederick Kurr had arrived at a Rotterdam hotel where Benson was staying, under yet another alias – 'George Washington Morton'. Unfortunately for the fraudsters this was one alias too many, as Benson had not informed his colleagues that he had assumed yet another name and Bale and Kurr had therefore not known the name of the man they were supposed to be meeting. In addition, Benson had foolishly changed one Clydesdale note at his hotel and was found to be carrying more notes in a money belt.[21]

Feeling pleased with themselves, the Rotterdam police were not expecting to receive the following telegram from London the next day: 'Find Morton and the two men you have in custody are not those we want – Officer will not be sent over – Liberate them – Letter follows – Williamson, Superintendent of Police, Scotland Yard, London.'[22] Fortunately, the Dutch police decided to await receipt of the letter before taking any further action, and the three men were retained in custody. No letter was forthcoming, however; the telegram had not been sent by Williamson or anyone else at Scotland Yard but had been sent at the instigation of William Kurr in an audacious attempt to free his colleagues. Druscovich travelled to Rotterdam on 5 December, armed with an extradition warrant for the three men. He was followed a few days later by Williamson. For much of the time until the prisoners' extradition was approved, Druscovich remained in Rotterdam, apart from a self-granted day's leave over Christmas when he returned to the UK, an action that incurred the displeasure of Williamson (who promptly sent him back to Rotterdam) and a censure from Commissioner Henderson.

The prisoners were meanwhile not enjoying their time on remand in a Dutch gaol. Bale, a family man, was writing wistful letters to his wife about how he would miss Christmas with his family. Frederick Kurr was more concerned about the prison food: 'The prison people ... are feeding us on black bread and warm water and if you can spare a few pounds ... it will be a godsend; two pounds will buy me and my friend Greengrocer white bread and coffee for a month – It is something horrible here, we are dressed in convict's clothes and in fact like felons convicted.'[23] Assistance was duly provided by Edward Froggatt, who had been engaged to represent the three prisoners, arriving at Rotterdam on 18 December to speak to his clients, and to provide £10 to the Dutch prison authorities so that Frederick Kurr and his colleagues could receive a modestly improved diet.[24]

William Kurr, on the other hand, had still not been arrested. Though his involvement was suspected, and his house was watched for several weeks before his arrest, the police were short of witnesses that could place Kurr at any of the offices that had been used by the fraudsters. However, by the end of December Abrahams and the police had accumulated sufficient information to justify a warrant for Kurr's arrest. On 31 December, following a robust chase through the streets near his house, William Kurr (who was armed with a revolver that he decided not to use) was arrested by Detective Sergeant John Littlechild.[25] Kurr's colleagues joined him in prison after the completion of their extradition hearings, returning on a steamer from Rotterdam on 12 January 1877 accompanied by Druscovich.

Meanwhile, Clarke was busy tackling other cases. At the beginning of December he successfully closed down a betting operation at the One Tun Tavern off Haymarket.[26] He also substituted for Williamson, who had travelled to Rotterdam during mid-December. On Boxing Day, he submitted a report on a 'Contemplated Fenian Outrage' in which he noted that small meetings had taken place organised by 'persons of little influence' and that his informers 'do not believe any outbreak is likely to take place'.[27] Then, while waiting for the weather to improve sufficiently to extradite de Tourville to Hamburg, he spent some time with family and friends. On 28 December he went to the Canterbury Music Hall with William Norfolk, a friend he had made through his daughter's marriage to Henry Payne. The two men saw the seasonal entertainment: 'Great attractions for the Christmas Holydays – Aquarium, Caverns, Sliding Roof, Grand Lounge, New ballet entitled Ceres. Première danseuse assoluta, Mademoiselle Pitteri. Operatic selection from La Sonnambula. Prima donna, Miss Russell, Prima tenori, Vincent Marmaduke, George Leybourne, Fred Albert etc.'[28] They also shared each other's company on the 29 December at the aquarium, and on New Year's Eve at the Paxton Head public house Knightsbridge, for a pipe and a glass.[29]

After several hearings at Marlborough Street Police Court the two Kurr brothers, Benson, Bale and Murray were all committed for trial at the Old Bailey. The foregoing account has provided the main elements of the case against the fraudsters, but the hearings were not without interest.[30] On 1 January 1877, when William Kurr first appeared to answer the charges against him, Kurr's friend, Harry Stenning (a professional billiard player), who had tried to prevent Littlechild from arresting Kurr, was spotted in court and arrested. He was carrying a plan of the court with a marked escape route. Stenning was later tried and sentenced to a year's imprisonment for obstructing a constable, plotting Kurr's escape and attempting to suborn a key witness. The witness in question was George Flintoff, the landlord of the premises rented by the fraudsters at 8 Northumberland Street. At Stenning's trial in February, Flintoff also claimed that Froggatt had tried to bribe him not to give evidence against Kurr. This prompted Froggatt to issue a writ against Flintoff for perjury; a confrontation that ended in legal impasse.[31]

The Old Bailey trial of the fraudsters took place over eight days between 12 and 23 April 1877. The five accused were charged with obtaining £10,000 by false pretences and 'forging and uttering with intent to defraud, checks [sic] drawn on the Royal Bank of London'. Montagu Williams, counsel for Edwin Murray, later commented on the case and the prisoners:

> The frauds that had been perpetrated were, I think, the cleverest that have ever come under my notice, and this being so, it will, perhaps, not be out of place if I briefly describe the appearance of the various prisoners.
>
> Benson, who was unmistakably a Jew, was of a very different stamp from his associates. He was a short, dapper, well-made little man … he was described as being twenty-six years of age, but he had the appearance of being somewhat older. It was clear that he was a man of good education. His hands and feet were remarkably small, and he was dressed well, and in perfectly good taste, which is more than can be said of the majority of those who make their appearance in the dock at the Central Criminal Court. Benson had charming manners, and it

transpired in the course of the trial that, during his sojourn in the Isle of Wight, and other places, he had moved in the very best society. There could be no doubt whatever that Benson's had been the master mind in a long series of frauds.

William Kurr, the culprit next in importance, was described as being twenty-three years of age. In appearance he was more like a well-to-do farmer than anything else ... His face wore an honest expression; but it does not always do to judge by appearances. I think that both in ability and craft he ran Benson very close.

My client Murray, whose age was stated to be thirty-two, was described as a clerk, and looked that part exactly. He, too, was scrupulously well-dressed, and I could not help feeling that, if he had really been a clerk, and an honest one, his services would have commanded a handsome salary ... The other two prisoners, Bale and Frederick Kurr, were mere nonentities, having been tools in the hands of their more astute confederates.[32]

Solicitor General Sir Hardinge Giffard led the prosecution. Unusually, the Treasury had transferred the responsibility for assembling the prosecution case to Michael Abrahams. Clarke was called to give evidence of the arrest of Edwin Murray and mentioned that Murray had denied any direct involvement in obtaining money from the Comtesse de Goncourt. With William Kurr's counsel trying to undermine the evidence of George Flintoff, Clarke was asked whether he had seen Kurr at Sandown Park Races on 31 August 1876. (Flintoff's evidence had placed Kurr at the gang's operational headquarters at 8 Northumberland Street on the morning of that day.) Clarke confirmed that he had. This information was to receive greater attention than it deserved later in the year.[33]

Amongst more than eighty witnesses, including the Comtesse de Goncourt, Charles Chabot was once more deployed to confirm the identity of the handwriting on various incriminating documents. Evidence also emerged that Benson had found a means of communicating with the outside world from his Newgate Prison cell and, later, it became clear that he and William Kurr had been able to maintain some dialogue in this way. That too is important in the context of subsequent events. There was only passing mention of Meiklejohn during the trial, and no reference to Palmer. Meiklejohn was mentioned in the evidence of the landlord of the Queen's Hotel, Bridge of Allan, and also in that of Alexander Monteith, manager of the Clydesdale Bank at Alloa, who said that Meiklejohn had been the means of introduction between himself and Kurr and Benson.[34] However, no specific references to police corruption surfaced at the trial; rather intriguing in view of subsequent events. There had undoubtedly been a concern not to compromise a successful outcome to the turf fraud trial in both the Treasury Solicitor's and the commissioner's offices.

The jury did not deliberate for long before returning a 'guilty' verdict against all the accused. Ironically, the Comtesse de Goncourt made a plea for clemency, possibly appeased by the successful outcome of the trial and the impending return of most of her money. Speaking quietly, and in French, her intervention had little effect on the sentences passed down. Benson received fifteen years' penal servitude, and Bale and the Kurr brothers ten years' penal servitude each. Only Murray escaped relatively lightly, having been found guilty as an accessory after the fact, and sentenced to eighteen months' imprisonment.[35] Benson, Bale and Frederick Kurr started their sentences at Pentonville Prison with a period of nine months' solitary confinement, before being transferred to the public works prisons at Portsmouth, Portland and Dartmoor, respectively.[36] William Kurr began his sentence at Millbank.

Investigations of Police Corruption

There was probably some satisfaction in the Scotland Yard Detective Department at the outcome of the trial, but it must have been muted by the apparent police corruption revealed during the investigation. Although an official inquiry had been implemented by the Treasury, it is unclear by late in 1876 precisely what immediate action, if any, was taken against Palmer and Meiklejohn.[37] Palmer was, however, recorded to have visited the Metropolitan Police Chief Surgeon in January and February 1877 and was probably on sick leave for some time.[38]

Apart from his friendship with Williamson, Clarke was probably closest with Palmer in his relationships with his other senior colleagues. They had both started work in the department in 1862, and some of their social activities and interests had coincided when Clarke became a Freemason in 1869. On 8 October 1869, at the age of 51, Clarke had been initiated into the Freemasons, joining Domatic Lodge No 177.[39] Palmer was also a member and former Inspector Richard Tanner was a well-regarded acting secretary of the lodge during the early 1870s.[40] 'Freemasonry historically attracted two different types – the philosophical intellectuals and the gentlemen who thought that a Masonic lodge was a useful and agreeable social gathering.'[41] Clarke was presumably in the latter group. He attended dinners at the lodge and the Lodge's Annual Festival to the Ladies where, in July 1875 at The Greyhound, Dulwich: 'A first-rate band played during dinner. The speeches were necessarily short as the Brethren and the ladies had made up their minds for dancing ... [and] kept up till a late hour.'[42]

Whatever Clarke's reasons for joining, he appears to have been committed to Freemasonry's aims and objectives, as he also chose to become a Royal Arch Mason, joining on 23 November 1871, and remained a Mason until his resignation in June 1890, long after his retirement from the police.[43] At the end of 1876, both he and Palmer were officers of the Domatic Lodge. Palmer had the more senior position of junior warden while Clarke was a deacon, whose responsibilities included guarding the inside of the main door of the lodge during the arrival of members for their meetings. This was a task that he fulfilled on the 10 November 1876 when the lodge met at their usual venue, Anderton's Hotel in Fleet Street.[44] For reasons that will become clear later, the date and location of this meeting became significant in subsequent events.

Apart from Meiklejohn and Palmer, Druscovich also had some questions to answer concerning his conduct of the investigation into the turf fraud. Firstly, what had happened to the letter that had been sent by the Chief Constable of Leeds to Williamson, which should have arrived in the detective department on 26 September 1876 when Druscovich was in charge of the office? Druscovich had denied knowing anything about it, and the letter was never found. Secondly, it was discovered that Druscovich failed to report that he had received a compromising telegram from Meiklejohn, when in Edinburgh in November 1876. When asked to explain the omission, Druscovich said that he thought it hardly worth mentioning, only later telling Williamson that he had withheld the telegram to shield Meiklejohn from trouble.[45] Thirdly, Druscovich's colleague, William Reimers, had told Williamson in early December 1876 of a conversation that took place between Reimers and Druscovich in late November that year:

> I said, 'How are you getting on with the turf swindle?' He [Druscovich] said, 'Damn the turf swindle! I wish I had never heard anything of it'. He then added 'I have documents in my hand with which I could smash two'. Just before he said this I had said 'I believe there is some one else in it besides Meiklejohn'. Then he made the remark about the documents. I then said to him 'Have you told the Governor so?' (Meaning Mr Williamson.) To that he replied 'No, I have not; let him find out like I have done'. I then said to him 'Surely you will not jeopardise your position for the sake of screening others'. He made no reply.[46]

Reimers was not the most impartial observer at that time. He had been promoted to inspector in October 1876 following the secondment of Meiklejohn to the Midland Railway. However, in late December he had been 'busted' back to sergeant and believed that Druscovich had been responsible for this demotion.[47] All in all, the Scotland Yard Detective Department was not a happy place to be in during 1876–77, except perhaps for George Greenham, who was promoted to inspector in place of Reimers. Undoubtedly Druscovich was feeling the pressure of events and it is probably no coincidence that this generally highly regarded young officer received a caution for irregular conduct in June 1877, when he was found to have been at fault in 'failing to differentiate clearly between charges made and legally proved' when giving evidence at a magistrate's court.[48] One imagines that his mind was on other things. Someone else who was being scrutinised was Froggatt, who was suspected of having offered to bribe a court official at Marlborough Street Police Court in 1876, to provide early warning of any warrants that might be issued against William Kurr. In addition, he had probably tried to bribe George Flintoff.[49]

Actions to investigate the suspected corruption became more apparent after the turf fraud trial. On 18 May 1877, Treasury Solicitor Sir Augustus Stephenson sent a confidential memorandum to the Home Secretary, stating that 'there is no doubt of the complicity of Meiklejohn and Palmer', but expressing uncertainty whether the men had committed an indictable offence, or whether they should be dismissed without attempting to prosecute them. Stephenson recommended that a submission should be made to counsel for advice.[50] By then, Benson and Kurr had decided to make their own contribution to the investigations. Whether they initiated the approach to provide information, in the hope of getting a deal for an early release, or whether the Treasury approached them first is not known for certain.[51] However, from Benson's account of events, on 24 April 1877 he asked Stephenson to see him. This was followed on 9 May 1877 by a visit by William Pollard, assistant to the Treasury Solicitor, who questioned Benson in Pentonville Prison in the first of six meetings that Benson had with him and with Abrahams.[52] Similar meetings were held with Kurr.

While these activities were underway, Clarke was preparing to travel to Austria with Detective Sergeant von Tornow for the trial of Henri de Tourville. The two men were away from Scotland Yard for three weeks from 15 June. For von Tornow at least, it seems to have been a bad time to be away because, on his return, he discovered that an accusation had been made against him that he had been seen drinking with William Kurr and, worse, that he had taken a bribe from Kurr to ensure that he would not locate the second cabman who had picked up Benson on 4 October 1876; accusations which von Tornow denied. Von Tornow's reaction further enhanced suspicion, as he went missing in late July, returning to his family home in Germany. However, in his later and more considered response (which in the circumstances seems courageous rather than suspicious) he returned to Scotland Yard in August to 'face the music', and was reinstated in his post albeit with a reprimand and caution. Ultimately, he was never charged with any offence and remained in the detective department at Scotland Yard, later achieving promotion to inspector.[53]

Whether Clarke had been in communication with the office while he was away in Austria is not known, but he was soon to discover on his return that things had moved on. The Treasury Solicitor's office had finally reached a decision on the actions that they should take. On 11 July 1877, arrest warrants were approved by the chief magistrate at Bow Street, Sir James Ingham, and on 12 July Williamson arrested Meiklejohn, Palmer and Druscovich, while Clarke was sent to arrest Froggatt. All four men were charged with conspiring to defeat the ends of justice. When they were placed in the dock at Bow Street Police Court, Williamson and Clarke gave formal evidence of the arrests. Their three colleagues were remanded in custody and only Froggatt received bail despite Palmer's insistent efforts to achieve the same outcome.[54]

The magistrate's committal hearings started on Thursday 19 July at Bow Street and continued intermittently until Saturday 22 September. The arrests had created a sensation. Although police officers had appeared in court before for various offences, nothing on this scale or level of seniority had previously been seen: 'The three officers were brought up in custody and an immense concourse had gathered in front of the court to witness their arrival ... The court was most inconveniently crowded and business was frequently interrupted by the struggles of persons to enter or to leave the building.'[55] As several of the key witnesses were convicted criminals, the hearings attracted huge crowds who applauded and shouted encouragement to the Black Marias carrying the convicts and hissed at those containing the accused policemen. As a consequence, Bow Street was frequently blocked by large numbers of spectators throughout the summer of 1877, much to the annoyance of residents and local tradesmen.

The prosecution case was led by Harry Poland. The four accused were variously represented: Palmer by Mr Besley, Druscovich by Mr St John Wontner, Meiklejohn by Montagu Williams (on this occasion most certainly 'the defender of lost causes') and Froggatt by George Lewis (now famous for his inquisitorial performance at the Bravo inquest). Poland's opening statement made it clear that the key witnesses against the accused were Kurr and Benson. The evidence against Meiklejohn was that he had been providing useful information to Kurr since 1872, which had been of value in helping Kurr and the other fraudsters to conduct their frauds and to evade arrest during their involvement in several criminal betting schemes. Meiklejohn had received substantial amounts of money from Kurr in return. Corroborative evidence included incriminating letters that Meiklejohn had written to Kurr (which Kurr had kept), and also evidence that Meiklejohn had purchased a house in 1874 with banknotes traced back to Kurr. It was claimed that Druscovich had fallen under the influence of Kurr in April 1876 when he had needed money to meet an outstanding debt that he had incurred on his brother's behalf and, at Meiklejohn's recommendation, had accepted a £60 loan from Kurr. As a consequence, from the first day that he was given responsibility for the turf fraud investigation, the prosecution case was that Druscovich had conducted his enquiries in a manner that had given the fraudsters every opportunity to evade arrest, receiving some additional money and jewellery from Kurr in the process. Evidence against Palmer consisted of the letter, in his handwriting, from 'W. Brown', addressed to 'W. Gifford' at Bridge of Allan, to warn Kurr of the imminent arrival of Druscovich. Further incriminating evidence had been found in the form of a telegram which had been sent on 10 November from the telegraph office in Fleet Street (close to Anderton's Hotel where Palmer and Clarke were attending a Freemasons' dinner that night). Kurr's reply had been sent to Palmer's home address. Finally, the case against Froggatt included evidence that he had sought to bribe a court official as well as the witness George Flintoff, and had been, in several other ways, involved with the fraudsters; being implicated in drafting the telegram that had been sent to Rotterdam in an attempt to free Benson, Bale and Frederick Kurr, and in discussions to 'launder' some Clydesdale banknotes.[56]

Clarke and Williamson appeared to be free of suspicion. Indeed, it seems plausible (though not certain) that Clarke's plans to retire in 1876 may have been halted at the request of Williamson or Commissioner Henderson to help maintain a functioning detective department during the corruption investigations. However, with three senior members of his staff being apparently involved in criminal activity, Williamson must have felt vulnerable. One would think that his apparent lack of awareness of what seemed to have been going on should have raised questions at a higher level. However, there is little or no indication that it did, which says a great deal for the trust that his superiors placed in him. Indeed, even before matters were fully resolved, the Home Secretary approved a restructuring of the detective department early in October 1877 and Williamson, as superintendent, received a substantial pay increase of £100 a year.[57] During late July and August, however, Williamson was 'specially employed', (probably assisting the Treasury legal team and planning changes to the structure of the department) and Clarke was once again placed as inspector in charge.[58] The detective department was busy with at least two murder investigations during August, which temporarily became Clarke's overall responsibility.[59] Yet, as events unfolded at Bow Street Police Court, Clarke's mind soon became engaged on even more important matters: self-preservation.

On the first day of the hearings at Bow Street, Clarke's name had cropped up during Poland's introductory statement. It was mentioned that Clarke had previously met Benson (as 'Yonge') in 1875 on the Isle of Wight, and secondly that he had been present at a Masonic dinner with Palmer on 10 November 1876, the night a telegram had been sent to Bridge of Allan. On 26 July, Clarke was again mentioned in court during Kurr's evidence when several letters written by Meiklejohn to Kurr were read out in court. Several of these made reference to Clarke, including a letter from Meiklejohn postmarked 11 October 1875:'... I had a letter from Poodle this morning, in which he says that he expects a letter from Chieftain saying that the matter of mine will be settled in my favour. I simply told him the matter was settled Saturday week, and C. never intended me to get it, as he recommended D. himself.'[60] The letter requires some translation: 'Poodle' was Benson; 'Chieftain' and 'C.' refer to Clarke; 'D.' was Sergeant Davey who, at Clarke's recommendation, had been promoted to inspector instead of Meiklejohn. One implication of this letter was that Clarke had been in correspondence with Benson (as Yonge), several months after he had first met him in the Isle of Wight in April 1875.

At Bow Street on 2 August, Kurr stated that he had not been at Sandown Races on 31 August 1876, although it had previously been stated at his April trial that he had been there on that day. Clarke had given evidence at the same trial that he had seen Kurr on that day at Sandown, and the inference was, if Kurr was now telling the truth, that Clarke must have lied. On 12 and 16 August Kurr gave evidence that he had bribed Clarke and had received up-to-date information of the turf fraud investigations from Clarke, via a pre-arranged signal in which Clarke would send a piece of blotting paper in a self-addressed envelope that Kurr had supplied. Kurr claimed that the blotting paper bearing the text 'Keep the lame man out of the way' had been sent by Clarke. Claiming that he had been sent other such envelopes, Kurr said that he had several meetings with Clarke at his home at 20 Great College Street, and elsewhere, including the Duke of York steps. On 17 August, Kurr mentioned the subject of the unsigned letter that Clarke had written to William Walters in 1874, a copy of which had been given to Kurr by Meiklejohn. The implication that Kurr put on this letter was that Clarke had also been in league with Walters and had accepted bribes from him. However, Kurr also confirmed that he had originally told the Treasury Solicitors that Clarke 'was an honest man and not to be bribed'.[61]

Kurr was followed into the witness box by Harry Benson. On Saturday 25 August, Benson was in his fourth day of evidence when he also claimed that Clarke was in his pay. When cross-examined he claimed that Clarke had visited Rose Bank on at least three occasions during 1875. In addition, there had been meetings between the two men at the Langham and Westminster Palace hotels, and Benson said that he had given Clarke money on several occasions.[62] Many of these comments had been extracted from Kurr and Benson during cross-examination by Meiklejohn's counsel, Montagu Williams, who brought things to a head when he expressed the hope that it would be possible to cross-examine Clarke on 8 September.[63] He explained later, during the subsequent Old Bailey trial, that his strategy for Meiklejohn in the magistrate's court had been to ensure that Clarke was called as a witness:

> ... in order that he [Clarke] might have an opportunity of contradicting upon his oath the statements which had been made about him and asserting that they were a tissue of lies from the beginning to the end. If that course had

been allowed, the magistrate would have had the alternative of either believing Clarke or the two convicts … Did the jury believe that such a man like Clarke, with his character, antecedents, and the position he had occupied for 35 years, would be guilty of this fraud? Did they believe he would be such a lunatic or candidate for Colney Hatch [lunatic asylum] as to put himself in the power of two such arrant knaves as those who gave their evidence?[64]

It was a strategy that did Clarke no favours, but it undoubtedly concentrated the minds of the Treasury legal team.

The claims made by Kurr and Benson, and the fact that several aspects of their 'story' appeared to be consistent, must have been enormously discomforting to Clarke, regardless of whether they were a fabrication or not. He therefore started to produce reports to rebut the accusations made. Meanwhile, the senior lawyers in government were increasingly concerned. Attorney General Sir John Holker and Solicitor General Sir Hardinge Giffard wrote to the Home Secretary on 29 August expressing their view: 'We have come to the conclusion that Inspector Clarke ought to be charged along with the men now in custody. We may add that in our view the prosecution which has been instituted would probably be prejudicially affected unless such charge against Clarke is preferred at once.'[65] Clearly, the two politicians felt that the charges against Meiklejohn, Druscovich, Palmer and Froggatt would be undermined unless Clarke was also charged, even though any case against Clarke at this stage was based solely on the uncorroborated evidence of two convicted criminals. This caused some disquiet and a measure of support for Clarke in the Home Office. The permanent secretary wrote to the Home Secretary suggesting that it would be better:

to see the whole case of Clarke's statements before the final step is taken which is a very serious one for Clarke. I infer that the LO's [Law Officers] have come to their decision upon the Newspaper reports:– which in effect is upon the uncorroborated statements of the convicts. Clarke professes in his statement to explain much of that and particularly the letter [to Walters] about which so much has been said, and I confess it seems fair to me that any thing that he has to say should be considered before the statements of unmitigated rascals uncorroborated should be taken as sufficient to inflict so serious a blow on so old and hitherto so trusted an official as Clarke. For whether he were convicted or discharged the blow would be fatal to him. I have seen Hodgson of the Treasury and he takes the same view.[66]

By 2 September, Poland and Abrahams were in favour of Clarke's arrest while Williamson and Pollard were still of the view that Clarke was innocent, though Pollard's opinion 'was somewhat shaken on Friday [31 August]', after Benson had described several meetings between Clarke and himself.[67] Meanwhile, Clarke continued to assemble his response to the evidence given by Kurr and Benson, and submitted his final report to the Treasury Solicitor's office on 7 September.

Arrest of Chief Inspector George Clarke

On the morning of Saturday 8 September, Clarke was arrested by his friend and colleague, Williamson, and suspended from duty without pay. The event became national news:

> No subject has been so much talked about this week in London as the arrest of Chief Inspector Clarke. He is a well known and highly respected man, and I have heard more sympathy expressed for him than for the other three detectives put together. Why this should be I cannot say; but that is a fact, I can vouch. The arrest was made by Supt. Williamson, the Chief of the Detective Department, and I suppose he never did this duty more unwillingly in his life. He and Clarke had been neighbours and bosom friends for 29 years; and it is not surprising, under the circumstances, that he should have wept, as I am informed he did, when he told his lieutenant that he must consider himself in custody.[68]

Whether the increased expectation that Montagu Williams had created – that Clarke would be available for cross-examination on 8 September – was the principal trigger that influenced the timing of his arrest is not certain. It could be that the Treasury had finally made up their mind that there was a case against Clarke that needed to be answered in court. However, the fact that the prosecuting counsel, Harry Poland, was not fully prepared on 8 September to present the case against Clarke (his presentation was delayed until 13 September) suggests a degree of unplanned haste in the final decision to arrest him. Indeed, if Clarke had not been arrested when he was then he would have been eligible to give evidence at the magistrate's hearing, and the Treasury case against the other prisoners could have been undermined in the way that Montagu Williams was seeking to achieve for his client. Once arrested and charged with the same offence, Clarke could not now give evidence on his own behalf or as a witness.

Immediately after his arrest Clarke found himself in the dock at Bow Street alongside his police colleagues and Froggatt. There was not room to fit them all in, so Froggatt was moved down to the front of the court. There are reports that Palmer and possibly Meiklejohn were in tears when Clarke entered the dock, and the events that morning were quickly captured in courtroom verse:

Clarke's arrest at the Court was so suddenly planned,
It gives all the prisoners a shock;
But whilst the detectives are moved where they stand,
Mr. Froggatt's moved out of the dock.[69]

At the end of the momentous day's events, Poland did not oppose Clarke's
request for bail, which was granted on total sureties of £1,000.

Clarke's arrest did not prevent his statement to the Treasury emerging into
the public domain, and it soon appeared in the press. The fact that this did
not raise any issues of contempt of court suggests either that Clarke released
it himself before his arrest or that the Treasury Solicitor's office, for reasons of
their own, arranged for it to be available to the press. The following version
was published in the *Hertfordshire Express* and would have been seen by friends
and family living in the area where he was born:

I first became acquainted with the associates of these men [Kurr and Benson]
in 1871, by complaints being received respecting a betting agency carried on
at Myrtle-terrace, Hammersmith, and I ascertained that it was carried on by
the man Walters. I obtained evidence, and submitted a report of details to the
Treasury. In the result I obtained a warrant and arrested Walters, who pleaded
guilty, and was fined £100. In 1872 I ascertained that this man was again carrying on betting. Again I reported to the Treasury. Again obtained a warrant
against him. Again arrested him and he was fined £100. I lost sight of him until
1873, when Walters applied for a transfer of the license of the Grapes public
house, Red Lion-street, Holborn. I gave evidence to the licensing magistrates
of the two convictions, all I then knew of him; and on his counsel (Mr Besley)
stating that Walters wanted the house for his mother, who had formerly kept
a public house at Kingsclere, Berkshire, and would give up betting, the magistrates granted the transfer. Walters followed me out of the building, and said that
he intended to conduct the house in a respectable manner, and that if he could
assist me at any time by giving information he would be glad to do so. I never
entered his house, and I saw nothing more of Walters until the spring of 1874,
when the late Inspector Pay having informed me that there was every reason
to believe a burglary with violence at Nayland, Suffolk, had been concocted at
Walter's public house, that one of the men arrested on the charge had had his
defence paid for by Walters, I, at Pay's request that I should see Walters, wrote
a letter to Walters asking to meet me. Before sending that letter I submitted it
to Superintendent Williamson. I met Walters, who denied all knowledge of the
burglary and of the men, who, however, were all arrested, the last exclusively
through my exertions.

I heard nothing more of Walters until January 1875, when a betting man
named Charles Berkley [sic], together with Daniel Potch [sic] and George

Manning, called at Scotland Yard. Berkley stated that his name was being improperly used by some men having offices in the City, and carrying on a betting swindle under the title of 'The General Assurance Society Against Losses on the Turf'; that the principals in the 'Society' were a man named Edwin Murray and William Kurr; that upon Berkley complaining of his name being improperly used, the man named gave him a document holding him harmless, and promised him a sum of money for the use of his name; that by false telegrams and letters he had been induced to meet them at a wine shop in the Holloway-road for the purpose of settling the matter; and that on going there he was invited into a back parlour, where Murray, Walters, Kurr, and four or five others, armed with revolvers, under threats of his life, took the documents he possessed from him. I submitted a report to the Commissioner, and accompanied by Berkley I obtained warrants at Clerkenwell against the men named. I apprehended Murray on the same evening, but Walters and Kurr absconded. The evidence of Berkley and his friends before the magistrate was very confused, and Murray was remanded on bail. I was directed by the magistrate not to execute the other warrants, but to give the parties charged notice to attend on the remand day. I succeeded in arresting Walters on the 18th of February, and used, without success, every endeavour to arrest Kurr. During the remand till the 26th I obtained evidence connecting these men to the fraud (the 'General Assurance Against Losses on the Turf'). I submitted a report to my superiors, asking for legal aid, and the solicitor of the Treasury obtained warrants at the Mansion House for the arrest of these men. The men in custody at Clerkenwell, Murray and Walters, were discharged, and I re-apprehended them, Kurr still keeping out of the way. They were remanded from time to time until the 27th of April. By that time, by my own exertions, I had obtained a chain of evidence connecting these men and others with the frauds which had been extensively practised in Russia, Germany and France – this evidence being reported verbally and in writing to the solicitors to the Treasury. After the committal for trial an application was made by the late Mr. Justice Archibald to the admission to bail of Walters and Murray. This was granted, though at the time I reported that the men would abscond. I said to Mr. Thomas at the Treasury, 'I feel sure these men will abscond,' to which he replied 'We cannot help it, we cannot resist any longer'.

The men did not appear at the Central Criminal Court, and I found that they had absconded to America. I made inquiries from time to time, and in January, 1876, I was informed that they were in Havre, in France. I reported this to the Commissioner, and at my suggestion my report was forwarded to the French police on January 19th, 1876. The man (convict) Kurr had succeeded in keeping out of the way, but during June 1875, I heard that he was in London, and I had several conversations with Mr. Pollard as to the steps to be taken if he should be found. It was decided that it would not be advisable to apprehend him in the

absence of the other two, and I inserted a 'memo' in the 'police information' to
the effect that Kurr was not to be apprehended, but that if found a report was to
be made in order that the solicitor might be consulted. No report was received
from divisions as to Kurr's being seen in London. During that autumn (1875),
however, I received a letter from Kurr, offering to surrender himself. This I submitted to the Treasury but no steps were taken in this matter.

During the remands of Murray and Walters in 1875 I was made aware that
the letter I had written to Walters respecting the burglary, asking him to meet
me, had been photographed and copied and put in the hands of counsel for
the purpose of making an accusation against my honesty. This was not carried into effect, owing, I believe, to the honest advice given by their counsel,
Mr. D. Straight. I felt much annoyed that my letter should be in the hands of
this class, and I endeavoured to recover it. Early in 1876, upon going home
one evening, my wife handed me the identical letter and a copy of it. These
had been left by a man in my absence. I have no doubt now that it was Kurr
who left the letter. As soon as I found that this letter was of importance in the
inquiry at Bow-street I handed it to Mr. Pollard and by the newspaper reports
I see that it is admitted by Mr. Poland that the letter was honest, and written
in the interests of justice. It follows, therefore, that the present convicts, wilfully and deliberately contemplated in 1875 making a false charge against me
in respect to this very letter.

I now commence the history of my acquaintance with the convict Harry
Benson.

On a Sunday, about the 11th of April 1875, a Mr. Andrews of 9 Mincing-
lane (a merchant and a gentleman of undoubted respectability), called at my
house, and said that a friend of his, 'Mr. Yonge', of Rosebank, Shanklin, Isle
of Wight, could give me some information respecting the frauds I was then
inquiring about, and the persons who had committed them. Mr. Andrews
offered me £5 to pay my expenses as 'Mr. Yonge' was an invalid, and could
not come to London. I declined to receive the £5, but promised Mr. Andrews
to attend to the matter. The next day I was instructed by the Treasury to see
'Mr. Yonge' at Shanklin, and on arriving there late in the evening, I was by
Mr. Andrews introduced to the convict Benson, who was then passing under
that name. 'Mr. Yonge' was living with all the surroundings of wealth. He was
spoken of as the proprietor of the principal newspaper in this island, kept a
carriage, upon the panel of which was a coronet; he lived in a villa standing in
its own grounds, and in all kept an establishment such as only the wealthy could
keep. He professed to have become acquainted with men of the description of
Walters and Murray through an advertisement, and that he had been engaged
in drawing up newspaper articles for them for a mining speculation in Wales.
He promised me information regarding the men on the conditions that his

name was not to be mentioned, and by reason of his being a helpless cripple, he was not under any circumstances, to be required to give evidence. I told him that I would be glad of any information, and that I would report his helpless condition to the Treasury. I then left 'Mr. Yonge' and spent the night with Mr. Andrews at an hotel, seeing 'Mr. Yonge' in the morning before I returned to London, to ask him some questions which had occurred to me in the interval; and on my return that morning I reported all the particulars in writing. During these interviews 'Yonge' told me incidentally that he had met with his lameness by a railway accident, and that he had recovered large compensation. He showed me a bill of Mr. Andrews's for £1,000, and led me to believe that he was connected with a firm of money-lenders. As I have said, I found him living in apparent wealth, and finding him associated with a gentleman of undoubted respectability like Mr. Andrews, perhaps I spoke more freely of the persons connected with the fraud than I should have done to the ordinary class of 'informants'. Before leaving Yonge I had a strong suspicion that he was a mischievous, cunning man, and this suspicion I mentioned to Superintendent Williamson on my return. Some time after my return to London I received a few communications from Yonge, but they were confused, and did not afford any information, but I have no doubt I acknowledged the receipt of these letters by replies to Yonge. I visited the island in June, 1875, to seek for lodgings for my daughter, who was ill, and I took this opportunity to call upon 'Yonge' to see if he had any information. The interview was short, and I returned with my wife to London, not having taken lodgings as I found them more than I could afford. In August I took my sick daughter a trip to the Isle of Wight during the time I was on leave, and I had again a short interview with Yonge. I was only in the island from the 14th to the 17th. Shortly after this date a gentleman from the Isle of Wight called at the office. His name was either Young or Harvey; both names were mentioned but I do not remember which was the gentleman's. [It was Harvey.[70]] He told me that 'Mr. Yonge', the proprietor of a newspaper, had slandered every one of any respectability in the island, and as 'Mr. Yonge' had publicly stated that he was attached to the French Embassy to England, the gentleman was anxious to establish who Mr Yonge really was. I referred the gentleman to the Commissioner who directed me to make enquiries at the French Embassy. I inquired, and reported in writing that Mr. Yonge was in no way connected with the Embassy. Soon after Yonge called at my house one evening with a man-servant, and said he wished to speak to me at the Westminster Palace Hotel. I promised I would call upon him in the course of the evening. I did so. 'Mr. Yonge' then stated that he had reasons to believe that I was in correspondence with a private inquiry agent named Nichols respecting his (Yonge's) antecedents, and that he thought it very unfair that the police should be engaged with private inquiry men. I told him that his belief was not founded on fact; that I had not seen Nichols [who was employed by Harvey[71]]. Yonge told me either that he had communicated with the Commissioner or that he was about to communicate with the Commissioner on this matter. I told him he was at liberty to do as he pleased; adding the remark, 'There's a good deal of mystery surrounding you'. To this he replied, in seeming confidence, that the fact was he was one of the Princes Murat, and was here on a political mission, showing at the same time a handkerchief with a coronet upon it. I doubted his statement, but I do not recollect whether I told 'Mr. Yonge' my doubts. He appeared to me altogether a romantic man, whom I could not understand. I saw him again at the Langham Hotel, and later at 3, Bentinck-street, at his invitation, both times. These interviews were very short, and with those I have already spoken of, are all I have had with him. On every occasion he professed to be anxious to give me information respecting the turf frauds, and particularly mentioned the name of Trevelli (who under some name is undergoing penal servitude) as being engaged in a similar fraud; but I could never get 'Yonge' to enter into definite details. Shortly before the Christmas after I saw him last I received a letter from him, saying that he had given me a great deal of trouble and asking me what wine I would prefer for Christmas. I made no reply. During all the time I knew him he was living in excellent style. I had strong suspicions he was telling falsehoods, but I never understood his true character. The statement that he gave me £100 and the construction he puts on my acquaintance with him is wholly untrue, and I beg to point out there were no secrets in the case which it was possible for me to have told him; that I had no control on any action which might be taken by the Treasury respecting Kurr; that I used every endeavour to rearrest Walters and Murray; that by my exertions I completely exposed the whole system and broke it up for the time being, and I was the means of recovering a large sum of money which would have fallen into the hands of these men; that I knew nothing of this man 'Yonge' at the time I was in communication with him, and could not suspect that he was one of the principals in the fraud; and that I did not know Kurr but by his bad repute, and should not have known him if I had met him. In further proof of my innocence of all complicity with these men or their actions, I submit the letter I received from Yonge in September 1875, and copies of these he returned to me of my own, dated 14th, 22nd and 28th September, 1875.[72]

Clarke went on to deny in detail the statements of Kurr as to meeting him at Clarke's house, the alleged payment to Clarke of £200, and appointments at the steps of the Duke of York's Monument. He concluded:

I beg to state that these allegations can only have been made from motives of revenge against me for the active part I have taken in the prosecution of this class. From the fact that Kurr made no mention of my name in his original statement to the Treasury, which is admitted in his evidence, the statements regarding myself show them to be self-contradictory and an afterthought. I had no control in conducting inquiries respecting the fraud on Madame de Goncourt. I had nothing to do with sending the information to the several ports. I personally arrested the first prisoner in connection with the case, Murray, on the 27th of November, the information which led to his arrest being in my possession from the 25th; and the least word from me would have been sufficient to have prevented this initial step in bringing those who are now convicts to justice. I submit all my reports on these turf frauds and my correspondence with Yonge. Any letters which have passed, and are not here, were destroyed at the time when I had sought to retire from the service (before these frauds were discovered) and about which I spoke to Superintendent Williamson. The letters which were not destroyed at this time were preserved by accident.[73]

Returning to the Bow Street dock on 13 September, Clarke faced the rare experience of being on the opposite 'side' in a courtroom to Harry Poland, and at the receiving end of Poland's prosecution case against him. The principal evidence, relating to the charge of conspiring to defeat the ends of justice, was based on the statements made in court by Kurr and Benson. The main accusations were:

1   That Clarke had been bribed by William Walters not to oppose the granting of a publican's licence. In addition, the unsigned letter written by Clarke to Walters provided grounds for suspicion of their relationship, particularly because Clarke had been anxious to recover his letter when he discovered it had fallen into the hands of Kurr and Benson. Kurr had also claimed that when Clarke had searched Murray's lodgings after arresting him in November 1876, Walters had also been at the property and that Clarke had allowed Walters to escape.

2   That Clarke corruptly instigated the withdrawal of the arrest warrant that had been issued for William Kurr's arrest in 1875 (in the context of the 'General Society for Assurance against Losses on the Turf').

3   That Clarke had accepted money from Benson since 1875. The fact that he had only reported one of three meetings with Benson on the Isle of Wight was seen as suspicious. In addition, Clarke had maintained a subsequent correspondence with Benson; copies of several letters had been kept by Benson and his housekeeper Mrs Avis, and several others (that had been misdirected in the post) were discovered in a 'dead letter office' in late August 1877. The late discovery of these letters only reinforced suspicions that the relationship between Clarke and Benson was not an innocent one.

4   That Clarke had accepted money from Kurr during 1876 and had provided information that had assisted the fraudsters to evade arrest during

the turf fraud investigations. The failure of Druscovich and Clarke to send a telegram (rather than a letter) to the Glasgow police on 3 October 1876, after Bank of England notes obtained by the fraudsters had been 'passed' in Glasgow, was interpreted by the prosecution to have been a contributory factor in delaying the arrest of the fraudsters. In addition, Kurr claimed that he had several meetings with Clarke during this period, at Clarke's house and other venues.

5   That Clarke had committed perjury at the turf fraud trial by stating that William Kurr had been at Sandown Park on 31 August 1876; Kurr now denied that he had been there on that day.

After Poland had finished his presentation of the evidence, the hearing for the rest of the day moved on to other prosecution witnesses including Superintendent Williamson.[74]

Up to this point, Clarke had not obtained legal representation but, by 14 September, he had arranged for George Lewis to represent him. This was a good choice, not only because Lewis was an extremely competent solicitor, but also because he had been in court throughout the magistrate's hearings (representing Froggatt) and was therefore well acquainted with the case. As soon as he was engaged, Lewis asked the court for permission to recall those prosecution witnesses who had earlier given evidence relevant to Clarke's circumstances. With the agreement of Sir James Ingham, and deep sighs from the press correspondents (who had already fought for seats in the crowded Bow Street Court for about twenty days and would now have to continue), Lewis' request was granted. Once more, Kurr's and Benson's solitary confinement was interrupted; however, their cross-examination added little. In contrast, when Superintendent Williamson was recalled, Lewis extracted several helpful comments. Firstly, that Clarke's use of Walters and Benson as potential informants was not unusual:

> He [Williamson] considered it was the duty of any detective officer to visit persons who volunteered to give valuable information relative to the commission of crime, and to report the results to him. They might volunteer the names of their informants, but were not bound to do so … He considered that there was nothing even suspicious in Clarke's calling on Benson when he was in the Isle of Wight with his wife and daughter. He would not be required to report small details like that.[75]

Secondly, in relation to the frequent visits that Kurr claimed to have made to Clarke: 'He remembered being told by Clarke that some of this class had been watching and making mysterious inquiries about him in the neighbourhood of his own residence.'[76] Thirdly, Williamson indicated that none of the money alleged by Kurr and Benson to have been paid to Clarke had been traced to him, as far as Williamson was aware (and that remained the situation).[77]

The next day, Lewis completed his cross-examination and presented his rebuttal of the accusations against Clarke. He then called witnesses in Clarke's defence in the hope of achieving a discharge of the case against his client. With the considerable experience that both men had in assembling evidence and witnesses, this was undoubtedly worth a try. The first of these witnesses was Inspector John Shore, a colleague of Clarke's at Scotland Yard, who was questioned by Lewis about his experience with informants. Shore stated that he:

> Had found it necessary at times to receive information from suspected persons, from thieves, and from persons of the lowest grade … Had written hundreds of times to persons making appointments to meet them, and had kept up correspondence where necessary. All this was required to get the information they desired. Their associates at times were betting men of the lowest type, thieves, and all kinds of persons. If certain information was obtained and no result came of it, the inspectors would probably not report upon it … It was not the habit of the authorities to ask the names of informants. It was not true that witness ever had a conversation with Chief Inspector Clarke with respect to having received £400 in the Walters and Murray case, or with a Mr. Levy, about Clarke having received any money over the affair. Kurr's statements he did not value in the least. It was known, he believed, to every inspector that Mr. Clarke reported in the interest of justice, with regard to the burglary at Stannard's mill. Had always regarded Mr. Clarke one of the steadiest men in England. He was a man who evidently never lived beyond his means. He had always borne an irreproachable character, and witness had never known anything against him in his life.[78]

Amongst the other defence witnesses, Sergeant Littlechild reported that there was no truth that William Walters had been at Edwin Murray's house when he and Clarke had searched it. Inspector Cruse confirmed that when Walters had been granted a licence for the Grapes public house, Clarke had informed the magistrate of Walters' previous betting convictions. Clarke's youngest daughter, Catherine, said that she often opened the door to visitors, and that she had never seen William Kurr in her life before seeing him during the court proceedings. Mary Booker, a part-time servant of a lodger in Clarke's house, gave similar evidence. Clarke's daughter-in-law, Louisa Clarke, stressed the frugality of the Clarke household, and stated that, on 25 September 1876, Clarke and she had spent the late evening waiting at Kings Cross Station for Clarke's wife Elizabeth to return from visiting her sick brother-in-law. The significance of this evidence was that Kurr claimed that he had met Clarke elsewhere that evening. In a similar manner, William Norfolk confirmed that he had been out with Clarke on other nights in late December 1876 at times when Kurr had stated that he held meetings with Clarke. Norfolk's evidence was reinforced by the landlord of the Paxton's Head, Knightsbridge, where Clarke and Norfolk had spent an evening together. Likewise, the landlord of Clarke's local public house, Charles Jackson, also contradicted Kurr by stating that he had never seen Kurr and Clarke together in his pub, though Clarke himself was a regular customer. Frederick Andrews, the accountant who had introduced Clarke to Yonge (Benson) in 1875, confirmed the manner of the introduction and that 'from his knowledge of Benson he would say that he was a man who was not to believed on his oath'. Finally, James Griffin swore that William Kurr had been present at Sandown Races on 31 August 1876, as he had previously done during the turf fraud trial in April.[79]

When given the opportunity to speak, before a final decision was made by the chief magistrate, Clarke said:

> I wish to say that I am perfectly innocent of the charge made against me by the convicts. It is made to destroy me for having honestly and fearlessly performed my duties towards the public in protecting them against the frauds committed from time to time, and especially during the last six or seven years, and for having brought them and their friends and associates to justice.[80]

However, despite the efforts of George Lewis and the defence witnesses, Clarke was probably sufficiently experienced and sanguine not to be surprised when he and all the arrested men were committed for trial at the Old Bailey. Only Clarke and Froggatt were permitted bail.

The Trial of the Detectives

The Old Bailey trial covered the same ground as the proceedings at Bow Street, notwithstanding the appearance of some new personalities amongst the prosecution and defence teams, and some additional witnesses.[81] For this reason, the following account will not repeat aspects previously covered and will focus on the case against Clarke and the events and personalities that only emerged during the Old Bailey trial.

After his committal for trial, Clarke needed to find a counsel who could represent him at the Old Bailey and to raise the funds to pay for legal costs. On 25 September, and again on 10 October, his solicitors wrote to the Home Secretary asking for payment of Clarke's defence costs. The letters highlighted the service he had provided to the Home Office in shutting down betting offices and stressed that Clarke was a poor man 'and is quite without means to defend himself against the charge which has been made against him'.[82] The Home Office replied that he would only have a fair claim if acquitted; in the meantime his case could not be distinguished from that of the three other inspectors. However, Secretary Cross was sufficiently intrigued to ask Commissioner Henderson 'whether this representation as to his poverty is correct and, if so, how the fact can be explained and when it first became known to the Commissioner'. Henderson duly provided Cross with a reality check:

> … Chief Inspector Clarke joined the Detective Department in May 1862. He was previously a Serjeant in the S Division his pay being £1 4/- per week. He was a Detective Serjeant until November 1867 pay £2 2/- per week, promoted then to Inspector at a salary of £200 per annum. In May 1869 he was promoted to Chief Inspector. Salary £250 per annum and in 1872 his pay was increased to £276 per annum.
>
> I am informed that he has brought up a family of five children, three boys and two girls. He has assisted two of his sons with money to start in business, and has still one son and a daughter dependent on him. His wife has had frequent attacks of illness, his daughter also requiring expensive medical treatment. He also has to contribute to the maintenance of his aged mother.
>
> At present he receives no pay, being suspended. Under these circumstances it is not surprising that he has no funds to draw upon to meet the heavy expense of legal assistance … an expense which probably would fall little short of £100.[83]

Although he was unsuccessful in raising additional funds for legal costs, there was a moment of happiness for Clarke when his daughter Emily's first child was christened on 30 September. His grandsons's birth had prevented Emily from giving evidence on his behalf at Bow Street, but she would be well enough to appear at the Old Bailey.

Following discussions with George Lewis, Clarke followed his solicitor's recommendation that an up-and-coming barrister, Edward Clarke (no relation), should be asked to represent him at the Old Bailey. Edward Clarke had recently added to his burgeoning reputation as an advocate during the Staunton murder trial (often referred to as the Penge murder case).[84] In his autobiography, Edward Clarke described the first meeting of the two men:

> Clarke came to me with an introduction from Mr. George Lewis, assured me that he was innocent, and begged me to defend him, and in consideration of his slender means to accept a small fee and very small refreshers. I believed him and sympathised with him, and agreed to a refresher of five guineas a day, half the amount which had been paid me in the Staunton case.[85]

At nineteen days the trial of the detectives was, in its time, the longest criminal trial that had been held at the Old Bailey. The prosecution for the Crown
was in the hands of Attorney General Sir John Holker and Solicitor General
Sir Hardinge Giffard. Edward Clarke later described his strategy as counsel
for Clarke: 'My cross-examination in the Detective case was careful but by no
means long. It is a very useful general rule that you should not cross-examine
when you cannot contradict. By provoking a repetition of the story you fix it
on the minds of the jury, and you run the risk of the mention of some fresh
detail.'[86] For these reasons, he decided to keep short his cross-examination of
Kurr and of Mrs Avis (Benson's housekeeper who had produced copies of
Benson's correspondence with Clarke). As the committal hearings had shown,
Clarke and Lewis had assembled a number of defence witnesses able to provide evidence that contradicted Kurr's statements relating to his 'meetings'
with Clarke. There was only one witness who provided partial corroboration
of one aspect of Kurr's story. This was a cabdriver who had taken Kurr to the
end of Great College Street on two occasions during the autumn of 1876.
However, the cabdriver had not seen whether Kurr had called at Clarke's
house, or could simply have been one of the men that Clarke had reported to
Williamson, who 'had been watching and making mysterious inquiries about
him in the neighbourhood of his own residence'.[87]

Far more difficult to deal with was Clarke's correspondence with Benson
during 1875. Clarke had either not received or had not preserved some letters
that Benson claimed to have sent him. However, copies of some of Benson's
letters and Clarke's replies had been provided to the Treasury by Benson's
housekeeper, Mrs Avis, or had been recovered from a 'dead letter office' –
having been sent originally to an incorrect forwarding address by an Isle of
Wight resident who was clearing Rose Bank after Benson had vacated it
during 1876. The recovered correspondence started with a letter from Clarke
of 19 April 1875, sent shortly after his first meeting with Benson (as Yonge) in
the Isle of Wight, followed by a second letter a few days later. Clarke's initial
tone had been robust:

> Scotland Yard April 19th 1875
> Dear Sir, In reply to yours of the 11th inst., I am utterly astonished that you,
> as a stranger, should have heard anything of my character, good, bad, or indif-
> ferent; but, thank God, I am not afraid of any man, and do not care one pin if
> all my actions through life were published to the world to-morrow. You have
> certainly excited my curiosity, and I appeal to you as a gentleman to let me
> know what you have heard about me, and you may depend that I will in no way
> compromise you. It is quite impossible for me to see you at the Isle of Wight.
> Yours respectfully, G. Clarke.[88]

Detective Office April 26th 1875

Dear Sir, Your letter of the 19th only reached me yesterday, having been absent from London. You must have misunderstood me when at Rose Bank, as I certainly said that my visit was purely official, and that I could not enter into any confidential correspondence respecting the two men Walters and Murray, but I did express my astonishment when you told me that the secrets of the office were betrayed by some one, whose name you may decline to give. I further said that I should be glad to hear from you on that subject. I am still prepared and anxious to hear on that matter. Yours respectfully, G. Clarke.[89]

By June 1875, Clarke's tone had softened:

20, Great College Street, Westminster June 16th 1875

No doubt you have heard that the two men, Walters and Murray, did not appear to take their trial and have not been heard of since. I hear they have left the country. I should be glad to see you to talk over the matter, but I cannot spare the time this week. I feel that I want a run out somewhere for a blow. Kurr and Montague have also left the country. Yours truly, G. Clarke.[90]

That letter had been written in response to one from Benson:

15th June 1875

My Dear Sir and Brother, We exchanged promises at our last interview. Yours was that [you] would give me an early opportunity of proving my friendship; mine that I would show you how kindly I feel towards you, and how anxious I am to pay my debt to you. I have also news of great importance to communicate with you about the letter you know of [Clarke's letter to Walters]. I will show you how thoroughly you can trust me. Will you, therefore, oblige me by coming down as soon as possible – Thursday or Friday? By leaving Waterloo at 3 p.m. you can return next morning in time to be in your office by 10. A line from you in return announcing your visit as requested will oblige yours sincerely, G.H.Y. If you do not like to write, merely let me know what time I may expect you, as it is urgent I should see you before Saturday.[91]

Subsequent letters from Benson also mentioned his 'debt' to Clarke, references that the prosecution interpreted as circumstantial evidence that Clarke had accepted money from him, though Clarke's letters to Benson contained nothing specifically compromising in their content.[92]

Edward Clarke was also concerned that many aspects of Kurr and Benson's 'story' were consistent, though the two men, in prison, were 'without any opportunity of communication'.[93] In this regard, Edward Clarke failed to recognise that Kurr and Benson had found ways of communicating while in prison, at least before their own trial. Nonetheless, Clarke's counsel was undoubtedly right to adopt a strategy that would highlight Benson's potential to fool not only the gullible, but also to compromise a hardened veteran of the detective department like Clarke:

> My chief object was to show him [Benson] at his best; as the polished and educated man who was capable of deceiving and outwitting even a trained inspector of police. He looked little like that when my turn came to cross examine him. He was ill; it was the afternoon of his third day in the witness box; and all that morning he had been cross examined with just severity, but with some roughness by Montagu Williams. As he sat in the chair put for him in the witness box, in the ugly convict's clothes, hair cropped, face worn with illness and fatigue, he was a pitiful object. My first words brought a change. 'Now Mr. Benson, I have a few questions to ask you.' It was the first time for months that he had been spoken to in any tone of courtesy. His face lit up, he rose to his feet, bowed in acknowledgment, and stood with an air of deference, waiting to reply … I felt that my object had been attained.[94]

During his cross-examination, Edward Clarke was successful in extracting confirmation from Benson that he had passed on information to Clarke about another fraudster, Victor Trevelli, who was later apprehended and sentenced to five years' penal servitude for forgery in March 1877.[95] This was proof that Clarke had gained information of value to the police during his dialogue with Benson.

Other prosecution witnesses who yielded a positive outcome when cross-examined were Superintendent Williamson and William Pollard (Clarke's principal point of contact over many years at the Treasury Solicitor's office). On the subject of whether a telegram or letter should have been sent to Glasgow police on 3 October 1876, Williamson confirmed that telegrams were only sent where essential and that 'if information had to be sent after bank hours with a view of stopping notes on the following day a letter would answer the same purpose as a telegram'. Pollard confirmed that he had never had the slightest reason to suspect Clarke.[96] When it came to the defence witnesses for Clarke, those previously examined at the Bow Street hearings re-appeared. Their number was also added to by Clarke's daughter Emily, and by Commissioner Henderson. Emily described the excursion that she had taken to the Isle of Wight in August 1875, during which her father had left her in Shanklin for half an hour while meeting Benson (a meeting that Clarke had never denied having).[97] Commissioner Edmund Henderson's evidence was consistent with the considerable trust placed in Clarke by his superiors:

I am the Chief Commissioner of Police – besides my having the superintend-ence and command of all the ordinary police business, there is business of a special and confidential character in my case relating to personages of State upon which reports come directly to me – in that sort of business I have for some years employed Inspector Clarke; he has been employed and trusted in matters of the most confidential character, and has been in the habit of making to me personal reports which would not pass into ordinary police work – so far as I have been able to form an opinion I have found him thoroughly trust-worthy – I have never had the least cause to suspect either the information connected with his work or his want of faithfulness in any way at all – on 18th Oct., 1876, I had some communication with him with regard to a threat-ened attempt on the person of the Prince of Wales – the reports with regard to that matter were made on the following day, the 19th ...[98]

When it came to Edward Clarke's closing speech for Clarke's defence, he has provided his own perspective:

My speech for Clarke was the most elaborately prepared of all my forensic speeches ... My scheme was to throw all my strength into an exordium which might make the jury feel that such an accusation made against a man of stainless reputation and long-continued public service was really incred-ible. Then, when I came to deal, discreetly and not in too great detail, with the serious evidence against him, each of the twelve minds which it was my duty to influence would be predisposed, and even eager, to reject or explain away, or wholly to ignore, facts which were inconsistent with the conclusion at which it had already, if unconsciously arrived. The peroration was intended to sweep away any lingering doubts by the confidence of its rhetorical appeal for an acquittal.[99]

The advocate's strategy was therefore similar to that earlier adopted by Montagu Williams for his client, Meiklejohn, which had contributed to Clarke finding himself in the dock in the first place. Would it now prove to be his salvation?

The last tense day of the trial was vividly described in the *Daily Telegraph*:

For forty-eight days, at Bow-street and at the Old Bailey, the trial of the detec-tives has dragged its slow length along, with the inevitable recurrence of the same facts, the same witnesses, the same arguments; and at the opening of the court yesterday – the last day of the trial – it really looked as if the excitement had exhausted itself. Everyone who possessed a curious mind or whose strange idiosyncrasy it was to watch the long mental agony of five of their fellow-creatures – unfortunate, however guilty; miserable, however innocent – had made himself or herself familiar with the features, the nervousness, the stolidity, or the anxiety, as the case might be, of the four police officers and the solicitor. Students of physiognomy have remarked on the undisturbed gloom which made Meiklejohn's features a placid mask; had noticed the quick nervous changes playing over the lively face of the foreigner Druscovich; had likened the tall figure of Palmer to some well-drilled, non-commissioned officer in a line regiment; had watched the colour coming and going as Froggatt's name was mentioned incidentally or directly; and had expended pity on the venerable look and gray hair of Clarke ... At ten o'clock in the morning when the doors were undisturbed, when the passages leading to the court were comparatively free, when the barrister's benches were half empty, and when it was possible to conduct the business of the court in order and silence, every seat allotted to the ladies had been secured. Ladies well-known in fashionable society, ladies related to the bench and the bar, ladies celebrated in art, had evidently postponed until the last moment their visit to a court of justice during a celebrated criminal trial. Though the very circumstances of the case prevented any idea of novelty or excitement during the summing-up, and though the plan of the learned judge was to deal with the evidence in order of witnesses, instead of in personal or chronological order, still it was clear that the ladies anticipated sufficient interest to reward them for sitting in the same seat for six or seven hours. The summing-up was anything but interesting even to the judicial mind. The evidence was wearisome from repetition, and the judge's system necessitated constant allusion to the same circumstances. However, there were the prisoners exposed to the public gaze, and subjected to determined scrutiny. Whenever Druscovich stood up, whenever Froggatt sat down, whenever Clarke leaned upon his elbow, whenever Meiklejohn scrunched up a pen in his strong fingers, whenever a note was passed down from the dock to the barristers or solicitors, each one of these facts was duly recorded and whispered about by the unprofessional spectators in court. But as the lengthy list of witnesses was wearily exhausted, on one face only was seen a sign of expectancy or a ray of hope, and that was the face of Inspector Clarke. Anxiety seemed to fade from him as the end drew near. Meiklejohn never stood for a second. His features never relaxed their gloom. Druscovich and Froggatt were nervously anxious and apprehensively fidgety, were often whispering and constantly writing during the early morning hours. But Clarke's face was comparatively cheerful and illumined with hope. When the hour for the adjournment came the case of the detectives was summed up and finished. The jury was fully charged as far as four of the prisoners were concerned. Froggatt's was purposely kept apart by the judge all through, and this was taken after luncheon. And so without much solemnity, and with scarcely any deviation from an even and unruffled course, the jury retired to consider their verdict at twenty-five minutes past three.

The court was now full to overflowing. There were more people present – many more – than when the Penge convicts were sentenced to death. At the entrance to the bench there was not standing room. Barristers struggled to their seats with difficulty. Every avenue was blocked, and there were almost as many visitors standing as sitting. The counsel connected with the case returned to their seats, and all was anxiety, crowd, confusion, intolerable heat and expectancy. The jury only asked, through their foreman, for some documents to verify the handwriting of Palmer, and then they retired. At this moment there was – naturally perhaps – some little hesitation on the part of Clarke and Froggatt in following the other prisoners down the stairs into the gaol. Hitherto they had been on bail and up to this moment they were free men. Going down those stairs accompanied by the warders, certainly looked like going to prison, and both Clarke and Froggatt hesitated. They did more: they looked appealingly to Mr. Sidney Smith [Governor of Newgate Prison], who was in his old painful corner in the wide dock, as if to ask protection from this first step to gaol. But it could not be, and it was far better as it was; for who would willingly expose himself to the cruel gaze of a crowded court during those dread moments, when the jury is deciding the fate of prisoners? For then, when the judge is absent, when formality is comparatively at an end, the long pent up silence gives way to a period of what looks like heartless animation. There is a buzz of conversation, the usher indignantly calls to some daring personage instantly to remove his hat, the ladies are escorted into inner apartments for consoling cups of tea, there is an in-coming and out-going of City magnates in purple robes and chains of office. Anything but solemnity prevails while the jury deliberate in their room, and the prisoners wait below with visions of the treadmill and oakum-picking before their eyes. The more crowded the court the greater the gossiping; and if in a murder case actual levity is not restrained, how much less can silence be expected when it is whispered about that 'after all they can only get two years'. Painters have given to us scenes of intense dramatic effect as conveying the horror and despair of those who 'are waiting for the verdict'. But they are ideal. They do not occur at the Old Bailey when the rope is dangling in mid-air, and they are not expected when the ultimate doom will only be the crank and cropped hair. The prophets were true who anticipated that the deliberation would not be long. There had been plenty of time to consider the case in all its bearings before this, and there is one consolation in a long trial. It means a short deliberation. So the five o'clock tea was curtailed and the fashionable gossip was cut short by the arrival of the usher, who, fighting his way through a desperate crowd, announced that the jury would be back in three minutes. Back came the ladies, off went the obstinate hats, silence was emphatically pronounced, and at seventeen minutes past four the jury had returned, preceded by the young foreman, who held in his hand an ominous paper. This was the verdict. He had not returned to ask any questions as some asserted. The fate of the prisoners was now in the foreman's hands. But now there was a painful interval. The prisoners were arranged in front of the dock, all terribly distressed and nervous. But the judge had not returned. It seemed a long time this delay to all in court. It must have seemed hours to the accused. The longer the delay, the more the whispering, and once more, when the red curtains were parted and the judge appeared, it was necessary to command silence authoritatively. At last the names of the jurymen are called over, and the Clerk of the Arraigns asks the dread question in order and in deep silence. Meiklejohn? Guilty. Druscovich? Guilty. Palmer? There is an anxious hesitation, and the young foreman, who is terribly nervous, wishes to go back and recommend Druscovich to mercy. So Palmer's fate hangs in the balance, and the presentment of the jury is made commending Druscovich to clemency. Once more the questioning begins again. Palmer? Guilty. Once more there is some hesitation. Clarke? No; the foreman wishes to do everything in order, and goes back instantly to Palmer. He, too, is recommended to mercy, because he was not bribed. And now comes Clarke's turn, and apparently the most anxious moment of all, for the silence deepens. Clarke? Not guilty. The words were scarcely uttered before a burst of cheering rang through the court – not from one corner. Not from gallery alone, not merely the delighted relief of friends; but a sudden, strong, sympathetic cheer. The authorities of the court tried vainly to silence the noise, and it required the firm, indignant voice of the judge to restore silence. The court was to be instantly cleared if such indecent exhibitions of sentiment were heard again. Instantly Clarke appreciated his position and fell back from the rank with a smile on his face. He looked young again, and beamed, as he stood back with folded arms, almost a free man. Froggatt, terribly agitated with all this delay and excitement, closes up, and bows his head as the question is asked. Froggatt? Guilty.[100]

Druscovich, Palmer, Meiklejohn and Froggatt were sentenced to two years' imprisonment with hard labour, the maximum allowed for the offence committed, and inadequate punishment in the view of Judge Baron Sir Charles Pollock. As the jury had been charged with reaching a verdict on only part of the indictment, Clarke was released on his own recognisance of £100 to appear, if called upon, to answer other counts.

The Aftermath

By 13 December 1877, the decision had been made not to pursue any further charges against Clarke. His first task was to write to Edward Clarke:

I have much pleasure in informing you that all accusations against me have been withdrawn and I am now fully reinstated in my former position. I beg to thank you very much for the very able manner in which you conducted my defence. The Solicitor to the Treasury has been most grossly deceived by the woman, Mrs. Avis, as I most solemnly declare I never received a letter in her handwriting, the drafts of which she produced. I am informed by her own family that she was entirely a creature of the convict Benson, and would perjure herself to any extent to serve him. As to the evidence of the convicts, Kurr and Benson, I can only give it my solemn denial that ever I received even one penny at their hands, or ever gave them the slightest information.

Again thanking you most heartily.[101]

Clarke's next task was to try to get his legal costs refunded, and he sent a memorandum to Commissioner Henderson, which was duly forwarded to the Home Office with Henderson's support:

Having been acquitted of the serious charges preferred against me by the Solicitor to the Treasury, and being reinstated in my former position as Chief Inspector with full pay during my suspension: I beg in accordance with the recognised custom of the Service, to ask that Colonel Henderson will be kind enough to submit my application to the Home Office, that Mr. Secretary Cross may be pleased to authorize my legal expenses being paid out of the Police Funds.[102]

It was at this point that Clarke discovered that he had committed the most heinous of all 'crimes': he had become a political liability. The Home Secretary's response made Clarke's position abundantly clear: 'I should never have allowed him to be reinstated save for the ... purpose of pension. He has been acquitted by the jury. He has had long service. Let him have his pension but I cannot keep him in the force. He must ... retire at once [the last two words being doubly underlined].'[103] An escape route was obligingly found. Henderson reported that 'Chief Inspector Clarke's health is so seriously impaired that I apprehend he will probably be considered by the Chief Surgeon as unfit for further service'.[104] That prediction was conveniently confirmed by the police surgeon on 18 December, and, on 4 January 1878, Clarke retired from the Metropolitan Police on an annual pension of £184.[105] The Home Office letter confirming this could not resist rapping Henderson over the knuckles for reinstating Clarke in the first place.[106] Despite his acquittal and the strong support that Clarke had received from his superiors in the police, he was not successful in gaining Home Office approval for the payment of his legal fees.

Froggatt, Druscovich, Palmer and Meiklejohn, having served their sentences, were released from Coldbath Fields Prison, Clerkenwell, in October

1879.[107] Froggatt was immediately rearrested for the misappropriation of trust funds for which he was tried, found guilty and sentenced to seven years' penal servitude.[108] Druscovich returned to his wife Elvina at their home at 64 South Lambeth Road and established himself as a private inquiry agent; one of his jobs involved investigations into bribery in the Oxford parliamentary constituency in the May 1880 election. He did not survive long, dying on 29 December 1881 at the age of 39 from tuberculosis. Pensionless after his conviction, he left £448 7s.[109] Palmer, also pensionless, returned to his family and became manager of the Cock public house at 340 Kennington Road, Lambeth, having been helped to obtain a licence by Edward Clarke. He died from pneumonia, aged 53, on 8 January 1888, leaving £283.[110]

John Meiklejohn proved to be the most resilient of those imprisoned. Soon after his release he purchased four houses in Battersea at a cost of £1,025, and lived in one of them with his wife and children.[111] He set up a private inquiry agency and worked on several occasions for the solicitor George Lewis. When Lewis' client William O'Brien, an Irish Nationalist MP and editor of *United Ireland*, was sued because of an article reporting a homosexual scandal at Dublin Castle, Meiklejohn was called in and discovered a network of homosexual activity which helped *United Ireland* win the libel case brought against them.[112] When the Tichborne Claimant was released in October 1884, Meiklejohn's name was bandied around by the Claimant and his friends as having helped 'pack the jury' against the Claimant in 1873, under instructions from Scotland Yard. Counter reports indicated that Meiklejohn was preparing to respond to these claims by an action for libel, though ultimately no such action appears to have been taken.[113] During the furore surrounding the 'Jack the Ripper' inquiries in the autumn of 1888, he advertised in *Reynolds's Newspaper* that 'Mr Meiklejohn being instructed in the matter of the Whitechapel mystery, is prepared to liberally reward any person who can afford him information of a satisfactory nature'; like others he failed to solve the mystery of who committed the murders.[114] In 1890 he wrote a series of articles for the *Leeds Mercury* about his life as a Scotland Yard detective.[115] In 1903 the self-destructive side of his personality re-surfaced when he decided to pursue a libel action against the former prison governor and author Arthur Griffiths over his references to the Trial of the Detectives, in the book *Mysteries of Police and Crime*. The three-day hearing became effectively a re-run of the trial and, once again, Meiklejohn emerged the loser, probably facing considerable legal costs in the process.[116] In 1912 he published more accounts of his working life in his book *Real Life Detective Stories*. In this he referred, for the first time, to the events of 1877: 'I left the police force, under circumstances to which I can and shall, if I am spared, give a very different colouring to than usually accepted.'[117] He was not spared, and died from acute pleurisy on 12 February 1912 aged 71. He appears not to have left a will, and was buried in a pauper's grave at Grove Park cemetery.

With regard to the men who had played some part in bringing the detectives into the dock, William Walters was sentenced at the Old Bailey on 23 March 1880 to twenty years' penal servitude, after pleading guilty to forgery. While in Newgate Prison awaiting trial and anticipating a long sentence, he produced a statement accusing George Clarke and others, including von Tornow, of accepting bribes. Walters claimed that he had met Clarke on a number of occasions, but not since he had been bailed in 1875. The document was forwarded to Scotland Yard where the head of the new Criminal Investigation Department (CID), Howard Vincent, commented that 'this statement of Walters contains nothing new'.[118]

In September 1882 William Kurr, Frederick Kurr and Charles Bale were released on licence having served just over five years of their ten-year sentences.[119] Harry Benson was released on licence on 9 October 1885.[120] Within two days, Benson had written to the Home Secretary complaining that he had been 'followed in a most marked manner by detectives everywhere I have been'. Commissioner Henderson confirmed that Benson had been placed under observation, that Kurr was already out of prison 'concocting some fraud' and that Benson's liberation 'has been anxiously awaited by his former associates'.[121] Benson eluded his 'minders' and travelled first to Paris to establish whether his father (who had died while Benson was in prison) had left him anything; he hadn't, and it is believed that Benson then rejoined the Kurrs.

During the next two years they conducted frauds in Europe and America. In February 1886 Benson was convicted for fraud and false representations in Belgium and was sentenced to two years and sixteen days' imprisonment, later reduced to six months. He then travelled to North America, meeting up with Kurr, and it is 'tolerably certain that they made a great deal of money'.[122] In September 1887 the two men were arrested in Bremen on a charge of defrauding an English gentleman in Geneva, through a fraudulent business – the '*Agence Financière de Génèvre*'. Benson had passed himself off as an American banker, and had become engaged to the daughter of a retired surgeon general from the Indian army. He had given his fiancée jewellery (later found to be fake) and advised his father-in-law-to-be to invest £7,000 in the fraudulent scheme. However, the two men escaped prosecution when they refunded £5,000 to the angry but embarrassed ex-surgeon general and his daughter. Travelling once more to the American continent, in Mexico, Benson impersonated the impresario of Madame Patti, the acclaimed opera diva who, in her prime, received $5,000 a night for each performance.[123] After siphoning off some $25,000 from ticket sales, Benson was arrested in America and held in the Tombs Prison, New York. Expecting to be extradited to Mexico, he slipped back into the black depression that had caused him to set fire to his Newgate cell many years previously.[124] The *Liverpool Mercury* was amongst the first to report his death in September 1888: 'A telegram from New York announces the termination by suicide of the career of Henry [sic] Benson, perhaps the most accomplished swindler of the century. Whilst in jail he is said to have thrown himself from a staircase on to a stone floor below, and to have sustained injuries which caused his death.'[125]

Beyond the personalities involved, the events of 1877 also contributed towards changes in the organisation and management of the detective force. On 13 August 1877, the Home Secretary had appointed a departmental commission to inquire into the 'State, Discipline and Organization of the Detective Force of the Metropolitan Police'.[126] While there is no doubt that the establishment of the commission was linked to the investigations of corruption within the detective department at Scotland Yard, the report's conclusions and the eventual outcome, in terms of reorganisation, are not as simplistically linked to the fallout from the Trial of the Detectives as most general histories of the Metropolitan Police suggest. Chaired by Undersecretary of State at the Home Office Sir Henry Selwin-Ibbetson, the commission members also included Colonel William Feilding, who had been head of the short-lived 'secret service department' during the Fenian conspiracy. The commission started to collect its evidence on 23 November 1877, three days after the end of the Old Bailey trial; Superintendent Williamson was amongst the first witnesses to be called. In the commission report it is remarkable how little reference is made to the personalities and events that had been involved in the corruption trial. To employ a modern metaphor, the events surrounding the trial seem to have represented 'the elephant in the room' that was acknowledged but rarely spoken about. Clarke was mentioned twice in the minutes of evidence, on both occasions in a positive light. Firstly by Williamson, who described Clarke as 'a very unusual article' and highlighted his abilities in tracking down criminals: 'a man of about as much shrewd common sense as any man in London.' Secondly, Commissioner Henderson commented on the use of informers and referred to the now notorious letter to William Walters: 'Take the case of Inspector Clarke – he wrote to a publican to come and give him information. I believe that was perfectly legitimate.'[127]

Beyond such passing references, the principal issue addressed was the perceived failure of co-operation between the detectives based within divisions, and those in the department at Scotland Yard. This was an issue that Williamson had raised as far back as July 1870, suggesting then that the divisional detectives should be managed by the Scotland Yard Detective Department.[128] It was considerations of this nature that led the commission to put forward its first two recommendations: 'an amalgamation of all the detective bodies into one force' and 'that they be separated from uniform branch, and placed under officers of their own'.[129] Some other recommendations could be more readily traced back to issues relevant to the Trial of the Detectives, including proposals for higher pay to attract better recruits; reconsideration of travelling expenses and other allowances; the banning of gratuities from members of the public 'on pain of dismissal'; and the establishment of a reward fund administered centrally.[130]

On 6 March 1878 a young barrister, Howard Vincent, was appointed director of criminal investigations, having previously taken the initiative to produce a report on the police system and crime detection in Paris.[131] Judging by comments made by the Police Commissioner James Monro in 1888, Vincent's input was a greater influence in the establishment of CID than the 1877 departmental commission report:

> In reply to your letter of 8th [November], conveying a report of the Departmental Commission appointed on the 18th [sic] August 1877 and requesting marginal notes thereon or otherwise a report on the subject, I have to state that this Report appears to be quite unknown in the Commissioner's Office as a document and never appears to have been brought to the notice of the Commissioner for any action to take place upon it ... Yet for all this the greater part of the recommendations have been more or less carried out. So far as this office is concerned a new Criminal Investigation Department sprang into being without any action on the part of the Commissioner ... I am under the impression that most of the changes were arranged direct between Mr. Howard Vincent and the Secretary of State; Sir Edmund Henderson probably giving his concurrence verbally, saying that he had no objection.[132]

Superintendent Williamson remained at Scotland Yard, initially as Vincent's right-hand man. In March 1883 a bomb explosion in London marked the start of another Fenian campaign, and a 'Special Irish Branch' was established under Williamson's leadership later that month.[133] The Branch later suffered the embarrassment of a Fenian bomb exploding in a urinal beneath their offices on 30 May 1884; no one was injured.[134] Williamson died on 9 December 1889, still in post, though for some months prior to his death his health had failed. By then he had received personal promotion to the rank of district superintendent – equivalent to chief constable. The Home Secretary expressed his '... deep regret with which he hears of Mr. Williamson's death, and of his sense of the great loss which the Police and Public have sustained in being deprived of an Officer distinguished for his skill, prudence and experience, and whose life has been unsparingly devoted to the Public Service'.[135] The Prince of Wales expressed similar sentiments.[136] Williamson's well-attended funeral service was held at St John Evangelist church in Smith Square. He left £1,887 12s 7d.

Sir Edmund Henderson's term as Metropolitan Police commissioner came to an end in February 1886 and he was knighted in 1878. After almost twenty years without riotous public demonstrations in London, Henderson had been lulled into a false sense of security. When riots occurred in Trafalgar Square which were not adequately controlled by the police, his resignation was accepted. He died on 8 December 1896, leaving £7,273 3s 3d.[137]

George Clarke's pension provided a modest income, though he had still to recover from the legal costs he had incurred. For some years Clarke became a publican at the Bulls Head, Hyde Street, Oxford Street, and appeared once more at the Old Bailey as a prosecution witness in the trial of a customer accused of trying to pass counterfeit money; she was convicted and sentenced to five years' penal servitude.[138] However, between 1884 and 1891 he returned to the trade he knew best and advertised his services as a private inquiry agent, a business in which he was joined by his son Harry (Henry John Clarke).[139] His activities did not hit the newspaper headlines again in his remaining lifetime, though in 1886 the *Northern Echo*'s London correspondent mentioned: 'I saw Clarke the other day looking pink, healthy, and contented.'[140] By June 1890 his health was failing and he resigned his membership of the Freemasons.[141] On 31 January 1891, he died at his home in Great College Street, aged 72. As central London's graveyards had been full for many years, his body was transported by the London Necropolis Company to Brookwood cemetery near Woking, where he was cremated and his remains buried. In his will, he left everything, £949 2s 6d, to his wife Elizabeth.

Clarke's private inquiry business continued, after his death, to be marketed under the name 'George Clarke', by his son Harry. Little is known of the clientele that requested the company's services. However, in October 1892, Harry found himself in the witness box at the Old Bailey, giving evidence in the trial of the serial poisoner Thomas Neill Cream.[142] Cream, who was convicted and subsequently executed for poisoning several prostitutes in Lambeth, also had the bizarre habit of sending anonymous letters to the police and to others (of which 'George Clarke Private Inquiry Agents' was one), claiming to have identified the murderer as being a young medical student at St Thomas' Hospital.[143] Harry's evidence was simply to confirm that he had received such a letter. Three years later Harry was back at the Old Bailey, but this time in the dock, which he shared with a colleague, Ellen Lyon. Both were charged with keeping a brothel, and specifically with 'unlawfully conspiring by false representations to procure Gertrude Alexandra Barrett, not being a common prostitute, to have carnal connection with Charles Wilson'. During the trial it became clear that much of Harry's business, like that of many private detectives, involved divorce cases. He and his colleague had been unlawfully providing their clients with a service in which they would arrange for adultery to be proved, if necessary by offering themselves or hiring others for that purpose. Harry Clarke and Ellen Lyon were found guilty and sentenced to two years' hard labour and twelve months' hard labour, respectively.[144] By then, Elizabeth Clarke had moved to live with her daughter Emily and family in East Dulwich, where she spent her time conversing with her grandchildren, visiting relatives and friends, and playing cribbage. When she died, in April 1907, Harry was to find that his criminal behaviour had tested his mother's patience too far; he had been excluded from her will.

EPILOGUE

We often hear (almost invariably, however, from superficial observers) that guilt can look like innocence. I believe it to be infinitely the truer axiom of the two that innocence can look like guilt.

Wilkie Collins[1]

George Clarke's career with the London Metropolitan Police spanned a period of great technological and social change. Improvements in transport and communications allowed Clarke and his colleagues to pursue criminals from the meanest streets and tenements of mid-Victorian London to continental Europe, America and beyond. Crime and its detection were already international in their scope. The detectives also had to adapt to the social changes being engineered by increasingly moralistic attitudes and legislation to restrict betting, to moderate drinking and to reduce infanticide. With limited resources, Clarke and other members of the very small team in the Scotland Yard Detective Department individually tackled a diverse range of investigations: on one day hunting down a vicious murderer; another day functioning almost as a 'social worker' following tip-offs about farmed-out children; spending half the day or night undertaking surveillance of suspected criminals, before travelling to the racecourses of Epsom, Newmarket, Sandown Park or Goodwood to catch the 'swell mob' in action; and then returning to the office to sift through the reports for a court appearance the following day. Taken together with the long working hours, it is indeed little wonder that the principal medical reason for early retirement amongst the police was being 'worn out'. Indeed, with such pressures, what drove

George Clarke to spend thirty-eight years in the service? What type of person was he?

It has been reasonably straightforward to locate sources of information on the Scotland Yard career of George Clarke, but it has proved less easy to obtain other information about the man himself. None of his colleagues made direct reference to Clarke by name when they wrote about their experiences at Scotland Yard (e.g. Cavanagh, Greenham, Lansdowne, Littlechild and Meiklejohn). Perhaps they were seeking to distance themselves from (or in Meiklejohn's case, to forget) any association with the events of 1877. A similar reticence and embarrassment may also explain why I did not inherit any information about George Clarke from my ancestral connections.

In terms of his private life, there is enough information to suggest that, despite the intensity of his job, Clarke took his family responsibilities seriously; not least in helping to support his mother, wife and children financially. As he had no other source of income, like most of us he needed a job. In all ways he seems to have lived within his means, even frugally. When time permitted, he was no different to the majority of Victorian men in a similar financial position in enjoying company (predominantly male company) through his membership of the Freemasons, visits to the local public house with friends and colleagues, and the occasional visit to the music hall.

On a professional level, Clarke displayed considerable dedication to his job. His ability to survive the physical and mental pressures of his long service suggests a remarkable resilience, displayed when dealing with the 'roughs' and 'swell mob' at the racecourse, and when he found himself in the dock at the Old Bailey. He was a survivor. He was not an 'inspirational' detective in the sense that the fictional Sherlock Holmes would be regarded, but there seems to have been little need for such at Scotland Yard, as the Victorian criminal (with at least two notable exceptions) was rarely astute. What was needed was someone who could assemble evidence and build a convincing case for the prosecutor to secure a conviction. Throughout his career at Scotland Yard this seems to have been George Clarke's great strength. From 1870 onwards he was also deployed to tackle issues that were politically sensitive. As a result he acquired a reputation of trust and responsibility. But did he deserve that trust and was he innocent of corruption?

As far as the Old Bailey jury was concerned in 1877, Clarke was innocent of the conspiracy charges laid against him, or at worst was given the benefit of any doubt. The contemporary press coverage of the trial verdicts, such as that in *The Times*' leader column, was essentially content with the outcome: 'The conduct of Clarke in keeping up acquaintance with Benson after he had told the authorities at Scotland-yard that the latter was a "blackguard" may be regarded as indiscreet [sic], but it must be remembered that it is an ordinary duty of detectives to cultivate the intimacy of persons whom they suspect of crime.'[2] Though there must have been some 'there's no smoke without fire' conversations at the time (in which Home Secretary Cross appears to have joined in), it is interesting to note that Clarke's son, Harry, continued to run his private inquiry agency, even after his father's death, under the name 'George Clarke'. So his name cannot have been bad for business, although the nature of Harry's clients and 'inquiries' left something to be desired.

The revisionist view regarding George Clarke's innocence or guilt emerged in the twentieth century. This was first expressed by Dilnot in 1928, and subsequently reported by others: 'Although Clarke got off there can be small doubt that he was seriously mixed up with the conspirators.'[3] At the heart of this statement were comments made in the 1914 autobiography of Clarke's counsel, Edward Clarke, at the trial:

> It will be realised that my task in defending my client was a very difficult one. It would, indeed, in my opinion have been practically impossible to obtain an acquittal if at that time the law had permitted accused persons to be called as witnesses. The strange rule which then prevailed by which neither a prisoner nor his wife was a competent witness, a rule which was the worst example of judge-made law which I have ever known, often operated cruelly against an innocent person, but in nine times out of ten it was of advantage to the guilty.[4]

Setting aside the implausibility of the statistics that Edward Clarke cited, Dilnot and others have interpreted Edward Clarke's comments to mean that George Clarke was guilty in the eyes of his counsel. However, Edward Clarke had also written in the same autobiography that he believed George Clarke when the latter had proclaimed himself innocent of the charges![5] I do nevertheless agree with the wider implications of Edward Clarke's statement. The case for the defence would undoubtedly have been a lot more difficult to manage if accused persons had been eligible to be called as witnesses, not least because there were five men in the dock, each charged with the same offence, each of whom might have given a different representation of their part in the events.

In view of the gratitude that George Clarke expressed to Edward Clarke in December 1877, it now seems somewhat churlish to question the advocate's autobiographical comments. However, his recollections do strongly accentuate the positive aspects of his career (of which there were many), and omit reference to some events which he probably wished to forget.[6] He was also unusual in expressing so frankly his reasons for writing his autobiography:

> No one will doubt that vanity, the only universal weakness has something to do with my desire to leave a record of the events of my life ... I think if I tell it myself simply and briefly it will be more likely to do good than if I leave material from which, when I am dead, someone might compile a larger and more elaborate biography.[7]

Has Edward Clarke's role in Clarke's acquittal been exaggerated? Maybe. Were Edward Clarke's comments misinterpreted by Dilnot? Probably.

The most recently published analysis of the turf fraud and the Trial of the Detectives is that by Richard Stewart – a well-researched, cogently argued and beautifully written book.[8] Stewart's analysis leaves the reader with little doubt that he regards Clarke as being guilty of conspiracy. However, both Dilnot's and Stewart's retrospective analyses of the trial demonstrate little awareness of Clarke's fifteen-year track record as a detective; a record which would have been known to the 1877 trial jury. In addition, I find it difficult to place as much faith, as Stewart and Dilnot appear to have done, in the otherwise uncorroborated evidence against Clarke of two highly plausible fraudsters. Indeed, it is possible that they may have allowed themselves to be swayed, from beyond the grave, by the undoubted guile of Harry Benson and the audaciousness of William Kurr.

Nonetheless, I do think it appropriate that some questions remain about George Clarke's innocence. My reasons for saying this relate to that period at Scotland Yard during the turf fraud inquiries when, in October 1876, Clarke was inspector in charge. During that time Druscovich was generating descriptions of the men believed to have been involved in the fraud. One of these was 'Jacob Francis', a small man who was possibly French, lame and walked with two sticks. Did Druscovich show this description to Clarke? If so, why did Clarke fail to identify this description as the Mr Yonge (Harry Benson) that he had met on several occasions? Why did it have to wait until 8 November, when the Shanklin postmaster responded to a reward poster with these details? Perhaps Druscovich kept the information to himself? Perhaps Clarke was simply too busy with his own cases? With such questions remaining unanswered, Clarke's innocence or guilt, to my mind, remains unconfirmed. However, whether he was innocent or not he proved astute enough to escape the worst consequences of the attempt by two unscrupulous criminals to compromise him.

ACKNOWLEDGEMENTS

This book has only been feasible because of the patience, support and encouragement that I have received from my wife Meg and our children, Robert and Katherine. The realisation that one of my great-great-grandfathers had been a detective in the London Metropolitan Police emerged from research that I was undertaking on family documents written by my grandfather, Charles Payne. Without these papers and the care taken to preserve them by my grandmother, Ida Payne, and my father, Rupert Payne, there would have been no such book.

The research that I have undertaken has been greatly assisted by a number of outstanding national and regional archives and libraries. In particular, my thanks go to the following organisations and their staff: The National Archives (Kew), the British Library (St Pancras) and the British Newspaper Library (Colindale), Westminster City Archives, the Parliamentary Archives London, the Metropolitan Police Historical Collection, Cumbria Libraries (Kendal), Lancashire Libraries (Carnforth), Warrington Library, the Bodleian Library at Oxford University, the University of Lancaster Library and the Library and Museum of Freemasonry. Online facilities that have been invaluable have included Wikipedia, Ancestry.co.uk, Old Bailey Proceedings online, the Cengage digital archives of *The Times* and nineteenth-century British Library Newspapers.

I have been helped and advised by several people who have read and commented on draft sections of the book. Clive Bravery and Robert Payne have kindly read all chapters and provided helpful comments. Vincent Comerford, Padraic Kennedy, Rohan McWilliam, Canice O'Mahony, Michael McCarthy,

Stefan Petrow and Niall Whelehan have given me the benefit of their academic expertise on individual chapters. Particular thanks go to Niall Whelehan for introducing me to the first-hand accounts of the Fenian conspiracy written by Octave Fariola, and to Padraic Kennedy for providing me with references to George Clarke that he had located in the National Archives of Ireland. Other individuals who have provided information and encouragement that has been beneficial to the content and progress of this book include: Nene Adams, John Archer, Phillip Barnes-Warden, the late Maggie Bird, Phillip Bonney, Andrew Brooks, Sioban Clarke, His Honour Judge Peter Clarke, Nanette and Michael Crenol, Paul Dew, Gillian and Graham Douglas-Smith, Rod Elwood, Clive Emsley, Anne Featherstone, Martin Hagger, John Hicks, Carla King, Joan Lock, Peter and Jonathan Meiklejohn, Alan Moss, Neil Paterson, Paul Rason, Keith Skinner, Linda Stratmann, Eileen Summers, Donald Thomas, Margaret Webb and the members of the South Lakes U3A Genealogy Group. The final content and style, as well as any overlooked errors and omissions are, of course, my responsibility.

I would also like to thank Diane Clements of the Library and Museum of Freemasonry, Freemasons' Hall, London, for permission to include information on George Clarke's membership of the Freemasons. For advice on copyright issues affecting text and images from documents held in the National Archives, I am most grateful for the guidance received from Tim Padfield and Paul Johns.

I am most grateful for permission to include extracts from the following sources:

Axon Ballads, No 16 (Chetham's Library)

Bowen-Rowlands, Ernest, *Seventy-Two Years at the Bar* (Macmillan Publishers, 1924)

Comerford, Vincent, *The Fenians in Context: Irish Politics and Society, 1848–82* (Wolfhound Press, 1985)

Howard, Sharon, *Old Bailey Proceedings Online* (University of Sheffield, 2010)

Jenkins, Brian, *The Fenian Problem* (McGill-Queen's University Press, 2008)

Kennedy, Padraic, *Intelligence and National Security* (18, 2003), pp. 100–27

O'Mahony, Canice and Ferguson, Kenneth, *The Irish Sword* (22, 2000), pp. 36–50

Petrow, Stefan, *Policing Morals: The Metropolitan Police and the Home Office, 1870–1914* (1994, by permission of Oxford University Press, Inc.)

Ridley, Jasper, *The Freemasons* (Constable & Robinson, 1999)

Thurmond Smith, Phillip, *Policing Victorian London* (Copyright 1985, reproduced with permission of ABC-CLIO, Santa Barbara, CA, USA)

Images have been reproduced with the permission of the copyright or collection holders, where appropriate. Thanks are due to:

Mary Evans Picture Library – for photographs of Sir Richard Mayne, the Earl of Cardigan, Fenian Guy Fawkes, Michael Davitt, Sir George Lewis and Sir Edward Clarke
Getty Images – for photographs of Charles Bravo and Florence Bravo
Peter Meiklejohn – for the photograph of John Meiklejohn
Kjell Hoel and Brian Attree – for the photograph of George Hammond Whalley
The National Archives – for photographs of William Henry Walters, Charles Howard, Harry Benson, Charles Bale, Frederick Kurr and Edward Froggatt; with particular thanks to Paul Johnson
The Metropolitan Police Historical Collection – for the photographs of Superintendent Robert Walker and A Division colleagues and of Sir Edmund Henderson
The Parliamentary Archives, London – for photographs of the Tichborne Claimant and Sir Richard Assheton Cross

Every effort has been made to secure necessary permissions to reproduce copyright material, though in some cases it has proved impossible either to trace copyright holders or to generate a response. If any omissions are brought to my notice, I will be pleased to include appropriate acknowledgements on reprinting.

Finally, I would like to express my gratitude to Reuben Davison for introducing the concept of this book to The History Press, and to thank Simon Hamlet, Lindsey Smith, Chrissy McMorris, Abbie Wood and the team at The History Press for their enthusiasm and skill in generating the finished product.

NOTES

Main Abbreviations used
OBP – Old Bailey Proceedings Online (www.oldbaileyonline.org) as consulted on
    30 September 2010.
TNA:PRO – The National Archives: Public Records Office (Kew, United Kingdom).
The full details of all cited published books and papers in academic journals are
    provided in the Bibliography.

Preface
1   The National Archives (TNA): Public Records Office (PRO) HO
     45/9442/66692: 1878 Report of the Departmental Commission to Inquire
     into the State, Discipline, and Organisation of the Detective Force of the
     Metropolitan Police. Minutes of Evidence, paragraph 2032.
2   Summerscale (2008).

1 The Journey to Scotland Yard
1   Bratton and Featherstone (2006), p. 215.
2   TNA:PRO MEPO 21/14/4724; Census records.
3   Hertfordshire Archives and Local Studies (HALS) document DP/107/8/7.
4   Armstrong (1988), pp. 23–73.
5   TNA:PRO MEPO 21/14/2504; MEPO 21/14/4750.
6   TNA:PRO MEPO 4/333/84.
7   Cobb (1957), p. 43.
8   Kingston House and the Kingston House Estate, British History Online (www.
     british-history.ac.uk/report.aspx?compid=45934).
9   HALS document DP/107/29/10-12 and microfilms 466 and 467: 'Parochial
     Pedigrees compiled by the Reverend John G. Hale'.

10 Hart-Davis (2001), pp. 13–4, 206; White (2007), p. 10; Wilson (2002), pp. 9, 16, 24, 28; Paterson (2006).

11 Ascoli (1979); Browne (1956).

12 Taylor (1997), p. 15; Emsley (2005), pp. 221–30.

13 Smith (1985), pp. 33–6.

14 White (2007), p. 401; Ascoli (1979), pp. 129–30.

15 White (2007), p. 392.

16 Author's italics. Smith (1985), p. 23; Emsley (2005), p. 301.

17 Emsley (2005), p. 241.

18 TNA:PRO HO 45/9442/66692: Minutes of Evidence, paragraph 5105.

19 Emsley (1996), p. 86.

20 Emsley (1996), p. 186; Petrow (1994).

21 Emsley (1996), p. 26; Hart-Davis (2001), p. 204.

22 Cavanagh (1893), p. 4.

23 Emsley (1996), p. 254.

24 Emsley (2009), p. 43; Taylor (1997), p. 46.

25 Smith (1985), p. 45.

26 Browne (1956), p. 81; Critchley (1972), p. 151.

27 Currency conversions have been made using the Currency Conversion tool at The National Archives website (http://www.nationalarchives.gov.uk). The British currency in Victorian times was not decimalised. The main units of currency were pounds, shillings and pennies. One pound (one sovereign) contained 20 shillings (20s), and each shilling contained 12 pennies (12d).

28 Emsley (1996), pp. 191–8.

29 Moylan (1929), p. 98.

30 Fuller (1912), p. 21.

31 Ascoli (1979), p. 107.

32 Emsley (1996), pp. 28–30; Moylan (1929), p. 149.

33 Emsley (1996), p. 206.

34 TNA:PRO MEPO 4/333.

35 TNA:PRO MEPO 21/14/4724.

36 Smith (1985), p. 39.

37 Cobb (1957), p. 43.

38 Emsley (1996), p. 206.

39 Emsley (2009), p. 118; Smith (1985), pp. 40–1.

40 Ibid.

41 Emsley (1996), pp. 58, 225.

42 Critchley (1972), p. 168.

43 Moylan (1929), p. 112.

44 TNA:PRO HO45/10002/A49463.

45 TNA:PRO MEPO 21/14/4724; MEPO 21/14/2504; MEPO 21/14/4750.

46 TNA:PRO HO27 England and Wales, Criminal Registers, 1791–1892.

47 Information from census records and birth certificates. The five children were George Leonard Clarke (b. 2 July 1845 at Chipping Barnet); Henry John Clarke (b. 21 November 1846 at Highgate); Emily Bent Clarke (b. 28 September 1853 at St John's Wood); Herbert Edwin Clarke (b. 4 October 1855 at St John's Wood); Catherine Louisa Clarke (b. 3 September 1859 at St John's Wood).

48 Emsley (2005), p. 15.
49 Ibid., pp. 13–4.
50 Thomson (1935), p. 115; Stratmann (2010), pp. 9–18.
51 TNA:PRO MEPO 21/2/947; MEPO 21/2/743; MEPO 21/14/2504.
52 OBP (April 1844), John White (t18440408-1287); OBP (February 1849), John Cummings (t18490226-746); *The Times* (30 June 1860).
53 Begg and Skinner (1992), p. 27; Hibbert (1963), p. 275.
54 Moylan (1929), p. 153; Begg and Skinner (1992), pp. 35–6.
55 Smith (1985), p. 65.
56 TNA:PRO HO 45/9442/66692: Minutes of Evidence, paragraphs 4–7; Smith (1985), p. 62.
57 The term 'detective department' has been used throughout this book. Browne (1956), pp. 121–2; Wade (2007), p. 40.
58 Thomson (1935), p. 156.
59 Ascoli (1979), p. 120.
60 Smith (1985), p. 67.
61 Begg and Skinner (1992), p. 27; Hibbert (1963), p. 275.
62 Dickens (1850), *Household Words* (27 July).
63 Begg and Skinner (1992) p. 27; Hibbert (1963) p. 275.
64 Dickens, *Household Words* (27 July 1850).
65 *Leeds Mercury*, Weekly Supplement (1 February 1890).
66 Begg and Skinner (1992), p. 46.
67 TNA:PRO HO 45/9442/66692: Minutes of Evidence, paragraphs 4–7; Smith (1985), p. 62.
68 TNA:PRO HO 65/24 Waddington to Mayne (January 1862); Cavanagh (1893), pp. 98–100.
69 Campbell (2002), pp. 75–6; TNA:PRO HO 45/9442/66692: Minutes of Evidence, paragraph 1929.
70 TNA:PRO HO 65/24 Appointments.
71 Cobb (1956), pp. 28–9.
72 Summerscale (2008), p. 56.
73 Griffiths (1901), p. 366.
74 Cavanagh (1893), p. 67.
75 Lansdowne (1890), p. 1.
76 Browne (1956), p. 149.
77 TNA:PRO HO 45/9442/66692: Minutes of Evidence, paragraphs 63–6.
78 Ibid., paragraphs 282–6. It is these case reports that have sometimes survived in the National Archives though, unfortunately, many have been discarded over the years.
79 Lansdowne (1890), p. 39.
80 Fuller (1912), p. 214; Greenham (1904), p. 78.
81 Greenham (1904), p. 61.
82 TNA:PRO HO 45/9442/66692: Minutes of Evidence, paragraphs 597–8.
83 Ibid., paragraph 2080.
84 Ibid., paragraph 4766.
85 Ibid., paragraph 4663.
86 TNA:PRO HO 65/24 Appointments.
87 *Leeds Mercury* (21 February 1863); *Liverpool Mercury* (30 March 1863).

88   *The Times* (10 June 1863); *The Times* (14 July 1863); OBP (July 1863), David Charles Lloyd (t18630713-94 889).

89   *The Times* (20 January 1864); OBP (February 1864), Charles Alberti (t18640201-227).

90   TNA:PRO MEPO 7/24 (22 January 1863); MEPO 7/25 (25 February 1863); MEPO 7/25 (19 March 1864).

91   TNA:PRO MEPO 7/25 (5 March 1864).

92   TNA:PRO HO 45/9442/66692: Minutes of Evidence, paragraphs 4569–79.

93   Ibid., paragraphs 917–20; Greenham (1904), pp. 7–8.

94   Ibid., paragraphs 979–84, 1880.

95   Ibid,, paragraph 1887.

96   Wallachia and Moldavia are regions within what is now Romania. TNA:PRO HO 45/9442/66692: Minutes of Evidence, paragraphs 425–7.

97   TNA:PRO HO 45/9442/66692: Minutes of Evidence, paragraphs 2040–2.

98   TNA:PRO HO 65/24 Appointments; MEPO 7/24 (25 March 1864); MEPO 7/25 (29 March 1864); MEPO 7/24 (31 October 1863); Lock (1990), p. 163; MEPO 7/25 (30 April 1864); MEPO 21/11/3775.

99   Diamond (2003), p. 52.

100   Smith (1985), pp. 150–9.

101   TNA:PRO HO 45/9442/66692: Minutes of Evidence, paragraphs 542–3.

102   TNA:PRO MEPO 7/25 (21 May 1864).

103   Personal Notebook of Richard Tanner. Metropolitan Police Historical Collection.

104   Meiklejohn (1912), p. 13.

105   TNA:PRO HO 45/9442/66692: Minutes of Evidence, paragraphs 4794–5.

106   TNA:PRO MEPO 7/25 (31 May 1864); Wikipedia, 'Henri d'Orleans, Duke of Aumale'.

2 A Murderous Year

1   Hindley (1871), p. 209.

2   Irving (1911).

3   *Daily News* (27 September 1864).

4   Irving (1911), p. 21.

5   TNA:PRO MEPO 21/7/2201.

6   TNA:PRO MEPO 21/12/4022.

7   Irving (1911), p. 27.

8   Browne (1956), p. 164.

9   *The Times* (12 July 1864).

10   Ibid.

11   Sellwood and Sellwood (1979), p. 18.

12   *The Times* (14 July 1864); Brandon and Brooke (2010), p. 47.

13   *The Times* (18 July 1864).

14   *The Times* (20 July 1864).

15   Irving (1911), p. 51.

16   Ibid., p. 33.

17   Hart-Davis (2001), p. 34.

18   *The New York Times* (6 August 1864).

19   *The New York Herald* (8 August 1864).

20 Hart-Davis (2001), p. 100.
21 TNA:PRO MEPO 3/75.
22 Wikipedia, 'Lancashire Cotton Famine'.
23 Wikipedia, 'CSS *Alabama*'.
24 *Freeman's Journal* (19 September 1864); *Glasgow Herald* (19 September 1864).
25 TNA:PRO MEPO 3/75 Report from Tanner to Mayne (9 August 1864).
26 *The New York Herald* (7 August 1864).
27 TNA:PRO MEPO 3/75 Report from Tanner to Mayne (16 August 1864).
28 Ibid.
29 Wikipedia, 'CSS *Tallahassee*'.
30 *The New York Tribune* (15 August 1864); *The New York Times* (15 August 1864).
31 TNA:PRO MEPO 3/75 Report from Tanner to Mayne (23 August 1864).
32 Goodman and Waddell (1987), p. 133; *Liverpool Mercury* (8 September 1864).
33 OBP (October 1864), Franz Müller (t18641024-920).
34 Irving (1911), p. xviii.
35 *Liverpool Mercury* (8 September 1864); *Glasgow Herald* (19 September 1864).
36 TNA:PRO MEPO 3/75 Report from Tanner to Mayne (26 August 1864).
37 *The Times* (13 September 1864).
38 Ibid.
39 Ibid.
40 TNA:PRO MEPO 3/75 Report from Tanner to Mayne (28 August 1864).
41 *The Times* (19 September 1864).
42 Ibid.
43 Ibid.
44 Ibid.
45 *Liverpool Mercury* (19 September 1864).
46 TNA:PRO MEPO 3/75 Memo from Williamson (15 September 1864).
47 Irving (1911), p. xvi.
48 Ibid., pp. 70–1.
49 Williams (1890), Vol. 1, p. 256.
50 *The Times* (20 September 1864).
51 *Daily News* (27 September 1864).
52 *The Times* (27 September 1864).
53 Wikipedia, 'Sir Robert Collier'.
54 Wikipedia, 'William Ballantine'; Wikipedia, 'Hardinge Giffard'.
55 *Oxford Dictionary of National Biography*, 'John Humffreys Parry' (2009).
56 Wikipedia, 'Sir Frederick Pollock'.
57 *The Times* (28 October 1864).
58 Ibid.
59 Ibid.
60 Irving (1911), p. xxv.
61 Ibid.
62 *The Times* (29 October 1864).
63 Ibid.
64 Ibid.
65 *The Times* (31 October 1864).
66 *The Times* (29 October 1864).

67   Ibid.
68   *The Times* (31 October 1864).
69   Ibid.
70   Irving (1911), p. xxix.
71   *The News of the World* (30 October 1864).
72   *The Times* (31 October 1864).
73   *The News of the World* (13 November 1864).
74   Ibid.
75   TNA:PRO MEPO 3/76 Memo from Williamson (10 November 1864).
76   *The Times* (14 November 1864).
77   Ibid.
78   *The News of the World* (20 November 1864).
79   Ibid.
80   Goodman and Waddell (1987), p. 36.
81   Jenkins (2008), p. 127.
82   *The Times* (15 November 1864).
83   Ibid.
84   Ibid.
85   Goodman and Waddell (1987), p. 97.
86   Sellwood and Sellwood (1979), pp. 66–9.
87   O'Neill (2006), p. 140.
88   TNA:PRO MEPO 7/26 (8 February 1865); HO 45/7078.
89   TNA:PRO MEPO 3/77; Stratmann (2010), pp. 205–11.
90   OBP (January 1865), Ferdinand Köhl (t18650111-142).
91   Ibid.
92   *The Examiner* (12 November 1864).
93   TNA:PRO MEPO 3/77 Report from Howie (9 November 1864).
94   OBP (January 1865), Ferdinand Köhl (t18650111-142).
95   Ibid.
96   Ibid.
97   Ibid.
98   *The Times* (10 November 1864).
99   Ibid.
100 Greenwood (1874), pp. 264–8.
101 Ibid.
102 OBP (January 1865), Ferdinand Köhl (t18650111-142).
103 Ibid.
104 Ibid.
105 Ibid.
106 *Daily News* (11 November 1864).
107 TNA:PRO MEPO 3/77 Report from Howie (10 November 1864).
108 Ibid.
109 TNA:PRO MEPO 3/77 Report from Howie (11 November 1864).
110 *The Era* (13 November 1864).
111 *Daily News* (14 November 1864).
112 Ibid.
113 Ibid.

114 *The Times* (15 November 1864).

115 TNA:PRO MEPO 3/77 Translation of Report from Carl Paterson to Captain W.L. Harris (11 November 1864).

116 *Manchester Times* (26 November 1864).

117 TNA:PRO MEPO 3/77 Report from Howie (16 November 1864).

118 OBP (January 1865), Ferdinand Köhl (t18650111-142).

119 Ibid.

120 Ibid.

121 *The Times* (17, 18 and 24 November 1864).

122 *The Times* (28 November 1864).

123 TNA:PRO MEPO 3/77 Report from Howie (27 November 1864).

124 TNA:PRO MEPO 3/77 Letter from Greenwood to Mayne (17 December 1864).

125 TNA:PRO MEPO 3/77 Report from Clarke (5 January 1865).

126 Wikipedia, 'Hamburg'; Wikipedia, 'Lüchow-Dannenberg'.

127 TNA:PRO MEPO 3/77 'Extraordinary Expenses' claim from Clarke.

128 *The Times* (12 and 13 January 1865).

129 Ibid.

130 Ibid.

131 Ibid.

132 *The Times* (28 January 1865).

133 *Leeds Mercury* (24 January 1865).

134 Goodman and Waddell (1987), p. 133.

135 Bent (1891), p. 214.

3 The Fenians are Coming

1   Hindley (1871), p. 113.

2   TNA:PRO MEPO 3/77 Letter from Treasury to Mayne (21 January 1865).

3   *The Newcastle Courant* (10 February 1865).

4   *The Times* (2 March 1865); *Lloyds Weekly Newspaper* (5 March 1865).

5   TNA:PRO MEPO 7/30 Police Orders (7 November 1868).

6   O'Broin (1971); Smith (1985); Kee (1980); Kee (2000); Comerford (1998); Jenkins (2008).

7   Kee (1980), p. 66.

8   Wilson (2002), pp. 74–83.

9   Kee (1980), p. 104.

10 Ibid., p. 106; Comerford (1998), p. 18.

11 Comerford (1998), p. 39.

12 Devoy (1929), p. 97.

13 Anderson (1906), p. 50.

14 Kee (2000), pp. 309–13; Campbell (2002), p. 55.

15 Vincent Comerford, Personal Communication.

16 Comerford (1998), pp. 47–8.

17 *The Times* (7 April 1868); Kee (2000), p. 300.

18 Kee (1980), pp. 299–300.

19 Kee (2000), p. 312; Comerford (1998), p. 68.

20 Jenkins (2008), p. 29.

21 Kenny (1994), p. 11.

22 Jenkins (2008), p. 28.

23 Kee (2000), p. 318.

24 Campbell (2002), p. 55.

25 Comerford (1998), p. 121.

26 Scanlon (1998), pp. 7–10; McCracken (2009), pp. 10–6.

27 TNA:PRO MEPO 1/47 Mayne to Greig (20 February 1865).

28 Kee (2000), pp. 317–21; Campbell (2002), p. 14.

29 TNA:PRO: HO 45/7799 part 1.

30 Ibid.

31 Kee (2000), p. 318.

32 TNA:PRO MEPO 7/26 (27 May 1865); OBP (December 1865), Nathaniel Holchester, Samuel Berrens, Jules Bayer, Abraham Davis, Gershore Silverman, Philip Braun (t18651218-140).

33 Kee (2000), pp. 319–21.

34 Jenkins (2008), p. 36.

35 TNA:PRO MEPO 1/47 Mayne to Larcom (December 1865).

36 White (2007), pp. 371–3; Smith (1985), pp. 94–5, 193–4.

37 TNA:PRO HO 45/9442/666921878 Minutes of Evidence, paragraph 4640.

38 TNA:PRO HO 45/7799 Letter from Mayor of Birmingham (20 October 1865) and Cohen to Williamson (24 October 1865).

39 Anderson (1906), p. 75.

40 Kee (2000), pp. 328–30.

41 National Archives of Ireland. Fenian Police Reports, Box 3, 332: Report by Williamson (29 October 1865).

42 TNA:PRO HO 45/7799 part 1 (8 November 1865).

43 Jenkins (2008), p. 39.

44 Kee (2000), pp. 321–4; O'Broin (1971), pp. 17–29.

45 Comerford (1998), p. 130.

46 Campbell (2002), p. 61.

47 TNA:PRO MEPO 1/47 Mayne to Waddington (10 January 1866) and Mayne to Larcom (1 February 1866).

48 TNA:PRO MEPO 7/27 (12 January 1866).

49 Comerford (1998), p. 133.

50 Anderson (1906), p. 59; McCracken (2009), pp. 22–24.

51 Kee (2000), pp. 324–5; Campbell (2002), p. 64.

52 David (1997), p. 150; other background information on Lord Cardigan was also extracted from this reference and from Paxman (2009), pp. 168–72.

53 *The Times* (4 June 1866; 27 and 28 June 1867).

54 *The Times* (28 June 1867).

55 *The Times* (27 June 1867).

56 *The Times* (4 June 1866).

57 Ibid.

58 *The Times* (28 June 1867).

59 Countess of Cardigan and Lancastre (1909).

60 Anderson (1906), p. 36.

61 White (2007), pp. 371–3; Smith pp. 161–82.

62   Kennedy (2003), p. 104.

63   TNA:PRO MEPO 1/47 Two undated letters from Mayne to Greig
     (*c.* September 1866).

64   TNA:PRO HO 45/7799 Report from Inspector Williamson (15 September
     1866).

65   TNA:PRO HO 45/7799 Reports from Sergeant Mulvany (8, 12 and 24 October
     1866).

66   Jenkins (2008), p. 80.

67   TNA:PRO MEPO 1/47 1 Mayne to Whelan (4 and 18 September 1866).

68   Wikipedia, 'Gustave Paul Cluseret'.

69   Kee (2000), pp. 329–30.

70   TNA:PRO HO 144/1537/2 Confession of Fariola; 'Amongst the Fenians', *The
     Irishman* (1 August 1868 – 31 October 1868).

71   *The Irishman* (1 and 8 August 1868); 'Belgians in the American Civil War'
     (http://home.scarlet.be/gallez.nic/US%20Army/Colored/OctaveFariola.htm);
     TNA:PRO HO144/1537/2.

72   TNA:PRO HO 144/1537/2 Confession of Fariola, p. 7.

73   *The Irishman* (8 August 1868).

74   TNA:PRO HO 144/1537/2 Confession of Fariola, pp. 10–1.

75   Ibid., p. 8.

76   Ibid., pp. 18–20; *The Irishman* (29 August 1868).

77   *The Irishman* (15 August 1868).

78   Whelehan (2009), pp. 55–9; TNA:PRO HO 144/1537/2 Confession of Fariola,
     pp. 13–20.

79   TNA:PRO FO 5/1340 (7 December 1866); MEPO 1/47 Mayne to Larcom
     (14 and 20 December 1866), Mayne to Wood (18 December 1866) and Mayne to
     Walpole (2 January 1867).

80   Kee (2000), pp. 321–4; Campbell (2002), p. 73; O'Broin (1971), pp. 119–21;
     Anderson (1906), p. 63.

81   O'Broin (1971), p. 119.

82   Smith (1985), p. 186.

83   Ibid., p. 187.

84   TNA:PRO HO 144/1537/2 Confession of Fariola, p. 29.

85   *Daily News* (2 December 1867); *The Times* (2 December 1867).

86   MEPO1/47 Mayne to Greig (19 April 1866) and Mayne to Comte de Gernon
     (21 November 1866).

87   TNA:PRO HO 144/1537/2 Confession of Fariola, p. 81.

88   HO 65/8 Liddell to Receiver of Police (2 April 1868).

89   *The Times* (21 March 1867); *Pall Mall Gazette* (15 February 1867); *Glasgow Herald*
     (16 February 1867).

90   TNA:PRO HO 45/7799 part 4, telegram from Mayor of Chester (11 February
     1867).

91   Kee (2000), pp. 331–3; Devoy (1929), p. 187.

92   *Trewman's Exeter Flying Post* (2 October 1867).

93   Jenkins (2008), p. 93.

94   Kee (2000), pp. 332–4; *The Irishman* (10 October 1868).

95   TNA:PRO HO 144/1537/2 Confession of Fariola, pp. 57 onwards.

96   Ibid.
97   Novak (2007 and 2008); National Archives of Ireland CSO:LB 267; Matthews (2010), pp. 13–4.
98   Jenkins (2008), p. 84; Kee (2000), p. 104.
99   Anderson (1906), p. 71.
100   *The Irishman* (10, 17 and 24 October 1868).
101   Ibid.
102   Kee (2000), pp. 330–40; Murray (1878).
103   OBP (July 1867), Charles Stuart (t18670708-650); *The Times* (18 June 1867); *Daily News* (10 July 1867).
104   *The Irishman* (24 October 1868).
105   TNA:PRO MEPO 7/29 (11 July 1867); MEPO 7/30 (20 May 1868).
106   Diamond (2003), pp. 28–9.
107   *The Irishman* (24 October 1868).
108   *Freeman's Journal* (11 November 1867).
109   *The Times* (31 July 1867).
110   TNA:PRO MEPO 1/47 Mayne to Lord Naas (19 July 1867).
111   O'Broin (1971), pp. 200–1; Jenkins (2008), p. 171.
112   *The Times* (13 November 1867).
113   'Belgians in the American Civil War' (http://home.scarlet.be/gallez.nic/ US%20Army/Colored/OctaveFariola.htm).
114   National Archives of Ireland, F4067.
115   O'Broin (1971), p. 124; (www.lisburn.com/history/digger/Digger2010/digger-29-01-2010.html).
116   TNA:PRO HO 65/7 Liddell to Mayne (6 September 1867).
117   Jenkins (2008), pp. 104–46.
118   *The Times* (19 September 1867).
119   TNA:PRO HO 65/8 Ferguson to Mayne (1 October 1867).
120   Jenkins (2008), pp. 104–46.
121   Smith (1985), pp. 187–8, including quotation from Mayo MSS, National Library of Ireland.
122   Kennedy (2003), p. 106.
123   Kee (2000), p. 343; Jenkins (2008), p. 141.
124   TNA:PRO FO 5/1347 Report (4 August 1869).
125   Kennedy (2003), pp. 106–7; TNA:PRO HO 45/7799 part 1, Superintendent Ryan to Home Office (8 October 1867).
126   TNA:PRO HO 65/8 Ferguson to Mayne (7 October 1869).
127   TNA:PRO HO 45/7799 Part 1; MEPO 1/47 Mayne to Chief Constable of Aberdeenshire (14 October 1867); Smith (1985), p. 189.
128   *The Times* (14 November 1867).
129   *The Times* (11, 12 and 14 November 1867); TNA:PRO HO 65/8 Liddell to Receiver of Police (2 April 1868), includes reference to Reading expenses claim by Clarke.
130   Jenkins (2008), pp. 148–9.
131   TNA:PRO HO 65/8 Memo (4 December 1867); MEPO 7/29 (9 December 1867).
132   TNA:PRO HO 65/8 Ferguson to Mayne (9 November 1867).

133 TNA:PRO MEPO 1/47 Mayne to Hardy (1 November 1867).
134 TNA:PRO HO 65/8 Liddell to Receiver of Police (2 April 1868).
135 Kennedy (2003), pp. 110–3.
136 Ibid.
137 Anderson (1906), p. 75; Smith (1985), p. 190.
138 Smith (1985), pp. 190–2; Jenkins (1985), pp. 152–5.
139 Ibid.; Ibid.
140 Smith (1985), p. 192.
141 Ibid.
142 Moylan, p. 155.
143 Wade (2007), p. 171.
144 Browne (1956), pp. 141–3.
145 TNA:PRO MEPO 7/30 Police Orders (7 November 1868).
146 Kennedy (2003), pp. 110–22; Jenkins (2008), pp. 145–78.
147 Jenkins (2008), pp. 179–208.
148 Jenkins (2008), p. 180.
149 Fitzgerald (1888), Vol. 2, p. 312.
150 OBP (April 1868), William Desmond, Timothy Desmond, Nicholas English, John O'Keefe, Michael Barrett, Anne Justice (t18680406-412); TNA:PRO MEPO 3/1788 Report of Sergeant Sunerway.
151 National Archives of Ireland CSO LB 267 Mayne to Larcom (18 December 1867).
152 'Edmund O'Leary' (http://nga.ie/Fenians-Edmund_OLeary.php).
153 National Archives of Ireland CSO LB 267 Larcom to Mayne (28 December 1867).
154 TNA:PRO MEPO 1/48 Mayne to Home Office (2 January 1868); Mayne to Scudamore (11 March 1868).
155 *The Times* (21 April 1868).
156 Williams (1890), Vol. 1, pp. 182–4.
157 Ibid., p. 184.
158 *The Times* (28 April 1868).
159 Ibid.
160 Ibid.
161 Williams (1890), Vol. 1, p. 203.
162 Jenkins (2008), pp. 197–202.
163 *The Times* (27 May 1868).
164 Jenkins (2008), p. 181; OBP (April 1868), William Desmond, Timothy Desmond, Nicholas English, John O'Keefe, Michael Barrett, Anne Justice (t18680406-412).
165 Campbell (2002), p. 78; Devoy (1929), p. 249.
166 *The Times* (27 December 1867); TNA:PRO HO 65/8 Liddell to Receiver of Police (2 April 1868).
167 TNA:PRO HO45/7799 Report from Superintendent Butt (20 December 1867).
168 TNA:PRO MEPO 21/15/5056.
169 Jenkins (2008), p. 207.
170 O'Broin (1971), pp. 227–40.
171 TNA:PRO MEPO 1/48 Mayne to Larcom (13 April 1868).
172 Jenkins (2008), p. 188; Wikipedia, 'Alfred, Duke of Saxe-Coburg and Gotha'.

173 TNA:PRO MEPO 1/48 Mayne to Ferguson (9 May 1868); Wikipedia, 'SS *Great Britain*'.
174 *The Times* (14, 16, 22 and 24 July 1868).
175 Smith (1985), pp. 183–4.
176 Porter (1992), p. 81.
177 TNA:PRO HO45/10002/A49463.
178 Ibid.
179 TNA:PRO HO45/9442/66692 Minutes of Evidence, paragraphs 457–62.

4 Back to Basics

1 Davitt (2001), p. 1, the first verse of the poem *Innisfail*.
2 *Warrington Advertiser* (18 April 1868); TNA:PRO HO 45/9419/58406 Report from Inspector Clarke (24 April 1868).
3 TNA:PRO C16/828/T45; C16/829/T74.
4 *Warrington Guardian*, Supplement (18 April 1868).
5 Ibid.
6 Ibid.
7 Ibid.
8 TNA:PRO MEPO 7/31 (21 January 1869).
9 *Leeds Mercury*, Weekly Supplement (4 January 1890).
10 Cavanagh (1893), p. 80.
11 Ascoli (1979), p. 138; Browne (1956), p. 172.
12 TNA:PRO HO 65/8 Liddell to Henderson (6 July 1869).
13 Ibid. (12 May 1869).
14 TNA:PRO MEPO 7/31 (15 May 1869).
15 TNA:PRO HO 65/8 Knatchbull-Huguessen to Henderson (2 June 1869).
16 TNA:PRO MEPO 21/10/3018; *Pall Mall Gazette* (31 August 1869).
17 TNA:PRO MEPO 7/31 (6 July 1869).
18 TNA:PRO MEPO 7/32 (17 October 1870).
19 'The Police of London', *The Quarterly Review* (1870), pp. 87–129.
20 *The Times* (6 October 1868).
21 *The Times* (13 October 1868).
22 *The Times* (1 March 1869).
23 *The Times* (24 October 1868); *Lloyds Weekly Newspaper* (25 October 1868); *Reynolds's Newspaper* (25 October 1868).
24 *The Times* (1 March 1869).
25 TNA:PRO MEPO 7/31 (1 and 5 March 1869).
26 Meiklejohn (1912), p. 80.
27 Ibid., pp. 79–89.
28 *The Times* (1 November 1869).
29 Ibid.
30 OBP (November 1869), Hyppolite Longuay, Emile Antoine, George Christiens, Andre Berthier (t18691122-59).
31 *The Times* (6 and 15 December 1869); OBP (December 1869), Hyppolite Longuay (t18691213-117).
32 TNA:PRO MEPO 3/99 Report by Clarke (13 February 1871).
33 Ibid. (21 February 1871).
34 Paterson (2006), p. 200.

35 TNA:PRO MEPO 3/99 Report by Clarke (25 February 1871).

36 Ibid. (6 March 1871).

37 TNA:PRO MEPO 7/33 (21 April 1871).

38 Williams (1890),Vol. 1, pp. 291–2.

39 OBP (April 1871), Michael Campbell, John Calbraith (t18710403-332).

40 OBP (April 1871), John Calbraith (t18710403-333).

41 TNA:PRO MEPO 3/99 Letter from Henderson to Treasury (12 April 1871) and Memorandum from Clarke (2 May 1871).

42 OBP (April 1869), James Gambier, William Rumble (t18690405-432).

43 Ibid.

44 Ibid.

45 *The Times* (18 February 1869).

46 *The Times* (5 and 12 March 1869).

47 OBP (April 1869), James Gambier, William Rumble (t18690405-432); *The Times* (10 April 1869); *Lloyds Weekly Newspaper* (11 April 1869).

48 *The Times* (6 December 1864) and (6 and 7 February 1865); Wikipedia, 'CSS *Rappahannock*'.

49 Wikipedia, '*Alabama* Claims'.

50 Petrow (1994), p. 280.

51 Stewart (2000), p. 19.

52 Petrow (1994), pp 279–80.

53 Petrow (1994), p. 246.

54 Davies and Metcalfe (2010).

55 Williams (1890),Vol. 2, p. 113.

56 *The Times* (21 April 1869).

57 Ibid.

58 *The Times* (30 April 1869).

59 Ibid.

60 Ibid.

61 *Pall Mall Gazette* (6 May 1869).

62 *The Times* (16 and 21 October 1871), (21 January 1872) and (15 July 1872).

63 *The Times* (21 June 1869) and (5 August 1869).

64 Ibid.

65 *The Times* (24 January 1870).

66 *The Times* (14 September 1870), (2 and 3 November 1870), (4 November 1871), (19 July 1873), (11 March 1875), (22 and 31 May 1875), (11 October 1875) and (4 December 1876); *Illustrated Police News* (1 October 1870); *The Ipswich Journal* (25 December 1875); *Reynolds's Newspaper* (2 January 1876); *Penny Illustrated Paper* (3 June 1876).

67 Dilnot (1928), p. 182.

68 *The Times* (14 September 1870).

69 *The Times* (2 November 1870).

70 *The Times* (3 November 1870).

71 *Penny Illustrated Paper* (3 June 1876).

72 Petrow (1994), p. 250.

73 TNA:PRO HO 45/9526/34897.

74 Ibid.

75   Dilnot (1928), p. 214.
76   Petrow (1994), p. 280.
77   TNA:PRO MEPO 3/92.
78   TNA:PRO MEPO 3/92 Report by Inspector Druscovich (1 December 1869).
79   Arnot (1994).
80   Ibid.
81   Archer (2008).
82   Lowndes (1872–73), pp. 397–412.
83   Archer (2008).
84   Arnot (1994).
85   TNA:PRO MEPO 3/93.
86   TNA:PRO MEPO 3/94.
87   Ibid., Report by Clarke, concerning Mrs Clarke (7 October 1870).
88   Ibid., Report by Clarke, concerning Mrs Davis (7 October 1870).
89   Ibid., (2 January 1870).
90   Arnot (1994).
91   Ibid,
92   TNA:PRO MEPO 3/94 (23 December 1873).
93   TNA:PRO MEPO 3/95.
94   Arnot (1994).
95   Rattle and Vale (2007).
96   TNA:PRO MEPO 3/96 report by Chief Inspector Clarke (28 December 1870).
97   *The Times* (16 August 1870).
98   TNA:PRO MEPO 3/96 report by Chief Inspector Clarke (28 December 1870).
99   Ibid.
100   *British Medical Journal* (1 July 1871), p. 15.
101   *The Times* (15 July 1871); OBP (July 1871), Charles and Sarah de Baddeley
      (t18710710-560).
102   Bowen-Rowlands (1924), pp. 96–100; *The Times* (14, 16 and 17 December 1880).
103   TNA:PRO HO45/9329/19461.
104   TNA:PRO FO5/1347 US Legation to Earl of Clarendon (9 August 1869).
105   TNA:PRO MEPO 7/31 (23 October 1869).
106   Campbell (2002), pp. 14, 85–7.
107   Healy (2010).
108   *Freeman's Journal* (27 June 1870).
109   *Freeman's Journal* (28, 29 and 30 September) and (1 October 1869).
110   Ibid.
111   Ibid.
112   *Morning Post* (2 October 1869).
113   *Freeman's Journal* (18–21 February 1870); Wikipedia, 'Isaac Butt'; McCracken
      (2009), p. 37.
114   *Freeman's Journal* (24–27 June 1870).
115   Anderson (1906), p. 81.
116   Anderson (1910), p. 58.
117   OBP (July 1870), John Wilson, Michael Davitt (t18700711-602).
118   *The Times* (18 May 1870).
119   King (1999).

120 *The Times* (21 May 1870) and (3, 6, and 15 June 1870).

121 OBP (July 1870), John Wilson, Michael Davitt (t18700711-602); McCracken (2009), p. 35.

122 OBP (July 1870), John Wilson, Michael Davitt (t18700711-602).

123 National Library of Ireland: NLI 5697, Samuel Lee Anderson Papers; Journal and Date Book (7 July 1870).

124 *The Times* (16, 18 and 19 July 1870); OBP (July 1870), John Wilson, Michael Davitt (t18700711-602).

125 *The Times* (19 July 1870).

126 Davitt (2001), Vol. 1, pp. 43–80.

127 Kee (2000), p. 373.

128 Davitt (2001).

129 Wikipedia, 'Franco-Prussian War'.

130 TNA:PRO HO 45/8444 Report from Inspector Pay (6 September 1870).

131 O'Mahony (2000); McCracken (2009), p. 46.

132 *The Times* (24 and 28 September 1870).

133 TNA:PRO HO 45/8444 Report from Inspector Brannan (1 October 1870).

134 Ibid., Telegram from Frederick Bernal (8 October 1870) and Letter from Foreign Office (11 October 1870); TS25/1695 Legal Opinion (5 October 1870).

135 TNA:PRO HO 45/8444 Orders for Clarke (10 October 1870) and Report from Clarke (19 October 1870).

136 Ibid.

137 O'Mahony (2000).

138 Ibid.

139 TNA:PRO HO 45/8444 Report from Clarke (19 October 1870).

140 *The Times* (22 and 29 October 1870) and (4 and 21 November 1870).

141 TNA: PRO HO27.

142 Comerford (1999), pp. 81, 166, 185; *Leeds Mercury* (9 January 1872).

143 Porter (1987), p. 9; Porter (1992), pp. 81–98; TNA:PRO HO45/9303/11335.

144 TNA:PRO MEPO 3/1778 Report from Chief Inspector Clarke (27 August 1872); MEPO 3/3070 Report from Chief Inspector Clarke (8 January 1872), (30 December 1872), (28 June 1876) and (26 December 1876); Irish National Archives Fenian Papers R series Box 13 6992R and Box 14 7059R Correspondence and Reports by Chief Inspector Clarke relating to Arms Supplies; *Belfast Newsletter* (20 and 21 July 1871); *Freeman's Journal* (23 July 1873); *Pall Mall Gazette* (30 July 1873).

145 Porter (1992), pp. 101–10.

146 OBP (December 1871), William Anthony (t18711211-102); *Illustrated Police News* (7 October 1871).

147 Wikipedia, 'London Fire Brigade'; Wikipedia, 'London Salvage Corps'.

148 OBP (December 1871), William Anthony (t18711211-102).

149 Ibid.

150 *Illustrated Police News* (7 October 1871).

151 *The Times* (18 October 1871).

152 Ibid.

153 *Penny Illustrated Paper* (2 December 1871); *The Times* (8 and 23 November 1871).

154   OBP (December 1871), William Anthony (t18711211-102).

155   *Pall Mall Gazette* (14 December 1871).

156   *Liverpool Mercury* (15 December 1871).

157   TNA:PRO MEPO 7/34 (3 January 1872).

5   *The Tichborne Claimant, Theft and Fraud*

 1   Chetham's Library, *Axon Ballads*, No 16.

 2   McWilliam (2007), pp. 5–52; Maugham (1936), pp. 17–314.

 3   Ibid.

 4   Ibid.

 5   Ibid.

 6   Ibid.

 7   Ibid.

 8   McWilliam (2007), pp. 27–33; Maugham (1936), pp. 108–50; Summerscale (2008), pp. 263–6.

 9   McWilliam (2007), pp. 35–52; Maugham (1936), pp. 153–314; *Freeman's Journal* (7 March 1872).

10   TNA:PRO MEPO 21/18/6786.

11   Bowen-Rowlands (1924), p. 81.

12   Maugham (1936), p. 318.

13   *Manchester Times* (9 March 1872); *Bristol Mercury* (9 March 1872); *Lloyds Weekly Newspaper* (10 March 1872).

14   Williams (1890), Vol. 2, p. 1.

15   McWilliam (2007), pp. 53–82; Maugham (1936), pp. 317–21.

16   Maugham (1936), p. 322.

17   *The Times* (17 January 1874).

18   *Bradford Observer* (29 December 1873).

19   Summerscale (2008), p. 266.

20   *Leeds Mercury* (22 May 1873).

21   *Daily News* (28 May 1873) and (19 August 1873).

22   *The Times* (9–11 October 1873).

23   *The Times* (15–18 October 1873); TNA:PRO HO 144/1/4877a, Treasury Report (21 May 1879).

24   *Freeman's Journal* (15 December 1873); *The Times* (1 and 18 November 1873).

25   *The Times* (31 October 1873).

26   *The Times* (1, 18 and 27 November 1873).

27   *The Times* (28 and 29 November 1873).

28   Atlay (1899), p. 378.

29   *The Times* (1 December 1873).

30   *Pall Mall Gazette* (8 December 1873); *The Times* (9 December 1873).

31   *Liverpool Mercury* (9 December 1873).

32   *Pall Mall Gazette* (8 December 1873); *The Times* (9 December 1873).

33   *The Times* (19 January 1874).

34   *The Times* (12 December 1873) and (9 January 1874); *Lloyds Weeekly Newspaper* (14 December 1873).

35   *The Times* (5 and 13 December 1873).

36 *The Times* (9 January 1874).

37 *Daily News* (16 January 1874); *The Times* (19 January 1874).

38 *Daily News* (21 January 1874).

39 *The Times* (24 January 1874) and (2 April 1874); *Exeter Flying Post* (28 January 1874); McWilliam (2007), p. 71.

40 Kenealy (1875),Vol. 7, p. 380.

41 McWilliam (2007), pp. 107–8.

42 Hawkins (1904),Vol. 1, pp. 328–9.

43 Maugham (1936), p. 72.

44 *The Times* (7 March 1874); *Pall Mall Gazette* (19 March 1874).

45 *The Times* (10 and 11 April 1874); OBP (April 1874), Carl Lundgren and James Brown (t18740407-273).

46 McWilliam (2007), pp. 113–85.

47 TNA:PRO MEPO 7/37 (27 March 1875);TNA:PRO MEPO 7/38 (15 April 1876).

48 McWilliam (2007), p. 163.

49 TNA:PRO HO 144/1/4877a, Reports of Chief Inspector Clarke (7 February 1877) and (11 and 12 April 1877).

50 McWilliam (2007), p. 273.

51 *The Times* (26 June 1873).

52 *The Times* (5 July 1873);TNA:PRO MEPO 7/35 (5 July 1873).

53 *The Times* (11 and 20 May 1872) and (14 June 1872); *Illustrated Police News* (18 May 1872); OBP (June 1872), David Edwards, Sarah Edwards, Elizabeth Hopkins (t18720610-486).

54 Ibid.

55 *The Times* (14 June 1872); *Daily News* (14 June 1872); OBP (June 1872), David Edwards, Sarah Edwards (t18720610-487); PRO HO27.

56 Ibid.

57 Williams (1890),Vol. 2, p. 134; Hawkins (1904),Vol. 2, p. 15.

58 TNA:PRO MEPO 7/34 (18 June 1872).

59 *Morning Post* (7 March 1874).

60 *Birmingham Daily Post* (16 September 1872); *Hertfordshire Express* (15 September 1877).

61 Stewart (2000), p. 146.

62 Ibid., pp. 38–44.

63 Ibid., pp. 39–51.

64 *The Times* (12 February 1875).

65 *The Times* (13 March 1875).

66 *Daily News* (19 and 27 February 1875).

67 TNA:PRO HO 65/33 Liddell to Henderson (2 March 1875).

68 *The Times* (6 March 1875).

69 *The Times* (28 April 1875).

70 Stewart (2000), pp. 59–61.

71 *The Times* (6 and 21 May 1875); *Pall Mall Gazette* (20 May 1875).

72 *The Times* (10 June 1875).

73 Littlechild (1894), p. 138.

74 *Illustrated Police News* (3 April 1880).

6 *Suicide, Accidental Death or Murder?*

1   Hall (1923), p. 87.
2   TNA:PRO MEPO 3/120; *The Times* (28 February 1876) and (5 and 24 May 1876).
3   Greenham (1904), p. 136; TNA:PRO HO 65/35 Liddell to Henderson (2 March 1876).
4   TNA:PRO MEPO 7/38 (5 March 1876); PCOM 1/112, pp. 624–5.
5   Greenham (1904), p. 137; TNA:PRO HO45/9325.
6   *The Times* (22 April 1876).
7   Ibid.
8   Ibid.
9   Ibid.
10 OBP (May 1876), William Vance, Ellen Snee (t18760529-408); *The Times* (6 May 1876); Wikipedia, 'Thomas Bond (British physician)'.
11 *The Times* (29 April 1876) and (6 May 1876).
12 OBP (May 1876), William Vance, Ellen Snee (t18760529-408); *The Times* (1 and 2 June 1876).
13 *The Times* (18 May 1876).
14 Bridges (1956), p. 158.
15 Ibid., p. 160.
16 TNA:PRO MEPO 3/123 Clarke report (11 May 1876).
17 Ibid., Special Enquiry (10 May 1876).
18 *Morning Post* (9 May 1876); *The Times* (13 May 1876).
19 TNA:PRO MEPO 3/123 Clarke report (24 May 1876).
20 Ibid., Clarke memorandum (17 May 1876).
21 Ibid., Memorandum (prepared in 1929); *The Times* (18 May 1876).
22 *The Times* (27 June 1876).
23 TNA:PRO MEPO 3/123 Clarke report (29 May 1876).
24 Ibid., Memorandum (31 May 1876).
25 Ibid., Clarke report (5 June 1876).
26 Ibid.
27 Bridges (1956), pp. 293, 303; Ruddick (2001), p. 195.
28 *The Times* (12 August 1876); Hall (1923), pp. v, 1.
29 *The Times* (12 July–13 August 1876); Hamilton and Mooney (2010).
30 Juxon (1984), p. 163.
31 TNA:PRO MEPO 3/123 Clarke report (22 July 1876).
32 *The Times* (9 August 1876).
33 TNA:PRO MEPO 3/123 Clarke memorandum (20 July 1876).
34 Ibid., Clarke report (12 August 1876).
35 *British Medical Journal* (26 August 1876), pp. 264–6.
36 TNA:PRO MEPO 3/123 Clarke report (12 August 1876).
37 Ibid., Murder reward poster.
38 Ruddick (2001), pp. 134, 141, 183.
39 Juxon (1984), p. 137.
40 Bowen-Rowlands (1924), p. 135.
41 Hall (1923); Ruddick (2001).
42 Bridges (1956).

43 OBP (October 1876), Charles Howard (t18761023-511); *Reynolds's Newspaper* (5 September 1876); *Pall Mall Gazette* (5 September 1876).

44 Ibid.

45 *Reynolds's Newspaper* (3,5 and 10 September 1876); *Pall Mall Gazette* (5 September 1876); *The Times* (6, 12, 20 and 27 September) and (11 October 1876); Wikipedia, 'Robert Carden'; Wikipedia, 'Barnstaple (UK Parliament Constituency)'.

46 *Pall Mall Gazette* (3 September 1876).

47 *The Times* (11 October 1876).

48 OBP (October 1876), Charles Howard (t18761023-511); *The Times* (26 and 27 October 1876).

49 Ibid.

50 *The Times* (28 October 1876).

51 TNA:PRO HO 45/9419/58406 Letter from J. Oldfield (15 August 1876); Laws (1971).

52 Ibid.

53 TNA:PRO C16/829/T74 and C16/828/T45.

54 TNA:PRO HO 45/9419/58406 Clarke report (21 August 1876).

55 Griffiths (1901), Vol. 2, pp. 23–7; Kingston (1923), pp. 122–33; Kingston (1927), pp. 138–47; Ellis (1928), pp. 268–74.

56 TNA:PRO HO144/169/A43194.

57 *The Times* (15 May 1871); *Pall Mall Gazette* (20 November 1871); TNA:PRO C16/829/T74 and C16/828/T45.

58 TNA:PRO HO 45/9419/58406 Undated letter from John Jennings to Earl of Derby.

59 Ibid., Clarke report to Austrian Consul-General (22 September 1876).

60 Ibid., Clarke internal report (22 September 1876).

61 Ibid.

62 *Liverpool Mercury* (25 September 1876); *Warrington Advertiser*, *Warrington Guardian*, Supplement, and *Cheshire Observer* (all 30 September 1876).

63 *Warrington Guardian* (4 October 1876).

64 TNA:PRO HO 45/9419/58406 Letter from F. Krapf to Commissioner Henderson (11 October 1876).

65 Ibid., Clarke report (30 October 1876); MEPO 7/38 (28 September 1876); OBP (October 1876), Charles Howard (t18761023-511).

66 TNA:PRO HO 45/9419/58406 Clarke memorandum and report (28 and 30 October 1876, respectively).

67 Williams (1890), Vol. 2, pp. 32–4.

68 *The Times* and *Freeman's Journal* (31 October 1876); *Cheshire Observer* (4 November 1876); *Manchester Weekly Times* (4 November 1876).

69 *The Times* (6 November 1876); *Daily News* (6 November 1876).

70 *The Times* (17 November 1876).

71 *The Times* (30 November 1876).

72 *The Times* (7 December 1876).

73 Ibid.

74 Ibid.

75 *The Times* (7 January 1877).

76　*Cheshire Observer* (23 June 1877).

77　*The Times* (23 June 1877).

78　Ibid.

79　*The Times* (21 and 25 June 1877).

80　*The Times* (25 June 1877).

81　*The Times* (3 July 1877).

82　*Warrington Guardian* (4 July 1877).

83　*Lloyds Weekly Newspaper* (8 July 1877).

84　*The Times* (19 November 1877), (5 and 21 December 1877) and (28 January 1890); *Paddington, Kensington and Bayswater Chronicle* (30 August 1890).

85　Freeston (1900), p. 29.

86　Kingston (1927), p. 147; TNA:PRO C16/829/T74.

87　Kingston (1923a), p. 126.

88　Meiklejohn (1912), pp. 92–102; Littlechild (1894), p. 203; Kingston (1924), p. 268; Wikipedia, 'Adam Worth'.

89　Stewart (2000), p. 85.

90　*The Times* (12 September 1877).

7　*The Great Turf Swindle and Police Corruption*

1　*Fun* (29 August 1877).

2　Williams (1890), Vol. 2, pp. 48–55, 69–80; Clarke (1918), pp. 136–48; Dilnot (1928); Stewart (2000); Stratmann (2006), pp. 108–29.

3　Stewart (2000), pp. 73–84.

4　Ibid.

5　TNA:PRO MEPO 7/38 (28 September 1876).

6　Stewart (2000), pp. 85–6.

7　Ibid., p. 87; *The Times* (8 November 1876).

8　Stewart (2000), p. 123.

9　Ibid., pp. 126–7.

10　Ibid., pp. 86–8.

11　OBP (October 1877), John Meiklejohn, Nathaniel Druscovich, William Palmer, George Clarke, Edward Froggatt (t18771022-805).

12　Ibid.

13　Ibid.

14　Stewart (2000), pp. 124–5.

15　TNA:PRO HO144/21/60045 Liddell to Henderson (21 November 1876).

16　TNA:PRO MEPO 1/48 Henderson to R. Stuart, Procurator Fiscal (c. 10 December 1876) and Labalmondière to Stuart (25 November 1876).

17　*The Times* (9 July 1872); OBP (July 1872), Harry Benson (t18720708-502); Stewart (2000), pp. 9–14.

18　TNA:PRO HO144/21/60045; Stewart (2000), p. 91.

19　OBP (April 1877), Harry Benson, William Kurr, Charles Bale, Frederick Kurr, Edwin Murray (t18770409-391); OBP (October 1877), John Meiklejohn, Nathaniel Druscovich, William Palmer, George Clarke, Edward Froggatt (t18771022-805).

20　OBP (April 1877), Harry Benson, William Kurr, Charles Bale, Frederick Kurr, Edwin Murray (t18770409-391); *The Times* (1 December 1876).

21 Stewart (2000), p. 93.

22 Ibid.

23 TNA:PRO HO144/21/60045 Letter from 'Charles Collinge' (Frederick Kurr).

24 *The Times* (1 September 1877).

25 Stewart (2000), pp. 93–5; Littlechild (1894), pp. 45–7.

26 *Daily News* (4 December 1876).

27 TNA:PRO MEPO 3/3070 Clarke Report (26 December 1876).

28 *The Times* (28 December 1876).

29 OBP (October 1877), John Meiklejohn, Nathaniel Druscovich, William Palmer, George Clarke, Edward Froggatt (t18771022-805).

30 OBP (April 1877), Harry Benson, William Kurr, Charles Bale, Frederick Kurr, Edwin Murray (t18770409-391);

31 Stewart (2000), p. 96.

32 Williams (1890), Vol. 2, pp. 49–50.

33 OBP (April 1877), Harry Benson, William Kurr, Charles Bale, Frederick Kurr, Edwin Murray (t18770409-391).

34 Ibid.

35 *The Times* (24 April 1877); Stewart (2000), pp. 97–9.

36 TNA:PRO PCOM 2/77 and PCOM 2/99.

37 Stewart (2000), p. 129.

38 TNA:PRO MEPO 7/39 Police Orders for 23 January 1877 and 13 February 1877.

39 Information courtesy of the Library and Museum of Freemasonry, Freemason's Hall, London.

40 *The Era* (2 November 1873).

41 Ridley (1999), p. 93.

42 *The Era* (25 July 1875).

43 Information courtesy of the Library and Museum of Freemasonry, Freemason's Hall, London.

44 OBP (October 1877), John Meiklejohn, Nathaniel Druscovich, William Palmer, George Clarke, Edward Froggatt (t18771022-805); Wikipedia, 'Masonic Lodge Officers'.

45 Stewart (2000), p. 129.

46 OBP (October 1877), John Meiklejohn, Nathaniel Druscovich, William Palmer, George Clarke, Edward Froggatt (t18771022-805).

47 Stewart (2000), p. 140; TNA;PRO HO 65/35 Home Office to Henderson (23 December 1876) and (4 January 1877).

48 TNA:PRO HO 65/36 Liddell to Henderson (9 June 1877).

49 Stewart (2000), pp. 129–30.

50 TNA:PRO HO 45/9442/66692a Memorandum from Stephenson to Cross (18 May 1877).

51 Stewart (2000), p. 130.

52 *The Times* (27 August 1877).

53 Stewart (2000), pp. 166–8; TNA:PRO MEPO 7/39 Police Orders for 27 July and 8 August 1877; Greenham (1904), p. 137.

54 *The Times* (13 July 1877).

55 *The Times* (20 July 1877).

56 *The Times* (20 and 26 July 1877), (3–4, 6, 13, 17–18, 20, 24, 27 and 31 August 1877) and (1, 3, 7, 10, 14, 19, 21, 24 September 1877); OBP (October 1877), John Meiklejohn, Nathaniel Druscovich, William Palmer, George Clarke, Edward Froggatt (t18771022-805).

57 TNA:PRO HO 65/37 Lushington to Henderson (2 October 1877).

58 TNA:PRO MEPO 7/39 Police Orders for 27 July 1877.

59 TNA:PRO MEPO 3/128 and 3/129.

60 *The Times* (26 July 1877); Dilnot (1928), p. 88.

61 *The Times* (3, 13, 17–18 August 1877).

62 *The Times* (27 and 30 August 1877).

63 *The Times* (7 September 1877).

64 *The Times* (10 November 1877).

65 TNA:PRO HO45/9442/66692a Memorandum from Holker and Giffard to Home Secretary (29 August 1877).

66 Ibid., from Liddell to Home Secretary (1 September 1877).

67 Ibid., from Sir Augustus Stephenson (2 September 1877).

68 *Newcastle Courant* (14 September 1877).

69 *Hampshire Telegraph* (15 September 1877).

70 Williams (1890), Vol. 2, pp. 48–55, 69–80; Clarke (1918), pp. 136–48; Dilnot (1928); Stewart (2000); Stratmann (2006), pp. 108–29.

71 Ibid.

72 *Hertfordshire Express* (15 September 1877).

73 Ibid.

74 *The Times* (14 September 1877).

75 *The Times* (21 September 1877).

76 Ibid.

77 Ibid.

78 *Daily Telegraph* (22 September 1877).

79 *The Times* (22 and 24 September 1877).

80 *Daily Telegraph* (24 September 1877).

81 Dilnot (1928); Stewart (2000); OBP (October 1877), John Meiklejohn, Nathaniel Druscovich, William Palmer, George Clarke, Edward Froggatt (t18771022-805); national and regional newspapers (25 October–21 November 1877).

82 TNA:PRO HO45/9442/66692a Lewis and Lewis to R.A. Cross (25 September 1877) and (10 October 1877).

83 Ibid. Henderson to Cross (2 October 1877); Stewart (2000), pp. 117–8.

84 Juxon (1984), pp. 146–54.

85 Clarke (1918), p. 138.

86 Ibid., pp. 144–5.

87 *The Times* (21 September 1877).

88 OBP (October 1877), John Meiklejohn, Nathaniel Druscovich, William Palmer, George Clarke, Edward Froggatt (t18771022-805).

89 Ibid.

90 Ibid.

91 Ibid.

92 Ibid.

93 Clarke (1918), p. 141.

94 Ibid.

95 TNA: PRO HO27.

96 OBP (October 1877), John Meiklejohn, Nathaniel Druscovich, William Palmer, George Clarke, Edward Froggatt (t18771022-805).

97 Ibid.

98 Ibid.

99 Clarke (1918), p. 146.

100 *Daily Telegraph* (21 November 1877).

101 D. Walker-Smith and E. Clarke (1939), p. 106.

102 TNA:PRO HO45/9442/66692A Clarke memorandum (15 December 1877).

103 Ibid., Cross to Henderson (15 December 1877).

104 Ibid., Henderson memorandum (15 December 1877).

105 TNA:PRO MEPO 21/14/4724.

106 TNA:PRO HO 65/37 Liddell to Henderson (4 January 1878).

107 Ibid., (22 October 1879).

108 TNA:PRO CRIM 4/914; PCOM 2/77 and PCOM 2/103.

109 *Jackson's Oxford Journal* (4 December 1880); *New York Times* (31 December 1881); Probate records.

110 Clarke (1914), pp. 147–8; 1881 census; Probate records.

111 *Reynolds's Newspaper* (13 June 1880); 1881 and 1891 censuses.

112 Juxon (1984), pp. 223–4; *Freeman's Journal* (8 and 9 July 1884) and (3 October 1884); *Bristol Mercury* (22 December 1884).

113 *Northern Echo* (19 November 1884); *Aberdeen Weekly Journal* (16 December 1884); *Manchester Times* (30 October 1886).

114 *Reynolds's Newspaper* (18 November 1888).

115 *Leeds Mercury*, Saturday supplement (4 January–5 April 1890).

116 *The Times* (11–13 November 1903).

117 Meiklejohn (1912), p. 130.

118 TNA:PRO HO 45/9442/66692a Statement of William Walters (17 February 1880); *Newcastle Courant* (2 July 1880).

119 *Bristol Mercury* (22 September 1882).

120 *Daily Post* (8 October 1885).

121 TNA:PRO HO 144/21/60045 Benson to Cross (11 October 1885).

122 Fitzgerald (1888), Vol. 1, p. 338.

123 Wikipedia, 'Adelina Patti'.

124 TNA:PRO HO 144/21/60045 Benson to Cross (11 October 1885); Fitzgerald (1888), Vol. 1, p. 338.

125 *Liverpool Mercury* (18 May 1888).

126 TNA:PRO HO 45/9442/66692.

127 Ibid.

128 TNA:PRO MEPO 2/134 Williamson memoranda (6 July 1870) and (20 November 1871).

129 TNA:PRO HO 45/9442/66692.

130 Ibid.

131 Stewart (2000), pp. 200–3.

132 TNA:PRO HO45/10002/A49463 Monro to Home Office (5 November 1888).

133   Andrews (1985), p. 44.
134   Campbell (2002), p. 147.
135   TNA:PRO MEPO 2/238; HO 144/190/A46472E.
136   Ibid.
137   White (2007), p. 402; Emsley (1996), p. 66; Wikipedia, 'Edmund Henderson'.
138   *Kelly's Commercial Directory* (1882–83); OBP (November 1881), Mary Saunders (t18811121-11).
139   *Kelly's Commercial Directory* (1884–91).
140   *Northern Echo* (11 August 1886).
141   Information courtesy of the Library and Museum of Freemasonry, Freemason's Hall, London.
142   OBP (October 1892), Thomas Neill [Cream] (t18921017-961).
143   TNA:PRO MEPO 3/144 Report of Inspector Harvey (23 May 1892); Shore (1923).
144   OBP (March 1895), Henry John Clarke, Ellen Lyon (t18950325-334).

Epilogue

1   Collins (1868), p. 324.
2   *The Times* (21 November 1877).
3   Dilnot (1928), p. 54.
4   Clarke (1918), p. 144.
5   Ibid., p. 138.
6   Walker-Smith and Clarke (1939), pp. 243–5.
7   Clarke (1918), pp. 1–2.
8   Stewart (2000).

BIBLIOGRAPHY

Offices of the publishers are located in London, UK, unless otherwise stated.

Adam, H.L., *C.I.D. Behind the Scenes at Scotland Yard* (Sampson Low, Marston & Co. Ltd, 1930)
————, *Old Days at the Old Bailey* (Sampson Low, Marston & Co. Ltd, 1932)
Anderson, R., *Sidelights on the Home Rule Movement* (John Murray, 1906)
————, *The Lighter Side of My Official Life* (Hodder and Stoughton, 1910)
Andrews, C., *Secret Service: The Making of the British Intelligence Community* (William Heinemann Ltd, 1985)
Archer, J.E., 'Mysterious and Suspicious Deaths: Missing Homicides in North-West England (1850–1905)', *Crime, History and Societies* (12, 2008), pp. 45–63
Armstrong, A., *Farmworkers: A Social and Economic History 1770–1980* (B.T. Batsford Ltd, 1988)
Arnot, M.L., 'Infant death, child care and the state: the baby farming scandal and the first infant life protection legislation of 1872', *Continuity and Change* (9, 1994), pp. 271–311
Ascoli, D., *The Queen's Police: The Origins and Development of the Metropolitan Police 1829–1979* (Hamish Hamilton, 1979)
Atlay, J.B., *The Tichborne Trial* (Grant Richards, 1899)
Begg, P. and Skinner, K., *The Scotland Yard Files* (Headline Book Publishing plc, 1992)
Bent, J., *Criminal Life: Reminiscences of Forty-Two Years as a Police Officer* (John Heywood, 1891)
Bowen-Rowlands, E., *Seventy-Two Years at the Bar* (Macmillan and Co. Ltd, 1924)
Brandon, D. and Brooke, A., *Blood on the Tracks: A History of Railway Crime in Britain* (The History Press, Stroud, UK, 2010)
Bratton, J. and Featherstone, A., *The Victorian Clown* (Cambridge University Press, 2006)

Bridges, Y., *How Charles Bravo Died: The Chronicle of a Cause Célèbre* (Jarrold Publishers Ltd, 1956) (Edition published by The Reprint Society, 1957)

Browne, D.G., *The Rise of Scotland Yard: A History of the Metropolitan Police* (George G. Harrap & Co. Ltd, 1956)

Campbell, C., *Fenian Fire: The British Government Plot to Assassinate Queen Victoria* (Harper Collins, 2002)

Cavanagh, T., *Scotland Yard Past and Present: Experiences of Thirty-Seven Years* (Chatto and Windus, 1893)

Clarke, E., *The Story of My Life* (John Murray, 1918)

Cobb, G.B., *Critical Years at the Yard: The Career of Frederick Williamson of the Detective Department and the C.I.D.* (Faber and Faber, 1956)

———, *The First Detectives and the Early Career of Richard Mayne Commissioner of Police* (Faber and Faber, 1957)

Collins, W., *The Moonstone* (Wordsworth Editions Ltd, Hertfordshire, 1868) (1993 Edition)

Comerford, R.V., *The Fenians in Context: Irish Politics and Society 1848–82* (Wolfhound Press, Dublin, Ireland, 1998)

Countess of Cardigan and Lancastre, *My Recollections* (Eveleigh Nash, 1909)

Critchley, T.A., *A History of Police in England and Wales* (Second Edition. Patterson Smith, Montclair, New Jersey, USA, 1972)

David, S., *The Homicidal Earl: The Life of Lord Cardigan* (Little, Brown & Co., 1997)

Davies, D. and Metcalfe, E., 'Sir Harry Bodkin Poland (1829–1928)', *Oxford Dictionary of National Biography* (Oxford University Press [online], 2010)

Davitt, M., *Collected Writings 1868–1906*, Carla King (ed. and introduction), Five Volumes (Thoemmes Press, 2001)

Devoy, J., *Recollections of an Irish Rebel* (Irish University Press, Shannon, Ireland, 1929) (1969 Edition)

Diamond, M., *Victorian Sensation: Or the Shocking and the Scandalous in Nineteenth-Century Britain* (Anthem Press, 2003)

Dickens, C., 'The Detective Police', *Household Words* (27 July, 10 August and 14 September 1850)

———, 'Three Detective Anecdotes', *Household Words* (27 July, 10 August and 14 September 1850)

Dilnot, G. (ed.), *The Trial of the Detectives* (Geoffrey Bles, 1928)

Ellis, J.C., *Blackmailers & Co.* (Selwyn and Blount Ltd, 1928)

Emsley, C., *Crime and Society in England* (Third Edition. Pearson Education Ltd, Harlow, UK, 2005)

———, *The English Police: A Political and Social History* (Second Edition. Longman, 1996)

———, *The Great British Bobby: A History of British Policing from the 18th Century to the Present* (Quercus, 2009)

Fitzgerald, P., *Chronicles of Bow Street Police Office*, Two Volumes (Chapman and Hall, 1888)

Freeston, C.L., *Cycling in the Alps: With Some Notes on the Chief Passes* (Grant Richards, 1900)

Fuller, R., *Recollections of a Detective* (John Long Ltd, 1912)

Furniss, H. (ed.), 'The Cold-Blooded Crimes of Henri de Tourville', *Famous Crimes Past and Present: Police Budget Edition* (Vol. V., No 63, year unknown), pp. 242–6

Goodman, J. and Waddell, B., *The Black Museum Chamber of Crime* (Harrap, 1987)

Greenham, G.H., *Scotland Yard Experiences: From the Diary of G.H. Greenham, Late Chief Inspector Criminal Investigation Department, Scotland Yard* (George Routledge and Sons Ltd, 1904)

Greenwood, J., *The Wilds of London* (Chatto and Windus, 1874)

Griffiths, A., *Mysteries of Police and Crime*, Three Volumes (Cassell & Co. Ltd, 1901)

Hall, J., *The Bravo Mystery and Other Cases* (John Lane, The Bodley Head, 1923)

Hamilton, J.A. and Mooney, H., 'Sir John Holker (1828–1882)' *Oxford Dictionary of National Biography* (Oxford University Press [online], 2010)

Hart-Davis, A., *What the Victorians Did for Us* (Headline Book Publishing, 2001)

Hawkins, H., *The Reminiscences of Sir Henry Hawkins, Baron Brampton*, Richard Harris (ed.), Two Volumes (Edward Arnold, 1904)

Healy, A., 'Did the Evicted Tenant's Son Shoot the Landlord?', *Carnaun School Athenry 1891–1991* (Finbarr O'Regan, Athenry, Ireland [http://homepage.eircom. net/~foregan/adc/shoot.html], 2010)

Hindley, C., *Curiosities of Street Literature* (Reeves and Turner, 1871)

Irving H.B. (ed.), *Trial of Franz Müller* (William Hodge & Co., 1911)

Jenkins, B., *The Fenian Problem: Insurgency and Terrorism in a Liberal State 1858–1874* (McGill-Queens University Press, Canada, 2008)

Juxon, J., *Lewis and Lewis* (Ticknor & Fields, New York, 1984)

Kee, R., *Ireland: A History* (Weidenfeld and Nicolson, 1980)

———, *The Green Flag: A History of Irish Nationalism* (Penguin Books Ltd, 2000)

Kenealy, E.V. (ed.), *The Trial of Sir R.C.D. Tichborne Bart*, Eight Volumes (Publisher Unknown, 1875)

Kennedy, P., 'The Secret Service Department: A British Intelligence Bureau in Mid-Victorian London, September 1867–April 1868', *Intelligence and National Security* (18, 2003), pp. 100–27

King, C., *Michael Davitt* (Dundalgan Press, Ireland, 1999)

Kingston, C., *Dramatic Days at the Old Bailey* (Stanley Paul & Co. Ltd, 1923)

———, *Enemies of Society* (Stanley Paul & Co. Ltd, 1927)

———, 'Henri de Tourville: An Intriguing Study of a Ruthless Adventurer and Murderer', *The Detective Magazine* (2, 26 October 1923), pp. 1179–85

———, *Remarkable Rogues: The Careers of Some Notable Criminals of Europe and America* (John Land, The Bodley Head Ltd, 1924)

Lansdowne, A., *A Life's Reminiscences of Scotland Yard* (The Leadenhall Press Ltd, 1890)

Laws, J., 'Foxley House', *Lymm and District Society Newsletter* (37, 1971), pp. 1–2

Littlechild, J., *The Reminiscences of Chief Inspector Littlechild* (The Leadenhall Press Ltd, 1894)

Lock, J., *Dreadful Deeds and Awful Murders: Scotland Yard's First Detectives 1829–1878* (Barn Owl Books, Taunton, 1990)

Lowndes, F.W., *Infanticide in Liverpool* (National Association for Promotion of Social Sciences, 1872–73)

Matthews, A., *Renegades: Irish Republican Women, 1900–1922* (Mercier Press, Cork, Ireland, 2010)

Maugham, F.H., *The Tichborne Case* (Hodder & Stoughton, 1936)

McCracken, D.P., *Inspector Mallon: Buying Irish Patriotism for a Five-pound Note* (Irish Academic Press, Dublin, Ireland, 2009)

McWilliam, R., *The Tichborne Claimant: A Victorian Sensation* (Hambledon Continuum, 2007)

Meiklejohn, J., *Real Life Detective Stories* (John Dicks Press Ltd, 1912)

Moylan, J.F., *Scotland Yard and the Metropolitan Police* (G.P. Putnam & Sons Ltd, 1929)

Murray, S., 'The Fenian Landing at Helvic', *The Journal of the Old Waterford Society* (9 September 1878)

Novak, R., 'Ellen O'Leary, Irish Writer (1831–1889)', in Thesing, W.B. (ed.), *Dictionary of Literary Biography: Late Nineteenth- and Early Twentieth Century British Women Poets* (240) (Gale Group, Detroit, 2007)

———, 'Ellen O'Leary: A Bold Fenian Poet', *Éire – Ireland* (43, 2008), pp. 58–84

O'Broin, L., *Fenian Fever: An Anglo-American Dilemma* (New York University Press, New York, USA, 1971)

O'Mahony, C., 'The Irish Ambulance Corps 1870–1871 and the Dundalk Contingent', *The Irish Sword* (22, 2000), pp. 36–50

O'Neill, G., *The Good Old Days: Crime, Murder and Mayhem in Victorian London* (Viking, Penguin Books Ltd, 2006)

Paterson, M., *Voices from Dickens' London* (David and Charles, Cincinnati, Ohio, USA, 2006)

Paxman, J., *The Victorians: Britain through the Paintings of the Age* (BBC Books, 2009)

Petrow, S., *Policing Morals: The Metropolitan Police and the Home Office 1870–1914* (Clarendon Press, Oxford, UK, 1994)

Picard, L., *Victorian London: The Life of a City* (Weidenfeld and Nicolson, 2005)

Porter, B., *The Origins of the Vigilant State: The London Metropolitan Police Special Branch Before the First World War* (The Boydell Press, 1987)

———, *Plots and Paranoia: A History of Political Espionage in Britain 1790–1988* (Routledge, 1992)

Rattle, A. and Vale, A., *Amelia Dyer: Angel Maker* (Carlton Books Ltd, 2007)

Ridley, J., *The Freemasons* (Constable, 1999)

Ruddick, J., *Death at The Priory: Love, Sex and Murder in Victorian England* (Atlantic Books Ltd, 2001)

Scanlon, M., *The Dublin Metropolitan Police* (Minerva Press, 1998)

Sellwood, A. and Sellwood, M., *The Victorian Railway Murders* (David & Charles, 1979) (republished as *Death Ride from Fenchurch Street and other Victorian Railway Murders* [Amberley Publishing plc, Stroud, UK, 2009])

Shore, W.M. (ed.), *Trial of Thomas Neill Cream* (William Hodge & Co. Ltd, 1923)

Smith, P.T., *Policing Victorian Britain: Political Policing, Public Order, and the London Metropolitan Police* (Greenwood Press, Westport, Connecticut, USA, 1985)

Stewart, R.F., *The Great Detective Case of 1877: A Study in Victorian Police Corruption* (The Battered Silicon Dispatch Box, Shelburne, Ontario, Canada, 2000)

Stratmann, L., *Greater London Murders: 33 True Stories of Revenge, Jealousy, Greed and Lust* (The History Press, Stroud, UK, 2010)

———, *The Crooks Who Conned Millions; True Stories of Fraudsters and Charlatans* (Sutton Publishing, Stroud, UK, 2006)

Summerscale, K., *The Suspicions of Mr Whicher or The Murder at Road Hill House* (Bloomsbury, 2008)

Taylor, D., *The New Police in Nineteenth Century England: Crime, Conflict and Control* (Manchester University Press, Manchester, UK, 1997)

'The Great Detective Case', *Police News* (G. Purkess, Strand, London, *c.* 1877)

Thomson, B., *The Story of Scotland Yard* (Grayson and Grayson, 1935)

Wade, S., *Plain Clothes and Sleuths: A History of Detectives in Britain* (Tempus, Stroud, UK, 2007)

Walker-Smith, D. and Clarke, E., *The Life of Sir Edward Clarke* (Thornton Butterworth Ltd, 1939)

Whelehan, N., *Dreamers, Dupes and Dynamiters: Political Violence and the Transnational Flows of Irish Nationalism, 1865–1885* (PhD thesis, European University Institute [EUI], Florence, Italy, 2009)

White, J., *London in the Nineteenth Century: A Human Awful Wonder of God* (Random House, 2007)

Williams, M., *Leaves of a Life: Being the Reminiscences of Montagu Williams Q.C.*, Two Volumes (Macmillan & Co., 1890)

Wilson, A.N., *The Victorians* (Hutchinson, 2002)

INDEX

abortion 106, 126–9, 131–3

Abrahams, Michael 199, 203, 207, 209, 212, 216

agricultural labourers 11–12, 19, 127

Alabama 35–6, 39, 119

Alfred, Duke of Edinburgh, *see* Duke of Edinburgh

America 34–44, 48, 63, 68–75, 80, 82–4, 88–90, 93, 97, 100–2, 119, 133, 139, 147, 149, 153–4, 164, 166, 186, 219, 237, 243

American Civil War 35–6, 70–1, 80, 90, 119

Anderson, Sir Robert **Plate 8**, 68, 79, 87, 92, 97

Anderson, Sir Samuel 79, 90, 137

Andrews, Detective Sergeant Walter 171, 179

Anthony, William 142–4

antimony 170, 172–3, 175–7, 179, 181–2

arson 8, 106, 142–4

assault 28, 31–2, 116, 155, 163–4

Attorney General 44, 137, 182, 216, 228

Austrian Tragedy, *see* de Tourville, Henri

Avis, Ann 223, 228, 235

baby farming 8, 106, 127–8, 131

Bale, Charles **Plate 23**, 205–10, 214, 237

Balham Mystery, *see* Bravo, Charles

Ballantine, William 44, 61, 124, 150

Barnes, Police Constable John 115–16

Barrett, Michael 97–100

Barrett, Peter 134–5, 137

Beake, Louisa, *see* Clarke, Louisa

Bell, Dr Royes Hutchinson 171–4

Bella 147, 149, 153

Benson, Harry **Plate 21**, 165–6, 203–30, 235, 237–8, 244, 246

Bent, Superintendent James 65

Berkeley, Captain Henry 163–5

betting 8, 28, 106, 119–26, 159, 162–5, 201, 207, 213, 218–19, 225–6, 243

Betting Houses Act 1853 120, 125–6

Betting Houses Act 1874 126

Birmingham 13, 73, 83, 93, 135–7

Blackburn, Justice Colin 61

Blackett, Police Constable Edward 113, 116

Bond, Dr. Thomas 169, 195

Bow Street Police Court 26, 34, 43, 97, 118, 123, 155, 161, 169, 193, 213–14

Bow Street Runners 16, 20

Braddick, Detective Sergeant 21

Bradlaugh, Charles 84

Brampton, Lord, *see* Hawkins, Henry

Brannan, Inspector 139
Bravo, Charles **Plate 19**, 8, 170–84, 198
Bravo, Florence **Plate 20**, 170–84, 198
Bravo, Joseph 170, 173, 178–9, 182
Bridge of Allan 203–5, 209, 214
Brett, Police Sergeant Charles 91–2
bribery 106, 117–19, 198, 236
Briden, Police Sergeant 113–14
Bridgeland, Police Sergeant William 51
Briggs, Thomas 30–4, 38, 41–4, 46–7, 50,
    53, 58, 63–4
Brigham, Elizabeth 107, 187–8, 191–3, 195–8
Brigham, Henriette, *see* de Tourville,
    Henriette
Brookwood Cemetery 240
Brown, 'Captain' James 153, 155–6, 158
Bruce, Henry (Baron Aberdare) 119
Brudenell, James Thomas, *see* Cardigan,
    Earl of
burglary 106, 110–17, 162, 218, 220, 225
Burke, Ricard O'Sullivan 73, 83–4, 87–8,
    91, 93–6, 100–2, 112, 135, 151
Butt, Isaac 134–5

Calbraith, John 116–17
Calcraft, William 50, 93
Campbell, Michael 114–16
Campbell, Detective Sergeant William 73,
    135–6
capital punishment 50, 93, 100, 116, 197
Cappel, Revd. Dr. 50, 63
Carden, Sir Robert 186
Cardigan, Earl of **Plate 6**, 8, 75–8
Cardigan, Countess of 75–8
Carter, Mr. W. 172, 179, 182
Castro, T(h)omas, *see* Tichborne Claimant
Cavanagh, Detective Sergeant Timothy 15,
    109, 244
Central Criminal Court, *see* Old Bailey
Chabot, Charles 137, 144, 161, 186, 209
Chadwick, Sir Edwin 21
Chapman, Police Constable 114
'Chieftain', *see* Clarke, George
Chester Castle 85–6
chloral 168–70
Criminal Investigation Department (CID)
    237, 239

City of London Police 14, 166
claimant, *see* Tichborne Claimant
Clan na Gael 134, 142
Clappinson, Sarah 188, 195–6
Clark, Police Sergeant Henry 12, 18
Clark, Police Sergeant John 12
Clarke, Catherine 11, 227
Clarke, Catherine Louisa 225
Clarke, Sir Edward **Plate 28**, 227–31, 234,
    236, 245–6, 249
Clarke, Elizabeth 18–19, 240–1
Clarke, Emily Bent **Plate 29**, 131, 184,
    227, 230, 241
Clarke, Chief Inspector George **Plate 1**
  arrest 217
  children 19, 102, 131, 184, 225, 227, 230,
    240–1, 244, 252
  death 240
  early life 11–12
  grandchildren 133
  investigations
    abortion 126–9, 131–3
    arson 142–4
    baby farming 127–8, 131
    betting 119–26, 162–5
    bribery 117–19
    burglary 110–17
    conspiracy to murder 168–70
    Fenian and Irish affairs 67–75,
      79–105, 133–42, 198, 207
    forgery 26, 72, 150, 166, 230, 237
    fraud 8, 26, 118, 126, 146–59, 185–7,
      200–10
    murder 30–65, 92–3, 97–100, 106–8,
      112–17, 170–84, 187–98
    perjury 150–8
    robbery 25–6
    theft 66–7, 76–8, 160–1
  joined detective department 22
  joined Police 17
  marriage 18
  nicknames 8, 22
  promotion 7, 18, 94, 109
  relationships with colleagues 23–4, 111,
    210
  training 17
  trial 218, 223–34

Clarke, George Leonard 102
Clarke, Henry John (Harry) 240–1, 245
Clarke, Jane 12
Clarke, Leonard 12
Clarke, Louisa 102, 225
Clarke, Mrs 128–9
Clarke, Robert (brother) 12
Clarke, Robert (father) 11
Clarke, Susan 12
Clarke, Thomas 12
Clerkenwell Explosion **Plate 9**, 95–8, 106, 108, 151, 198
Clerkenwell Police Court 163
Cluseret, Gustave 80–1, 83–4, 88
Clydesdale Bank 202–4, 206, 209, 214
Coathupe, Detective Sergeant Edwin 25, 27, 29
Cockburn, Sir Alexander 99–100, 137, 151, 154–5, 157, 179
Coleridge, Sir John 150
Collier, Sir Robert 44, 61
Collins, Wilkie 23, 243
Condon, Edmund 92–3
Condon, Patrick, *see* Massey, Godfrey
corruption 8, 14, 200–38
Corydon, John Joseph 86–7, 89, 102–3, 137
Cox, Jane 167, 171–84, 198
Cream, Thomas Neill 240
Crimean War 76
Criminal Evidence Act 1898 64
Cross, Sir Richard Assheton, **Plate 30**, 179, 216, 227, 235, 245
Cubitt, Arthur 147
Cuff, Sergeant 23

Davey, Detective Inspector 167
Davis, Charlotte 129–31
Davis, James 14, 125
Davitt, Michael **Plate 13**, 86, 106, 135–8
de Badderley, Charles and Sarah 132–3
de Goncourt, Comtesse 200–2, 205–6, 209–10, 223
de Guillenan, Chevalier 192–3, 196
de Horsey, Adeline, *see* Cardigan, Countess of
de Morgan, John 159

de Tourville, Henri 8, 107–8, 187–98, 206, 208, 212
de Tourville, Henriette 188
de Tourville, Madeline 188–98
de Tourville, William 188, 196–7
Deasy, Captain Timothy 91–3, 95
Death, John 33–4
Death, Robert 33–4, 45
Denning, Chief Inspector Eleazar **Plate 3**, 150–2
Deptford Spec Lottery 121–3
Derby, Lord 79, 95–6
detective department (Scotland Yard)
establishment 14, 20–1
expenses 24–5, 61, 91, 104, 111, 239
operating procedures 24
staff 20, 21–4, 26–7, 67, 94, 109–10
Devany, John 102
Devonshire, Duchess of 199
Devoy, John 68, 70, 73, 75, 81, 133–4
Dickens, Charles 21–2, 40, 93, 116
Digance, Daniel 32, 42, 46
Dill, Dr 179–81
Dilnot, George 245–6
Disraeli, Benjamin 90, 95–6
Dougan, Police Constable Edward 31–2
Doughty, Katherine, *see* Lady Radcliffe 147, 158
Druscovich, Chief Inspector Nathaniel 27, 85, 94, 110–11, 126, 128, 141, 189, 198, 202–4, 206–7, 211, 213–14, 216, 224, 232, 234–6, 246
Dublin 13, 69, 70–5, 83, 86, 88–9, 92–3, 98, 102, 134–8, 141
Dublin Castle 70, 74, 79, 89, 98, 236
Dublin Metropolitan Police (DMP) 70–3, 92–3
Duke of Edinburgh 102
Duke of Wellington, *see* Wellesley, Arthur
Dyer, Amelia 131

Edward, Prince of Wales, *see* Prince of Wales
Edwards, Police Constable David 160–1
Ellis, Sarah 128, 130
Ergot of Rye 132
extradition 36, 38–40, 64, 185, 191, 193–4, 206–7

Fariola, Octave 80–5, 87–90
Farrell, Henry 102
Feilding, Lieutenant Colonel William 95, 97, 238
Fenians 66–105, 133–142
Fenian Brotherhood (FB):
  establishment 69–71
  invasion of Canada 74–5
Fenian conspiracy 66–105
Fergusson, Sir James 94
Field, Detective Inspector Charles 22
fire brigade, *see* Metropolitan Fire Brigade
Flintoff, George 208–9, 212, 214
Flowers, James 43–4, 161
Foley, Detective Sergeant 135–6
Fordham, Police Constable 94
Foreign Enlistment Act 119, 139, 141–2
Foreign Secretary 189
forensic methods 43, 46, 56–7, 60, 169, 181, 197
forgery 26, 72, 150, 166, 230, 237
Foxley Hall 188, 195
Francis, Jacob 201–203, 246
France 12, 29, 69, 71, 85, 100, 102, 133, 138–42, 147, 165, 194, 197, 219
Franco–Prussian War 138, 145
fraud 8, 26, 118, 126, 146–59, 185–7, 200–10
Freemasons 210, 214, 240, 244
Froggatt, Edward **Plate 26,** 206–8, 212–14, 216–18, 224, 226, 232–5
Führhop, Theodor 52–66

G Division (Dublin Metropolitan Police) 71, 73, 92
Gainsborough, Thomas 199
Gambier, James 118
Gambling, *see* betting
Garibaldi, Guiseppe 28, 80–2
General Society for Assurance against Losses on the Turf 162–6
Germany 49, 58–62, 64, 101, 165, 185–6, 212, 219
Gerrett, Detective Sergeant William 21
Giffard, Sir Hardinge 44, 60–1, 150, 205, 209, 216, 228
Gifford, William, *see* Kurr, William
Gladstone, William Ewart 119, 133

Goff, Detective Sergeant Charles 21
Goode, Inspector George 53
Great Britain (steamship) 102
Great Western (steamship) 34
Greenham, Inspector George 24, 27, 124, 165, 167, 193, 211, 244
Greig, Major John 71, 79
Griffiths, Arthur 236
Griffiths, George 177, 182
Gull, Sir William 172–4. 176, 184
Gully, Dr. James 173–7, 180–4, 198

Habeas Corpus, suspension of 74–5, 79, 83, 142
Haire, Police Constable James 139
Hall, Mary 128
Halpin, William 71, 73, 83, 87–90, 103, 133
Halsbury, Earl of, *see* Giffard, Sir Hardinge
Hamburg 56, 58, 60–1, 185–7, 195, 208
handwriting recognition 136–7, 144, 161, 186, 204, 209, 214, 233
hangman, *see* Calcraft, William
Harbison, William 90–1
Harding, Dr William 131
Hardy, Gathorne 92, 95–6
Harris, Assistant Commissioner William 58
Harrison, Dr George 171–2, 174
Harvey, John 185–6
Hawkins, Henry 150–1, 153–4, 156–8
Hayes, John 77–8
Haynes, Inspector John 21–2
Henderson, Commissioner Sir Edmund **Plate 11,** 109, 117, 125, 128, 159, 193, 205, 207, 214, 227, 230, 235, 237–40
Henderson, William 203
Henry, Sir Thomas 122, 141
Hodgson, Mr 216
Holker, Sir John 182, 216, 228
Holmes, Sherlock 7, 244
Home Secretary 13, 48–9, 79, 84, 92, 94–6, 100, 119, 179, 212, 214, 216, 226, 235, 237–9, 245
Howard, Charles **Plate 18,** 185–7, 193, 202–3
Howie, Superintendent Daniel 32, 52, 55–8, 60
Hyde Park 28, 79, 133, 159

Infant Life Protection Act 131
Infant Life Protection Society 128, 131
informers
    Fenian 80, 83, 86–90, 94, 97–9, 102–4,
        137, 207
    other 24–5, 117, 238
Ingham, Sir James 213, 224
International Working Man's Association 142
Irish Ambulance Corps 138–42, 145
Irish branch, *see* Special Irish Branch
Irish Constabulary 71, 97, 103
Irish famine 63, 136
Irish Home Rule 135
Irish National Land League 135, 138
Irish Provisional Government 83, 87, 90
Irish Republican Brotherhood (IRB)
        69–70, 73, 75, 82, 136
Irish rising 69–72, 74–5, 82–3, 85–90, 93,
        96, 98

Jennings, John 189–91, 194
John Bull (steamship) 139–40
Johnson, Dr. George 172–4
Judford, F.C, *see* Howard, Charles
Jury, Mina 152
Justice, Anne 97–9

Keeber, Mary Ann 171–2, 180
Kelly, Colonel Thomas 71, 73, 75, 83,
        87–93, 95, 103–4
Kendall , Detective Sergeant 22
Kenealy, Dr Edward Vaughan 151–6
Kerressey, Inspector Walter 32, 34, 36,
        39–40, 48
Kickham, Charles 70
Kingston, Charles 198
Knightsbridge Exchange betting club 124
Köhl, Ferdinand 52–63, 116
Kurr, Frederick **Plate 24**, 205–10, 213–14, 237
Kurr, William **Plate 22**, 166, 204–10,
        212–26, 228–9, 235, 237, 246

La Fontaine 138, 141
Labalmondière, Assistant Commissioner
        Douglas 108–9
Ladies Committee for the Relief of State
        Prisoners 87

Lambert, Captain Thomas Eyre 134–5
Lambeth Police Court 132, 165
Lansdowne, Detective Sergeant Andrew
        24, 123, 135, 244
Larcom, Sir Thomas 72
Larkin, Michael 92–3
laudanum 174–6, 178
Leeds 101, 136–7, 203–4, 211, 236
Letheby, Dr Henry 57, 59
Lewis, Sir George **Plate 27**, 182–4, 213,
        224–8, 236
Lilley, Robert 76–8, 88
Lincoln, Abraham 40
'Little Emily' 128, 131
Littlechild, Detective Sergeant John
        206–8, 225, 244
Liverpool 34–5, 37, 40, 63, 71, 79–80,
        82–3, 85, 89, 102, 105, 121, 144, 238
Loder, Mary 149
London Metropolitan Board of Works 101
lottery 120–3, 126
Luby, Thomas Clarke 70, 72
Luie, Jean 153–8
Lundgren, Carl Peter, *see* Luie, Jean
Lush, Sir Robert 116, 151, 187
Lushington, Colonel Franklin 150

McCafferty, Captain John 84–6
McDonnell, Joseph Patrick 141–2
McGregor, Elizabeth, *see* Clarke, Elizabeth
McGregor, John 18
McGregor, Louisa 127
Madame Tussauds 197
Maguire, Thomas 92
Manchester 25–7, 34–6, 65, 79, 83, 86,
        91–3, 95, 105, 136
Manchester Martyrs 93
Manners, Detective Sergeant 85, 89
Mansion House 165, 186, 219
Manton, Detective-Sergeant 168
Marlborough Street Police Court 208, 212
Martin, Baron 44, 48
Martin, Mrs 126
Marylebone Police Court 77, 136
Marx, Karl 142
Massey, Godfrey 83–4, 86–7, 102
Matthews, Jonathan 33–4, 39, 45–6, 48

Mayne, Commissioner Sir Richard
    Plate 2, 13–14, 16, 21, 23–5, 27,
    32, 36, 38, 40, 49, 52, 56, 58, 60, 66,
    71–2, 75, 79–80, 83, 85, 89, 94–6, 98,
    102–4, 108, 117, 188, 198
Mayo, Lord 79, 92–3, 95
Mazzini, Giuseppe 72, 84
Meiklejohn, Detective Inspector John **Plate**
    25, 29, 94, 103, 108, 110–11, 167, 199,
    203–5, 209–17, 231–2, 234–6, 244
Mellor, Sir John 151
Metropolitan Fire Brigade 143
Metropolitan Police, London
  beats 17
  corruption 200–34, 238
  detective department, *see* detective
      department (Scotland Yard)
  discipline 15, 238
  district 14, 16, 67, 160
  divisions 14, 17–24, 26–7, 32, 45, 48,
      51–2, 64, 94, 97, 104, 109–10,
      112–15, 122, 128, 139, 150, 152, 160,
      177, 220, 227, 238
  manpower 14–16, 94, 159–60
  pay 15, 18, 25, 61, 94, 104, 109, 116, 200,
      214, 227
  recreation 109
  recruitment 15, 17, 23
  staff turnover 15
  strategy 14, 17, 64, 79
  training 17–18, 25
  uniform 14–15, 19
  workload 18, 33
Millen, Francis 71, 73
Miller, Madeline, *see* de Tourville, Madeline
Montgomery, Andrew 200–05
Moore, Dr 171–2
Mullany, Patrick 97–9, 103
Müller, Franz **Plate 5**, 33–51, 54, 58, 61,
    63–4, 153
Mulvany, Inspector John 27, 79–80, 85,
    94, 110
Murder victims, *see* Briggs, Thomas;
    Bravo, Charles; Brigham, Elizabeth;
    Clark, Police Constable George;
    de Tourville, Madeline; Führhop,
    Theodor; Galloway, Samuel

Murderers, *see* Campbell, Michael; de
    Tourville, Henri; Köhl, Ferdinand,
    Müller, Franz
Murray, Edwin 163–6, 206, 208–10,
    219–20, 222–3, 225, 229
Music Hall 111, 208, 244

Naas, Lord, *see* Mayo, Lord
Napoleon III 29, 138
Nasir-al-Din, *see* Shah of Persia
New York 34–8, 40, 50, 54, 63, 69–70, 73,
    75, 80–4, 89, 93, 133, 153, 237–8
Norfolk, William 184, 208, 226

O'Brien, William 92–3
O'Keefe, John 97–9
O'Leary, Edmund 98
O'Leary, Ellen 87, 98, 133
O'Leary, John 70, 72, 87, 98, 133
O'Leary, Patrick 'Pagan' 70
O'Mahony, John 68–9, 71, 74
O'Neill, Colonel John 75
O'Sullivan, Jeremiah 100
Odger, George 84
Old Bailey 19–20, 26, 34, 42, 44, 58, 61,
    88, 98–9, 101, 112, 116–18, 122, 128,
    1312, 1367, 144, 158, 161, 166, 169,
    186, 193, 203, 205, 208, 215, 226–8,
    231, 233, 237–8, 240, 244
Oldfield, Jonathan 187
Onslow, Guildford 148, 151, 156
Orton, Arthur, *see* Tichborne Claimant
Osprey 149, 153–4, 157–8

Palmer, Chief Inspector William 23, 27,
    94, 110, 121–2, 128, 204, 209–14,
    216–17, 232–6
Paris 68–9, 79, 82–5, 88–9, 98, 138, 142,
    147–8, 188, 192, 237, 239
Parnell, Charles 138
Parry, John Humffreys 44–5, 47
Patti, Adelina 237
pawnbrokers 42, 44–5, 52–3, 58, 64
Pay, Detective Inspector James 138, 162, 218
Payne, Emily Bent *see* Clarke, Emily Bent
Payne, Henry Stableforth **Plate 29**, 184, 208
Pearce, Detective Inspector Nicholas 20–1

Pearson, Henry Hume 85
Peel, Sir Robert 3, 15, 44
Penge murder case 227, 233
Perreau, Henri, *see* de Tourville, Henri
Plaistow Marshes murder 8, 49, 51–63
poison 85, 168, 170, 172–9, 181, 184, 240
Poland, Sir Harry Bodkin **Plate 12**, 77,
    120–2, 125, 132, 136, 144, 165, 182,
    184, 186, 193–5, 213–14, 216–18,
    220, 223–4
Pollard, William 154, 156, 212, 216, 219–20,
    230
Ponchon, Pierre 203
'Poodle', *see* Benson, Harry
Portch, Daniel 163–4
portico burglary 112–15
Pollock, Sir Charles 234
Pollock, Sir Frederick 44, 48, 61, 63
potato blight 68, 136
prime minister 13, 95, 119
Prince of Wales 28, 102, 189, 231, 239
prisons
    Brixton 127
    Chatham 154–5
    Clerkenwell House of Detention 95, 97,
        155–6, 194
    Coldbath Fields 235
    Dartmoor 210
    Holloway 154–5, 157
    Ilford 56, 60
    Kilmainham 89
    Millbank 155, 210
    Newgate 44, 49, 100, 151, 186, 205, 209,
        233, 237–8
    New Bailey, Salford 93
    Pentonville 159, 210, 212
    Portland 210
    Portsmouth 210
    Richmond Bridewell 73
    Springfield, Chelmsford 63, 116
procurator fiscal 205
prostitution 47, 127, 130, 240
public house 31, 40, 52, 93, 114, 148, 208,
    218, 225–6, 236, 244

Queens Bench, Dublin 134
Queens Bench, Westminster 78, 152, 157, 179

racecourses
    Epsom 28–9, 72, 125, 243
    Goodwood 243
    Newmarket 243
    Punchestown 102
    Sandown 209, 215, 224, 226, 243
Radcliffe, Lady 147, 150, 158
Rappahannock 119
Redwood, Professor Theophilus 172
Reform Bill 79
Reform League 72, 79, 84
Reimers, Detective Sergeant John 101,
    110, 199, 211
Relf, Inspector Richard 128–30
Ricardo, Florence, *see* Bravo, Florence
Ripper, Jack the 169, 236
robbery 25–6, 110, 111–12, 114–15, 162, 200
Robinson, Detective Sergeant 23
Robson, Detective Sergeant 168, 206
Roots, Detective Sergeant 182
Rossa, Jeremiah O'Donovan 69–70, 72,
    103, 133, 142
Rotterdam 206–7, 214
Rowan, Commissioner Sir Charles 13–14,
    16, 21
Royal Bank of London 201, 203, 208
Rumble, William 117–19
Russell, Lord John 79
Russia 72, 76, 162, 165, 219
Ryan, Superintendent Daniel 72

Savory, John 206
Sayer, Detective Sergeant 117
Scotland Yard (location) 14
Scott, Miss 192–4
Selwin–Ibbetson, Sir Henry 238
Shaffer, Chauncey 39–40
Shah of Persia **Plate 14**, 159
Shanklin, Isle of Wight 165–6, 203–5, 220,
    230, 246
Shaw, Detective Sergeant Frederick 21–2
Shore, Detective Inspector 110, 225
Snee, Ellen 168–71
Solicitor General 44, 48, 61–2, 64, 110, 139,
    150, 209, 216, 228
Solicitor to the Treasury, *see* Treasury Solicitor
Somerset House 101, 117–18

Southwark Police Court 28, 165
Special Irish Branch 239
Spicksley, John 127
Stannards Mill robbery 162, 225
state visits 28, 89, 159
Staten Island 36–7, 64, 153–4
Stelvio Pass 189–90, 194, 197
Stenning, Harry 208
Stephens, James **Plate 7**, 68–75, 80–4, 86,
    104, 142
Stephenson, Sir Augustus 212
Stewart, Richard 246
strychnine 84
sugar-baking 54–6, 61–2
Suicide Act 1961 169
Sunerway, Detective Sergeant Henry 98,
    103, 112
Sultan of the Ottoman Empire 89
swell mob 22, 28, 102, 243

Tallahassee 36–7
Tanner, Detective Inspector Richard 23–4,
    26–9, 32, 34–43, 45–6, 48, 50–2, 64,
    89, 94, 109, 210
tartar emetic 179, 182–4
Tattersalls Racing Club 124–5, 163
theft 66–7, 76–8, 160–1
Therfield 11–12
Thomas, Detective Sergeant 41
Thomson, Detective Sergeant Alexander 23
Thomson, Superintendent James 7, 23,
    26–7, 72, 85, 89, 94, 109
Thorpe, Revd. Oscar 128, 130–1
Tichborne Claimant **Plate 15**, 8, 146–59,
    161, 163, 165, 236
Tichborne, Lady Henriette 147–9
Tichborne, Sir Roger 146–50, 153, 159
Tiernan, Sergeant John 36–9
Thornton, Detective Inspector Stephen
    21–3
Tower of London 88
Trafalgar Square 79, 240
transportation 63
Treasury Solicitor 144, 178–9, 183, 235
Trevelli, Victor 222, 230
Trial of the Detectives 226–34
turf fraud 8, 162–6, 200–10

Vance, William 168–70
Vaughan, James (Fenian) 97–8
Vaughan, James (Magistrate) 103, 193
Victoria, Queen 49, 76, 92–4, 108, 172
Victoria 34–8, 42–4, 49–50
Vifquain, Victor 80, 83, 87
Vincent, Howard 237, 239
Von Howard, Count, *see* Howard, Charles
Von Tornow, Detective Sergeant Charles
    167, 186, 193, 195, 203, 212, 237

Walker, Superintendent Robert **Plate 3**,
    22, 93
Walpole, Spencer 79, 84, 92
Walters, William Henry **Plate 17**, 162–6,
    215–16, 218–20, 222–5, 229, 237–8
Waters, Margaret 128, 130–1
Wellesley, Arthur 12
Wellesley, Gerald 12
Wellesley, Richard 12
Whalley, George Hammond **Plate 16**,
    151, 153, 155–8
Whelan, Captain William 80, 97
Whicher, Inspector Jonathan 8–9, 21–3,
    26, 149, 151–2, 157
Wilding, Thomas 188–9, 192
Williams, Captain Henry 186
Williams, Montagu **Plate 10**, 98–100, 116,
    121, 132, 151, 161, 164, 193, 208, 213,
    215, 217, 230–1
Williamson, Superintendent Adolphus
    Frederick **Plate 4**, 20, 23–28, 41,
    49, 60, 67, 73, 79, 85–6, 88–9, 91–2,
    94, 97–8, 102–3, 105, 109, 126,
    142, 150–1, 160, 165, 167, 170, 200,
    202–7, 210–11, 213–14, 216–18, 221,
    223–5, 228, 230, 238–9
Willmott, Temple, *see* Howard, Charles
Wilson, John 135–8
Windsor Castle 8, 63, 66–7
Worship Street Police Court 49
Worth, Adam 199

Yeats, William Butler 87
Yonge, George, *see* Benson, Harry
Young Ireland 68